From Richmond Barracks
to Keogh Square

First Published in 2014
RIPOSTE BOOKS
28 Emmet Rd Dublin 8. Ireland

ISBN 9781901596205

Front cover photo: 'Dismantling of the Empire:' demolition of the entrance arch to Richmond Barracks, 1926. Original photo, Irish Independent.

Back cover photo: Regiment in review, Richmond Barracks circa 1833: a lithograph by James Henry Lynch after Michael Angelo Hayes.

Pullout section: The 2nd Boer War. Lord Roberts' inspection of the Argyll and Sutherland Regiment, 1899 prior to departure: original photo, Stirling castle.

'At famed Waterloo
Duke of Wellington would have looked blue
If poor Paddy was not there too
Says the Shan Van Vocht.'

The Sean-Bhean Bhocht, (Irish for 'Poor Old Woman') often spelt phonetically in this song as 'Shan Van Vocht', is a traditional Irish song from the period of the 1798 Rebellion. Many different versions of the song have been composed by balladeers over the years, with the lyrics adapted to reflect the political climate at the time. It is reputed that one third of the British soldiers at Waterloo were from Ireland (including Wellington himself).

Members and friends of the Inchicore Ledwidge Society gathered at the installation of a plaque to the Irish poet and soldier, Francis Ledwidge on the wall of the former recreation room of Richmond Barracks. Included are (front row), from left to right: Liam O'Meara, Catherine Byrne TD. (who unveiled the plaque), Phyllis Mc Guirke, May Mac Giolla, the late Tomas Mac Giolla, Christine Broe, Margaret Somerville, Mrs. Dunne, Larry Mc Kenna, Kate Brophy, Helen Scott, Sr. Jo Kennedy, Rita Fagan, Marian Finan, Ann Graham- Area Manager, South Central Area, D.C.C., and Brendan Byrne, Labour History Museum.
(Photo taken by Michael O'Flanagan, Secretary of the Society.)

FROM
RICHMOND BARRACKS
TO
KEOGH SQUARE

RIPOSTE BOOKS DUBLIN

Acknowledgements

Special mention is due of the late Paddy Healy who, some 20 years, ago allowed me to copy a full set of his photographs of Keogh Square in the 1960's (now housed at the Irish Architectural Archives). I am grateful to British Ambassador Dominick Chilcott for his words of encouragement. The courtesy and helpfulness of the staffs of the various military museums in the U.K was much appreciated: in particular, I would like to thank Rod Mackenzie, Argyll and Sutherland Museum, Stirling Castle, Scotland; the Earl of March, Goodwood House, Sussex; Liz Bregazzi, County Archivist, Durham County Record Office; Ian Hook, Keeper of the Essex Regiment Museum; Giles Guthrie, Royal West Kent archives; Christine Pullen, Rifle Brigade/Royal Greenjackets Museum; Michael Cornwell, curator, The Rifles (Berkshire and Wiltshire) Museum; Ann George, Archivist, YMCA records, Cadbury Research Library, Uni. of Birmingham. Also my thanks to Victoria Burbidge, The British Memorial Association, Fromelles; The Imperial War Museum; Public Records Office, Kew, Richmond, U.K; Dennis Nelson for information on rifleman Fred Peters; Andrew Bonar Law (the Neptune Gallery, Dublin) and Bernard Heathcote, nephew of Major Harold. C. Heathcote.

Much of my research was spent at the National Library of Ireland, especially while compiling the list of regiments: this had to done by perusing the newspapers from 1814-1922 as the records at Kew only covered the latter period. My thanks go to Gerry Kavanagh and all of the staff at the library; also to The Representative Church Body Library-C.O.I; the Gilbert Library; Dublin City Archives; Irene Stevenson, *The Irish Times* photo archives; Kilmainham Gaol; James Langton, The Irish Volunteers Org. web site; Tom Burke, Royal Dublin Fusiliers Association; David McFarlane-Johnson of the British Legion; Muriel McAuley, grand-daughter of Thomas MacDonagh; Aengus O'Snodaigh TD; Frances Tallon, Meath County Library; Sr. Cecily and the Sisters of Mercy, Baggot Street.

I would like to mention author/historians with whom I was in personal contact: Seosamh O'Broin; Jimmy O'Toole; Diarmuid O' Connor; Martin O'Dwyer and Liz Gillis. Where would one be without family, friends and personal contacts; in this regard I must mention my sister, Sr. Johanna O'Meara; Michael O'Flanagan, Kilmainham and Inchicore Heritage Group; Shay Hurley, former Principal St. Michael's CBS; John Peacock (Keogh Square Facebook page); Damien Maddock, photographer; Deirdre Coffey, St. Michael's Parish Community Centre; Rita Fagan, St. Michaels Family Resource Centre; Eadaoin Ni Chleirigh, Richmond Barracks Advisory Committee; Aileen Balfe; James Spooner; Marie Mc Mahon; Anthony Larkin; Aubrey Bunyan; Terry Breen; Marion Davis, genealogist; Joe Lee, artist, independent film and video maker. Every effort has been made to credit sources. If any sources were omitted, please notify us for acknowledgements in future editions.

Contents

Calendar of Events- Richmond Barracks

1807   Duke of Richmond's Administration; overhaul of barracks and added fortification around the coasts.

1808   Land surveyed at Golden-bridge for barrack purposes.

1809   Map of area drawn up by Messrs Brassington and Greene.

1810   Tenders issued for building work; work commenced.

1811   Discovery of spa or chalybeate spring.

1812   Lease for Richmond Barracks issued.

1813   Appointment of Barracks Master.

1814   Arrival of Cheshire and Lancashire Militias.

1815   Waterloo.

1816   Disembodiment of Militia and reduction of Regiments Also, Sadler's balloon.

1817   The 94th Regiment- Fire at Kilmainham Gaol.

1818   Outbreak of Typhus: 50th Queen's stricken.

1819   The 42nd Royal Highland Regiment (The Black Watch) Also, George Maclean and the arrival of the 91st.

1821   William Leeke, Gawler, Rowen and Mac Nair, the 52nd - Heroes of Waterloo; also, Michael Keenan of the 39th.

1822   Whiteboy alert; also, more ground taken for barrack purposes.

1823   Typhus Fever-The death of the Hon. George Finch.

1829   Consecration of Golden-Bridge Cemetery.

1830   The Scandal of Captain Smith of the 32nd Regiment.

1834   Birth of Hans Garrett Moore, first V.C. on S. African soil.

1839   The Connaught Rangers / Night of the Big Wind.

1843   Extensive fortifications to resist Repeal insurrection.

1844   Colonel Thomas Makdougall Brisbane.

1845   The Death of Lieutenant Colonel John Shelton.

1846   The Great Southern and Western Railway Line.

1847   Famine.

1853   The Garrison Chapel.

1854   The Arrival of the Third West York Militia.

1855   The She Barracks; Golden-Bridge Prison.

1858   James Thomson (B.V.), Poet.

1859   Lord Viscount Gough & a Presentation of Colours.
1861   Meeting of Residents and Ratepayers at Golden-Bridge.
1864   The Recreation Room Opens.
1866   Devoy Averts a Mutiny at Richmond Barracks.
1867   The Fenian Rising;
         also the Church Row: Rev. Mills V Rev. Craig.
1868   Golden-Bridge Cemetery Closes;
         The Army Chaplains Bill;
         New Kilmainham Township Act.
1869   Plans for the building of a Gymnasium.
1870   John Mackenzie Rogan.
1877   Hans Garret Moore's deed of Bravery.
1878   Sale of the Chapel of Ease.
1880   Return of the 80th from Zululand;
         Charles à Court Repington.
1882   The Invincibles.
1886   The Crawford Divorce Case.
1889   Typhoid Fever, The Rogers Field Report;
         Evacuation of Troops to Phoenix Park;
         Winter Camp at Balls Bridge.
1895   Purchase of Lands for Enlargement of Barracks.
1897   Baden-Powell and the Scots Guards.
1899   Lord Roberts at Richmond Barracks,
         Departure of 1st Battalion Argyll and Sutherland.
1900   Duke of Connaught; departure of 4th Argyll & Sutherland.
1903   The Irish Guards; Billie the Bulldog.
1904   The Royal Berkshire Regiment.
1905   A visit by the Prince of Wales.
1906   The Fire at Mountshannon Mills.
1907   The Coming of the Royal Irish Constabulary
         also the 56th Royal Essex Regiment.
1910   The Cavalry Depot.
1911   The arrival of the Queen's Own, Royal West Kent Regiment.
1913   The Dublin Lockout: riots at Emmet Hall, Inchicore.
1914   The First Deserter of World War One: Thomas Highgate.
1915   Francis Ledwidge.
1916   The Easter Rising, Surrender, Courts Martial, Executions.
1919   Post war Peace celebrations.

1921	Bandsman, Mark Percival KORR ambushed at Inchicore.
1922	The Handover of Richmond Barracks.
1923	Richmond Barracks is renamed Kehoe Barracks; The Execution of Sylvester Heaney.
1924	A Daring Raid.
1925	Keogh Square.
1926	The Church of St. Michael of the Angels.
1929	St. Michael's C.B.S.
1933	St. Michaels Parish Church.
1934	Extension to the Church.
1968	A Fire at the Youth Club / Arrival of Fr. Brian Power.
1969	Demolition of Keogh Barracks.
1970	St. Michael's Estate.
2006	Closure of C.B.S.
2008	Collapse of the Public Private Partnership/ Brendan McNamara.
2012	HSE Primary Care Centre opens at Unit 1.
2013	Demolition of the last block of St Michaels Estate.

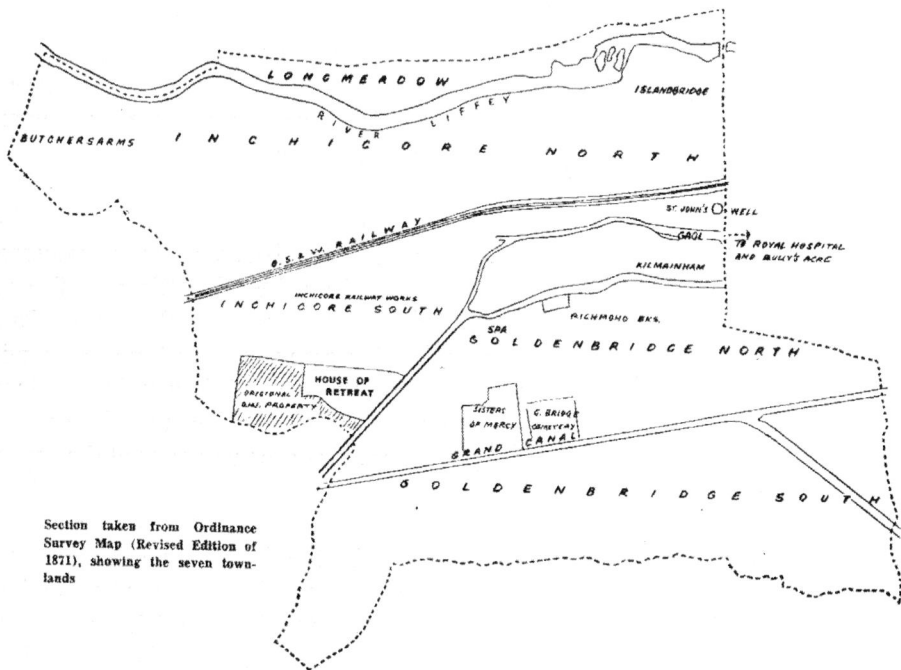

LONGMEADOW

RIVER LIFFEY

ISLANDBRIDGE

BUTCHERSARMS   I N C H I C O R E   N O R T H

G.S.& W. RAILWAY

ST. JOHN'S O. WELL

GAOL

KILMAINHAM

→ TO ROYAL HOSPITAL
AND BULLY'S ACRE

INCHICORE RAILWAY WORKS

I N C H I C O R E   S O U T H

SPA

RICHMOND BKS.

G O L D E N B R I D G E   N O R T H

HOUSE OF RETREAT

ORIGINAL
S.M. PROPERTY

SISTERS
OF MERCY

G. BRIDGE
CEMETERY

GRAND   CANAL

G O L D E N B R I D G E   S O U T H

Section taken from Ordinance
Survey Map (Revised Edition of
1871), showing the seven town-
lands

12

Goodbye to the Square

When I first set my mind on writing this history, I thought that it would be double themed as a story of soldiery followed by a story of families struggling against the odds; however, I found that it was one continuous struggle; Richmond Barracks was not just a base for soldiers, it also had a 'Married Quarters' for their wives and children. During its 108 years history almost every British regiment was represented here. Many people living in the Inchicore and Kilmainham areas, whether they know it or not, have ancestry dating back to Richmond Barracks.

In 1541, when the possessions of the Knights Hospitallers were commandeered by King Henry VIII, a mill was mentioned situated on the River Camac. The same enquiry into monastic settlements mentioned the 'Glydon Bryge' over the Camac. In more recent times, Inchicore was an adjoining area to the east and north with a small village, which together with Islandbridge village and Golden-Bridge formed the township of Kilmainham. The bridge, from which this area took its name, can still be seen after the turn from 'The Black Lion,' licensed premises at the corner of Grattan Crescent, onto Emmet Road.

Golden-Bridge, north and south was intersected by the Grand Canal. The ordinance survey map of 1871 shows the south as a wide expanse of open ground, that which is today taken up by Davitt Road and the beginning of the district of Drimnagh. Along this route the Luas tram can now be seen whizzing back and forth, chiming its mellow bells, so reminiscent of former times when trams were such an integral part of everyday life in Inchicore. To the north, from the canal to the present Emmet Road and involving some of the Bulfin Estate was the area occupied by the Sisters of Mercy Convent, Golden-Bridge Cemetery, Richmond Barracks and the barracks training ground and fields.

Standing on the vacant green area today, occupied until quite recently by St. Michael's Estate flats complex, one can still experience the feel of the barracks square and can easily imagine the tramp of soldiers, the drilling and the sergeant majors' shouted commands. This square, also remembered as Keogh Square, was but half of the barracks, that used by the ordinary soldiers; a second square for the officers' quarters and a training ground continued behind the three units of the old

Christian Brothers School and took in all of the Bulfin Court area. Little of the barracks remains now: part of the perimeter walls, scaled down, can still be seen where the old Health Centre stands (the site of the old Guard House), and a larger portion at St. Vincent's Street; the Garrison Church with added south wing which is today the Parish Church of St Michael; three units, two recreation rooms and a gymnasium comprised the local boys C.B.S national school; finally, a mortuary chapel at the rear of a garden in Connolly Avenue has survived the recent construction of senior citizens apartments at Emmet Court.

During the last three hundred years Dublin has witnessed the construction of numerous army barracks, some permanent and many others temporary. Only a small number of these barracks have survived to the present day, in use as museums or military archives, and there are still active army bases at McKee and Cathal Brugha Barracks. Most of the rest have disappeared without trace and without any lasting impact on the areas in which they once stood. Not so, however, in the case of Richmond Barracks. This year marks the bicentenary of the opening of this barracks. While just three of the units that formed its huge presence remain, its memory has endured both at national and at local level; nationally, because of its association with the events immediately following Easter, 1916; locally, because of its notorious afterlife as Keogh Square, and because even when the latter was finally demolished the families were then housed in new high rise flats built on the same site.

Now that ill conceived complex of flats, St. Michael's Estate, or 'Michael's Mistake,' is also gone. Those who have lived on the site, in particular, those born there and a number of the older generation (the 'Barrackers') will not tolerate a negative word spoken about the place. Indeed, there were tears quietly shed and many glazed eyes among the former residents gathered as the walls of the blocks were being torn down by the excavators. It will be among these people and their children that some of the good and fond memories will endure.

Thornton Heights (named after Dr. Brigid Lyons-Thornton), a new development of 75 houses and apartments was opened by President Michael D. Higgins in September 2014. However, because of the long delays in bringing the project to fruition most former inhabitants have put down roots elsewhere. Just 11 of the previous tenants and their families, now live in the new complex. When the Dublin City Council's regeneration plan is eventually completed it will radically reshape the area and a chapter lasting two centuries in local social history will finally close. For that reason, this is perhaps the ideal opportunity to reflect on the events of former times.

Liam O' Meara

The 4th.Duke of Richmond

Aristocrat, soldier, sportsman, MP, Lord Lieutenant and Governor of Ireland, Governor in Chief of Canada

It is appropriate to give an account of the Duke of Richmond, as the life and times of this Lord Lieutenant make a perfect backdrop to the circumstances in which Richmond Barracks was constructed. Few Irish commentators today record anything but a scant negative review of his office; they make no allowance for the fact that he was sent here for the purpose of keeping the Irish down at a time when echoes of the Emmet insurrection still hung in the air and the heavy handed response of the British through its yeomanry had further alienated the peasantry. Given that, he managed the first half of his tenure with remarkable diplomacy and was even considered popular!

In 1807, the *Dublin Evening Post* set the tone right for the arrival of the Duke of Richmond when they recalled former Viceroy, Marquis Townsend's boast that it had cost him £60,000 as Lord Lieutenant to drink down the aristocracy of that country. The editor wryly remarked that the Duke of Richmond had as strong a head, and, as the resident aristocracy was thinned since the Union, he would be able to accomplish that task with less expense to his purse or to his constitution. This was a reputation to which the Duke of Richmond certainly proved worthy, and, as far as he was concerned, such overindulgence came with the job. For all that, however, his own beginnings were humble enough; indeed, it was a great irony that it could finally be said of him, "He seems to have been born, just as he died, *in a barn*." [1]

Charles Lennox was born in Scotland on 9th September 1764, the son of Lieutenant-General Lord George Henry Lennox, brother of the 3rd Duke of Richmond, and his wife, Louisa, daughter of William Henry Kerr, Marquis of Lothian. Apparently his pregnant mother was on a fishing party when she suddenly went into labour. She was rushed to a nearby barn where young Charles first came into the world. He was educated by a private tutor in Paris, where he was joined by his cousin, the fourteen year old, Lord Edward Fitzgerald. Both studied at a military academy, perfecting their skills at fencing and riding 'and probably began their social and sexual education.'[2] The two boys then entered the Sussex Militia on the payroll of their uncle, the 3rd Duke of Richmond, who was master-general of the Board of

Ordnance. Charles and Edward were destined to follow different paths thereafter, though Edward later formed a romantic attachment to Charles's sister, Georgiana. Charles was promoted to a lieutenancy in 1778. Six years later, he became secretary to his uncle.

In 1787, he was commissioned a captain in the 35th Foot Regiment, and in 1789, with the influence of Prime Minister, William Pitt, secured a captaincy in the Coldstream Guards. This was a big promotion as it carried with it a lieutenant-colonelcy in the army at large. The Duke of York, second son of King George III, was incensed that Lennox, his political opponent had been granted this position in his company without his approval. There was great odium between the followers of both. Soldier friends of Lennox, allegedly, made their feelings towards the Duke of York known at Daubigney's army officers' club in the presence of Colonel Lennox. News of this conversation was relayed to York, who was greatly upset and said that the Colonel had subjected himself to comments which 'no gentleman would have tolerated'. *'Of course,'* he added, *'the Lennoxes don't fight.'* This inevitably led to a duel, which took place on Wimbledon Common on 26th May 1789.

As the King's son was involved there was great public interest. Lennox fired first and grazed the Duke's curl. The latter, refused to return fire despite repeated demands by Lennox to do so; instead, he suggested that Lennox fire again. Colonel Lennox naturally declined and the seconds then intervened, calling an end to the affair. Such was the value of honour, that most men would have rather taken a bullet (ball) than this perceived humiliation. Cartoonists of the day, biased in favour of royalty, depicted 'The Prince and the Poltron,' with Lennox in his familiar blue Goodwood colours, the latter of the two: a poltron, a bird of prey, with the talons of the hind toes cut off to prevent its flying at game (or more generally, a coward).

It had been a no-win situation for Lennox: had he seriously wounded the Duke, the repercussions would have been tremendous. As it was, he had to suffer being snubbed at a ball to which both parties were invited. It was the occasion of the Queen's birthday. The ball was opened by the Prince of Wales and the Princess Royal. The Queen, noticing that the prince was agitated, inquired why and was told that the Prince was uncomfortable in the presence of Lennox; whereupon the Queen retired, and 'the ball broke up with the same abruptness as the banquet in Macbeth.'[3]

The general consensus among his fellow officers was that Lennox had 'behaved with courage, but from the peculiarity of the circumstances not with judgement". After this ambiguous verdict, Lennox quit the Coldstream Guards, exchanging with Lord Strathnairn, his captaincy for the command of the 35th Foot, then stationed in Edinburgh.

Gentlemen who had failed or been compromised on the field, often welcomed the chance to restore pride at the earliest opportunity, and so it was with Lennox who was again involved in a duel near Uxbridge Road, London, just a little more than a month later, on 3rd July 1789. The unlucky man on this occasion was Theophilus Swift, who had published a pamphlet reflecting on his opponent's character. Swift was wounded, but not fatally: satisfaction was served and some pride and credibility restored. When Lennox arrived in Edinburgh, to take up his position with the 35th, the castle was illuminated in his honour. He was also presented with the freedom of the city.

Charles was fond of sports, having come from a great sporting family; his uncle was the founder of the Goodwood horse-races. He, himself, was a versatile competitor, excelling in the foot-race, at which it was said that few men could compete with him.[4] His family had contributed a lot to the growth of cricket and Charles, in the course of his life, played for twenty-two seasons, renowned as a wicket-keeper and right-hand bat. He was a founder member of the Marylebone Cricket Club. In 1786, together with the Earl of Winchilsea, Lennox had offered Thomas Lord a guarantee against any losses Lord might suffer on starting a new cricket ground. This had led to Lord opening his first cricket ground in 1787, known to this day as 'Lord's.' In this way, he immediately made himself popular with the soldiers of the 35th by joining them in playing cricket, something that was considered unusual for an officer to do. At tennis too, an officer of the garrison once described him as, *'One of the finest tennis-players in England and an excellent-baller who joined the officers around him in all manly games with an unaffected urbanity and good nature that endeared him to all.'*[5]

On 9th September 1789, he married Charlotte, heir to the last Duke of Gordon. This was seen as an important marriage for the future of the family as it would, in time, unite the estates of Lennox and Gordon. Although she was known to be excessively proud and disdainful of persons of inferior rank, she too enjoyed great affection and admiration among the people. They would have seven sons and seven daughters together. He served in the Leeward islands in the West Indies and on various campaigns with the 35th, steadily rising in rank to become an ADC to the King and, in 1814, a full General. In 1790, again with the influence of his uncle, he became MP for Sussex in succession to his father as a supporter of William Pitt. He continued to represent the county until the death of his uncle on 29th December, 1806, an event which was to prove momentous in the life of Charles Lennox.

The Dukedom of Richmond was a peerage which had expired and which was given new life (literally) by Charles II, when he bestowed it upon his natural son Charles Lennox, born in 1672 of his mistress, Louise Renée De Penancoët de Kéroualle, (nicknamed 'Fubbs,' an old English word meaning chubby). With the peerage came an income of £2,000 a year and a royalty on coal dues which the King set on coal at the port of Newcastle. As manufacturing increased, so did the wealth of the Lennox dynasty. It is thought that Goodwood House was purchased from the proceeds of this tax, known as the 'Richmond shilling.' The title passed from father to son until the 3rd. Duke, who died without an heir, although he did provide in his will for three illegitimate daughters by his housekeeper. The title and estate encumbered by debts of £180,000 went to his nephew Charles Lennox.

The following April 1807, Lennox, now the newly installed 4th. Duke of Richmond was appointed Lord Lieutenant of Ireland. A young Colonel Arthur Wellesley (later Duke of Wellington) 'who had returned home covered with Indian laurels and full of the promise of other honours and victories to come,'[6] was, at the same time, sworn in as Chief Secretary. The office of the Lord Lieutenant-General and Governor General of Ireland (his full title) was in Dublin Castle and his residence was at the Viceregal Lodge in the Phoenix Park. During his stay at the latter, which was once a plain building- a gentleman's private residence-Richmond added the north portico, a structure of the Doric order, and the lodges by which the demesne is entered on the side of Dublin.

The function of the Viceroy (as he was also known) was largely ceremonial:
'A Lord Lieutenant of Ireland has now little more to do with the measures of government than the postman with the incendiary letter he is the bearer of; he is a mere chair of state, and has little more real power than a village magistrate or parish constable: all he has to do is to fall in with the temper of the people, and keep them in good-humour, if he can.' [7]

It has to be said that this was a card played to perfection by Charles Lennox, who was more intent on the pursuit of pleasure than attending the affairs of state; it was a role that was tailor-made for him. On the 21st April, the honour 'Freeman' of the city of Dublin was conferred on both the Duke and Arthur Wellesley. That same year the honour was repeated in other counties such as, Waterford, Tullamore, Enniskillen, and Drogheda. The Duke and Duchess made their first public appearance on May 5th 1807, at a reception held at the Rotunda Rooms, followed (much to the delight of the Dublin citizens) by a visit to a play called 'The Honeymoon,' at the Theatre Royal.

Dinner party after dinner party followed at the Viceregal Lodge, at Dublin Castle, or the home of some titled gentleman. Often, His Grace would leave one function to attend another where there would be just as much wine and food. At a dinner on St. Patrick's Day, for instance, there were so many people to be 'toasted,' that the party went on until 4 o' clock in the morning. Another, was 'a turtle feast' given by Wellesley in his private rooms; turtles were a bit of a fad at this time- 'Leeches' Royal Hotel, Kildare street, advertised them at a half a guinea a quart. It was even claimed that the Duke dined in a tent at the notorious Donnybrook Fair in 1808,[8] forsaking the safety and comforts of a neighbouring hotel. It is easy therefore to understand why he soon became known as the 'duke of poitín.' Another event was the annual pattern at St. John's Well, near Kilmainham, where he presided over sumptuous feasts laid on for his cronies and hangers-on.[9] The most notable event was a Jubilee Ball and Dinner (1809) at the Rotunda, in celebration of the 50th anniversary of the accession of George III; this lasted 3 days and catered for 1000 guests.

A contemporary report gives us a glimpse at his character:

> He is, by a bottle, at the least, the best Lord Lieutenant that has been in this country for half a century:—he has taken several excursions to the country parts of the kingdom, where he is as famous for his conviviality as his high rank. He is what is called here a five-bottle man, and after supper drinks grog and smokes tobacco like a West India planter... He was spending a few days at a gentleman's house in the south of Ireland; — there was a good deal of other company, all great topers, and invited for that reason: they were milksops, however, compared to his Excellency; who, having soon laid them under the table, was reduced to the unpleasant alternative of either drinking by himself, or not drinking at all. In this melancholy predicament, his host dispatched a messenger for a young curate of good family, in high estimation for the strength of his head, who lived a few miles distant; he begged of him to come to him immediately, and strive to keep company with his Excellency. The clerical Bacchus did not refuse so agreeable a summons, and next day was seated at table opposite the vice-regal one.
>
> After the rest of the party were dispersed or fallen, the two champions were left alone. *'This is poor pitiful work, your grace,'* said the Curate: *'the wine is getting cold on my stomach; what do you think of a bumper of brandy?"* His grace had no objection to so spirited a proposition, and two large glasses were instantly swallowed; two others were as instantly filled up. The Curate drank part of his, but could proceed no further; his jaw became fixed, and he rolled motionless on the floor: the Duke coolly finished his own glass, and, smiling on his prostrate antagonist, walked steadily to his chamber.[10]

There are many more laughable and ludicrous stories on record concerning the 4th Duke of Richmond, but the most extraordinary one is associated with an official visit he paid to Mullingar to witness a pattern (festival or fair) for which at that time Lough Owel was famous. Lord de Blacquiere was the host at Portomon, and after a lively stay, the cellars were drained of their wines and at the close of the pattern there was not a drop to be had in the house. The Duke was furious and de Blacquiere in a quandary, retired to think out a scheme for getting a supply. He was so long away that Lennox, left holding an empty glass, lost his patience and when the crowds returned from the pattern, he had them rounded up to an auction of some of his host's furniture. When sufficient money was secured, a quantity of wines and spirits was obtained from the village of Bunbrusna and the house party (with the exception of Lord de Blacquiere) retired highly pleased with the last night of the Lord Lieutenant's visit. [11]

Another story concerns his love of sport coupled with his love of gambling. Apart from cricket, at which he excelled and athletics, Lennox was a frequent visitor to cock-fighting bouts in Clarendon Street and was also fond of boxing. His favourite pastime however, was the game of rackets- an early form of tennis- which he played regularly at the rackets hall in John's Lane. He invited some of the finest players in England to join him here and often a match would be arranged for a wager. Lord Sydney Osborne prided himself on his skills with a racket and he challenged the Duke to find him a suitable opponent, *'any man in the world'* brave or foolish enough. The bet was an enticing one thousand guineas. The Duke, straight away thought of someone, a Dublin tailor named Flood, who also happened to be a highwayman and a pickpocket in his spare time. He had seen Flood play at John's Lane court and knew his strengths. Having accepted the bet with Osborne, the Duke set out to find Flood at John Lane, only to discover that the rogue was lodged in Newgate prison awaiting hanging that Saturday for highway robbery. Flood could scarcely believe his luck when the Duke organized his release and a full pardon. Privately, Lennox informed him that there were certain conditions, which the tailor was only too glad to honour. Osborne knew nothing of this arrangement and the date for the bout was fixed. On the day of the match Osborne took an early lead, but soon this was reversed and Flood seemed to be getting the upper hand. Osborne, frustrated at the prospect of being beaten by a lowly tailor lost his temper and ultimately the match and the wager. The grateful Duke gave Flood £50 and advised him to leave the country. [12]

Other official business for the Duke involved inspection of military displays. These ranged from witnessing, with Wellesley at the Pigeon House fort, the throwing of shells and red hot balls, to the annual reviewing of troops. At the Phoenix Park in June 1807, a two gun salute announcing the approach, followed by a twenty one gun salute heralded the arrival of His Grace to review 20,000 soldiers. The location of this salute battery, where twelve pieces of cannon fired salvos on 'rejoicing days,' would later be the site of the Wellington Monument. Lennox was immensely popular with the soldiers. As he had done in England, he engaged in sporting activities with them, displaying his considerable and varied talents.

Lennox had only been appointed Lord Lieutenant after two others had refused the job. The country was prone to sudden incidences of rebellion. Lennox's conditional acceptance of the role of Governor- that he would only do so if nothing were done for the Catholics- has to be seen in this light. It was very much the attitude that his Prime Minister would have expected of him, for while Richmond could boast that he was the great-great-grandson of the King of England, his detractors could equally remind him that he was the cousin of the treacherous Lord Edward Fitzgerald[f]; Such were the complexities of the Lennox family; another cousin was Charles James Fox, whose followers were known as 'Foxites,' anti-Tory, opposed to the Union and the war with France and in favour of Catholic Emancipation. Even so, Richmond was anxious, not to add to the unrest of Catholics and once, on a tour of Ireland, he is said to have refused a toast to the Protestant Ascendancy, in a public display meant to portray his willingness to deal fairly with all groups. His Secretary (Wellington), likewise, is said to have repressed with the same firmness the excesses of those he called 'red-hot Protestants,' as he showed in resisting, at that period, what he considered to be the unconstitutional pretensions of the Catholics. He even dissuaded the Wexford yeomanry from celebrating the anniversary of the battle of Vinegar Hill, as he regarded such celebrations likely to 'exasperate party spirit,' and to 'hurt feelings.'

For the first half of his tenure in office, Richmond managed to stay out of trouble. Even the two main organs of Catholic opinion the *Freeman's Journal* and the *Dublin Evening Post* had to concede that he was liked by all sections of the community. Both newspapers followed the movements of the Duke and Duchess almost on a daily basis, always commenting in the most flattering tones. This would all change during the second half of his reign. However, let us first view the often forgotten (positive) side of his Lord lieutenancy.

During these first years, the Duke and the Duchess were anxious to show that they were caring individuals. They attended many charity lectures to raise money; their very presence, ensuring large audiences of benevolent subscribers. When the idea was mooted for a memorial to the late Admiral Nelson to be erected in Sackville Street, the Duke and his predecessor Bedford were the first contributors to the public sponsorship fund, each personally donating £200. The Duke, himself, laid the foundation stone on the 15[th.] February 1808, dressed in regimentals, but with a Freemason's apron around his waist and a black scarf draped over his left arm. Richmond was patron to the new and very popular Subscription Bath Houses-vapour medicated baths. Indeed his name attached itself to more places and things than almost anyone else in Irish History. There was even the *Duke of Richmond Streamer*, a new elegant copper-bottomed cutter from Dublin to Liverpool named in

---

[f] After the death of Lord Edward in Newgate Goal, his wife Lady Pamela and their children crossed to Goodwood where they were shown much kindness by the 3rd. Duke and his daughters.

his honour. He not only gave his name to, but was sponsor and founding member on the committees of several institutions which have survived to this day. Among these were, the Richmond Surgical Hospital and Dispensary, the Richmond Institution for the Instruction of the Industrious Blind (for which he gave a personal donation and laid the foundation stone) and the Richmond General Asylum, which was expecting upwards of 200 lunatics; the Duke here again laid the foundation stone and "graciously permitted it to be named after him". In a very personal way too, he was known to have sent money (usually £20) to widows of murdered husbands. A Mr. Palwert Russell, tried convicted and awaiting execution for horse stealing, was granted a reprieve owing to the Duke's intervention.

In particular, the Gaol Act, enacted during his administration and the introduction of the penitentiary system were seen as great improvements. At that time, convicts were often sent to New South Wales at a cost of £150 each and the additional loss to the Irish labour force. It was found that criminals seldom reformed following transportation. A penitentiary formed at Kilmainham, and other local gaols proved successful. Here prisoners were put to work and allowed to keep half of their earnings as incentive to labour. Occasionally, Richmond visited himself and advised the directors. The 'idle and refractory' prisoners were remanded to Gaol and pardon was extended to the 'orderly and industrious.' Encouraged by the success of this small scale experiment, he extended the system by the building of the Richmond General Penitentiary for receiving, reforming and employment of criminals.

Richmond's record on army reform holds up well. Being a soldier himself he was in a good position to know what was required. Volunteers from the militia, forming large drafts into the regiments of the line and the interchange of militia between Great Britain and Ireland were both measures of sound policy, well calculated to benefit the military establishment of the Empire. The construction of fortifications, magazines, military roads, depots etc., while necessary of course, gave employment to indigent workmen while providing a lasting monument to their founder. Other outstanding features of his term in office were: the Paving Board; improvements to harbours and docks and the erection of lighthouses; loans to merchants during a period of stagnation in trade (1810) and the preference by the Duke and Duchess to the manufactures of Ireland.

His Grace the Duke of Richmond
LORD LIEUTENANT OF IRELAND, &c. &c.

In dealing with the negative aspects of the Duke's term in office, we have to distinguish between Richmond personally and the Richmond administration. Indeed, even when things started to go wrong, the *Freeman's Journal* was loath, at first, to apportion blame to the Duke and described him as 'harmless, fond of amusement and the convivial circle' They wondered, however, if these were the necessary qualities required for his office and warned, that there was a limit to which he could distance himself from the actions of those in his employment. Long afterwards, Wellington, then, *'The most high, mighty and noble prince, whom all England and nearly all Europe delighted to honour,'* defended the Administration of which he had formed a part, for its habitual use of corrupt means and influence. He denied that: 'The whole nation is, or ever was corrupt,' but said that *'almost every man of mark has his price'* and he was obliged to use corrupt influences *'to command a majority in favour of order,'* arguing that, however the particular kinds of influence might go against the grain, he had no option but to use them.[13]

The administration soon showed that it meant business when it came to establishing law and order, and although some of the measures taken were surely necessary at a time of widespread lawlessness, there can be no doubt that they added to the difficulties of Catholics in particular. Wellesley's Police Act (1808) abolished the old City Watch and replaced it with a new police force that had jurisdiction over 8 miles around Dublin. The Insurrection Act was re-enacted with additional powers calling for the registration of all arms and allowed for houses of suspects to be searched. Richmond, however, did not impose martial law and instead placed corps of yeomanry in the most disturbed districts. The expectations of the Catholic body, raised during the previous administration (Bedford), were soon dispelled and it became obvious that the Duke of Richmond was fully committed to the Union and against Emancipation. Indeed, it is a measure of his charm that he managed to placate the Catholics for so long while not giving an inch on their demands. He told them fairly:

'You must expect no increase of privilege from me; but you may expect that the law shall be equally and justly administered and you may expect that every office which the constitution has left open to you shall be distributed to the meritorious amongst you, and that no association shall be encouraged or spirit countenanced calculated in the slightest degree to insult your feelings.' [14]

He had tried to appeal to all of moderate inclination and was not directly opposed to every measure of the interests and objects of the Catholic religion. Then, out of the blue, came the notorious Circular of his new Secretary, Wellesley Pole, which would undo all the diplomatic work he had undertaken to keep the Catholics on his side.

Arthur Wellesley, who of course had unfinished business with Napoleon, was succeeded as Chief Secretary in 1810, by his brother, William Wellesley Pole. From the outset, this was an unpopular appointment. The Catholics, for so long, deprived of a parliament were driven to permanent association as the only means of effecting changes in the legislature. In addition they were forbidden from meeting in convention and so had to assemble voluntarily from various quarters without delegation. They met habitually in the disused theatre in Fishamble Street and outdoors, where they gathered in large numbers. Such assemblies were known as 'aggregate meetings' and were, supposedly, only for the purpose of petition. These meeting had taken place frequently and were well signalled in advance in the newspapers. The Duke had to have known, but chose to ignore them. In a dramatic change of policy, Pole's Circular effectively enforced the Convention Act suppressing the Catholic Committee. Under the Act, Catholics attempting to convene could be dispersed, but Pole's Circular ordered magistrates of respective counties to, **'Arrest or hold to bail all persons who shall attend or vote or act for such purpose.'**

No account, it seems, was taken of people who were observers, or who had come to oppose the petitions sought at these meetings. The letter which, if implemented to the full, could have led to the confinement of three fourths of the population, outraged the Catholics and provided great substance for the opposition in the House of Commons. When, in 1811, Lord Fingal and some of his friends convened a Catholic Assembly of the leading Catholics in contravention of the Act, he together with Drs. Sheridan and Kirwan and secretaries were arrested and the concourse dispersed. Lord Fingal was not prosecuted, but the secretaries were. After that, the Catholic Committee ostensibly dissolved but continued to lobby under the title of the Catholic Board.

Other deeds of the Duke were then questioned, for instance: his appointment of Sir Edward Stanley, on a huge salary as Barrack Master of Dublin (The Royal Barracks); another contentious issue was a very harsh tax on tea in the amount of £10,000 per annum, coincidentally the same as the Duke's annual salary. Catholics were now set against the Lord Lieutenant and his Secretary. A petition containing 26,000 signatures calling for the removal of Richmond and Pole was presented to the Prince Regent.

To add to the Duke's woes, he was forced to initiate proceedings in two separate libel suits defending charges perceived to have been made against his administration. One was brought against the proprietor of the *Dublin Evening Post*. In 1813, John Magee, a champion of the Catholic cause, was tried on corruption charges before an all Protestant jury and found guilty of 'a wicked malicious and 'seditious libel.' The offending quote was cited thus:

> As the Duke of Richmond will shortly retire from the Government of Ireland it
> has been deemed necessary to make a review of his administration as it may at
> least warn his successor from pursuing the errors of his Grace's conduct…the
> people of Ireland must find themselves at a loss to discover any striking
> features of his Grace's administration, that makes it superior to the worst of his
> predecessors… They insulted, they oppressed, they murdered they deceived ---
> the profligate unprincipled Westmoreland, the cold hearted cruel Camden, the
> awful and treacherous Cornwallis… etc.

Daniel O'Connell, defended the editor and, with his usual robust oratory, subjected
attorney-general, William Saurin to a harangue of humiliating personal abuse.
Nevertheless, Magee was sentenced to 2 years. The Kilkenny Catholic Committee
passed a resolution condemning the Government's treatment of Magee, which he
unwisely published in his paper and for which he received an additional 6 months.
As a further penalty, stamps for mailing Magee's paper were withheld forcing him
to transfer ownership to his brother James. He was eventually freed from Newgate
prison in 1816, after paying £1,500 in fines.

The second libel action concerned, Hugh Fitzpatrick, a printer and bookseller for
the college at Maynooth, who had issued an anonymous book titled *A Statement of
the Penal Laws Which Aggrieve Catholics.* It was objected to by the authorities and
Fitzpatrick rather than reveal the identity of author Denis Scully, went to jail for 18
months and paid a fine of £200. The following was the inflammatory piece from that
work:

> At the Summer Assizes of Kilkenny, 1810, one, Barry was convicted of a
> capital offence for which he was afterwards executed. This man's case was
> tried tragically. He was wholly innocent- was a respectable Catholic farmer in
> the County Waterford, in good circumstances. His innocence was clearly
> established in the interval between his conviction and execution and yet he was
> hanged publicly avowing his innocence. There are shocking circumstances
> attending this case, which the Duke of Richmond's Administration may yet be
> invited to explain to Parliament.

Barry is alleged to have been 40 miles from the scene, according to an article in the
newspaper in Feb. 1813. Although the administration was successful in both cases
much damage was already done. The Duke was no longer of a conciliatory
disposition and his ire was especially reserved for the Catholic Committee. When
Grattan's Relief Bill was being debated, Peel, the new, more capable Secretary,
advised Lennox that should the Bill be defeated it would result in violence. The

Catholics were excited following the Clare election victory and, with so many of them infiltrating the police and army, the Government could not be sure what way they would react. His Grace was almost gleeful at the prospect of this:

'Please God, if we are obliged to draw the sword, the Committee gentlemen shall have their full share of it if I can catch them.'[15]

Support for the demands of Catholics was growing with the popularity of their great leader, Daniel O'Connell. In a letter to his sister, Richmond confided that, given the stance he had taken, he would have to resign if these demands were met. However, the Corporation of Dublin submitted their own petition of approval to the Prince Regent and the Duke saw out his term of office.

Together with his wife and children he returned briefly to their home in Goodwood, Chichester, West Sussex. At the time of death of his predecessor, the 3rd Duke was in the process of extending the house. He had built an extra room to accommodate rare tapestries and other works of art and had begun to build two additional wings to cater for an art collection salvaged from (the uninsured) Richmond House, on the Thames, destroyed by fire in 1791. The 4th Duke thus had the makings of a fine house. He arranged for the completion of the work, but because of outstanding debts he and his family moved to Brussels.

It was here that Charlotte gained notoriety in her own right. The Duchess, if anything, craved power even more than her husband. Besides her interest in gaming, a vice that left her husband on the brink of ruin, her talent for organising drawing rooms and balls was renowned. Of course, she had plenty of practice during the years of her husband's tenure in Ireland and loved to be paraded in the finest gowns. To her credit, when she was in Ireland she had always insisted on wearing cloth of Irish manufacture; the ladies of the court being encouraged to do likewise. On the 15th June, 1815, Charlotte planned a ball (what has since been referred to as 'the most famous ball in history') to be held in a coach-maker's depot adjacent to their home in the Rue de la Blanchisserie. For obvious reasons, she asked the Duke of Wellington if she could continue: he replied, 'Duchess, you may give your ball.'[16] By that time Wellington was a close family friend and military colleague of the 4th. Duke. He may have counted on Napoleon believing that the British were frivolous and unready. Also, he knew that his presence at the ball would help to allay the considerable disquiet and near panic which circulating rumours were causing amongst the inhabitants of Brussels. At the height of the ball, in the early hours of the 16th June, just as Wellington was retiring to bed, an urgent message was brought to him and he asked the Duke of Richmond if there was a good map in the house. Richmond took him into his dressing room and Wellington, having closed the door, confided to him some startling news: *'Napoleon has humbugged me, by God! He has gained twenty-four hours' march on me.'*

When Richmond asked what he intended doing, Wellington replied*: 'I have ordered the army to concentrate at Quatre Bras; but we shall not stop him there, and so, **I must fight him here,**'* (at the same time passing his thumb-nail over the position of Waterloo). [17] ...

The Duchess of Richmond's ball

Napoleon had entered Belgium that evening, and many officers left the ball for the battlefield, some to their deaths. The French were contained in a holding battle at Quatre Bras the next day, two days before the battle of Waterloo. Richmond was present at Waterloo, unofficially with Wellington's suite, though Wellington had tried to send him home saying 'Duke, you have no business here.' [18] If, however,

28

Wellesley thought that the Duke would keep quiet, he was mistaken, as this lovely cameo from the battlefield, recently retold, captures:

When the Inniskillings were beginning to gather speed many of them saw a man in civilian clothes on horseback waving a hat and shouting *'now's your chance!'* Next to him, likewise on horseback, a boy with an arm in a sling and a bandaged head stood upright in his stirrups, thoroughly excited. The man shaking his hat was his Grace, the Duke of Richmond, who although he possessed the rank of general had been assigned no command in Wellington's army. Nevertheless, he had come to Waterloo to observe the battle, in which three of his sons were serving as aide-de-camps. The boy beside him was Lord William Pitt Lennox, at fifteen the youngest of the three... A few days before, the youngster had fallen from his horse, breaking his arm, cracking his head, and loosing the sight in one eye... Sir Peregrine would not permit him to serve in his present state so the fifteen year old had resigned himself to watching the battle at his father's side. Whenever the Duke, heedless of the bullets that were whistling all around, stopped to converse with one General or another it was all Lord William could do to steady his frightened horse which seemed on the point of bolting off and perhaps carrying him into the midst of the French; but he felt immense pride when his father turned to him and said *'I'm glad to see you stand fire so well.'* Then the cavalry began to move forward and the boy remained there, lighting with excitement, standing up straight in his stirrups to see what would happen.[19]

The Duke seemed to regard the Battle of Waterloo as a cricket match! There had been talk of forming a third corps for Richmond to command, but this never materialised, and Wellington kept the Reserve under his own hand. What followed, of course, was the decisive British triumph on 18th June 1815.

The Richmond family continued to live in Brussels until 1818, when the Duke was appointed Governor-in-Chief of British North America. It is not within the scope of this book to record his activities there, but as we commenced with the curious comparison of the details of his birth and death it is now appropriate to give some account of the latter. During the summer of 1819, he undertook a tour of Upper and Lower Canada. At William Henry's residence (Sorel, Que.) he was bitten on the hand by a pet fox. There were no symptoms at first, indeed not for a further 40 days. The injury apparently healed and he returned to Toronto. Returning to Kingston, he planned a visit to the remote settlements on the Rideau. He had to walk 30 miles from Perth in excessive heat through woodland where there was not even a path to accommodate a saddle horse. It was in the course of this journey that he was overcome by hydrophobia. He recognised his situation from the start. On attempting to descend the Ottawa River, the sight of water instantly threw him into convulsions and in little more than 24 hours he was dead. He died on 28th August, in extreme agony in a barn only a few miles from a settlement named in his honour. Richmond's body was brought back to Quebec, where on the 4th September 1819, it was buried in the Cathedral of the Holy Trinity. A timber ship brought the news of his death. The colours of the fort were at half mast and the town of Quebec in universal lamentation for the loss of 'such a worthy character.' He was 55 years of age. On his death he was: Duke of Richmond, in England; Duke of Aubigney in France; Duke of Lennox and Earl of Darnley in Scotland; Governor General of Canada; Governor of Plymouth; High Steward of Chichester; he was also on the Privy council and was a Knight of the Garter. Military titles included, Lieutenant General in the Army and Colonel of the 35th Regiment.

And there we leave this outline of the colourful aristocrat, Charles Lennox, 4th Duke of Richmond; but as we now return to 1810, and the building of Richmond Barracks, you we may expect to encounter him from time to time throughout the first decade of that period.

Memorial to the Duke of Richmond in Ontario, Canada

Proposed New Barracks
at Golden-Bridge

The Threat from Napoleon

The British were in constant fear of an invasion by Napoleon. A measure of this paranoia can be had from their reaction to an elaborate hoax which suggested that the French dictator had determined to use the powerful Danish navy for an attack on Ireland. On 29th April 1807, Napoleon wrote an instruction to his naval minister, Denis Decrès, instructing him to undertake preparations at Brest which would give the impression that an expedition to Ireland was underway and to spread the rumour amongst the exiled Irish Republicans of the plan to free the island from English rule. The report of the British agent to the British foreign secretary was just as Napoleon had anticipated. It said that Napoleon's navy was planning a two-pronged advance on Ireland – one of them involving the Danish navy. First, a French fleet was to leave from Brest, Brittany, to take Southern Ireland. The second step was to seize the Danish navy and, with its help, attack Northern Ireland. The response of the British, however, was not what Napoleon had hoped. Still smarting from his defeat at Trafalgar, he had thought the intelligence would force the British Government to concentrate on strengthening its defences nearer home. This was later the case, as we shall see, but the immediate action taken by the British was to go on the offensive. Instead of sending troops to Ireland to tackle unrest fuelled by the rumours, Prime Minister William Pitt opted to take direct action against his supposed enemies, the unsuspecting citizens of Denmark.

British troops were mobilized in a matter of weeks. The navy landed in Copenhagen on 16th August 1807, with the intent of taking the Danish navy by force. Batteries were set up around the city and for three nights the city was subjected to artillery fire as well as mortar and rocket destruction. The rockets, called 'Congreve rockets,' named after their inventor William Congreve, were described by a British soldier as *'fiery serpents in the sky.'* The brutal bombardment was intended to force the surrender of the Danish navy by instilling terror in the capital's civilians. It destroyed a third of the city, killing 2,000 civilians, ten percent of Copenhagen's population.*ʃ* It was only after the surrender that the British realized what a blunder the operation had been. The 20 battleships lay idle in port without rigging and were clearly not going anywhere. The whole affair was a deliberate scheme of misinformation perpetuated by their arch rival. [20]

Where Ireland was concerned, the British had the additional dilemma of internal conflict, since even the bloody retribution wrought in the aftermath of the 1798 rebellion had not prevented a further insurrection in 1803. Repeal of the Act of Union had already become the new cause for the Irish. Napoleon had taken full advantage of this state of uncertainly to hatch his plot of deception and was relying on an uneasy British Government to stretch their military reserves in this direction. Even the revelation that there was no truth in the story about an invasion of Ireland involving the Danish fleet, still the fear remained and needed to addressed. First, a firm-handed administration under the Lord Lieutenancy of the Duke of Richmond

---

ʃ 'The attack itself is a historic landmark - the first deployment of terror tactics on civilians to cause a nation's surrender and also the first example of rockets being used in Europe. The attack's largely been forgotten, and even brushed under the carpet by the British. I think it's important that we put it back on the map again. It has definite relevance to readers today and people will see the parallels with the intelligence that led Britain to war in Iraq. That too was a pre-emptive attack that was founded on shaky intelligence and the credulity of politicians,' **Dr. Thomas Munch Petersen.**

was put in place. The considered solution to quell any unrest and to safeguard the country without weakening the regular army was to build up the army to capacity. The Duke of Richmond's scheme of augmenting the regular army with regiments of militia was a way of achieving this. Extensive fortification was another measure taken; the introduction of Martello towers[f] and a complete overhaul of the barracks system which would see the closure of many small barracks throughout Ireland and the creation of newer larger ones. In addition to the Royal Barracks, from 1793, the city had acquired 10 more sets of temporary barracks. These were necessary, not just for the protection of the city, but because of the increased size of the garrison. Soon after, however, these barracks proved inappropriate: they were overcrowded and the troops were too widely dispersed. The revised plan, expedited by the threat of Napoleon, resulted in the closure of all temporary barracks in Dublin with the exception of George's Street. In their place, two new large edifices were to be erected, a cavalry barracks at Portobello and an infantry barracks at Golden-Bridge.

William Smith and Golden-Bridge House

The name Golden-Bridge is said to date back at least five centuries and takes its name from the little bridge which to this day still spans the River Camac. For three hundred years of that time Golden-Bridge House has stood here and it is with this house, its grounds and occupants that the area is more commonly associated. The occupants of this house and lands were descendants of Heriz of Withcote in the county of Leicester in England, who in turn claimed to be descended from the ancient family of Heriz of Wiverton, whose lineage could be traced to King Henry I. The earliest reference is of William Heriz, who in 1492 married Katherine Ashby and assumed the name and arms of Smith in consideration of the manor of Withcote, which was bequeathed to him. His descendants included his grandson, Roger (1571-1603)) who was a Captain of a column of 100 men in Ireland, and his great-grandson, Sir Roger Smith, a knight of the manor whose tomb can be seen at Edmondthorpe in Leicestershire. The Smiths lived at Dunlavin in county Wicklow for a few generations before coming to Dublin.

---

[f] These towers were cheekily modelled on a similar type tower at the Cape of Mortella in Corsica, which had made a strong resistance to an English naval force in 1794. Each had its own cannon manned by one officer and between 5-27 artillery men. A furnace was provided to heat the cannonballs so that a missive could fire the sails of an advancing ship. 28 such circular tapering towers of stone were built on the east coast to oppose possible Napoleonic landings. In 1812, a fresh threat by the French saw the addition of more towers in other coastal areas such as, Magilligan Tower in Derry.

A lease for lives dated 1716 and registered in 1720, under the name of William Smith, Farmer, Kilmainham, City of Dublin, granted 'the tenement known as the Three Chimneys near Golden-Bridge with the farm and the quarry by the River *Cammock*, Rent £60 annually.' Viscount Wolseley referred to it as being 'a red-brick domestic dwelling of King William or early Queen Anne in design.' The forename, William continued to be passed down the line from father to eldest son.

Golden Bridge House

Viscount Wolseley's maternal great-grandfather, William Smith was born in 1717. According to the Dublin Assembly Roll of 1751, he was appointed city scavenger for a portion (lots 2 and 3) of the north side of the Liffey, the cleansing for which he would be paid £312. [21] It was when he was in his 83rd year that a stirring event, now long forgotten, occurred at this house: a tale of a daring robbery and murder, which resulted in a young man being sent, rather controversially, to the gallows. That this man deserved the ultimate penalty, was perhaps borne out by the discovery of a previous murder he allegedly committed, but for the crime for which he was

34

indicted, it was considered harsh even by the standards of those times. The case was considered interesting both on account of the law of the case and the singularity of the facts of which the law arose.

On the evening of the 22nd March 1800, shortly after dark, a band of robbers entered the home of this elderly gentleman. They had reconnoitered the property for some time in separate groups; two of them stationed opposite to the kitchen door next to Mr. Smith's orchard, and the rest at the front of the house close to the hall entrance. Their opportunity came when a carter for the family, William Donnelly, opened the kitchen door. (It later emerged, that on the previous night Donnelly had been seized by the gang as he returned from town with some articles for his master; he was dragged into the orchard and interrogated as to the particulars of the house, its security- arms and ammunition, whereabouts of articles of value and the persons likely to be present. The carter, in peril of his life, had given the information.) The gang now rushed into the house, much to the consternation of the servants and two sons of Mr. Smith's who were present. As the rogues were engaged ransacking the place and stripping the sons of expensive items of clothing and watches, one of their number, John Quinn, ventured around to the front parlour where Mr. Smith senior and his wife, Elizabeth (nee White) were sitting together.

He ordered the pair to lower their heads, but the old man not hearing the instruction properly, instead rose up with candle in hand to enquire what was going on? Quinn panicked and discharged his pistol at Smith. Fortunately, its contents, a ball and some swan shot went above him and lodged in the wall behind. However, the candle fell over leaving the house in a darkened state. Another of the gang, Farrell, convinced that Mr. Smith had fired on Quinn, rushed to his assistance. He saw a figure in the darkness which he took to be a son of Smith's and fired a shot. When the other gang members restored the light they were all dismayed to find that the shot person was in fact Quinn.

They were further alarmed to find that he was dead. Initially they were still convinced that it was Smith who had killed Quinn and they swore to take the lives of every being in the house. They soon realized however, that it was Farrell who had inadvertently shot his accomplice. The pillage of the house continued, and old Mr. Smith, in particular, was subjected to much cruelty; on his knees throughout, he was repeatedly questioned as to where he kept his cash. Mrs. Smith was crying and screaming throughout this ordeal. It was only when one of the sons produced a receipt for a large sum of money paid for rent the previous day that the gang were persuaded to desist. Their final nefarious act was to wrap the corpse in a tablecloth and to dispose of it in the Grand Canal nearby.

Farrell was later arrested on Aston's Quay, as he was leaning against the Liffey Wall. A pistol was found in his possession. Shortly after, all of the gang members were in custody. One gang member had been admitted a King's witness (an approver). In addition, the evidence against the men was overwhelming; items were recovered, including a great coat, property of Francis Smith, and a silversmith in Dame Street came forward with a gold watch, property of Robert Smith, sold to him by the prisoner Shea. The most serious charge, of course, was levelled at Farrell. The prosecution conceded that Farrell had not intended to kill Quinn; however, he had intended to kill Mr. Smith. A case was cited, of a man who attempted to murder his wife by giving her a poisoned apple. The woman unknowingly passed the apple over to her child who ate it and died. The husband was found guilty of murdering the child:

> If the intention was to kill or wound one of Mr. Smith's family or domestics, and death ensued, the offence will be murder, though the party who fired the shot had mistaken his victim, and though the person actually killed was one of the very banditti engaged in the robbery- a homicide was committed, and that homicide was at all events the result of the wicked and murderous workings of an abandoned and profligate heart - that malice which the law requires, existed, therefore, in the case, and the offence of murder became in every legal point of view, complete and consummate.'

At first, all of the prisoners were charged with murder, but only James Farrell was found guilty on this charge and sentenced to death; the others were found guilty of felony. The speed of the proceedings in this saga was surprising: the offence was committed on 22nd March; Farrell was tried on 15th July, found guilty and sentenced on 17th and executed on 26th July at Kilmainham Jail; his body thereafter sent for dissection.[22] There was little sympathy for him when it emerged that he had allegedly killed another of his 'confederates' in Drumcondra some years before. The two had apparently gone to dig up a booty of plate and, on completion of the task, Farrell killed his associate, took the plate and buried the corpse in the hole, a deed worthy of 'Long John Silver!' [23]

Mr. William Smith, it seems, led a charmed life, having survived two murder attempts in one night alone; he died on the 28th September, 1810, at the age of 93 years. His wife died around the same time and their burials are recorded on opposite pages of the register at St. James's Church. In 1809, a map was signed by Mr. R. Robinson showing 'ground contiguous to Kilmainham in the County of Dublin taken for Barrack purposes,' having being surveyed by Sherrard Brassington and Greene, the previous year, 1809.[24] The ground in question, consisting of 23 acres, was in the holding possession of William and Francis Smith. The Smith's retained that area of land which was situated in the immediate vicinity of the house. As we shall see, in due course, this land including the house was later acquired by the

36

Sisters of Mercy; but not before a marriage of significance between the families Smith and Wolseley which produced one of the most celebrated Irish born British soldiers of all time.

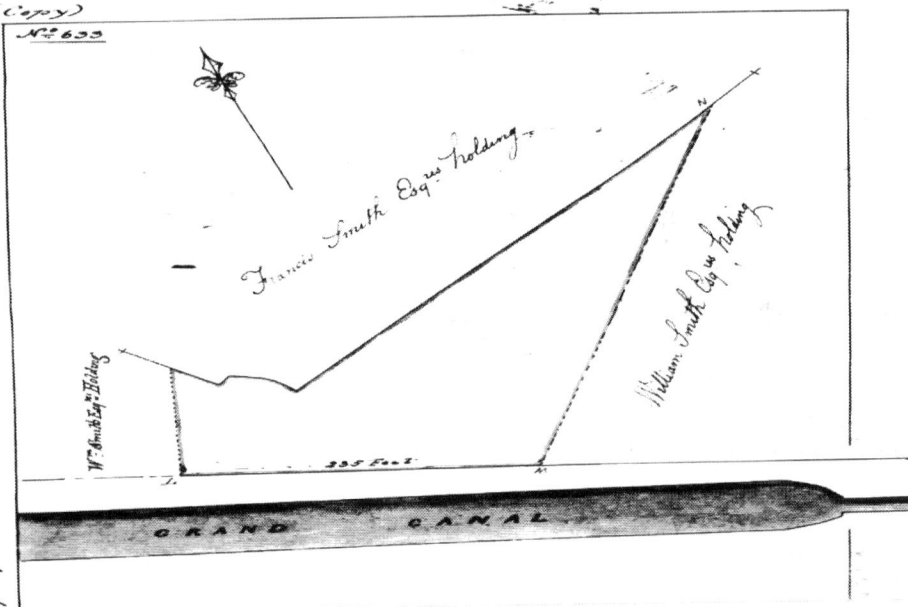

Tenders for the building of the two new Dublin barracks at Portobello and Golden-Bridge appeared together in the newspapers on 23rd January, 1810. The Parliamentary Papers also give 1810 as the date for the erection of these barracks.[25] The principal buildings of Richmond Barracks were to be built from rubble masonry and set a plateau 80 to 90 feet above sea level, with a valley on the west and north sides through which ran (as it still does) the curving River Cammock or Camac, a tributary of the River Liffey. It is likely that convicts from Kilmainham were involved in the construction work. The stone was quarried locally (behind the present Emmet Crescent housing estate) on Mr. Smith's land and in the course of excavations at this quarry the discovery was made of a chalybeate spring which gathered, attracting much attention. The spring (not unusually) had another exit at the bottom of the hill still known to this day as Spa Road. We know that this was sometime in 1811, because a visitor to 'the new spa' in April of that year was so impressed that she was moved to write poetry, published in the Hibernian Magazine.

On Seeing the New Spa at Golden-Bridge

O! Pause awhile, who e'er thou art,
That drink'st this healing stream,
If e'er compassion o'er thy heart
Diffuse its Heavenly beam!

Think on the wretch, whose destined lot
This friendly aid denies;
Think how in some poor lonely cot,
He unregarded lies:

Hither the afflicted stranger bring,
Relieve his heart-felt woe:
Even let thy bounty (like this stream)
In genial currents flow!

So be thy years from want and pain,
And pining sickness free;
May thou from Heaven that debt obtain
The poor man owes to thee.

Hibernian Magazine, April 1811

Chalybeate waters are natural mineral waters containing minute quantities of iron salts. On the 17th February 1813, a leading authority on such matters, Professor Higgins, sent in the following report of the analysis of this spa to the Dublin Society:

Golden Bridge Spa

	Grains
Of Sulphate of Potash	7.00
Crystallised Carbonate of Potash	8.12
Crystallised Carbonate of Soda	25.38
Carbonate of Lime	13.50
Total	54.00

'With the portion of Sulphurated Hydrogen usually condensed in sulphurous mineral waters and a quantity of carbonate of iron too minute to be collected. The above analysis proves the Golden-Bridge Spa to be one of the safest and most valuable mineral waters in the United Kingdom, and to possess properties of the most beneficial nature, and we must congratulate the inhabitants of Dublin and the country at large upon an acquisition of such importance to the health of the metropolis.'

TO BUILDERS.

BARRACK OFFICE, DUBLIN,

16TH JANUARY, 1810.

MAJOR GEN. FREEMAN, Commissioner for Barracks, &c. hereby gives notice that he will receive proposals, on or before the 17th of February next, for building an Infantry Barrack at Kilmainham, near the city of Dublin, according to plans, specifications, and instructions, to be seen at this Office, from 11 to four o'clock each day.

Security will be required for the performance of the contract ; and each proposer (who must be an experienced professional builder) will observe, that no proposal will be received after the 17th February, nor any attended to but such as have transmitted therewith the written consent of two respectable persons to join in the security.

The proposals to be sealed, and endorsed " Proposals for building an Infantry Barrack at Kilmainham."

By order,

JOHN HUGHES, Sec.

Michael Ryan, in his *'Treatise on Mineral Waters,'* (1824) found the waters at Golden-Bridge 'strong and sulphurous and much frequented; good for the treatment of skin and bowel disorders.' A total sulphur bath was recommended. The discovery of this spa caused great excitement locally and comparisons were soon drawn with a similar spring from which the Phoenix Park had derived its name -from the Gaelic, 'Fionn uisce.' The latter, an ancient spring was neglected for most of its history, but gained notoriety in the 1800's, following several reported 'cures.' At one time it attracted over 1,000 visitors a week. It was located just outside the Vice Regal Lodge and was vouched for by three Lord Lieutenants, Bedford, Richmond and Whitworth. The Duchess of Richmond, at her own expense had a beautiful rustic grotto created and a seat placed round the entrance. A tablet fixed in the walls was inscribed thus: *'This seat is given by Charlotte, Duchess of Richmond for the accommodation and comfort of the inhabitants of the City of Dublin.'* - August 19th 1813.

Meanwhile progress was being made on the building of Richmond Barracks. The lease was signed on 24th September 1812 and in 1813, the first Barrack-Master, Lord Dunboyne [26] was appointed, indicating that the barracks was in readiness to receive troops. Barrack-Masters had a term of 10 years or so. In his last year of term (1823) Dunboyne was also Barrack-Master at Portobello. This appointment ties in with the following letter sent sometime before 1813. It reveals how the poor and prison inmates were further used with regard to the Barracks:

The Governors of the House of Industry

To His Grace, Charles, Duke of Richmond,

Humbly Sheweth,
    That your Memorialists have been directed by the Barrack Board to prepare against the 24th June next 12,000 pairs of sheets, 6,000 bed ticks and 6,000 bolsters for the use of the Richmond Barracks, Kilmainham...and that two of your Memorialists have preceded to Tuam..etc... and as they have not received the Parliamentary grant for the support of the House of Industry they have not the means of purchasing the necessary articles required by the Barrack Board ...and humbly submit that it would be advantageous that they should be enabled through their agents to obtain small supplies (of linen) weekly for the purpose of employing the Penitentiary Prisoners and the Poor and Children of the House of Industry. [27]

Then, in 1814, Rev. Dr.Vesey complained in a Memorial to Lord Lieutenant Whitworth, the Duke of Richmond's successor, *'My duties are enlarged while my pay is not and my youth is gone… The main Barracks at Richmond has been lately occupied by a large number of troops…* '[28]

An early impression of the Barracks was recorded by Warburton in his famous History of Dublin (1818):

> 'It is erected on an elevated and healthy situation; not far from the prison of Kilmainham, between Golden-Bridge and the banks of the Canal. It consists of two fronts, with extensive courts, open to north and south; these are connected in a right line by a row of elegant houses, 300 yards in length; on the east and west fronts are two spacious areas, and in the centre a communication, through a large portal, surmounted with a cupola and spire.'[29]

In all, the Barracks enclosure occupied an area of 14 Irish acres (23 statute acres). There were two entrance gates, the north gate and the south gate with a guard house at each end, just inside the gate. The construction of the Grand Canal was instrumental in the decision to establish Richmond Barracks on this site, sandwiched between two major transport arteries. The north gate fronted onto what is now Emmet Road,[f] but which then formed part of the Great Southern Mail Coach Road. The south gate led onto the Canal, serving a dual purpose: the military could offer protection against the conveyance of rebel arms and supplies in boats on the canal, and in the case of a revolt, the military could themselves use this convenient waterway. In time, the presence of the of the barracks would give rise to an influx of army personnel and their families, and the development of shops, pubs and rooming houses to serve them.

Within the walls there were two parade grounds, the Officers Square to the east and the Soldiers Parade Square to the west. Both squares were divided by a two storey block running north-south with an archway at its centre for access. Accommodation provided for 76 officers, 1,600 non commissioned officers and men, with stabling for 25 horses and a hospital for 100 patients. Ancillary buildings, which followed comprised a military stores, armoury room, a forge, a tailors shop, and a detention centre.

Arrival of the Militia

The Militia was a military force raised in the counties by the Lord Lieutenant, the men undergoing one month's training each year for which they received payment.

---

[f] Emmet Road, since 1890; from The Black Lion to the old Police station, the area formerly known as Richmond; even after this it was still divided into terraces such as Madelaine Terrace, Barnett Villa and Ellen Villa.

The Militia was formed when the country was threatened with invasion: it was called out in 1715, 1745, during the several wars with France, 1759-62, 1778-83, 1792-1802, and 1803-16, during the Crimean War, 1854-55 and the struggles against the Boers, 1899-1902. In 1907, the Militia was merged into the Territorial Force. After 1757, each parish was obliged to furnish men, drawn by ballot, for the militia, but persons on whom the lot fell could pay a substitute.

In May 1813, the 3rd Lancashire Militia was given the honour of the designation 'Prince's Own Regiment of Royal Lancashire Militia.' Col. Bradyll, commander of the Regiment, to complete his corps to full strength requested of the Secretary of State permission to use additional means to raise men by 'Beat of Drum.' On the 16th July, the Militia with their new recruits, mainly from Manchester, received orders to march to Bristol where they arrived in August. They sailed on 12th August, in transport ships to Ireland, but were severely hampered by the weather conditions. Because of contrary winds the fleet took shelter at Tenby Bay; a second attempt was made and this time the fleet again took shelter at Milford Haven until 23rd August. On 27th August they finally arrived in Dublin. The whole of the regiment was given temporary accommodation at George's Street Barracks.[30]

The first regiment to arrive at Richmond Barracks, however, was the Royal Cheshire Regiment of Militia, commanded by Col. Parker. They disembarked on the 5th January 1814, at Sir John Rogersons's Quay, where they had come from Gloucester via Plymouth and Liverpool:

THE ARMY.

The Royal Cheshire Regiment of Militia, commanded by Colonel Parker, disembarked at Sir John Rogerson's Quay on Friday last, from Liverpool.— This very fine body of men are to remain to do duty, in this garrison. They have taken up their quarters at the new Richmond Barracks, near Golden Bridge.

They were joined, soon after, on the 3rd. March 1814, by the 3rd Lancashire Regiment of Militia, who had marched from Georges St. where they had remained since the previous August. They consisted of two companies of riflemen, 900 strong. A sad incident occurred shortly after their arrival. On the 15th April, an inquest was held in the barracks by Mr. Pasley, the coroner, on view of the body of John Miller, one of the Privates of the Lancashire Regiment. It appeared in evidence, that the deceased fell from one of the top windows of the barrack, by which his skull was fractured. The unfortunate man lingered in pain for 14 hours; verdict- accidental death.

We should have no illusions regarding the life of a soldier in the early part of the 19th century. The new barracks at Golden-Bridge were certainly better than the makeshift barracks they replaced, which in some cases were no more than converted dwelling houses; they were even superior to the Royal Barracks, which, although more spacious, were a hundred years older. Even so, conditions at Richmond Barracks were that of a grim discomfort. There was poor lighting, heating and sanitary conditions; a sewage problem, constant throughout the lifespan of these barracks, coupled with the poor quality of drinking water, periodically led to fever or disease. The lack of a 'married quarters' (in the early years) meant that wives and numerous children shared the squalid quarters with the men, rendering over-crowded rooms still more congested. Food was often bad and always inadequate. For the officers, conditions were much better, as the following report reveals:

Fete at Richmond Barracks

On Tuesday evening the 21st, June the officers of the 3rd or Prince Regent's Own Royal Lancashire Regiment, stationed at Richmond Barracks gave a most elegant ball and supper to a numerous and fashionable party of their friends. The Mess Room was appropriated for dancing and was decorated in a style of tasteful elegance which reflects the highest credit on the ingenuity of the gentlemen who superintended its execution. At each end of the room a brilliant star formed of bayonets enclosed the one, a Regal Crown, and the other, the Arms of the County Palatine of Lancaster. Muskets, swords, pistols, and other military weapons were fancifully disposed throughout the room, interspersed with flowering shrubs and evergreens, occasionally relieved with draperies. The floor was classically decorated with emblematical allusions to the present happy times. The most conspicuous of those decorations were the lion and the harp, the *fleur de lys,* and the red rose, that ancient badge of the House of Lancaster- entwined with wreaths of shamrocks. An adjoining room was very neatly fitted up for cards. Dancing commenced about half past ten and continued till one o clock, when the company adjourned to supper, provided in a spacious tent pitched upon the parade ground in front of the Barracks and connected with the ball room by a temporary passage representing a grove ornamented with arches of coloured lamps.

On entering the tent a scene met the eye which beggared description. A table nearly 80 feet in length, covered with every delicacy of the season, was brilliantly lighted up with massy silver branches. The pillars of the tent were handsomely ornamented with wreaths of laurel and a profusion of flowers, an abundance of which were distributed in festoons throughout the sides and roof of this fairy palace. The fine band of the regiment gratified the company with several martial airs during supper to which upwards of ninety persons sat down. About three o clock, dancing recommenced, and continued with unabated ardour till six o clock *in the morning,* when the company departed highly gratified with an entertainment which, in point of tastefulness and splendour has seldom been equalled in the Irish metropolis. Among the company present were: Lord and Lady Dunboyne, General and Mrs. Barry, Col and Mrs. Ready, Col. and Mrs. Browne; Mr. and Mrs. and Miss Lockwood, Mr. and Mrs. Palmer of Rush-house, Col. Ramsay, Mr. and Mrs. Mitford, Col and Mrs. Grogan, officers of different regiments in the garrison and etc. [31]

The following year was to prove momentous and one which would affect the fortunes of every British soldier. The feared invasion of Napoleon 1st. never came to pass; it ended with his absolute defeat by the Anglo Prussian forces of Wellington and Blücher at the Battle of Waterloo on 18th June 1815. The victory was celebrated universally and honorary titles showered on Wellington, considered a hero, even before Waterloo, and now a legend. For the ordinary soldier, however, with peace would come change. The army was not disposed to finance a militia in peacetime and even regular soldiers in barracks could not expect the same pay as when they were on active service. The huge reduction in British army personnel and disembodiment of militia forces in Ireland at this time bore testimony to how much the army had been built up during the Napoleonic years. All regiments in the higher numbers- all above the 90th regiment- were reduced; by March 1818, this would amount to 30,000 men. Of course, some regiments were reduced through battle losses; the 42nd regiment was, in this way, reduced from 1,100 to 400. There now began the usual business of 'promotion' of half pay soldiers of lieutenant rank or higher exchanging with others of different regiments on full pay who were either of retirement level or willing to opt for less of an active role in the army; a sum of money, representing the difference, was often a part of the transaction. An anonymous soldier-poet poured out his grievances to the local newspaper:

'...Such is the man who lately led his crew
To fight, to conquer, and to bleed for you:
Such is the man, who late in proud affray,
Shone with the proud, the Great, the fair, the Gay;
But who, alas! now scans with wary eye
Each group, each equipage that passes by,
(*'The Half Pay Officer'*- an extract)'[32]

The scaling down of militia had begun even before Waterloo, during Napoleon's exile in Elba. A warrant for the disbandment of the Lancashire Militia was issued as early as 20th June 1814, but was deferred. On 12th June 1815, the regiment quitted Richmond Barracks and moved to Palatine square, The Royal Barracks, where it remained until 1st September. Nothing remarkable happened in their short time there and on 2nd September, all regiments left from Dublin on transport ships taking them to England. Full disembodiment took place on December 1815. In what was described as an act of 'liberality,' gifts of Bibles were issued in some cases.

On Feb 1816, the Royal Cheshire Militia who had, by that time, moved from here to Cashel marched back to Sir John Rogerson's Quay where they departed for Liverpool. At Chester they were disembodied.

The 40 years between Waterloo and the Crimean War was a time of relative peace with some rioting in England and isolated incidences of rebellion in Ireland. The authorities here could now focus on this internal discord; we have the example, for instance, of the entire 49th Regiment stationed on the banks of the Grand Canal to prevent interruption of the transport of corn to the metropolis.[33] Richmond Barracks, *in a sense* already redundant having only been built, became a Depot with the nucleus for the formation and training of draft recruits, as well as a stopover for regiments en route overseas for foreign service and for those regiments returning from the colonies. Barrack life must have seemed dull for the experienced soldier and diversion, of any kind, was welcomed: they could be sent to escort convicts to a transportation ship; to meet and lead a regiment, to and from barracks; to help put out fires; to form a guard at a public execution, and other garrison duties. Towards the end of 1816, however, the barracks was used for something completely out of the ordinary- and you might say, out of the blue!

'So on the shoreless Air the intrepid Gaul,
Launched the vast concave of his buoyant ball.
Journeying on high, the silken Castle glides,
Bright as a Meteor through the azure tides.'[34]

Erasmus Darwin, *The Loves of the Plants*

MR. W. SADLER

Most respectfully informs the Nobility and Gentry of Dublin,
that on

*This Evening, Wednesday, November 20th, and on
Friday, the 22d,*

IN THE THEATRE OF

THE DUBLIN SO IETY-HOUSE,

Hawkins's-street,

He will deliver his

LECTURES

UPON THE HISTORY AND PRACTICE OF

ÆROSTATION;

With a Detailed Account of the

LATE ÆRIAL VOYAGE,

With Mr. EDMOND D. LIVINGSTON,

FROM RICHMOND BARRACKS,

Near Kilmainham.

The Lecture will be illustrated by a variety of Brilliant
Experiments on the Nature and Properties of the Gasses.—
PHILOSOPHICAL FIRE-WORKS will be exhibited, with additions
since the last Lecture. Small BALLOONS, on the principle of
Montgolfier, and with inflammable air, will be made to ascend;
and in the course of the Lecture the Theatre will be brilliantly
illuminated with

GAS LIGHTS.

At the conclusion, Balloons will ascend from the Court-yard
of the Society-house, with Fire-works attached.

*To open at Seven, and to commence at Eight o'Clock
precisely.*

TICKETS, 2s. 6D. EACH,

To be had at the Society-house, Hawkins's-street, and of Mr.
Tyrrell, 17, College-green.

46

Sadler's Balloon

The Richmond and Portobello Ascents

The military and inhabitants of Golden-bridge were greatly excited at the prospect of Mr. Sadler's famous balloon making an ascent from the square of Richmond Barracks.[35] The fact that it was not the illustrious James Sadler, but his son, Windham made little difference, since the latter had established himself as the worthy successor to his father; besides, it was the balloon that was the real star of the show. The balloon would be on display at a venue in Hawkins Street for several weeks in advance of the flight and a lecture on aerostation would follow the ascent. This was a major attraction for Dubliners and far outshone any other spectacle of the day: such as, the 'scientific' elephant which could be seen for 10 pence admission at 'the large wooden building on D'Olier Street.' In addition, was the anticipation that Mr. Sadler might parachute live animals or scatter fistfuls of lottery tickets from the heavens.

There are many recorded incidences of the military overstepping the mark when supporting a weak police force. At Richmond Barracks, the police and infantry were joined by the cavalry in presenting a guard at the launch of Sadler's Balloon. Their combined, excessive, zeal, on this occasion, evoked a public outcry. On the 5th November 1816, notwithstanding the gloomy aspect of the morning, the flags waved on Nelson's Pillar and at the Post Office announcing to the anxious public that Mr. Sadler would fulfill his pledge, and consequently at an early hour, every avenue from the Richmond Barracks was crowded. The interior of the Barracks was soon filled also with an immense concourse of people, and the process of inflation began at 11 o' clock, in a compartment made up of sailcloth to defend it from the wind. The apparatus for extracting the hydrogen gas was simple and complete and the process went on successfully till about 2 o' clock, when the top of the balloon rose majestically above the fence around it.

It was then found that by some mistake a sufficient quantity of sulphuric acid had not been provided, the procuring of which delayed the inflation for a further hour, much to the frustration of those assembled. Impatient members of the public moved closer to the balloon to ascertain the nature of the delay, and perhaps some were a little unruly. Entertainment was to be provided by military bands; instead the military now moved in to restore order. Unbelievably, the cavalry (very likely, the 5th Dragoons from Portobello) drew their sabres, although there is no evidence that they actually used them.

At 3 o'clock, a gun announced the ascension of the Pilot Balloon, which was liberated to mark the course of the 'Grand Machine.' Sadler's balloon was spherical, made of fine silk. When inflated, it presented a splendid appearance, being composed of alternate stripes of crimson and white, connected in the centre by a *zone*, decorated with appropriate and emblematic devices. The car was of an extremely light texture suspended to a hoop formed of cane and which was attached by twenty four cords to a net of Italian hemp, with which the balloon was entirely covered. Mr. Sadler attached the hoop himself, and when the car was affixed another gun was fired. All being now complete, the whole was removed to a platform to the centre of the square, by a 'committee of scientific gentlemen,' to whom the cordage was entrusted. Mr. Sadler was borne in the Car from the place of inflation and was then joined by Mr. Edmund D. Livingston, a balloon pilot who was to accompany him on the voyage. This man, always referred to as a 'gentleman of the city' had raised a lot of money for the poor and distressed regions of the south and west of Ireland. As soon as Mr. Livingston had taken his seat opposite Mr. Sadler, the final gun was sounded, followed by an expectant hush:

'It was as if the general pulse of life stood still.'

Special guest, Lady Castlecoote, advanced and gave the usual salutation: *'Gentlemen, I have the heartfelt satisfaction of presenting you these flags, and I sincerely wish you success in this brave and hazardous undertaking. - May God preserve you.'*

The Balloon ascended with great beauty and sublimity, but at one point, was heading towards the roof of an adjoining building, when Livingston, with great presence of mind, threw out sufficient ballast to cause its immediate and safe elevation. The aeronauts were at this time waving their flags and hats towards the multitude below who responded with greetings and acclamations that, it was said, 'tore Heaven's conclave.'

The 'floating wonder' ascended at 3.30, two and a half hours behind schedule, on that overcast November afternoon, by which time the light had begun to fade. It was in the air less than five minutes when it seemed to take a south-westerly direction and disappeared into the dense clouds. Today, most of us have had the experience of air travel and know of the beauty that lies above the stratosphere. A reporter in 1816 was able, even then, to conjure a picture of *'The declining sun; the sprightly buoyancy of the cloudless ether and the variegated tints of the bright beams, refracted in a thousand lively colours.'* This though, was in stark contrast to the view beheld by the unfortunate people below who had paid 5 shillings for the privilege of being left in the dark. Meanwhile, the aeronauts were being borne in the direction of Kildare, and when there were no further sightings of the intrepid adventurers, up to a late hour that night, fears grew concerning their safety. However, the balloon having risen to a height of four and a half miles, and 'sailing on the bosom of air,' had come down at Ticknevin, some 30 miles outside Dublin. The aeronauts had been in the air for only three quarters of an hour. They then found themselves traversing, at a late hour and without prospect of any certain guidance from the darkness of night, through the Bog of Allen. After three hours thus, walking in hope in such perilous conditions, they were alerted to the sound of a dog's barking and this directed them to a nearby cabin. The cottagers within, conducted them to the house of Mr. William Smith of Ballybrack, where they stayed overnight. The following morning they returned by post-chaise to Dublin bringing with them the 'honest dog,' which they considered to be the instrument in preserving their lives. They arrived at 9 o'clock in the evening with the 'exhausted' Balloon on the roof of the chaise, by which they were recognized by the people, who congratulated their safe return with cheerful shouts of regard.[36]

It may well be that this man was the son of William Smith of Golden-Bridge; that the reception at this property was prearranged with the military; and that they had fallen short, when they descended in Ticknevin; or it may simply have been a coincidence. The actions of the military brought a strong response from the media. The staunchly Catholic, *Dublin Evening Post*, (editor, Magee, who was only out of jail!) could not miss the opportunity to have a go at the authorities. He described it as,

> A serious cause of complaint; one amounting to insult, to public grievance; in every respect an unnecessary use of military power. Why introduce *mounted* cavalry within the barrack walls? Why make such a display of cavalry and infantry, under arms, in a place where no one could enter who had not paid *five shillings?* Was it likely that such a description of people would riot or mar the object to promote which, in these times of distress, they had paid so much money?

The curious facts of this voyage, however, fuelled public imagination and prompted journalist, Charles O'Flaherty, to pen a poem immortalizing the event. Sadler made many ascents that were much more notable (especially Portobello), but it was their precarious walk in darkness in bog-land, never knowing if the next step would be sure-footed or lead to their drowning, and the oddity of the dog being their saviour, that gave the witty poet his inspiration.[f]

---

[f] Charles O'Flaherty was a pawnbroker's son who rose to become editor of the Wexford Evening Post. He was part of a *convivial society* known as 'The Hermits.' and performed regularly at the Theatre Royal. Among other songs/poems is his Humours of Donnybrook.

The Aeronauts [37]

(Air- 'The Irish Phantasmagoria')

Oh! did you not hear of the famous Balloon,
Sing farina na, sing farina ne,
How SADLER shook hands with the Man in the Moon,
Sing farina na, sing farina ne,
The Mob was so eager, the sight to behold,
Such Noddies, and Jingles, and Carriages roll'd,
And myself run so fast, faith I caught a big cold,
(*Spoken*) – That very nearly spoil'd my singing –
"Chick a chee, ouralee, fa, lal de ral,
lal de ral le."

The day was so hazy, 'twould hardly go up,
Sing farina na, sing farina ne,
So to keep out the cold, faith myself took a sup,
Sing farina na, sing farina ne,
And soon the two heroes were lost in the fog,
They reckon'd no mile stones – but fell in a bog,
And both were ask'd home by a true Irish Dog
That sung "Chick a chee, ouralee," &c.

'Twas Night when they follow'd their four-footed guide,
Sing farina na, sing farina ne,
The door of his Cabin stood smiling so wide,
Sing farina na, sing farina ne,
That each whisper'd th' other, "We now have the odds,"
"This visit is better than that to the Gods;"
So the Dog stirr'd the fire, and put down a few sods,
Singing, "Chick a chee, ouralee," &c.

When the blazing turf warm'd the wanderers' legs,
Sing farina na, sing farina ne,
The Dog did the honours – but *they* did the eggs,
Sing farina na, sing farina ne,
But first they drank, out of the real Innishone,
The health of the Dog, and they then drank their own,
And bless'd their kind Host, who such favour had shewn,
With his "Chick a chee, ouralee," &c.

50

In the morning then, after their rural shake down,
Sing farina na, sing farina ne,
To the Village they walk'd, for a Carriage to Town,
Sing farina na, sing farina ne,
And says SADLER, "We surely may now travel post,
"For there's You and there's I, and the third is our Host,
And sure *among three* 'tis a trifle at most.
We'll sing "Chick a chee, ouralee,'" &c.

In a Post-Chaise and four, then they gallop'd away,
Sing farina na, sing farina ne,
And wherever they came sure the mob did "Huzza,"
Sing farina na, sing farina ne,
For Jowler was placed, and two heroes between,
And the ship-wreck'd Balloon, on the roof it was seen,
And they made no delay, until in College-green
They sung, "Chick a chee, ouralee," &c.

Charles O'Flaherty

On November 20th and again on 22nd, Windham gave his usual lectures on the history and practice of Aerostation at the Dublin Society House, Hawkins' Street, where the Balloon had been on display for several days prior to the ascent. Always, Sadler would update his talk with details of his latest ascent. These lectures were never dull; a constant ascension of a variety of small balloons and decent of parachutes gave a peculiar degree of interest and grandeur; every exhibit illuminated by gas light- itself a wonder and a novelty at this time. To cap it all, was a 'philosophical display' of fireworks.'

The ascent from Richmond Barracks had followed an ascent, just a few weeks previously, from Cork and there were many other ascents during this period. All of which might be seen as a preparation for his attempt from Portobello Barracks on 22nd July 1817, when Windham sought to cross the channel. His father, the great James Sadler had been thwarted in his much chronicled attempt from Drumcondra in 1812; an illustrious affair in which the Duke and Duchess of Richmond, presided at the launch. Sadler senior, had successfully negotiated the Irish Sea, but was determined to land in Liverpool. Strong winds, however, carried him along the

Welsh coast, where he descended precariously into the water. Windham, on the other hand, no doubt benefiting from his father's experience, made no mistake. Together with Livingston, they passed perpendicularly over and saw very clearly the packet which sailed from Holyhead. The sun was inconveniently hot at first and then later there was a snow shower. The pair descended in a field of oats, two and a half miles south of Holyhead. A Captain Skinner took them the rest of the way to the port. Here, Sadler, in a further display of bravado, descended in the diving bell at the new pier. On return to Dublin they went straight to the Phoenix Park for a celebratory reception with the Lord Lieutenant. Windham was presented with a piece of plate funded by public subscription. It was a magnificent achievement to have surpassed, in this single aspect, at least, the efforts of his ingenious father.

Windham Sadler was later killed in a ballooning accident in 1824, when he struck a chimney in the course of a descent and was thrown to the ground.[38] It showed how dangerous was his occupation and also, what might have happened eight years earlier at Richmond Barracks when, but for the quick thinking of Mr. Livingston, Windham might not have survived to make that historic voyage.

The coming of the 94th Regiment & the Fire at Kilmainham Gaol

Another public episode concerning the military at Richmond Barracks occurred in 1817. The year began quietly for the soldiers in peacetime at their quarters along the Grand Canal close to the second lock. A newspaper report however, shows that even the presence of this military force did not deter the local criminals:

At between 8 and 9 o'clock on Sunday last, the house of Mr. Edward Knightly at the 1st Lock of the Grand Canal was attacked by a group of four or five robbers, one of whom demanded admission, alleging that he had a letter from the Canal Company. On being desired to hand it in, the fellow immediately presented a horse pistol, saying 'Here it is,' with which he kept the door partly open for some time. Mr. Knightly having had the precaution to keep on the chain, Mrs. Knightly with much presence of mind, in a very spirited manner gave the alarm and called her brother who was then in bed in the house, threatening to blow out the fellow's brains should he advance a single step. After several efforts to get into the house and seeing that they were likely to meet a warm reception, the villain withdrew the pistol and the party scampered off. The vigilance of the Horse Police should be directed to lonesome parts of the suburbs of the city where these predators usually resort. [39]

Mr. Knightly, who was presumably the Lock-Keeper, made another headline within twelve months:

Disgraceful Outrage- Mr. Knightly, of Parnell Place, near Harold's Cross was returning home from the first lock when he observed a number of grown-up boys bathing there. He having expostulated with the boys to the impropriety in polluting the water which supplied that part of the city, they immediately seized this old gentleman, who was upwards of 80, and beat him so unmercifully that they left him for dead. He was shortly afterwards taken home by some person who happened to know him, where he has since been confined to bed. It is lamentable to say that there is very little hope of his recovery. On Sunday last, two young ladies were walking up the line of the Canal leading from Portobello to Parnell Bridge when they were pursued by two naked men who had just come out of the water after bathing, but fortunately the ladies had sufficient time to make their escape. It is to be hoped that proper steps will be taken to prevent a continuance of such practices, which are at present daily committed, particularly on Sundays. [40]

We have no account of what happened to the rogues who beat poor Knightly; a spell in Kilmainham Gaol would have sorted them out. It was at Kilmainham that the next significant incident occurred. In the upper storey of the old west wing (the hospital part) a disastrous fire broke out at approximately 4pm on Wednesday 3rd. December 1817. Until the moment of the fire everything had seemed normal: the prisoners were under lock-up having had their last meal of the day at 2pm. followed by an hour's exercise. The turnkey had completed his inspection and was just about to have a break when the alarm was raised. As the officer in charge of this wing had only moments before passed through it without noticing anything irregular it was initially assumed that the fire was started deliberately. Almost instantaneously the roof burst into flames and soon the whole of the wing was engulfed.

Lord Dunboyne, 'with his usual promptitude, activity, and humanity, whenever any occasion requires it,' arrived at the scene with a contingent of the 94th Regiment from Richmond Barracks under the command of Colonel Campbell; also present were Colonel Wulff and the Officers and men of the Artillery at Islandbridge Barracks; the entire police force; the Lord Mayor and Sheriff Long, Capt. Stanhope and many others including a lot of excited local people. These were the days of bare-fisted boxing bouts on Kilmainham common, sword and pistol duels in the park nearby, and executions; this was yet another unexpected spectacle with the public taking full advantage. The prisoners were led out and detained in one of the yards after a cordon of soldiers had been placed around the jail to prevent any escape.

Then Lord Dunboyne and the troops entered the prison and escorted the prisoners to a safe part of the building. Gaoler Dunn, was absent at the time, as he was 'on business at the Special Commission.' He was actually delivering eight prisoners to Green Street Courthouse where they were to be served with notice of charges meriting the death penalty. On hearing of the news, he left the men in the temporary custody of Newgate prison and returned to Kilmainham. On the day in question, in addition to the ordinary prisoners, there were 200 convicts awaiting removal to Transport ships.[41]

The engines of the London Globe and the Union Fire Company were in attendance with great speed, but the firemen were hampered by an inadequate water supply. Earlier that year a trio from the Dublin grand jury had inspected the ineffectiveness of the water supply and had voiced concern at its inadequacy. Fortunately, because of the structure of the prison the fire was contained in that part of the building. With the large military and police presence it is hardly surprising that none of the prisoners escaped and their 'diabolical plot' was foiled. There were no fatalities either and no member of the authorities or rescue crew was a casualty, though two inmates were injured by falling molten lead. Notwithstanding the trauma or minor injuries which any of the convicts may have suffered, all 200 of those under sentence of transportation were the next day conveyed, to New South Wales.[42]

Gaoler George Dunn was a callous man, a stooge for the infamous 'Doctor' Trevor.[*] Between them they employed a regime of fear and unspeakable punishments. In the eyes of the authorities, of course, they could do no wrong. This was reflected in the report, a week later, that resulted from the enquiry chaired by Sir Compton Domville, the High Sheriff, into the cause of the fire. The Magistrates singled out Dunne for his clear thinking and immediate response.

'He arrived at the gaol in a few minutes, where his presence and exertions completely quieted the apprehension of all for the safety of the gaol and prisoners.'[43]

Doubtless he did return immediately on learning of the fire, but, according to the newspapers of the time, he did not affect his return until 6pm., two hours after the blaze started. It is unlikely that he was able to do very much at that stage. No blame was attributed as a result of the investigation to any member of staff. Despite rumours circulated among the public it would seem that the fire had happened due to natural causes. The officials report was quite convincing. On a thorough

---

[*] Ann Devlin was arrested on 29th August 1803, with her parents, brother and sister, who were given over to Doctor Trevor's custody. They were interrogated on the authorship of letters found on Robert Emmet. For Ann it was the beginning of a three year nightmare.

examination of the western wing they were satisfied that the fire was accidental:

'The sheet iron which passed over the flue to deprive any communication from the flue to the beam which supported the rafters had rusted and decayed away, and the construction of the stack of chimneys was so bad that the flue ran alongside of the beam, so that there was nothing to prevent the communication of the fire.'[44]

No mention here, of the report in *The Times* that it was common practice to set the chimneys alight in order to cleanse them and that this procedure had been carried out at least once in the week prior to the fire. The chimney stacks were rendered useless and unsafe; there was also extensive fire and water damage. Within a week of the event, work commenced on rebuilding the wing. There was some assistance from the prisoners in the old carpenters shop. In addition, tenders were placed in the *Freeman's Journal* for reconstruction work.[45] Some cells were lost and this allowed for the creation of day rooms for male and female prisoners where they could be given tasks to occupy them. [f] These areas were fitted with looms, and it is said that the entire prison population of Dublin was soon clothed from these workrooms.[46]

This 94th Regiment or Scotch Brigade was a Highland Corps raised in Scotland in 1793. They wore the Mackay tartan and had links with an older Scottish regiment which had fought with the Dutch in the mercenary days. The regiment fought in the Indian wars of 1799-1807, then in the Peninsular War under Wellington, before being stationed in Ireland from 1814. In addition to the 'elephant' emblem they were entitled to bear the words, Seringapatam, Cuidad Rodrigo, Badajoz, Salamanca, Vittoria, Nivelle, Orthes, Toulouse and Peninsula.

The incident of the fire at Kilmainham provided them, perhaps, their last public service in this formation. The following March 1818, they were called to Belfast and from there, in September, to Carrickfergus. Disbandment began on 24th December 1818. The regiment was later reformed in 1823 and in 1881 became the 2nd Battalion of the Connaught Rangers.

---

[f] Niamh O'Sullivan, former archivist at Kilmainham showed me the west wing, which is not part of the tour programme owing to the fact that it is yet to be restored and is generally unsafe; there is also the fear that inscriptions on the walls made by the women prisoners held here during the Irish Civil War could be erased simply by brushing against the old plaster walls. What struck me most was the narrowness of the corridor in the wing: the acute angle of the winding stairway at the rear; one can imagine the consternation at the time of the fire. An interesting fact was that the four condemned cells once present in the yard below and which featured in the original plan of the Gaol were no longer there. These were destroyed by falling debris from the roof and never replaced. The space was instead used as a debtors exercise yard.

Ensign Wm. Leeke, youngest British officer at Waterloo
Below, Major Geo. Gawler Governor of South Australia

Gawler, Rowen and Leeke
The 52nd Reg. in Dublin

Famous Men and Regiments at Richmond Barracks

Usually, at any given time, detachments from two different regiments would be accommodated at Richmond Barracks. They would remain for one year and would then be replaced by men from two other regiments. In the course of the next 100 years almost every British regiment spent time there. In the 1820's, in particular, some of the most notable of these were present and included soldiers, already famous from service in the Napoleonic wars and a few who would go on to achieve success and fame in later life. While space will not allow me to comment on every regiment, I will attempt in this chapter to give a sample of these regiments and men.

Some detachments of the 94th were still listed as being in Dublin up to June 1818, when the 50th Queen's Royal Regiment arrived here from Strabane. In July, this regiment was reviewed at the Phoenix Park prior to overseas service. In August there was an outbreak of typhus at the barracks, but apparently this did not deter their embarkation, the following January 1819, for the West Indies. Tragically, by April 1820 the men, then in Jamaica, were stricken with yellow fever and this, coupled with the insalubrious climate, reduced them to near skeletons. Escape was made on board the *Serapis*, but 200 men perished from the 50th alone. The 91st Argyllshire Regiment from Cork had replaced the 50th at Golden-Bridge and were soon joined by another detachment from Edinburgh. Among their number was Ensign George Maclean, a man who would later distinguish himself. Maclean served with the 91st until July 1821, when, having been put on half pay he exchanged with an officer of the 88th Foot, the Connaught Rangers. From there on, his career took off. He went on to become governor of the Gold Coast (now Ghana) and husband (1838) of English poet, Letitia Elizabeth Landon (better known by her initials (L.E.L.) one of the most widely read British poets of the early nineteenth century.[47]

In May 1819, the 42nd Royal Highland Regiment arrived at Richmond Barracks. Seldom has any body of soldiers gained the dual admiration of civilians and military, as that of the 'Black Watch,' the oldest Highland regiment (dating back to

1624); the first kilted regiment in the British Army and the first to introduce the bagpipe. The intriguing nickname came from the time of the 1715 Scottish rebellion, when companies of trustworthy Highlanders were raised from loyal clans. They became known as 'The Black Watch' for the watch they kept on the Highlands and from their dark government tartan. When King George II authorized the companies to be formed into a regiment of foot, in 1739, he also decreed: '...the men to be natives of that country, and none other to be taken.' Their pedigree included Flanders- the Battle of Fontenoy; the Americas, most notably in Ticonderoga; and the Napoleonic Wars -Alexandria (hence the Sphinx and the word Egypt on its colours), the Peninsula, including Corunna, Quatre Bras and Waterloo. In 1819, the *Dublin Evening Post,* lavished praise on them even before they had set foot in Ireland:

...the 42nd who in Egypt overthrew Napoleon's troops, the far famed 'Invincibles' under Menou. At the Battle of Corunna the 42nd acted a noble and distinguished part. The words' *'Highlanders remember Egypt'* addressed to them by Sir John Moore, recalled to their minds the memory of their glory and with a simultaneous movement they precipitated themselves on the French... When the ammunition was expended their gallant general cried aloud to them- *'My brave 42nd, ammunition is coming- you have your bayonets-give them steel- give them steel.'* Again they rushed to the contest and were again victorious. When Sir John Moore was struck to the ground by a cannon ball, he raised himself a little and with unaltered countenance gazed attentively at the Highlanders. Animated by the grateful intelligence which Captain Hardringe brought him, that they were rapidly advancing, he smiled in his agonies and the conduct of these valiant warriors cheered his spirits amidst the tortures he endured. It is scarcely necessary to remind our readers of their exploits in the Peninsula and in France. In vain they were assailed by the French Cuirassiers, clad in panoplies of steel. They presented an impenetrable front.[48]

Another report is more particular of the way in which the regiment was attired at this time while stationed in Dublin:

Before the adoption of the tartan trousers, the officers' dress was a strange mixture of Highland and line. For instance, at the guard mounting parade in Dublin in 1819-20, could anything, in the way of dress, be more absurd in a Highland regiment than to see the officers for the Castle guards in full Highland dress; the field officer, adjutant, quarter-master, and medical officer, in white Cashmere pantaloons, and short (under the knee) Hessian tasselled boots, and that with a feathered bonnet? ...Until 1822, to have trousers was optional, even on guard at night. Many men were without them, and cloth of all colours, and fustian, was to be seen. From soon after the return of the regiment to Edinburgh after Waterloo, long-quartered shoes and buckles were worn on all occasions. The shoes were deserving of the name given to them — 'toe cases.' To such a ridiculous extent was the use of shoes and buckles carried, that after a matching order parade, the spats had to be taken off, and buckles put on before being permitted to leave the barracks.... At this time the regiment was in Richmond Barracks, Dublin and, consequently had to go to the Royal Barracks for guard mounting, and often from a mile or two farther to the guard, in the shoe already described. In rainy weather, it was quite a common occurrence to see men reach the guard almost shoeless, with the hose entirely spoiled, and no change for twenty-four hours.[49]

Michael Keenan and the 39th Regiment

Among other duties, the 42nd were involved in escorting prisoners due for transportation. On their return from one such escort to Cork in August 1820, they were ordered to Kilkenny. It was here that Michael Keenan was born in 1797, at the parish of Durrow (now Laoise). He is deserving of special mention, having been in Richmond Barracks twice with two different regiments. On 30 January 1816, when the regimental recruiting party was in Kilkenny, Michael took the King's colours for unlimited service in His Majesty's 94th Regiment of Foot. He was 19 years old, and was one of that party of 223 men who marched from Kilkenny to Richmond Barracks in March 1817. He spent the next year training, drilling and on ceremonial and guard duties. In 1818, the regiment moved to Belfast. He was by now married and resolved to providing for his wife and family. However, when the regiment was reduced in December of that year, Keenan was discharged. His bride of six weeks was the sixteen year old, Susannah Lennon of Belfast. Life for this couple was difficult for the next two years. Not only was there widespread unemployment following demobilization, but without the war to fuel demand, prices for grain and other agricultural stocks fell, leading to even less employment and depression and unrest. Keenan learned that the 39th were stationed at his old training ground in Richmond Barracks. He applied there (with his wife and son) and was accepted into the Dorsetshire Regiment on the 24th January 1821.

Just two months later, this regiment was dispatched to Munster where, owing to a resurgence of the Whiteboys, the civil authority had lost control. Michael was in a party of 150 of the regiment who marched from Dublin to Cork in eleven days, with Susannah (it is claimed) walking along behind with the baby. The regiment spent the next four years deployed in the counties of Cork, Kerry and Limerick in small detachments. Wherever the regiment was moved, Susanna followed, even to New South Wales, on board a convict ship escorting 100 prisoners. They would not return to Ireland again. Despite the tragedy of the loss of two children, Michael and Susannah could see the opportunities for settlers in the expanding colony. Michael applied for discharge, and on 30th June 1832, after 14 years with the colours, he became a civilian. The life and times of the Keenan family in Australia thereafter, was long, eventful and colourful, and is today respectfully remembered:

'Military men and their families provided a large proportion of Australia's early settlers. Much has been written about the officers who administered the early colony, and of the military explorers who traced the Rivers and commanded distant settlements. Keenan's story is that of a private soldier and his colleagues, and their contribution to the early settlement west of the Blue Mountains.'[50]

****

On 21st September, 1821, the 1st Somerset Light Infantry Regiment arrived after being in various stations for the last ten months of that year. By the time that they departed, bound for East India, on 16th July 1822, they had made a lasting impression:

That very fine regiment of infantry the (old) 13th on its way to embark for England, passed between 5 and 6 o' clock this evening through College Green, attended by an immense crowd of people, cheering them as they passed along- the bugles were sounding; when they came to the statue of King William, they suddenly ceased, then the band struck up the enlivening national air of *Patrick's Day*. Though it rained heavily for a time, the multitude still followed them, giving expression to the warmth of their feeling by repeated huzzas, interjected with prayers for their future welfare.

Reports, such as the above always have to be balanced against the less glamorous side of things: the news, for instance of the 91st who had left here to face atrocious conditions in Jamaica. And as if typhus was not enough to contend with, the disciplinary regime at Richmond Barracks was as unrelenting as it was at any garrison:

'**Punishment:** consisted of a log or a large round shot, or shell which was connected to a delinquent's leg by means of a chain; and he was obliged to drag or carry this about with him on all occasions, except when he mounted guard. In one regiment, which was quartered in Richmond Barracks, Dublin in 1821, from twenty to twenty-five men were frequently seen marching round the barrack square, each dragging a log behind him, The log was interdicted in the garrison of Dublin by order of Sir Colquhoun Grant.'[51]

Overcrowding was another issue and in 1822 more ground was taken for barracks purposes; an area previously the property of St. Patrick's Hospital, and a lane to the east, property of Mr. Tyndall.

William Leeke and the 52nd Regiment

The 1820's were proving to be a volatile period domestically, despite the concentration of troops, particularly yeomanry, in the troubled areas. The harvest in 1821 was a disaster resulting in a famine in 1822. This only added to the misery of unemployment in a country where the population had risen since the return of war veterans and where there was an economic slump. As always in this situation, with tithes still having to be paid, there was the perceived threat of rebellion in the rural areas. Since the 1760s successive revolts of the rural poor had broken out across Ireland. These were led by a variety of underground movements with varying names but common characteristics. The best known of these were the Whiteboys and involved labourers, both agricultural and those working in minor industries, and cottiers. Whiteboys were usually, as the name suggests, young boys in their teens. In January 1822, they attacked and set fire to a police barracks at Churchtown in Cork killing four policemen and several horses. Three youths were later hanged for this. Before the year was out, there were two major 'battles' against the Whiteboys at Millstreet and Ichigeelagh in Co. Cork. 16,000 troops were deployed and 300 persons awaited trial for crimes associated with the 'Munster War,' with the likelihood that most would be sentenced to death. However, the new Lord Lieutenant, Marquis Wellesley, was anxious to avoid a situation which, 'neither humanity nor policy could sanction,'[52] and so 172 prisoners were transported on the convict ship *Brampton* to Port Jackson in November, 1822. The hostilities would continue throughout the decade, and while Munster was the region most afflicted, no area was safe. At Richmond Barracks, intelligence of an attack was received with great alarm by the garrison, which comprised the 52nd or Oxfordshire Regiment. This was the situation that William Leeke met with on his arrival there.

Leeke, or 'Waterloo William,' as he became known, joined the army as an Ensign five weeks before the Battle of Waterloo. He was a mere boy of eighteen years, yet he famously carried the colours of the 52nd Regiment and later in his partly autobiographical account, *A History of Lord Seaton's Regiment*, (1866) made the controversial statement:

'The author claims for Lord Seaton and the 52nd the honour of having defeated single-handed, without the assistance of the 1st British Guards, or any other Troops,

that portion of the Imperial Guard of France, about 10,000 in number which advanced to make the last attack on the British position, which defeat was immediately followed by the flight of the whole French army.'

On 25th July 1821, Leeke returned from extended leave in England to meet up with the Regiment already stationed at Richmond Barracks. One of his first duties, in August, was to command Major McNair's company at a review of the Regiment before the King, at the Phoenix Park, Dublin. The exuberance of this event was soon followed by consternation. Here, in his own words, is how Leeke described the preparations against the Whiteboys attack:

> One evening, in consequence of some intelligence that an attack was meditated that night on the Richmond Barracks by some thousands of Whiteboys who, I suppose, thought to take us by surprise, suitable preparations were made for their reception; men were told off to occupy the officers' barracks, in case they should be wanted, and the sentries were doubled in some places, and their muskets loaded, and the troops were ready to turn out. These preparations could not have been made unless there had been some ground for expecting an attack. The night, however, passed over without anything happening.

In January 1822, Leeke was sent on detachment under the command of Captain Macpherson, of the 13th Regiment, to the Pigeon House. Officers sleeping conditions there were rough and Leeke endured many sleepless nights fighting off rats, which were even eating the candles he was using to light his room. When he eventually did sleep he awoke one morning to find that the 14 inch candle, together with the extinguisher that covered it, had been carried off during the night. Goodness knows what the private soldiers had to endure.

Leek returned to Richmond Barracks on the 24th February 1822. In his absence the regiment had been kept busy with a local fire at Mr. Willan's Hibernian Woollen Mills at Kilmainham. The fire was contained thanks to the exertions of the commanding officer of the garrison, together with the insurance company's fire engine service and that of the Arthur Guinness Company. Towards the end of March, Leeke went on a detachment with McNair's company to Wicklow. He began a savings fund for the men in Wicklow, receiving small sums of money to hold for them. This led to the formation of a Regimental savings' bank a few months afterwards, and also, in 1824, to the first establishment of a savings' bank in the province of New Brunswick, in North America. On arrival back in Dublin in early May 1822, Leeke found that there was no room for him in the barracks. He stayed with his friends the Gawlers; Major George Gawler [f] was a married soldier and, there being no married quarters at that time, lived some distance from the barracks. Three weeks later on the 27th and 28th May the regiment, in two divisions, headed south for Tipperary.[*]

****

In October 1825, the 58th regiment occupied one side of the square and the 66th the other side. The greatest harmony prevailed between the two corps, who dined frequently together, and attended whist parties at each other's mess rooms. There was a billiard table at the bottom of the hill on the road to Dublin where the two sets of corps would meet. Walter Henry, an officer and surgeon with the 66th recalled one sad occasion:

'One day I was playing with a remarkably fine young man of the 58th named Bell; quite an Apollo Belvedere in face and figure, and much liked by all who knew him. We played till the dinner bugle sounded, and then agreed to meet at the same place for a conquering rubber next day. The morning after, I cantered down the side of the canal, towards Portobello strand, where I saw the 58th at ball-practice; whilst, as I approached a vague presentiment of evil, which I have sometimes felt immediately before a great calamity, crossed my mind. As I rode up I previewed a group assembled, and individuals hurrying towards it from all parts, and on reaching the ground I was shocked beyond expression to find my poor friend Bell just breathing his last, with the blood still gushing from his side. He had heedlessly passed in front of some awkward recruits who were firing with their eyes intent upon the target, and was shot through the body.' [53]

Both the 58th and 66th left Richmond Barracks the following summer.

---

[f] **Major George Gawler** became the second governor of South Australia. He replaced John Hindmarsh who was recalled to England in 1838. He was governor from 17 October 1838 until 15 May 1841. Although sometimes a controversial figure, he has earned an honoured place among the founders of South Australia. The town of Gawler was named after him, as it was surveyed soon after he arrived. The Gawler Ranges at the north end of Eyre Peninsula are also named after him.

[*] **William Leeke** was promoted to Lieutenant in 1823, but left the army in 1824. He was ordained in the Diocese of Chichester in 1829 and became Curate of Westham, Sussex, then of Brailsford, Derbyshire, from 1831-40. He was Perpetual Curate of St. Michael's Church at Holbrooke in Derbyshire from 1840 until his death about 1877, serving as Rural Dean of Duffield for 25 years.

63

Major Garnet Wolseley, who was born at Golden Bridge House

Golden-Bridge
& Golden-Bridge Cemetery

Golden-Bridge village was in the mid 1830's described as a parish of St. James, in the Barony of Upper Cross, 2 miles west of Dublin on the road to Naas. It comprised an area of 162 acres and by 1850 had a population of 1,090 persons inhabiting 180 homes. The area was for centuries known as Glyndon Bridge, from the bridge which still spans the Camac. Milling was one of the main industries: local mills were producing such useful products as paper, flour and pearl barley. The paper mill was later to become a large saw mill owned by the Brassington family and was in existence up until the 1960s. It was these mill owners, and later the Great Southern and Western Railway Company (1845) who would shape and continue the development of the area. The growth of this area was not gradual; it developed rapidly following the opening of the Grand Canal in 1755. Then in the beginning of the 19th, century this growth continued with the coming of the military and also, such people as Obadiah Willan. In 1814, Willan, a Yorkshire man, opened a mill on Inchicore Road using the water from the River Camac. He built a house, Susandale, (later Silverdale) and a row of houses for his workers. He also built the Congregational Church, originally named Salem Chapel.

Many other classes of people followed and as the area expanded, churches of various denominations were added. A school was erected in 1827 near Richmond Barracks, the cost of which was met by military and civilian subscription and a government grant of £250. [54] On Sundays, this was used as a chapel for the troops and the inhabitants of the neighbourhood. The village also had a Methodist church known as 'The Bethel,' having been leased to the Methodists on 7 July 1828, at a rent of £2-10-0 per annum. This lease stipulated that they could not sell or let for any manufacture or trade that might be a nuisance to the lessor or to William Smith, Gentleman. Apparently, a Mr. and Mrs. William Haughton of Dublin, feeling a deep interest in the spiritual welfare of the soldiers at Richmond Barracks resolved if possible to supply them with a chapel and *Methodist means of grace.'* Most of the money was raised by Mrs. Bessie Haughton with a generous donation of £20 from the Earl of Roden. The building was sold in 1884 and the proceeds were used towards the building of the new church on Tyrconnell Road.

'The Very Model of a Modern Major– General'

The inspiration behind the character in the famous Gilbert and Sullivan opera, 'The Pirates of Penzance,'was a real major general, one of the most decorated, most celebrated and most popular in the history of the British army. Wolseley knew it was based on him, but reportedly took no offence at the friendly satire — in fact, he often sang the part himself to entertain his family. He was born at Golden-Bridge. His mother was Frances Ann Smith, youngest daughter of William Smith and Martha Collins of Golden-Bridge House. He later described his maternal grandfather as, 'a typical spendthrift Irish landlord, who lived recklessly beyond his means.' He remembered his mother as,

'A beautiful, tall and stately woman, full of love and tenderness for all about her. Her smile was most fascinating and the poor and sorrowful of heart never came to her in vain for help and sympathy. Her white well shaped teeth, very regular features, dark, nearly black hair, and an almost southern complexion, made her more Spanish than English in appearance. She was very clever, capable, tactful, of sound judgment, and as a girl had read much. Her religion- devoid of everything approaching to priest-craft- was the simplest Bible form of worship.' [55]

In 1825, aged 24 years she was married by license at St. James's Church to the 49 year old Major Garnet Joseph Wolseley. [56] She was the second of Mr. Smith's daughters to marry into the Wolseley family, the other being Elizabeth who became the third wife of the Rev. Sir Richard Wolseley, 4th Baronet. Major Garnet came from a family of a long military tradition originating in Tullow, Carlow, where the home was burnt down by rebels in 1798. At the time of marriage, he was a soldier with the King's Own Borderers (25th Regiment), who were stationed at Richmond Barracks. Shortly after, however, he sold out as a major and rented Golden-Bridge House from his father-in law, who had settled in England. It was at Golden-Bridge House that their eldest son Garnet was born on 4th June 1833. Of their other children, another son, Frederick, would one day, like his brother, make a name for himself, but in a different way.[*]

---

[*] Frances Ann's second son, Frederick, born in on 16th March 1837, was not "cut out" for the army and realized this early in life. At the age of just 17 years, he went to seek his fortune in Australia. He developed several versions of a sheep-shearing machine. In 1887, 'The Wolseley Sheep Shearing Machine Company' was formed in Sydney with a capital of £20,000. By 1906, 3,000 sets were sold to a total of 300 sheds countrywide and by the 20th anniversary of the invention of the sheep shearing machine in 1907, 20,800 sets had been sold. The new equipment was so successful that it won every competition at the Melbourne Show. Frederick York Wolseley, J.P. passed away on 8th, Jan, 1899 and is buried at Elmers End Cemetery London. His business associate, Herbert Austin, became Works Manager of the firm in England in 1893, designed and made the first Wolseley motor car in 1895 and started the Austin Motor Co. in 1905.

In 1835, the family moved to a new home at Rathgar Road, Rathmines. Not surprisingly, Garnet Jnr. had little recollection of his birth place when, as a Viscount, he came to pen the autobiography of his illustrious career, *The Story of A Soldier's Life*. The little he did have to say was rather disappointing. In a reference to the house and to the place more recently known as 'The Puck,' he said:

'Like most of the old country houses near Dublin, it is now a convent, and a dirty slum has grown up in and around what was once its undulating and well-watered little park.'

Wolseley inherited strong religious beliefs from his Protestant mother and an interest in the military from his father. After the death of his father, when Garnet was seven, his mother was left with only a small income to provide for her seven children. Through her intercession with the Duke of Wellington, he was made an ensign in the 12th Foot, without purchase, at the age of 18. In those days, such ranks were usually bought. However, Wellington took into account his father's service, (unusually, since he had sold out) together, perhaps, with the Wolseley military record of many generations and made a concession. As with most of Wellington's military decisions, it was the right one.

He went on to have a glittering career. No Victorian was a greater hero for a longer period than Sir Garnet. The leading British general of the second half of the nineteenth century, he personally took part in and significantly influenced every campaign between the Crimea and the Boer War. Yet, ironically, he is best remembered today for one of his few failures: his unsuccessful attempt to rescue Major-General Charles Gordon, who was speared to death and beheaded by the Mahdai in Khartoum (1885); though it has to be said, that no blame was attached to Wolseley for this. In fact, he wrote a letter from Cairo in June 1885 to the publisher MacMillan, primarily attacking Prime Minister William E. Gladstone for his vacillation which resulted in the failure to reach Gordon and the Egyptian forces in time to save them from destruction by the Sudanese rebels attacking the city. [57] Wolseley (already a Baron) was made a Viscount in recognition of his efforts.

In the course of his distinguished career he had been severely wounded in Burma, and again, in the Crimea, where he had lost an eye. Apart from his deeds of valour, Wolseley is accredited as having modernized the British army, a feature latched onto by Gilbert and Sullivan. When the fictional Major-General Stanley of *The Pirates of Penzance* was created in London by George Grossmith he was given the elegantly twirled moustache and slightly imperious manner of the dashing British commander, on whom Gilbert had, at least partly, based his character. At the time when the musical was being written Lieutenant-General Wolseley was leading a successful expedition to capture the rebellious Zulu king Cetewayo. He returned to the War Office as quartermaster-general with specific responsibility for reforming the structure of the Army. Unlike Major-General Stanley, Sir Garnet Wolseley *was* the very model of a modern military commander. A prolific author, he wrote the classic *The Soldier's Pocket Book for Field Service,* in which he details how to prepare soldiers for anything they might experience in the field, from surveying and reconnoitering to the care and feeding of elephants and the proper method of burial at sea. This book was both highly popular and highly controversial. While many soldiers needed and loved it, the book offended many of the higher-ups because it talked about the lack of preparation and the inefficiency of the British army. He also offended both the public and the military elite by suggesting that soldiers be taught to despise those in civil life and by suggesting that false news be planted in newspapers to deceive the enemy, thus anticipating twentieth century tactics.

Wolseley's opponents in the army considered him to be a dangerous radical, but the Liberal leadership treated him almost as a colleague. He died in retirement (aged 80) at Mentone in southern France in 1913, and so, did not live to see the 1916 Rising, an event which no doubt would have caused great dismay to this Empire builder and protector: *'To see England great is my highest aspiration and that I might have a*

leading part in contributing to the attainment of that aspiration, is my only real ambition.' [58]

He had utter contempt for party politics - the curse of modern England- and the 'dirty dunghill sort of democratic wave… now passing over the world.'[59] Foreigners, he despised and especially the Irish nationalists, frequently alluding to the desirability of his filling some pro-consular role in Ireland and, on at least one occasion, of putting himself at the head of the loyalists to resist the hoisting of a 'filthy green flag.' [60]

As with the elite of British historical figures, he was buried in St. Paul's Cathedral in London.[61] The cathedral was packed with people for the funeral and immense crowds formed along the whole line from the War Office to St. Paul's. His only child, Frances, (by marriage to Louisa Erskine 1867) was allowed succeed to the viscountcy under special remainder

Golden-Bridge Cemetery

From where the southern gate and perimeters of the Barracks once stood, is Golden-Bridge Cemetery. Opened in 1829, this was the first Catholic Cemetery in Dublin. Since the time of the Reformation, Roman Catholics of Dublin City had no proper burial grounds. By law, burials could only take place in Protestant churchyards. The main churchyards used were St. James's, James's Street, Bully's Acre, Kilmainham and St. Kevin's, Camden row. The Protestant Church was quite happy with this arrangement as it provided easy revenue in the form of burial fees. At St. James's graveyard, alone, in 1823, £2000 per annum was being collected.

In the years prior to this, some gruesome scenes had often been evidenced. Bully's acre at that time was an area of open ground (actually about three acres) close to St John's Well, a place of pilgrimage. Because of this, it had once been the desired burial place of many distinguished people with grand headstones marking the graves; but it later became a convenient repository for executed criminals and Catholic corpses. This report from 1795:

> The great number of dead bodies carelessly left there, many of them not interred, for the sprinkling of earth thrown over them is insufficient to conceal from the eye the coffins and shells which contain them. Danger to the health of the public is to be apprehended. In this once highly venerated repository for the dead, but now a common on the verge of the highway, scenes shocking to

69

minds capable of reflection and horrid to relate are frequently exhibited: swine devouring human bodies which are in the most pernicious state of putrefaction and torn remains of males and females left exposed to public view. [62]

Attempts to build walls and gates around the area had proven futile. What was built by day was torn down at night by the public who considered they had right of access to it at all times. Even the levelling of the graves and removal of headstones by General Dilks, Master of the Hospital in 1755, had not deterred the people from coming here to congregate and pray for departed relatives. Soon after these reported incidents and following representations from the public, the Royal Hospital were held responsible for the area. A cemetery keeper was appointed and a high perimeter wall was constructed to enclose the site. With the relaxation of the Penal Laws at this time also, Catholics were, at last, allowed to use the facilities and a Catholic Chaplain allowed to work there as in other places. In 1823, however, an incident took place at St. Kevin's, Camden Row that would forever affect the nature of Catholic burials.

It happened at the funeral of Mr. Arthur D'Arcy, a prominent and popular Dublin citizen. The Rev. Dr. Michael Blake, who was Archdeacon, was officiating at the graveside when he was interrupted in his delivery of the 'De Profundis' and issued with an order which forbade him from saying any words for the deceased. The order had come from the Protestant Archbishop, Dr Magee and stated that, *'The burial service in any churchyard within this jurisdiction should not be read by a Roman Catholic clergyman.'*

This caused great dissatisfaction at the graveside among the large number of clergy and public figures who had assembled. To add to the insult, Mr. D'Arcy's family had already paid £10 in burial fees. Although the quick minded Archdeacon was able to diffuse the situation by suggesting that the mourners say the prayers to themselves, the affront remained and was much talked about thereafter. This was the impetus that Daniel O'Connell needed for his campaign for reform and he called together the old Catholic Committee under the new name of The Catholic Association (to avoid prosecution, the former were a suppressed organisation). O'Connell, who was himself the appointed chairman of this Association, was a brilliant lawyer and found that, contrary to popular belief, there was nothing to prevent them having a burial ground outside of the precincts of a town. He told the assembly:

'I have looked into the law authorities and I am happy to inform the meeting that neither by the common statute nor ecclesiastical laws are there any obstacles opposed to having a piece of ground where remains might be deposited without the eternal recurrence of insult, to which they were at present subject.'

This led to a great debate on the subject in the House of Commons and the 'Easement of Burials Bill' was the result. The problem of land acquisition remained, however, with much of the land in the possession of Protestant landlords who were not inclined to facilitate the Catholics in this cause. Eventually, however, in 1828, the persistent efforts of the Catholic Association were rewarded. By all accounts, 'a kindly Protestant', one, Mathias O'Kelly agreed to sell a tract of land on the southern side of Richmond Barracks and the Grand Canal. The purchase price of the land was £1,000, of which a down payment of £600 acquired as a loan by the Association was remitted to the land owner. After a meeting of the Catholic Association on the 7th June, 1828, a committee of trustees was set up to look after the finance of the cemetery.

Work commenced on the building of a high limestone wall. The builder was a Mr. J. Graham and the first stone was laid by Patrick Joseph O' Kelly, on the 26th. May 1829. In August of that year, the Rev. George Canavan advanced another loan to enable the wall to be completed. The cemetery opened on the 15th October 1829, six months after the passing of the Act of Catholic Emancipation. A newspaper report of the day puts us clearly in the picture:

Consecration of the New Catholic Burial Ground

Yesterday, this really Catholic cemetery was consecrated. The field, which contains two Irish acres, is situated between the Richmond Barracks and the Grand Canal; it is well enclosed by a stone wall, about nine feet high. At the entrance, which is at the south-western angle, is a very neat and commodious two stories high house, which is to contain apartments for the chaplain and the sexton. The ground is nearly square, and is intersected with neat gravel walks. A number of young trees, comprising willows, weeping ash, larch and sycamore, are planted at distances of eight feet asunder, in straight lines, which intersect each other. In the centre, is a small eclipse, within which there is to be erected a chapel, the foundation of which is already laid. *This temple is to be open for the performance of the burial service, to the clergymen of **all denominations of Christians**, without expense and without distinction.* On the southern and northern walls are painted, at equal distances, the letters of the Roman alphabet-and, on the eastern and western walls, are legibly inscribed, the numbers from one to 36; so that, by means of an alphabetical registry of internments, to be kept by the sexton, the friends of one, who may be buried here, can, in a century hence, ascertain in a moment where the ashes of their relatives lie.

The Catholic Archbishop having been unable to attend, the ceremony of consecration was performed by the Rev. Mr. Canavan, curate of James's, who officiated at the solemn Mass, which was celebrated in a temporary chapel, erected for the occasion. The Rev. Mr. Laffan, of St. Michael's and John's, and the Rev. Mr. Walsh, of St. John's-lane convent, officiated in Dalmatics, as deacon and sub-deacon... Charles Stuart was Master of Ceremonies. A number of other priests also attended in suitans, surplices, and stoles. The price of admission was 2s.6d. There were about 200 persons present, besides a few officers and a good many soldiers present, from whom no money would be received. The receipts are to go to the Parochial Free School Fund. Such was the desire of some families to have their deceased relatives interred here that four coffins, with their contents, were already deposited in the vaults, beneath the temporary chapel, and as soon as the ceremony of consecration ended, these were buried in the outer sections of the grave-yard.'[63]

Just days after the consecration, an unusual burial took place. It followed an angry discussion in the Dublin newspapers relating to the conduct of the curate of St. Thomas's Church in refusing to permit a Catholic clergyman to read the funeral service over the remains of a lady named O' Brien. As a consequence of this the coffin had to be removed into the street, where the ceremony was gone through. Protestants in common with Catholics felt indignant at such a reprehensible proceeding. The relations of the deceased lady went so far, in order to mark the sense of the insult offered to their religion, that they had the remains disinterred and reburied in the new cemetery at Golden-Bridge.[64]

Many thousands attended the burial of Rev. Lawrence Sylvester Whelan, a priest who had charge of the chapel at Dolphin's Barn in the penal days. His body was dug up from under the chapel's earthen floor and re-interred at Golden-Bridge. Thereafter, funeral processions, many of which had been postponed until the cemetery was opened, wended their way under the loop-holed ramparts of Richmond Barracks. In the course of the next two years a further twelve thousand people were buried there. During those years, of course, it was still the only Catholic burial ground in Dublin and funerals were averaging twenty a day, six days a week. Many were victims of cholera and fever; but consider, that this was well before the famine of 1845-47, which was to account for the whole south east corner of this cemetery; a mass grave containing an unknown number of persons.

Burial fees were used to discharge all outstanding loans. In time further work was carried out in order to enhance the grounds. Evergreen trees and decorative shrubs were planted. A path was laid, known locally as the 'chapel circle' and this became the chosen spot for many of the wealthy families, leading to the erection of large impressive tombstones. Over the iron gateway entrance were inscribed the letters D.O.M. (Deo Optimo Maximo, meaning 'to God, who is the best and the greatest') and just inside this, a bell was installed which is still in place today. The most striking addition was a beautiful Ionic temple. This structure has fortunately survived and was recently restored. It was a mortuary chapel where masses were said for the dead. The temple is reached by a flight of granite steps and supported by pillars. Beneath, is a darkened chamber once used as a room for storing bodies awaiting burial. These bodies were attended by sentinels who remained at night, accompanied by Cuban bloodhounds, whose duty it was to preserve the dead from body snatchers. 'Sack-'em-ups,' were so called because of the method used to acquire the corpse; they would dig at the end of a freshly made grave, place a noose around the feet of the body, which was then pulled up and placed it in a sack. It is recorded that in addition to guard-dogs, firearms were provided for some of the watchmen at Golden-Bridge.

As expected, Resurrectionists visited in the first years after the opening of the new burial ground. At that time only the bodies of criminals executed for murder were allowed to be given for anatomical research and with growing advances in medical studies there was a great shortage of supply. Where there is a demand there will always be someone ready to fill it and certain unscrupulous individuals were prepared to cash in on the needs of desperate students and doctors. While it was common to see the desecrated graves and torn cloths of shrouds strewn about the cemeteries, the problem never reached the level that it did in Edinburgh where sixteen people were murdered in one year to procure corpses. A pair of Irishmen, Burke and Hare, were charged with the crime. Burke turned King's evidence while Hare was hanged and publicly dissected. His skeleton is preserved in the anatomical museum of Edinburgh University; a fitting recompense, you might say, for his dastardly deeds.

Resurrectionists: an illustration by Hablot Knight Browne (Phiz).

The most renowned corpse to be stolen in Ireland was that of Dan Donnelly, the celebrated boxing hero who was removed by moonlight from Bully's Acre and returned after much hue and cry, though minus his famous right arm. Here also, the unfortunate surgeon, Peter Harkan, came unstuck when he tried to do the job of body-snatching. Harkan, who was a demonstrator at Crampton's anatomical school, presumably did not want to acquaint himself with the lowly villains usually associated with the trade and decided to do it himself. This proved to be a mistake, as Dr. Harkan was not nearly as street wise as he needed to be and was soon spotted. He was virtually pulled in two while he tried to make his escape over the cemetery wall. His helpers (students) were holding one of his legs while the cemetery watchers, from inside, were holding the other. It is said that the injuries he sustained led to his early death.

The presence of bloodhounds at Golden-Bridge Cemetery ensured that the incidents of body snatching were kept to a minimum. The problem was greatly eased with the opening of Glasnevin Cemetery in 1831, and the passing of the second Anatomy Act in 1832, allowing doctors and students to dissect donated bodies. That same year the notorious Bully's Acre, swollen with typhus victims, was officially closed. The bloodhounds, however, were destined to patrol the cemeteries of Glasnevin and Golden-Bridge for the next twenty years, an indication that the problem had not entirely gone away.

There is more to be said of Golden-Bridge Cemetery, the circumstances leading to its eventual closure and of the famous Irish statesman buried there in recent times; but for now, we must return to 1830, and to a long forgotten episode, which was then a thrilling sensation.

An artist impression of a typical 'meeting.'

Smith and Markham

The Killing of Standish Stamer O'Grady

For a number of years since its opening, Richmond Barracks languished in a state of relative anonymity, but all that changed in the spring of 1830, due to the exploits of two officers of the 32nd Regiment of Foot who were stationed there at that time. What should have passed off as a minor incident, led instead to a vicious attack, a resultant duel with fatal consequences, and the most talked about trial for years. Here was a case that involved the nephew of the Chief Baron and later Viscount Guillamore; an intervention by the Duke of Wellington; a trial in the Commission Court which was prosecuted by Lord Plunkett, the Irish Lord Chancellor; and which included as witnesses, some titled, high ranking officers of the 8th Hussars, the 12th Lancers and the 32nd Regiment, together with numerous Dublin shop proprietors such as Alexander Reid of York Street, John Walter Carroll of Lloyd and Carroll, Nassau Street and Robert Morrison (Morrison Hotel buildings).

Today, were you to hear the expression 'a melancholy occurrence,' you might reasonably suppose it to refer to some gloomy event; the passing of a friend, for instance; but in the times that we are here revisiting, a melancholy occurrence always meant a savage and bloody slaying or gruesome accident. Melancholy occurrences happened quite frequently during a period when duelling was the accepted, if illegal, manner by which scores were settled. And that brings us to another phrase: 'a meeting,' was not a talk followed by tea and biscuits, but pistols at dawn. Duelling was indulged at the highest levels of society in what was considered 'a court of honour.' We have already seen how easily the Duke of Richmond could be incited to enter the field. Daniel O' Connell too, whose derision of the 'Beggarly Corporation of Dublin,' had led to a duel where he shot dead his opponent, member Norcot d'Esterre. An alarming feature of duelling for the authorities at this time was that it usually involved soldiers in conflict with other soldiers or members of the wider community. It seems that having been trained in the ways of killing, they were not always prepared to wait for a war to come their way. Things had gotten completely out of hand; there is a contemporary account of an officer challenging someone to a duel because he sat in the wrong seat at the theatre; another of a duellist who, on missing the target, felt so humiliated when his opponent discharged his weapon in the air that he went home and shot himself. But the best one, to illustrate my point, has to be of the officer who administered a horsewhipping to a gentleman because of an incident with a lady. A meeting was arranged with unsatisfactory results; the offended party missed and although the officer did not return fire, he failed to apologise. Moreover, he repeated the flogging the next day and refused a rematch on the field!

The police were concerned only with the consequences and the not the prevention of such meetings. It has to be said that sometimes nothing much happened. The pistols used, whether flint or detonating, were not the most reliable of weapons, except in very experienced hands. Usually, there would be an agreement beforehand of just one shot and an apology. In that instance, if the offended party missed he would not reload and the offender would offer an apology. The matter would end there. If, having received his opponents fire the offender was unscathed, the honourable thing was to fire his pistol in the air and not to return fire. The 'etiquette' of duelling, however, was uncertain and many a man lost his life in its interpretation. Where there was no serious injury the police did not become involved, but if there was a fatality there would be a trial and one could expect to be charged with murder as the act was premeditated. There was also the possibility of a civil prosecution by the victim's family. Considering that it was illegal, it is surprising how much of the detail of this so called 'etiquette' was examined in the case of Standish Stamer O'Grady.

This story has a prelude. The 32nd regiment were for some time before the incident quartered in Dublin and had made themselves unpopular in social circles, due, it is said, to the haughty manner of some of the officers. The following unreported facts were divulged by reliable sources at a time when they were still fresh in the memory:

One evening a small party of these officers, amongst whom was a Captain Smith, were standing on the staircase of the Theatre Royal, close beside the Box Office. A young lady stood beside them, waiting, while a gentleman, who had come in with her, was arranging with the Box- keeper for seats. The lady was veiled, but her lithe and graceful figure was enough to make some of the party conclude that she was young, and someone conjectured, innocently enough, that she was beautiful. In an evil moment something prompted Smith to lift a corner of the girl's veil, and peer into her face. Perhaps he would not have dared to do so had not a glance at the lady's companion showed the latter to be, in appearance at least, a mere boy. But just as the veil had been touched, the "mere boy" turned round, and saw what he considered a most outrageous insult about to be perpetrated upon the lady in his charge. In an instant, swifter than the Captain's "thoughts of love" if he had any, a blow straight from the shoulder and worthy of a giant, was landed in the face of the gallant who fell sprawling down the stairs. Then, before the officer could recover himself, the youth, as coolly as if nothing had happened, offered his arm to his companion, and escorted her to her box.[65]

Smith's instinctive reaction was to challenge his assailant to a duel, but he was dissuaded by a friend who informed him that the young buck was a crack-shot: *'He is Luke Dillon, a regular young Nimrod with a strong spice of the devil. I've seen him put a bullet through the ace of hearts.'*

Smith, abided by his friends advice and offered an apology. To his dismay, Dillon wanted it in writing couched in words of his choosing. The two adjourned to the manager's room where pens, paper and ink were produced and Dillon dictated a most abject apology, which Smyth obediently wrote down word for word. He thus avoided a meeting on the field, but was thereafter branded a coward. The regiment, by association were treated in like manner. The next time they appeared in the Theatre Royal the gallery greeted them with cries of *White Feather!* Smith had brought dishonour upon his regiment and he yearned for a chance to redeem himself. His opportunity came at the expense of a totally innocent, harmless gentleman of a good family with great prospects and who was engaged to be married.

Few people today know the name of Standish Stamer O'Grady, although we are familiar with his descendent relatives, Standish James O'Grady, the writer, and Standish Hayes O'Grady, the Gaelic scholar, both cousins. Standish Stamer (also Staoner) O'Grady was from a distinguished Irish family. His uncle was the Lord Chief Baron of the Irish Exchequer, who was later raised to the peerage of the title Viscount Guillamore. On the morning of the 18th March, 1830, O'Grady, a young man of about 28 years was involved in a duel in which he was mortally wounded in the groin. After the duel, he was conveyed by carriage to the apartments occupied by his relative Lieutenant McNamara in Portobello Barracks. All the way from the field the blood continued to flow from the wound, which was large enough, it was said, to admit three of the fingers of the surgeon who attended. On the 19th March, O'Grady died after lingering in dreadful agony for 32 hours. His social standing and the savage behaviour of his aggressor, a captain in the British Army, excited universal outrage among the people of Dublin.

The Inquest

The city coroner, Mr Pasley issued summonses and directed an immediate inquest at Portobello in a room adjoining the very room (no.3-letter H) where O'Grady had breathed his last. A highly respectable jury attended and witnesses included Lord

Hill and Lord Crofton, Col. Molyneux and other officers of the 8th Hussars. There was a wave of controversy from the beginning, with the three central figures, Smith, Markham and McNamara all reported absent without leave from their respective barracks. The jury having viewed the corpse proceeded on their inquiry in the school-room. Gradually, it was possible to put together an entire picture of the events leading to the incident and of the duel the following day.

On the afternoon in question, St. Patrick's Day, Mr. O' Grady, a barrister and commissioner for bankrupts, ordered his horse for the purpose of riding out and taking his usual daily exercise. He was proceeding up Nassau Street[f] in the direction of Merrion Square on the left hand side of the road near the wall of Trinity College. A cabriolet came at great pace down the road towards him heading in the Grafton Street direction. As there was another vehicle, a common cart, parked on the right hand side of the road, it was necessary for the driver of the cabriolet to manoeuvre around this vehicle bringing his carriage in close proximity to Mr. O' Grady. At the corner of Dawson Street and Morrison's Hotel buildings O 'Grady's horse was forced onto the flags (footpath) and in so doing his horse stumbled somewhat. In order to 'right himself in the saddle' the young man put out his hand, in which he was holding a small lady's whip (his mother's). It appeared as if he had struck the capote of the cabriolet. O'Grady thought no more of what had happened and rode on. However, the driver of the cabriolet, a uniformed soldier, jumped out and ran after him nearly to the corner of Frederick Street, where he flogged him at least a dozen times in the space of 20 seconds about the back until he was tired. The young man was unable to turn his horse around to face his attacker and had no option but to sustain the blows. As soon as the soldier relented, he returned in a frantic state to his vehicle at the corner of Dawson Street. It was then, O'Grady's turn to follow him.

There were two uniformed people in the carriage. It was customary at that time for all gentlemen to carry cards and it seemed that O' Grady asked for his assailant's card. This was not given. He then asked for the name of his assailant, whereupon the latter replied: *'You know me well. I am quartered at Richmond Barracks; I am Captain Smith of the 32nd, if you have anything to say to me.'*

O'Grady, in fact, had never met Smith before. He rode slowly on up Dawson Street to his father's house in Stephens Green. His father was Edward O'Grady, Registrar

---

[f] 'I remember the dirty-looking wall seven feet high that separated the College park from Nassau Street, A boon when it was pulled down and replaced by the present splendid railings- the street having also been widened at the same time, it is now a beautiful thoroughfare. Four o' clock is a most fashionable hour in Dublin, Nassau Street being greatly crowded at this time.'- *'Leaves From My Notebook,'* by a retired Constabulary Officer: Dublin Uni. Magazine, 1876.

for the Court of Exchequer, former Chairman of the County Waterford and a brother of the Chief Baron. The matter could not be left as it stood; there was a question of family honour to be addressed. Lieutenant McNamara of the 8th Hussars was a military friend and relative. He was sent for and asked to seek an apology and an explanation from Captain Smith. McNamara then went to Richmond Barracks where he interviewed Smith and his friend Markham of the same regiment. He first spoke to Captain Smith who was looking out of the barrack-room window at the time. Smith insisted that he had received a blow from O'Grady. The Lieutenant pleaded with him, relating in full O'Grady's statement that he was merely steadying himself and that no offence was intended. Smith however, said that there would be no apology forthcoming. McNamara then spoke to Captain Markham alone. The latter said that the only way to resolve the issue was in the field. The two went together that same day to a spot on the Grand Canal between the third and fourth bridges from Portobello, measured the ground and agreed on a duel to be held there the next morning.

The police showed no apathy on this occasion and when word reached Police Officer Campbell at College Street that 'young O'Grady' was 'fighting a duel in the morning,' he ordered his arrest with the intention of keeping him locked up overnight for his own sake. However, Standish spent the night at McNamara's room in Portobello. When the police arrived at the O'Grady home they arrested his bother William, who allowed himself to be arrested to facilitate the meeting taking place.[f] The other two rogues, Captains Smith and Markham spent most of the night at a ball at the Castle.

On the morning of the 18th March, Mr. John Burke of Golden-Bridge, a jaunting-car driver who was used regularly by the local garrison, collected Captains Smith and Markham and Surgeon Griffin from Richmond Barracks. A small parcel wrapped in a coat was carried down from the barracks and put in the car. The driver had no idea of what was in progress and thought they must be going on a hunt. He was instructed to drive through the barracks square and out the upper gate opposite the canal. They headed towards the Rialto Bridge.

---

[f] In a bizarre turn of fate, William O'Grady, the brother of the victim, who allowed himself to be arrested to facilitate the duel was himself violently murdered in Burnley Barracks on Nov. 17th. 1841. He had served with the 16th Lancers in India and the 60th rifles. The 26 year old was stabbed to death by a fellow soldier named Morris. The quarrel was over a young bride of an officer who had been shipped over seas. The amorous maid sought attention and found it, resulting in two men vying for her charms. Morris told her to stay away from O'Grady or he would kill him. She went to O'Grady's room to warn him and was seen by Morris coming out. Morris killed them both with a carving knife.

Meanwhile, Standish O'Grady and Lieutenant McNamara both got into a carriage on the banks of the canal outside the gates of Portobello barracks. They proceeded along the main route of the canal until they came to Camac Bridge, which they crossed over through the turnpike at Dolphins Barn. As they approached a spot between the Harburton and Rialto bridges the driver spotted a one horse car being driven furiously up along the canal.

The parties left their vehicles, stepped across a ditch to a spot known as 'Sir Simon Bradstreet's Field' [f] and then leaped across another ditch into another field, just as the town clocks were striking 6 o'clock. McNamara and Markham went in first, each carrying a pistol case concealed in a wrap. McNamara again stepped and measured the ground and at the signal of a handkerchief the duellists entered. Both walked up to their seconds, were handed their pistols, and took up their positions, 12 paces apart. O' Grady was facing east. The agreed words were 'Ready,' 'Fire.' However, O' Grady later alleged that Markham had used the words *'Are you ready gentlemen?'* This confused him, as he thought it was a preliminary inquiry. Smith, at once raised his pistol and O'Grady was only raising his when Markham, who was watching him the whole time, gave the word *'Fire!'*

It was recalled, at this point, how O'Grady on his deathbed had described a ringing sensation such as that when you strike your elbow, and then it was as though his leg was knocked from under him. He fell on his side and tried to get up again, but found that he could not. He was raising his hands and kicking his feet in pain. The seconds re-entered the field together with Surgeon Griffin. Smith proffered a hand to O'Grady and may have been seeking forgiveness. However, O'Grady levelled his hand at him as if to bid him get away. Smith then walked a few paces and when he got near the road began to run. As he came to the wall of the Rialto Bridge he laid his hand on it and cried *'Oh! Oh!'* and lowered his head at the time. He then went across the bridge to the gig and left without Markham and Griffin. Mr Burke, the driver, observed that he was lamenting the whole way back to Richmond Barracks.

Some local labourers from the Dolphins Barn area assisted in conveying the injured party from the field. These provided good eye witness accounts. Among them were: Pat O' Brien, whose house was just beside the field; Abraham Keating, Dolphins Barn; and William Salmon, who worked for Mr. Sheridan- a cotton dyer on the canal. As they lifted O'Grady into his carriage he complained that his thigh was broken. Smith's surgeon, Griffin, to his credit, accompanied O'Grady all the way back to Portobello. On arrival at the barracks his situation was pronounced perilous

---

[f] Sir Simon Bradstreet, 6th baronet; sub sheriff (the Margaret Aylward case) lived at Riversdale, also known locally as 'Shakespeare House,' Kilmainham.

and the Rev. Manly of the Established Church was called. The latter entreated him to forgive Smith, so that he could die 'in perfect charity' with his opponent. He did so, saying it was never his intention to cause him any insult. However, he predicted that Smith would be shamed in society and his conscience greatly troubled. He lived long enough to make a full statement of his view of the affair. In it, he displayed a naiveté and inexperience that doubtless contributed to his downfall. He had convinced himself that, as he was the offended party, Captain Smith would not fire on him. He did not allow that Smith also, considered himself wronged against and had made this quite clear in his refusal to grant the accepted code of one shot and an apology. And then, there was the confusion over the words used.

O' Grady was in great pain and anxious to have the ball removed. It was evident under the skin above the left hip. Surgeon Badenock of the Hussars complied, removing the ball, but there was nothing else he could do to save the patient. The ball was produced and shown to the jury. The post-mortem later showed that he had bled to death in consequence of a wound to an artery of the intestines. The ball having hit his watch entered the cavity of the belly and broke the haunch bone on the far side. Midway through the inquest, which lasted a full week, the remains of Standish O'Grady were removed from Portobello and interred in the family burial plot in Limerick. The jury, meanwhile were brought to view the scene of the duel. They discovered that O'Grady had been disadvantaged by a large hay-cock about 200 yards behind, and by the fact that he was placed in a field terminating in an angle to his rear: both features were deemed to have assisted the aim of his antagonist; but, was this simply O'Grady's misfortune? After all, McNamara had agreed on the position. Sadly, McNamara, as he admitted himself, knew nothing of the ways and strategy of duelling. The verdict came in on the 30th March. The following is an exact quote:

We find that Standish Stamer O'Grady came to his death by a pistol ball fired at him by Captain John Roland Smith of the 32nd Regiment, on the morning of 18th inst, at a field near the Grand Canal, near Kilmainham Commons, in the county of Dublin; and that the said **Captain J.R. Smith is guilty of manslaughter**, *and the jurors do further find that Captain Frederick Markham of the same regiment, was aiding and abetting the said Captain... and that the value of the pistol is 20 shillings... There are circumstances in this case which seem to require a military investigation. It should be ascertained whether Captain Smith was or was not the original aggressor, and if he was, what is the military opinion concerning his whole conduct in this melancholy affair.*

The result of the inquest proved most disappointing to the general public who felt that the military were in the habit of abusing their authority when it came to civilians. The media reflected this in their editorials questioning why a murder charge was not sought. According to the *Dublin Evening Mail,* Smith had displayed:

> 'a passion amounting to a frenzy influencing a brutal and ferocious castigation upon a man unconscious of offence- a chastisement which no conduct could justify, no provocation palliate. If O'Grady had insulted or even assaulted Captain Smith, the mode of retaliation was very unbecoming of an officer and a gentleman... Gentlemen of the army must be made to feel that they are not to indulge in acts of savage barbarity against civilians.'

Nor was any credit given to the police, despite their having put a guard on O'Grady's house when they discovered they had arrested his brother and not him:

> After the incident in Nassau Street, Smith returned to Richmond Barracks, dined, dressed, returned to town, attended the public ball at the Castle, where the transaction was the subject of general conversation, remained there until 2 am, again retraced his steps to Richmond Barracks, from where he took his departure on the following morning, openly and undisguised, almost ostentatiously in a public uncovered vehicle not previously hired.

In the days following the inquest it was reported that Captain Smith had fled to France. This caused the Duke of Wellington some concern and he asked if a military inquiry should indeed be instituted. He called on Mr. Pasley, the coroner to make a copy of the depositions taken before him in order that they were transmitted to the Horse-Guards. This was followed by a statement in the *Dublin Evening Mail* that Captain Smith would not be subjected to a military tribunal as the civil laws were paramount to any other and that he was ready, when asked, to surrender himself for trial. Smith and Markham surrendered themselves to Mr. Farrell, Chief Constable of the Head Office, on the 8th August and were confined in Newgate Prison to await trail. Lieutenant McNamara, had by this time, already presented himself and was released on bail of £1000 to appear to give evidence.

The Trial of Smith and Markham

The trial of Captains Smith and Markham began in the Commission Court on the 24th. August 1830. The courthouse was crowded from an early hour with a great portion of the most respectable inhabitants of the city. At 11 o clock, the judges took their seats on the bench. They were Lord Plunkett, Mr Justice Vandeleur, and Lord Dungarvan. Plunkett had spent most of his legal career in the company of O'Grady's uncle, Baron Guillamore; in particular they were both involved in the prosecution of Robert Emmet. The Hon. Mr. Thomas Barnwall, High Sheriff for the county sat in the sheriff's box. The prisoners stood at the bar charged with manslaughter. This trial covered much of the same detail as the coroner's inquest: many of the same witnesses repeated their testimonies; but the main difference was that the main three people in the affair were now before the court.

The prisoners were dressed almost the same in black frock coats; each wore a black cravat, a waistcoat and white trousers. Smith and Markham were only allowed to speak through council. Lieutenant McNamara's contribution, however, was pivotal to the outcome of the case. Although a friend and relative of the deceased he adopted an 'honour among soldiers' attitude which greatly assisted the defendants. He confirmed that O'Grady's pistol had been discharged and pointed out that the detonating pistol his companion used was superior to the flint pistol used by Smith. On cross examination, he said that he did not discern any deviation in the words agreed to start the duel. Then council for the defendants tried to explain Smith's actions in the incident that led to the meeting as having been provoked by what Smith regarded as a blow aimed at him, but this was fiercely contested by Lord Plunkett. He said that, if that were the case, he should have first enquired of O'Grady as to why he had delivered such a blow; instead of which, Smith had acted in an outrageous way, flogging the man without any prior warning or apparent just cause. At that point Robert Morrison was called and he testified that he was reading a book next to the window of his hotel when his attention was alerted to the sound of the vicious flogging. He also stated that afterwards, Smith came into the hotel and enquired of him the name of the party he had just flogged.

Before sentence was passed there were two telling interventions for the purpose of mitigation. First, Mr. Bennett for Smith said that because of the current conventions of society, Smith, having appeared to have received a blow in full public view, could not have let the matter stand. Were he to do so, 'he would be considered an anchorite at once, cashiered not just from the society of his fellow soldiers but from all intercourse with men.'

He went on to say that the apology demand by McNamara on behalf of the family had compounded the problem, placing a British soldier in a peculiarly difficult situation. O'Grady, had allowed his brother to be arrested to facilitate the duel and so must share responsibility for his own fate; he must have felt in some way responsible, or why was it he had instructed his family not to prosecute. Mr John Byng, Commander of the Forces in Ireland, made a special plea for leniency, saying that both man had lost their pay having been reported absent without leave and that whenever they returned to barracks they would be placed under arrest subject to military inspection by the Commander in Chief.

Judge Vandeleur charged the jury for a conviction, in which Lord Plunkett concurred. The jury then retired, and after a lapse of only ten minutes returned with the verdict of '*Guilty*' against both prisoners. Judge Vandeleur pronounced the sentence of the Court to be, that they be confined in the gaol of Kilmainham for the space of twelve months. As soon as sentence was pronounced, Capt. Smith swooned and leant upon his brother. Then throwing himself into Capt. Markham's arms, he cried: '*Oh! Markham, my dear Frederick-have I brought you to this- Oh! I wish to God they would take my life- shame, and disgrace, and everything else have come upon me.*'

The distraught prisoner then covered his face with a handkerchief, and burst into tears. It seems that O'Grady was right in his assertion that the shame would be too much for him. At this point the judge added that in passing the sentence, he ought perhaps to mention his opinion that the conduct of the prisoners when in the field was such as to leave no imputation on their character. This was a surprising statement in view of the behaviour of Markham. Captain Smith's friends, then collected round him, and he was removed from the court. An anti-duelling association was formed after this, some say, driven by the details of the case; but duelling continued for a time yet. In June 1830, the 32nd with their band and colours marched out of Richmond Barracks, amid cheers of the general populous, to Kingstown en route for Canada. Smith appealed his sentence, but in vain. Still, he did not serve the full term. In April 1831, on release from Kilmainham, both he and Markham joined the depot of the 32nd. [f]And so the saga ended. The real tragedy of this case is that O'Grady was forced into a duel because of the social mores of his class and time. The *Freeman's Journal* summed up the affair thus:

> As society is at present constituted, there was no alternative left him but to appeal to the pseudo honourable laws which it is high time the legislation should make subservient to the laws of reason and humanity.

---

[f] **Capt. Markham** remained with the 32nd and was promoted to Lieutenant-Colonel in 1842. Capt. Smith exchanged into the 16th Lancers had a series of military triumphs: '**Sir John Rowland Smith**, K.C.B. served with the 16th Lancers at the siege of Bhurtpore; in the Ghwalar campaign, 1843, he commanded the advanced wing of cavalry at Marahjapore- his horse being wounded (bronze star); in the Sutje campaign in 1849, he commanded the 16th Lancers at the battle of Aliwal, where he captured eleven pieces of artillery and drove the Sikh infantry completely off the field, charging them three times, at the first of which charges he was wounded in the thigh.'- *Hart's Army List* for 1873

Men of Courage and of Frailty

The hardship of the Catholic peasantry continued throughout the following decade, especially in rural areas. They were still called on to pay tithes and also the 'church-rate' or 'church-cess,' a tax to keep the Protestant churches in repair. In the 1830's, the Anglican population was less than the total of the diocese of Durham, but was governed by four Archbishops and twenty two bishops and had notional revenues of 800,000, three quarters of which came from tithes paid by more than six million Roman Catholics. Some could not pay and some simply refused and they continued to be harassed by the exactions of tithe-proctors and others, who, if the money were not forthcoming seized the poor people's cows, furniture, beds, blankets, kettles, or anything else they could lay hands on. This inevitably led to a Tithe war or armed resistance to the military and police who were constantly called out to support the collectors in making their seizures. Almost daily there were conflicts, often with loss of life. At Newtownbarry in Wexford, in 1831, thirteen peasants were killed by the yeomanry and police; in 1832 eleven police and several peasants were killed in a tithe-conflict at Carrickshock near Knocktopher in Kilkenny: and many other such fatal encounters took place. If that was not bad enough, 1832 was the year of the Cholera. In Dublin alone, both Bully's Acre and Golden-Bridge Cemetery were filled; the latter, within two years of its opening, had recorded 12,000 burials with 20 funerals taking place each day.

Cholera combined with poverty hit the west of Ireland terribly. Wealthy Dublin business people set up a fund for relief of the worst afflicted areas. Non-commissioned officers and privates of the 92nd, then at Richmond Barracks, elected to have a day's pay donated for the relief of starvation in Mayo and Galway. Still the regiment was swapped and changed; few regiments were ever here longer than a year at a time and some only for a few weeks en route to some other destination. This, despite the fact that they were as prone to infectious disease as anyone else; in fact, they were more likely to pick up something, having to share quarters which were often overcrowded. A return of numbers in 1831, concerning Chaplain's duties gives:

76th. Regt.		70th. Regt.
39	Officers	39
39	Sergeants	40

13	Drummers	14
692	Rank & File	671
69	Women	75
100	Children	131
953		970 Total 1923

This, in addition to the Royal Barracks was quite a job for poor old Dr. Vesey. In his correspondence of 1831, (after the 92nd had replaced the 76th) he also tells us, '*In Richmond Barracks were 2 Infantry Regiments- the 92nd Highlanders and the 70th Regiment of Foot...for religious purpose they have no house so they assemble on Sunday in the open squares.*'[66]

Life for the common soldier at Richmond Barracks was grim due to the overcrowding, lack of married quarters, no proper lighting or sanitary facilities, poor quality of drinking water, numerous diseases, [f] other ailments and a harsh disciplinary regime. Even the structure of the barracks was showing signs of wear after only twenty years. The private soldier longed for active service as a diversion from the monotony of barrack life; he sought solace in drink and often had to suffer the consequences. Everywhere the British soldier drank to excess, and although this evil was not confined by any means to soldiers, it was more serious in them because it led to crimes against the military code which no officer could overlook: absence without leave, insubordination, selling of equipment, theft from comrades, brawling in quarters, and even mutinous behaviour. For these offences punishment was severe, with flogging still in common use. This was usually administered by a team of drummers, because the strength of their wrists would empower them the desired efficiency for the task. A standard punishment would consist of anything between 100-500 lashes. The unfortunate soldier, though stout, hardy and bold as any to be found, would soon be pleading for mercy while his comrades, just as hardy, were known to faint during the ordeal. A man having received, say 300 lashes with the 'cat of nine tails' would, at the end of it, have the appearance of being flayed alive and likely to be hospitalized for a week. Barrack records countrywide showed that between the years 1831-1836, 1,227 people were flogged, in addition to naval returns of 332 marines; making a grand total 1559.

But for some it was all too much. There were a disturbing amount of suicides

---

[f] Aug 1839, Opthalmia, a type of blindness, attacked the men in Richmond Barracks causing the 97th to be moved to Newbridge and to Athlone. Richmond Barracks underwent a thorough cleaning. 50 men of the 27th were sent to the military hospital in the Phoenix Park.

throughout the years, the first recorded incident of which was in 1834, in the case of Lieutenant Roger Coghlan of the 83rd Regiment. He was new to the regiment having only transferred a month previously. Apparently he had an altercation with a Captain who had then put him under arrest. The first intimation of the disastrous event was discovered by the servant of the deceased who opened the Lieutenant's door by the aid of a latch key at his usual hour and discovered his master lying within a few feet of his bed, against the front wall of his bed chamber, with the clothes on his person which he usually wore, including an undress jacket, trousers and boots. The face of the deceased, the floor, and the wall, to the height of several feet, were covered with blood, which flowed so copiously from his right temple, in which the wound was inflicted, that a Lieutenant who slept in the room immediately under the deceased, upon awaking in the morning, observed two or three streams of blood trickling down the wall of his chamber.

Another soldier of the same regiment who was on guard duty said, on examination, that he heard the shot, but didn't think anything of it; he frequently heard shots fired in the grave-yard at Golden-Bridge near to where he stood, (body-snatchers?). The deceased was known to keep two loaded pistols in an open drawer, which he used to say were for shooting at the crows or rooks. For the past ten days previous to the event he had been acting strangely; was also sickly in appearance and complaining of bowel trouble. (Perhaps, he had first tried to poison himself?)

1837, was a particularly violent year in 19th century Irish history; workers were beaten up for refusing to join unions and for working under the prices asked by unions. To this situation were added bread riots during the summer. Workers armed with pitchforks attacked wagons loaded with bread destined for the soldiers in Richmond Barracks. These attacks reached a peak in July and died off in August. However trade union outrage still continued.[67] Of the many incidents of drunkenness, two at least are worth recording; the first, because in its reporting was captured an insight into the lively activity in the Goldenbridge area of bygone years in a house now long forgotten. Here is an edited account of the original newspaper summation. The year was 1838.

Assault At Moran's Public House, Golden-Bridge.

Patrick McDonagh, Michael McDonagh and Pat O'Hara were indicted for having maliciously assaulted Patrick Moran and his wife Mary Moran, whereby their lives were endangered, and Patrick McDonagh, the younger, and Michael McDonagh, for having assaulted Michael Byrne, Stewart Walsh and Mr. Harrison, on the same night. The prisoners pleaded not guilty so witnesses were called.

Michael Byrne was examined by Mr. Piggott, Q.C.

I am a private in the 38th Regiment and was at Moran's public house on 11th December, about seven o clock; it is near Richmond Barracks. I went in there to get a pint of porter; there were some persons dancing and others drinking; I know two of the prisoners at the bar-- Patrick McDonagh, jun., and Michael McDonagh. I got up to have a dance, and while at it got a trip from a man, and upon turning about, I saw the two McDonaghs, and said- "If you do that again you, I know, won't be pleased," when I was immediately knocked down. I can't say who it was that knocked me down, but it must have been either of them. While down they both beat me, when Stewart Walsh came to my assistance. He belongs to the same regiment. Stewart Walsh and Michael McDonagh fell into grips, and Patrick McDonagh and myself followed their example when we succeeded in putting them out. After a quarter of an hour I went into the street and was immediately knocked down. Stewart Walsh still remained in the house. I think it was with a spade shaft I was struck; but I can't say who did it; I have no recollection of what occurred till the next morning; the blow I got was across the loins; no person was with me at the time; my senses did not return till I found myself in the barrack room.

Cross examined by Mr. McDonagh-

None of the soldiers, to my recollection tripped up young McDonagh; I helped to beat him, but that was all, and my companion and myself kicked him and his father out of the house; it was very fortunate we had no side-arms; I was quite sober, having taken about two pints of porter.

James Robinson was examined by Mr. McKane:

I am a corporal in the 94th and was going to Richmond Barracks on the night in question at about eight o'clock, when I found Byrne of the 38th lying on the ground between McDonagh's house and Moran's public house; I found Michael McDonagh and Patrick beating him, and when I came up, young McDonagh said 'Here comes another soldier, we'll sarve him out too.' I was nearly struck down on my hands and knees, and on rising up, I took the spade handle from the elder McDonagh, who was advancing to strike me; the younger McDonagh then made another attempt to strike me, and I then hit him on the head with the spade handle. It was I who gave him the dreadful cut on the head, and did not much care if I had killed him; Byrne walked before me to the barracks, and I believe he was drunk at the time; I heard McDonagh was in hospital ever since, from the effects of the blow I gave him.

Patrick Moran, examined by Mr. Piggott, Q.C., -

I am the brother of John Moran, who keeps the public house at Golden-Bridge, and recollect going to his house about half past eight o' clock on the night of 11th December; that was after the soldiers were beaten; when I went over there was a great noise about the door, which was shut; Michael McDonagh was hammering the door as well as Patrick, his brother; they then went away, and came back in about two hours, calling out for my brother, and saying they would fight him or any soldiers that were in the house; they again began to hammer and broke in two panels of the door; I spoke to them to go away, and afterwards opened the door, having first armed myself with a poker; Michael put his head into the panel of the door, but I did not like to strike him; as soon as they found the door open they rushed in looking for my brother; and when I said he is not here, they replied, "no matter we have you." I struck at McDonagh with the poker, when I was immediately knocked down by a blow of a spade on the head given by O'Hara; I am still an inmate in Steevens's Hospital, but will be out in a few days; the persons who rushed in are Michael McDonagh, Patrick McDonagh, the elder, and Patrick O'Hara.

Cross examined by Mr. McDonagh-
It was about eleven o'clock at night when I was struck, but it was not dark, in consequence of the moon being shining; I didn't know whether the poker was red hot or not at the time; McDonagh and his brother came to me to the hospital, saying they were very sorry for what they had done, that I was a quiet boy, and asking would I forgive them; I said I would, and that if the judge and jury forgave them I had no objection; they gave me £2.6s for the purpose of supporting my family while I was lying ill; I am sensible if they were not drunk they would not molest me or my brother.

John Moran, examined by Mr. Plunkett
I was at Kilmainham on the night of the 11th of December, in my own house; I did not see the prisoners there, but I heard their voices, crying out if they had me they would murder me; they all appeared to be outrageously drunk; my wife advised me to go into a bedroom, and that they would go away; I did not see any of them strike my wife; it was not in the house my brother was struck, but outside, and I did not know of it; if I did, perhaps I would go out and get the same myself.

The prisoners were found guilty of malicious assault, as well as common assault on John Moran, but not guilty of assault on Mary Moran. [68] The military at Richmond Barracks took measures to curb the growing problem of inebriated soldiers, beginning at the barracks. Sergeant Henry Bens, of the 97th Regiment was court-martialled for 'conduct unbecoming a non commissioned officer and disobedience of orders on various occasions between by permitting his wife to serve out spirits to persons not belonging to the sergeants mess.'[69] Other offences were punished with equal severity.

Baron Alexander Fraser Saltoun

In his very amusing memoirs *Scraps, or, Scenes, Tales and Anecdotes from Memories of my Early Days,* Alexander Fraser Saltoun tells of his time at Richmond Barracks with the 96th Regiment (although he doesn't name the regiment in his book). He was the nephew of the 17th Baron Saltoun, the famous 'Waterloo Saltoun,' and eventually, upon the death of his uncle, became the 18th Baron. At the beginning of his military career, while stationed in Dublin he was in possession of a large dog, a cross between a German boar-hound and a St. Bernard. His room was on the first floor in a part of the barracks known as 'the rookery.' The room had two windows with very wide window-sills at about the height of four feet from the floor. Behind the door, as it opened, were his bed, and one old-fashioned iron bedstead with top curtains like a miniature four-poster. The head of the bed rested against one of the windows and covered about half of its breadth. His dressing-table stood beneath the other window, the fire-place was in the side of the room opposite the door, and a table in the middle of the room; a chest of drawers, chairs, etc., completed the furniture.

The dog's favourite resting place was upon the sill or ledge beneath the window, about two feet broad, behind the head of the bedstead, where a mat had been placed for his accommodation, and where he was entirely concealed from the view of anyone entering the room. Sometimes I was unable to take him out with me, and left him at home, and often, I am afraid, I carelessly left the latch lock of the door unfastened, so that anyone could enter during my absence. On one of these occasions, at my return I was surprised to find the door open, and, upon entering the room, to see the dog lying crouched in front of the door, with his eyes fixed on a tall, slim, rather respectable-looking young man, standing on the other side of the centre table, and between it and my dressing-table, pale as death, and shaking all over with terror. When I came in the dog never stirred, but merely wagged his tail; the man however exclaimed, *'Thank God you have come, sir! Call off your dog.'* 'No, my friend,' I replied, *'not until I know more of what you are doing here;'* and saying to the dog, *'Good boy! Watch him, then!'* I left the room and, going to the stairs, called up three or four of the servants that were in a room below. When they came up I relieved the dog from his guard, and made them search the man's pockets, when they found several things belonging to me, and some others purloined from other rooms before he visited mine. He was in a terrible state of fright, and told us that he had entered the room, and had swept my dressing-table of whatever he thought worth taking, and was about to leave when he heard a deep growl, and saw the dog standing at the door, with his bristles up and showing unmistakable signs of hostility. At first he tried to advance, but found that would only precipitate matters; then he tried to replace the things on the table, so that nothing might be found upon him; but at every movement he made the dog growled savagely and advanced upon him, so that he had nothing for it but to remain perfectly still, in mortal fear of being torn to pieces if he stirred.

It was getting dusk, and I did not want to have the bother of prosecuting the rascal, so, as soon as we were certain that he had disgorged every atom of his plunder, I told the servants to kick him out of barracks, which order they executed by taking him to the back gate and pitching him into the canal that runs past the rear of the buildings.' [70]

Before we leave Saltoun, there is another story of his that is well worth retelling. It was an incident which would have had serious consequences if the military authorities had learnt of it, but fortunately all those involved and those who witnessed it kept their silence. It all began when a party of officers met by arrangement in one of the rooms and became engaged in a game of cards. Sometime, not long before midnight they were joined by two other officers who had been in the company of the commander-in -chief and were thus in full uniform; they were also highly inebriated even before they sat down to more drink. Being of the same regiment, these two were usually the best of friends, but with the influence of alcohol became hostile towards each other. The result was a violent quarrel and they had to be kept apart by their comrades. In normal circumstances this would have led to a duel at dawn, but their friends held council and a solution was found:

The result of the deliberations being that it was a thousand pities two such good friends should quarrel in such a stupid way; that if the matter could be settled at once it might be treated as a joke, and the weapons manipulated so as to do no harm, and then in the morning, if they remembered anything about it, they might be told that all had been concluded the night before. But a difficulty arose: not one of the whole party had pistols, and the scheme seemed about to fall through, when one exclaimed, '*Why should they not fight with double guns?*' The suggestion was received with acclamation, and the two combatants would have agreed to fight with field-pieces if necessary, so that they did fight. All was soon arranged, and the party left the barracks by the back gate, and, crossing the canal by a bridge, struck off over the fields that then lay beyond it. After gaining a sufficient distance from the barracks they halted in the middle of a grass field; the moon was shining brightly, and objects could be distinguished at a considerable distance. In consideration of the description of weapon used thirty yards was the distance allowed, and it was arranged that both barrels should be loaded and that the combatants should fire as they pleased. The guns being loaded with large charges of powder and a couple of wads well rammed down were handed to the duellists, and then, as soon as the word was given, a most ridiculous scene took place.

Both blazed away together at first, then one fired his second shot, then the other, making sure that now he had his opponent, went down on one knee and took a long and steady aim, as well as his unsteady condition would permit, and loosed off his remaining barrel. The bystanders had enough to do to stifle the roars of laughter that would have spoilt the fun, and perhaps betrayed the hoax. To make an end, three times were the guns loaded, and thus six shots a-piece were fired by these desperate enemies, who certainly deserved credit for the pluck with which they stood against each other. Then the seconds interfered, and said enough had been done, that they could not allow the matter to go on any further, and that they must shake hands and forget and forgive everything; which they did, and then the party started for home again, to finish up with a last good glass of grog; and next morning, though the two remembered that they had quarrelled, they had no distinct recollection of what had happened, and, on being assured that they had given mutual satisfaction and made up the quarrel, they became firmer friends than ever.[71]

Saltoun's regiment left Richmond Barracks in January 1839, a notable time in history. The Night of the Big Wind, or as it was known to the Irish speaking people *Oidhche na Gaoithe Móire* was a severe European windstorm which swept without warning across Ireland on the night of January 6-7 January, 1839 causing severe damage to property and several hundred deaths; 20 to 25% of houses in north Dublin were damaged or destroyed and 42 ships were wrecked. It was the most damaging Irish storm in the last 300 years. At Richmond Barracks it caused great damage rendering many of the upper rooms uninhabitable.

The Connaught Rangers at Richmond Barracks

Personal recollections from these times are rare and those that do exist usually record little more than details of daily routine. Here then, is a colourful depiction of an officer's life in barracks and also a delightful portrait of Donnybrook fair given by Edward Herbert Maxwell, an Ensign in the Connaught Rangers who went on to become a General. He was a bestselling author of *Griffin Ahoy*, which was followed by *With the Connaught Rangers in Quarters, Camp and on Leave*, from which this extract is taken:

In the year 1839 I entered the Army as ensign in the 88th Regiment Connaught Rangers, which was then quartered in Dublin; and a merry life it was. What with drill and parties, hunting and field-days, the officers of the old regiment were always occupied. There were several packs of hounds within easy distance of Richmond Barracks; but the Ward Union was the one most patronised by my brothers-in-arms. The manoeuvres in the Phoenix Park were not much varied. I remember one day, when, my captain being absent, I was in command of the company in which I was ensign. The old colour-sergeant took the greatest care of me. We advanced in line, and so sure was the non-commissioned officer of what the manoeuvre would be that he whispered to me: 'When ye get to that black thing on the ground, ye must give the words, "*Form fours to the right; right wheel*," which, I think, was the form in those days. The black thing was a crow, which flew away before we got up to it. But, by my friend the colour-sergeant's help, I gave the proper word, and we retired in time to let the cavalry through. Week after week passed, and the same manoeuvres were executed. I always tried to be sub on the Castle Guard, for it was a pleasant lounge during the day, and in the evening a good dinner was served free of expense, while at night a supper of grilled bones, etc., was always ready for those who had been at the theatre, and who looked in on their way home. There was always a comical side to all the proceedings of our Irish friends, even when the affair was serious, or assumed an air of importance.

I remember going to Donnybrook fair—now a thing of the past—with two brother officers. When we arrived all was quite decorous. We observed many tents, in which the country people were apparently enjoying themselves peaceably, but, unfortunately, an urchin—a Dublin street Arab—came up to us, and said, *Give me half-a-crown, Captin, and I'll show ye the finest sport ye ever saw.* So we tossed him the money, and off he went. He crept up near a tent, where we saw him ' feeling for a head,' and, having found one 'convanient' belonging to some man inside, perhaps asleep, he took the stick in his hand, and hit the head as hard as he could. The effect was wonderful. All started up with such vehemence that the tent came down at once, and everyone began to fight with his neighbour. The clatter of sticks was incessant, and the uproar soon extended to the whole fair. Then the peelers rushed in, and were swayed from one side to the other by the contending parties. We left the scene of battle while the strife was still raging—many a cracked crown being the consequence of that miserable half-crown.[72]

Military Fracas- 84th and 88th Regiments

When groups of soldiers got drunk together the results could be calamitous. There was rivalry and sometimes enmity between troops at Richmond and the Royal barracks; this was strange given that at any time the regiment could be moved to the Royal or vice versa. Trouble usually began in some public house convenient to both. In September 1840, for instance, the inhabitants of Barrack-street, Ellis's quay, Arran quay, and that neighbourhood, were thrown into a state of 'considerable excitement and alarm,' following a confrontation between the men of the 84th from the Royal Barracks and the 88th from Richmond Barracks. The incident was related to an occurrence a few days previously when some men of the above regiments happened to meet in a public-house in Barrack Street. A difference had arisen between them and words were followed by blows. The men of the 84th, it would seem, suffered most on the occasion. Vengeance was in the minds of the men from the Royal Barracks and on the evening in question, a little after 7 pm, a considerable number of them issued from their barracks and commenced parading about in the neighbourhood, hurrahing for the 84th, *'down with the 88th,'* and manifesting a strong determination of using violence towards any of the latter corps who might come in their way.

It happened that four or five of the 88th were drinking at the time in Mc Quade's public house in Barrack Street. A number of the hostile party forced their way into the place. The 84th had provided themselves with sticks, but no other weapons were visible with them. The men driven from the public-house sought shelter in the barracks immediately opposite. All succeeded in getting inside the gate, except one; he was overtaken by some of the pursuing party, and by them tumbled into a cellar. It was later alleged that he sustained serious injury. The assailants then proceeded along Ellis's quay, where meeting one of the 88th he was knocked down by them, jumped upon, and very savagely maltreated.

By this time strong parties of the police division were out, and on the alert, for the protection of the inhabitants. They proceeded to where the soldier had been beaten, and where he still remained on the flagway and conveyed him to the station-house in Bride-well lane. There, on examination, it was found that, independent of bodily bruises, no less than four wounds had been inflicted on his head and some of them apparently as if by a bayonet. The rioters, breathing vengeance against the 88th, having searched some public houses on the quay crossed Queen's Bridge, and proceeded towards Thomas Street. This was between eight and nine o'clock, and in the meantime intelligence as to the disturbance having been received at the Royal barracks, strong parties of the military, under non-commissioned officers, were sent out to quell the disorderly proceedings, by arresting every individual who was found in any way concerned in them. Accordingly, a great number of the 84th were picked up, and sent back under escort to their quarters. A strong party of the soldiery was drawn up in Thomas street, to prevent an expected collision there between the two regiments, for by this time news of what was going forward had reached Richmond Barracks, and the 88th was pouring down in considerable force, in the direction of the above street, with the resolution of inflicting a bloody retaliation for the injuries done to their companions. Fortunately, however, the force that had been drawn out in Thomas street was sufficient to prevent any such confrontation, but some partial collisions did occur resulting in 'severe handling' on both sides.[73]

****

Of course one of the worst offences was that of desertion, but given the conditions, even the severest penalties could not prevent some of the men from taking risks. On October 1840, Privates Francis Read and Ephraim Jeffrey of the 20th Regiment suffered the intimidation of military degradation for frequent desertion and acts of theft. The word 'Thief,' in large letters, graced the breast of each and was seen by everyone in the regiment as they marched through the barracks while the drums beat *The Rogues March* at their heels until they fairly cleared the gate. Things resumed to normal quite soon afterwards and the 20th were observed at ball firing a few days later at Ringsend where 'many a good shot was marked by the riddled condition of the bulls-eyes.' [74]

In the midst of so much gloom came a welcome display of colour and excitement provided by a Scottish regiment whose exploits were legendary. In November 1841, the 78th Highlanders landed from Liverpool. The men were preceded by a fine young elephant brought from Ceylon, and who, '…by his roars, kept the crowds which had assembled at a most respectful distance from the main body of the regiment.' [75] What an impact they must have made on arrival at Richmond Barracks. The elephant was representative of a famous encounter near Assaye in western India where a major battle was won by the forces of the British East India Company. It occurred on 23rd September 1803, when an outnumbered Indian and British force under the command of Major General Arthur Wellesley defeated a combined Confederacy army. The battle was Wellington's first major victory and one he later described as his finest military accomplishment. In recognition the 78th was awarded an Assaye Colour together with the Elephant symbol. At Richmond Barracks, the 78th shared their accommodation with the 58th some of whom were drafted into the 78th. The volunteers received 30 shillings bounty, which was supposed to cover the expense of facings etc.; one of the et ceteras being the Highland bonnet, which alone cost nearly £4 pounds!

97

Colonel Thomas Makdougall Brisbane

The Turbulent 1840's

Famine, Repealers and Young Irelanders

From the beginning of the 19th century the Irish peasantry experienced periods of crop failure. As the population exploded, going from 4.5 million in 1800 to 8 million in 1841, the situation grew precarious. Land was being subdivided in ever smaller plots and more people were dependent on potatoes. The crop had already failed a number of times: 1807, 1817 (famine and typhus), 1821-22, 1833-34, 1836, 1845-49. This did not directly affect the British soldier who had his standard daily ration, meagre though it was, consisting of a pound of bread, eaten at breakfast with coffee, and three quarters of a pound of meat, boiled for a midday meal in large cookhouse coppers. However, for the Irish in the forces it was distressing, as they were likely to have family and friends suffering and there was little they could do to help. Indirectly too, the military were affected insofar as food supplies had to be protected en route to the barracks and troops were on constant call to guard food markets and food stores. Add to this the already volatile situation caused by the Repeal Movement and the threat of rebellion led by the Young Ireland Movement.

Typical of the times was a report in 1842, of an attack on a potato market in Cork. It was implied that suppliers were making a bad situation worse by forestalling or holding back stock when plentiful and then selling at inflated prices, too high for most people. This eventually led, one evening around 10pm, to a riot when about 1,000 starving, angry people broke into the market and began helping themselves to some of the potatoes stored there. Information was soon relayed to the police who duly arrived under the command of the mayor and a fresh lock was fitted on the gates. Eight members of the constabulary were also placed inside the market for its protection. At 12 pm a second attack was made, which the police foiled; after which the people proceeded to attack both gates at the same time, for the purpose of distracting the attention of the police. This attack also failed because the gates had been reinforced. The crowd then dispersed, but renewed their attacks the next night, again in vain. [76] Similar attacks, by armed and hungry people on stores of potatoes and bread, being only repelled by volleys of shots, were reported countrywide, despite crops being good that year. Worse was to follow, in just a few years, culminating in the greatest catastrophe ever in the history of Ireland.

In 1843, the Commander of the Forces issued orders for all men to be confined to barracks at the Royal, Island Bridge, Richmond, and Beggar's Bush and the guards doubled with readiness to fall in at a moment's notice. Although reductions of men had been made in the Army, extra troops were sent to Ireland together with a huge supply of arms and ammunition to counter any rebel activity. 3 Cavalry regiments: 4th and 5th Dragoons and 11th Hussars, and five infantry regiments, 54th, 60th, 61st, 69th, and 72nd. This was a considerable force; most other troops at this time were in India, China or New South Wales. As these troops were flooding in, a new Army Bill (1843) was issued banning the possession of pikes, pike-heads or spears.

It was also known as the year of Repeal frenzy and most of it centered on the activities of Daniel O'Connell. Once again the peasantry of Ireland contributed to a fighting fund, known as the 'Repeal Rent', collected mostly in pennies and farthings. With indefatigable energy O'Connell addressed a series of 'Monster Meetings' across the country. The excitement was intense. Vast numbers travelled great distances to hear O'Connell, the 'Agitator,' the 'Emancipator,' the 'Liberator.' 'Monster meetings' were causing great concern, attracting gatherings of upwards of 100,000 people. Even in the North, according to the *Belfast Newsletter*, the authorities were 'preparing for the worst.' The ordnance stores at Carrickfergus were nearly as full of implements of war as they were during the reign of Napoleon. A large quantity of provisions, consisting of beef, pork, and biscuits had been 'stored' of late as though the Government apprehended a siege. Extensive fortifications were made at Portobello and Richmond Barracks for safeguarding against any street insurrection. Public opinion was that these measures were excessive, being built to resist, as the press would have it, 'Priests and Repealers,' who had no intention of doing battle with England, — especially at a moment when her entire army and navy were unoccupied in any continental war:

> The most formidable preparations which have yet met the eye are to be seen at Richmond Barracks situate on the south side of the city, a little beyond Kilmainham, which are being put in a state of the most complete fortification, with portholes, loop holes, embrasures, breastworks, and all the other works deemed requisite by the science of war for successfully resisting the attacks of an enemy. Prevention is no doubt better than cure, but really, after the experience of some few weeks and after it was made as clear as noonday that the mere ordinary powers of the law, if only asserted with dignity and firmness were quite sufficient to repress any overt act of sedition, whether made manifest at monster meetings, or within the naked walls of the Conciliation-hall, these very imposing "preparations" seem at best calculated to excite alarm and distrust among the well-affected portion of Her Majesty's Irish subjects. [77]

Thomas Steele, or 'Honest Tom' as he known, was quick to get in on the act. Steel was one of the earliest members of the revived Catholic Association and became its vice-president. O'Connell gave him a new title, dubbing him the 'Head Pacificator,' with the duty of quelling faction-fighting. Secret societies and faction fighting were preventing the possibility of any united effort being made by the people towards securing emancipation. In 1828 he had seconded Daniel O'Connell's nomination for Clare against Vesey Fitzgerald. He further agitated successfully along with The Liberator for the cause of Catholic Emancipation. His position as a Protestant and a landlord made him particularly valuable to O'Connell. Following the Repeal meeting at Tara another was planned for Clontarf, but Thomas, Earl De Grey, the Viceroy, urged the Prime Minister to stand firm and: 'Let whatever you do be strong enough…Let no morbid sensibility, or mawkish apprehension of invading the constitution… be allowed to weigh.'

The Prime Minister acting on the advice banned the meeting and O'Connell reluctantly complied in order to avoid any violence and bloodshed. Notwithstanding, he was charged with conspiracy, arrested and sentenced to a year in jail and a fine of £2,000. The sentence was set aside after O'Connell had been three months in prison. Steel was left with deep resentment towards Earl Grey and never missed any opportunity to let him know. He was a master of satire. In an open letter to the Earl, Steele showed his Excellency how easily Richmond Barracks could be taken at any one of *three* unprotected points, notwithstanding that the government generals and engineers had exhausted their ingenuity in fortifying that fortress:

To His Excellency Earl De Grey,
Military Governor of Ireland

Lough O'Connell, County Clare,
February 1944.

'Illustrious Warrior,-
Passing yesterday along the Naas road by the Richmond Barracks, and gazing upon the stupendous quadrilateral fortification erected in front, sternly commanding the mail coach road both on the Fox and Geese and Dublin sides, and while, of course, meditating on the best manner of attacking and gaining possession of the barracks with that portion of the Irish Repeal army under my command, as O'Connell's Head Pacificator, I observed what appeared to me to be an oversight of the military engineer by whom those awful fortifications, about the size of a moderate hay-stack, were planned and upreared. The walls are perforated for musketry, commanding the mail coach road both on the Fox and Geese and the Dublin sides; but there are no perforations in front; and, as the angles of this fortalice are all right angles, and as the front is parallel with the barracks, and in the actual line of the road, it is evident

that this front (of an otherwise Irish Gibraltar) is quite undefended.

' In order that I may demonstrate this to your Excellency, let me suppose that a brigade of the Repeal Army were, as a feint, to make on the road demonstrations on the Fox and Geese and Dublin sides of the barracks, and that while the garrison of this deadly fortification was keeping our soldiers in check by its fire on both sides, a body of our Irishry, under the command of that experienced and gallant guerrilla chieftain, the Rev. Father Tierney, were carrying scaling ladders to throw themselves into the woods in the valley directly under the front of the barracks, and then suddenly wading the little River Cummoge, and ascending the declivity, to cross the road directly in front, where they would be entirely unexposed to its fire, the new fortress would be carried with perfect facility by escalade.

'I would not take a noble soldier like yourself at any disadvantage, and, therefore, throw out those suggestions that you may put the Richmond barracks in a more perfect state of defence before we shall have the honour of storming them on the return of Field-Marshal O'Connell to Ireland from the Imperial Parliament. I remain, illustrious Sir, with profound respect, your most obedient humble servant,

Thomas Steele

'P.S. - My Reverend friend and brother conspirator Father Tierney, neither takes nor gives quarter.'

The publication of Mr. Steele's plan for attacking the barracks created great merriment, which increased when it was acknowledged by some eminent English commanders that Steele was right, and still more when his Excellency ordered the weak points, noticed in his letter, to be strongly fortified.

The Duke of Cornwall's Light Infantry

The 32nd or Duke of Cornwall's Light Infantry arrived at Richmond Barracks in June 1844. Private Waterfield, in his memoirs, records that the Regiment 'had their heads shorn for fever or some other malady.' According to Waterfield, Dublin was a place which most men liked although the duty was heavy; field days were very hard, two or three times a week. [78] Another soldier of the same regiment was Private John Ryder. In the following account he gives a moving account of an unexpected reunion with his parents who had resigned themselves to not seeing him for a long time. Ryder, from Nottingham enlisted in the army much against the wishes of his father, a veteran of Waterloo:

'At this time Ireland was in a very disturbed state. On the 6th of June, 1844, we had the route for Ireland. We went by train to Liverpool. There were six companies of us. On the morning of the 8th, we went on board the Rhadamanthus steamship and set sail for Dublin. We did not land till about 10 o'clock on the 9th, at Kingstown. We then went by railway to Dublin, and then marched to Richmond Barracks, where we were quartered. I liked Ireland very well; but our duty was hard. We had many field-days in the Phoenix Park. While lying at these barracks, one day in March, two men asked the captain to let them go on furlough; but to one he said, *'I cannot recommend you, for you have not been long out of gaol;'* and to the other, *'you have not been back from desertion long, so I cannot recommend you.'* We were on parade, and he came to me, and said, *'Ryder fall out; you have never been on furlough, have you?'* I said, *'No.'* The captain then told me to get my recommendation made out, and he would sign it; but he did not wait for me to get it made out, as he did it himself. Now, if anyone had told me that I should have gone on furlough, an hour before, I could not have believed it; for I had never thought of such a thing, as I had only been twelve' months a soldier, and only the day before I had sent a letter home to say that I should ask next year for a furlough, not having been long enough yet to get one. I had my furlough signed by the Colonel by 4 o'clock, for six weeks; in fact from the 14th of February to the third of April, 1845. I set sail that night at ten o'clock from Dublin to Liverpool, and the day but one after I was at home at Twyford.

It was dark when I got home; I opened the door, and went in, to the no small surprise of my father and mother. My poor old mother (as soon as she saw me) fell down on the floor as if she had been shot; and I thought the poor old creature would have died, for she was a long time before she came round. I passed the first part of my time very well, but during the latter I was very unsettled; I was tired of being about, doing nothing. So I was glad when the time came for me to return, and I bade my friends farewell. I was in Ireland with my regiment in a day or two. Soon after I joined the regiment, we changed quarters. We then went to the Royal Barracks; and on the 31st of May, 1845, we marched from Dublin to Athlone, where we arrived on the 5th of June.' [79]

That visit home was to prove significant to Ryder who went on to spend 4 years in India and was raised to the rank of Corporal. Later in life he became a police constable of the county of Leicestershire.

Colonel Thomas Makdougall Brisbane

When we hear the word Brisbane today we immediately think of the capital city in the Australian state of Queensland, and few would credit that the man after whom the area was named was a soldier commanding the 34th Cumberland Regiment at

Richmond Barracks in 1844. Even at the time of his service here he was already Governor of New South Wales. Sir Thomas was a Scot, born in 1773 and became Governor in 1821. He took some impressive steps in encouraging property development in the colony, selling off Crown land at 5s per acre and demanding that settlers improve their holdings by investing their own capital. Brisbane reduced corporal punishment and stayed the execution of many condemned to death. 'Makdougall' was actually his wife's maiden name which he took as his own middle name.

Having served under the Duke of Wellington his military honours were many. They included the Army Gold Cross with one clasp for the battles of Vitoria, the Pyrenees, Nivelle, Orthez, and Toulouse; and the silver war medal with one clasp for the Nive. In other fields too, his talents were recognised: Oxford and Cambridge (1828) gave him the honorary degree of DCL; he won the Gold Medal of the Royal Astronomical Society (1828) and was elected president (1832), of the Royal Society of Edinburgh in succession to Sir Walter Scott. In 1836 he was created a baronet; a KCB in 1814 and GCB in 1837.

All of these things he had achieved before coming to Richmond Barracks; you can imagine the excitement on the arrival the gallant General, as Colonel of the 34th Regiment. While there he took the opportunity to review the distinguished corps and was honoured with a complimentary dinner by the offices and the elite of Dublin. Then, Sir Thomas with his 'wonted benevolence,' provided a sumptuous dinner in the Barrack Square for the whole of the non-commissioned officers and privates, with their wives and children. One wonders what the people of the neighbouring village of Golden-Bridge would have made of this, virtually on the eve of the great famine. The Colonel gave a lengthy speech in which he outlined the details his military career, with some style, and finished by saying:

'I was anxious that you should hear many of these important military facts, from an individual who has passed above fifty years in the service, and who, in following up his profession, has crossed the Tropics twelve times, the Equinoctial line twice, and circumnavigated the globe, besides having been in America and other parts of the world.' [80]

Among the places named after Sir Thomas Brisbane are: the Brisbane River and the city of Brisbane in Australia, the Queensland state capital; the Sir Thomas Brisbane Planetarium (in Brisbane, Australia) and the crater Brisbane on the Moon.

The Death of Lieutenant Colonel John Shelton

With the country in turmoil the press had no difficulty in finding stories of hardship and other related matters with which to fill its pages. Much too was taken up following the fortunes of Daniel O' Connell's trial and imprisonment. But there was still room for one event that was given a sizeable amount of coverage: the death of the illustrious Col. Shelton. Almost every newspaper, periodical and journal in the country reported the bizarre circumstances of his fatal accident. Just three weeks before the incident his arrival with the men of the 44th was heralded by the *Freeman's Journal*:

'**Colonel Shelton** who was engaged in the memorable disaster at Cabool arrived at Kingstown on Monday from Plymouth in the *Resistance* troop ship. The regiment came up yesterday by railway to Westland Row, and on quitting the train proceeded to Richmond Barracks. They appear to be a very fine body of men and are destined for Newry to replace the 36th ordered to Newcastle on Tyne.'[81]

In the afternoon of 13th May 1845, Colonel Shelton* left his quarters at Richmond Barracks for the purpose of taking a ride. The horse which the groom brought to him belonged to Lieutenant Phillips, the Adjutant of the 44th and the bridle was that with which his master always rode, but Colonel Shelton objected to it, and desired him to go back to the stables, and put on one belonging to the Colonel himself. The groom obeyed, and having put on the Colonel's bridle, the bit of which was less powerful than that belonging to his master, he brought back the mare. When the Colonel got into the saddle the mare set off at a gentle canter, but when she had proceeded a few yards he dropped the reins loose on her neck, apparently with the intention of a taking shorter hold of them. Having but one arm, he could not manage this without some difficulty, and in the meantime the mare, finding her head loose, started off at full gallop. The Colonel, in order to retain his seat, pressed his knees and heels into her sides, and after the accident her sides were found to be severely cut by the spurs. It was thought that the animal had tried to make for its stable, and, when prevented, ran between the cook-house and the wall, where there was a narrow passage and a

---

* Colonel Shelton landed at Mondego Bay in the beginning of August, 1808, and was present at the battles of Roleia, Vimiera, and Corunna. He served also in the Walcheren expedition and at the capture of Flushing in 1809, and subsequently in the Peninsula, including the siege and capture of Badajoz, battle of Salamanca, capture of Madrid, retreat from Burgos, battle of Vittoria, and the siege and capture of San Sebastian, where he was severely wounded and lost an arm. He served also in the campaign of 1814, in Canada, and subsequently for 21 years in the East Indies, and where he was employed in the campaign in Ava and taking of Arracan. He was second in command throughout the disastrous operations in Afghanistan, under Major-General Elphinstone.

sharp angle. When she started off she ran through the southern archway of the barrack at a furious pace, and Colonel Shelton very firmly seated. The horse galloped in the direction of the barrack wall, and went so close to it that the unfortunate soldier's head was dashed against it, and the force of the concussion threw him off onto the stone pavement. The horse attempted to turn, fell down, and slid several yards with Colonel Shelton under her. The animal then struggled to get up, and in doing so trod upon the breast of the Colonel, who lay on the ground throughout, as if dead. Having been carried into his room, he was immediately attended by the surgeon of the regiment. The injuries on the head were so bad that a portion of the brain was protruding through the ear. He was given no hope, but held onto life for three days before he expired on 16th May. The inquest jury returned a verdict of 'Accidental death,' and levied a deodand of 1shilling on the mare.[82]

By September 1845, potato blight hit hard; potatoes were said to 'blasted,' and unfit for man or beast; crops that appeared to be fine on Monday would be found ruined the following day. The English did not move quickly enough. Early warnings of impending major problems were ignored. Absentee landlords were interested only in the money made from use of the land. The tenants' main crops were potatoes which grew abundantly in small areas and provided food during winter. It is estimated that approximately two-thirds of the potato crops were destroyed by the blight. More than one million people died of starvation and disease. Another one million people, who wanted to escape or were evicted by absentee landowners, emigrated to distant shores. Many died during their journeys.

The Queen personally donated £2000 to the Irish people. In part because of the false rumour that she had only donated £5, she became known in Ireland as 'The Famine Queen.' When Sultan Khaleefah Abdul-Majid I of the Ottoman Empire declared that he would send £10,000 in aid, Queen Victoria requested that the Sultan send only £1,000 because she had sent only £2,000. The Sultan sent the £1,000 but also secretly sent three ships full of food. British courts tried to block the ships, but the food arrived at Drogheda harbour and was left there by Ottoman sailors. Irish soldiers in Calcutta and Irish people working for the East India Company raised a further £14,000.

In Dublin, soup kitchens were set up; the largest, with a 300-gallon cauldron, was situated in the field below the Royal Barracks. The famine was to last a full four years reaching its height in 1847. Records from Richmond Barracks are scant, so the following report from that year makes interesting reading.

Parliamentary Records
1847- Return from barracks in the UK relating to the date of erection, materials etc:

Richmond Barracks

Date built	Material	Rooms sleeping
1810-	rubble masonry	39 /80 total 119 rooms

Dimensions of Rooms

	L	W	H
39-	13ft.	9ft.6ins.	10ft.
80-	30ft.	20ft.	10ft.
119			

Number of men each room regulated to hold:

36 rooms	15 men	540
6	16	96
36	17	612
2	19	38
9	1	09
30	2	60
119		1355

1355   (actual number 1592) 237 extra.

<u>How Barracks is supplied with water and distance from building:</u>

3 pumps close to barracks, also good supply from Grand Canal and 4 fountains with cocks at suitable distance.

<u>Access for washing</u>

For men-   none for clothes   2 wash houses

Cooking-   4 cook houses

Ventilation- none

This report suggests overcrowding. The barracks were originally designed to accommodate over 1600 soldiers and there were more than 1900 there in 1831, but by this time some of the rubble masonry buildings were in disrepair. As we know, the 1839 storm was also a factor. A rebuilding programme would be undertaken between the years 1849-1859. At that time too, more buildings would be added on the east and west. Instructions issued to Corps doing duty in the Garrison of Dublin published in 1847, direct,

'Soldiers Wives washing linen in the Canal at Richmond and Portobello Barracks will be deprived of all indulgence, and turned out of barracks.'

This regulation may have been promulgated with a view to maintaining decorum in the discharge of domestic chores, but in view of the prevalence of Cholera in 1847 reasons of health and hygiene may have indicated the wisdom of avoiding the canal, for the order is associated with another directed at the men:

'No soldiers are allowed to bathe in the River or Canals in or near Dublin, but they may do so in the Sea at the end of the North and South Walls, under charge of Non-commissioned Officers.' [83]

In December 1847 the 74th Highlanders, replaced the 92nd Regiment here, where they joined the 3rd Buffs (East Kent) whose headquarters arrived via Belfast on board the *Birkenhead*, a paddle-steamer that had been converted to a troop ship. The 74th had spent the summer months in the neighbourhood of Tipperary in consequence of the disturbed state of that county. They were employed as part of a movable column under Major-General Macdonald. The regiment, along with the 75th and 85th a half battery of Artillery, a detachment of Sappers, and three companies of the 60th Rifles, the whole forming a movable column, was kept moving about in the region of Thurles and Ballingarry. They returned to Dublin without incident apart from having suffered much discomfort from the almost incessant rain which prevailed during the time the men were under canvas. The 85th came to Richmond Barracks in September and the 60th after Christmas.

1847 was also the year that saw the funeral of Daniel O'Connell who had died in Genoa; there was a great outpouring of grief at Glasnevin Cemetery where thousands gathered. To the peasantry it must have seemed as though the end of the world was near. To the military at Richmond Barracks however, the year marked the beginning of a new era with the opening of the Great Southern and Western Railway line at Inchicore, completed the previous year. Since 1834, the Dublin to Kingstown line had been in operation and was availed of by the infantry, but the line at Inchicore was a welcome addition. Not everything ran smoothly to start with. A correspondent of the *Railway Record* gave the following hilarious sketch of the new locomotive establishment, amid all of the gloom of that year:

An Irish railroad
On my approach to the locomotive works at Inchicore, to my astonishment I saw, in the midst of a very large field, a building to all appearance tumbling to decay. Every part was in utter confusion. There were no workshops of any description. The blacksmiths were working in canvas tents; the pattern-makers in a temporary wooden shed (the offices comprising a part of the same); the fitters tumbling about in the half finished running-engine shed and valuable machinery lying about exposed to the weather.

He also gave a narrative of the style in which they ran special trains:

On Sunday the 30th a special train from Dublin to Sallins and back was engaged by a party of gentlemen. On the return to the Dublin station, neither stationmaster nor porter was to be seen. The carriage doors were locked and the party could not get out. After a short period of excitement, a gentleman was seen crawling out of one of the windows. His example was soon followed, when the whole got out in the space of about three minutes. If you had witnessed the scene, you could not, while you condemned, but have laughed, for the last was a gentleman remarkable for rotundity, and it required three of his friends to drag him out. If this had been a stout lady or any lady at all, she would have been rather awkwardly situated. But the matter did not end with this. There was a number of gentlemen not connected with the specials (it was hunting day), who were at liberty to get into the train on condition that they should pay their fares on arrival at Dublin; but, as all followed the example of the stationmaster, no-one was there to receive the cash, and off the parties went, laughing at the joke- as they called it.[84]

******

The Young Irelanders grew out of the Repeal movement and in particular, the *Nation,* a repeal propagandist journal established in 1842 by Charles Gavan Duffy and Thomas Davis. The group's turn to violence was prompted by widespread deaths due to the famine, government inaction, and the evictions of numerous tenants. They were also inspired by the French Revolution and popular uprisings across Europe. William Smith O'Brien, the leader of the Young Ireland Party, launched an attempted rebellion in July 1848, in response to the introduction of martial law. Most of the rebels were quickly arrested and convicted of sedition. When Smith O'Brien was imprisoned, Mrs O' Brien took up residence at Golden-Bridge Spa, a short distance from Kilmainham Gaol, to which she had access at all hours of the day. Originally sentenced to death, the government commuted the rebels' sentences to transportation to Van Diemen's Land.

And so, the decade closed with the end of the famine, the end of the Young Ireland threat (though its influence would remain) and the death of Daniel O'Connell. A distinct sign of the times was the visit of Queen Victoria in 1849. Victoria's first official visit to Ireland, was specifically arranged by Lord Clarendon, the Lord Lieutenant of Ireland, to try to both draw attention from the famine and alert British politicians through the Queen's presence to the seriousness of the crisis. During her stay she visited the Royal Hospital at Kilmainham. She also, famously viewed the Book of Kells, but did not, contrary to folklore, commit the barbarous act of autographing it; she signed a piece of parchment which was later bound into one of the volumes.

Yours faithfully,

Thomas Faughnan

The Crimean War

One of the most entertaining of military memoirs was *Stirring Incidents in the Life of a British Soldier,* an autobiography, long out of print, which was written by Thomas Faughnan. This self published memoir sold more than 29,000 copies and was dedicated to the Marcus of Lorne, the widely popular Governor General of Canada. The book includes a long section dealing with Ireland during the 1847 famine period and is especially valuable for its documentation of Catholic sentiment in the army during this critical period. Faughnan was born in County Leitrim and when the famine struck and his sisters chose to emigrate to North America, he took the other option favoured by young men in Ireland at that time. He enlisted in the British army, in Her Majesties' 17th Regiment of Foot (known as the Royal Tigers). Five years later, and having seen service in Malta, the author was a private soldier stationed in Galway when the men received word of a change of quarters:

> Our expectations were fulfilled on the fifteenth of March, by the Colonel receiving a large official envelope containing the route for the 17th Regiment to proceed by rail on the 28th March 1852, to Dublin, there to be stationed and do garrison duty till further orders, to be quartered in the Richmond Barracks. The order having being read to the regiment, the news soon spread to the creditors of the town, when could be seen tailors, shoemakers, hatters, bakers, grocers and liquor merchants, all rushing into the barracks, looking for their debtors. Notwithstanding the credit of the regiment having being cried down on our arrival (credit at your own risk), many trades people had given credit to several parties, which they now were trying to collect; but all those who cannot collect it now, the first tap of the big drum will pay them, when we march out of town.

On the appointed day the regiment finally departed by rail for Dublin. He described his view of the countryside as the train sped along, the valleys interspersed with running streams, the peasantry gazing in wonder and the country girls waving their handkerchiefs as the long train of soldiers passed them by. Eventually, the Wellington monument came into view and the Phoenix Park. They were met at the station by the band of the 39th who played at the head of their regiment all the way to Richmond Barracks. The 17th were assigned garrison duties as follows: the Castle Guard, Lower Castle, Vice Regal Lodge, Old Man's Hospital, Kilmainham, Arbour Hill, Magazine, Mountjoy, Islandbridge, Picture Gallery, Bank of Ireland, and Richmond Barracks. Relieving the Castle Guard was a very imposing sight, and hundreds of people would assemble to witness this military performance, as well as to hear the martial music. Faughnan was detailed for 'The Old Man's Hospital,' or Royal Hospital, Kilmainham. This large establishment at that time comprised the Major General's quarters, the English Church, where the troops from Richmond Barracks attended divine service, as well as the "Old Pensioners," or 'Old Fogies,' as they were called:

'Sunday, church parade at 10.a.m; being inspected, we were marched off, the band playing through Kilmainham to the Old Man's Hospital, where the Protestants and the Catholics parted company for the time. I, belonging to the latter, marched to Arran Quay. As we marched along the Liffey the sweet strains of music, which re-echoed along the River from the different bands as they marched to church, caused a most pleasant sensation, which raised our thoughts heavenward.'

There was accommodation at the Royal Hospital for 800 men. They were required to pay in their pension for board and clothes; the latter consisting of cloth trousers, a red tunic, which came down below the knee and a Napoleon hat. They had no duty to perform, only to keep themselves and their quarters clean and tidy. Faughnan noted that they seemed happy chatting away to one another and reliving their battles. As for Thomas Faughnan, himself, he was very contended in his present position.

'Strict military discipline, numerous general field-days and reviews, drilling at tent-pitching in the nineteen acres, regimental drills and parades, with five nights in bed, kept our men pretty well employed. But the beautiful walks in Phoenix Park, and driving to the strawberry beds on side-cars, with our sweethearts on Sunday afternoons, together with theatre, concerts, museums, picture galleries, and the scenery of the city, compensated us well for all our strict discipline and we were well pleased with Dublin as a military station.'

Faughnan was one of the rank and file selected to attend the funeral of The Duke of Wellington in London. On return to barracks he was moved with the regiment to the Royal Barracks, interchanging with the 63rd. From there they were sent to the Crimea where they experienced the terrible conditions, so often spoken of, in the disease ridden camps. He was involved in most of the military campaign until wounded and sent to the infamous Scutari hospital. Fortunately, he was brought back to health by one of Nurse Nightingale's team, of whom he remarked, *'She never seemed to sleep.'*

His abiding memory was seeing the sad end of one of his military commanders, General Raglan, whose incompetence on and off the field has long since been debated. Lord Raglan and his staff were blamed by the press and the government for the hardships and sufferings of the British soldiers in the terrible Crimean winter before the Siege of Sevastopol, owing to shortages of food and clothing. Raglan was to blame not only for representing matters in a too sanguine light, but also refusing to purchase supplies of wood from the Ottomans to be used for making floors for the tented buildings of the British camp and also to allow the troops to light fires, essential in the bitter damp winter. During this unhealthy winter, the British contingent had 23,000 men unfit for duty due to ill health and only 9,000 fit for duty. In battle too, his failure to give coherent or timely commands on the field of battle led to numerous mistakes, and his blind ignorance of the growing rivalry between the Earl of Lucan and the Earl of Cardigan would have tragic consequences in the infamous "Charge of the Light Brigade." Nevertheless, his passing, due to dysentery, on June 29th 1855, evoked sympathy from the author:

'The body of Lord Raglan was placed on board of Her Majesty's Ship 'Caradoc,' and removed from that battle-field where both his body and mind had suffered for the last nine months and where many hundreds of gallant officers lie, in their gore and glory, waiting for the sound of the last trumpet.'

After the Crimea, Faughnan transferred to the 6th Regt where he became a Colour Sergeant, serving in Quebec and Jamaica. In retirement in Canada he wrote his classic memoirs. He was also a poet and wrote numerous poems inspired by his service in the Crimea. Finally, he was discharged in Edinburgh in 1868, with "an excellent character" after 21 years service.

The connection with the Crimea does not end there. The 63rd West Suffolk Foot Regiment, the 21st Royal Scots Fusiliers (who distinguished themselves at Inkerman) and the 90th Perthshire Light Infantry, all stationed at Richmond Barracks at the time when the conflict began, left from there directly for Turkey and the Crimea. The Connaught Rangers who were there some years before were also involved, and the 55th. A soldier of the 21st Royal Scots, who followed in October, was far from happy with the military authorities as he anticipated his service abroad. On February 11th 1854, he had written to the editor of *The Times* as follows:

'Sir, - Respecting the low rate of pay allowed to the soldiers of our army...I have taken the liberty of laying before you the following facts relative to the position of the married soldiers of the British Army. In the event of a war, which is generally expected, all regiments forming part of an army for active field service will be obliged to leave behind them their women and children which will be an average of 150 women and 300 children to each regiment, including those married without as well as on leave. Under the existing circumstances and regulations of the service there is no provision made for the support of the soldier's wife, which is the cause of a deal of uneasiness to many. I have no doubt, if the authorities allowed it, the whole of the married soldiers would consider it a great boon to be permitted to leave a

portion of their "small pay" to keep wives and children from starvation during their absence, fighting for the honour of their Queen and Country.
I remain, a bold, but unfortunately
Married Fusilier, *Richmond Barracks'*

The Garrison Chapel

As we know from Faughnan, the 'Old Man's Hospital' provided church services for the soldiers at Richmond Barracks. This was not an ideal situation. Plans for the building of a garrison chapel were prepared in 1853, and the project was completed by 1856. The chapel was situated just inside the boundary wall of the Barracks adjoining the main thoroughfare, which was to become Emmet Road, and towards the north-eastern corner of the perimeter. The Ordnance Survey Sheet for 1875 shows a rectangular building '110 feet by 40 feet, its long axis lying in an east-west direction. It has a timber roof supported by a Truss. The building is divided in half by a moveable screen; the portion at the east end is a denominated Chapel, while that at the west end, a denominated School.' The first birth record was registered on May 10th 1857; Sarah Ann Dormen was born to Sarah, and Edward Dormen, a colour sergeant attached to the 3rd battalion, 60th rifles. The Rev. William Hare, chaplain to the forces, presided.

The Third West York Militia

With the continuance of the war in the Crimea there was a dearth of men available for regular guard duties as well as the reserve forces. It was clear that volunteers would have to be recruited from the militia. At Richmond Barracks the 3rd West Riding of York Militia took occupation of the barracks, vacated by the 21st Scots Fusiliers, in August 1854. A second division, numbering 300 men followed a few days later on board the *Trafalgar*. This regiment was one of the first raised under the Militia Act in 1852. It numbered 1,190 rank and file, but in consequence of the greater number of married men remaining at home the service companies were considerably reduced in strength. The names of some of the officers accompanying the 2nd division have been recorded. They included: Col. Loftus, Adjutant- Capt. Brothero, Captains Bower, Kendal, Faywell, Wade, Sherburne and Chantrill; Lieutenants Smyth, Roger, Marshall and Loftus; Ensigns Hind, Blake, Loftus and Howeth. They were later joined by a division of the 48th or Northamptonshire Militia, commanded by Major Vivian, numbering 400 privates and non-commissioned officers and seven officers.

By Christmas, upwards of 200 of the Militia men had volunteered into the line. This figure would finally reach 540. The exploits of the militia while here were varied. In an area which, to this day, has a tradition of pigeon keeping and pigeon racing some will find it interesting that pigeons were involved in some of the sport taking place locally over 150 years ago. In January 1855, a pigeon match was arranged in the neighbourhood of Richmond Barracks between Capt. Wait and Lieutenant Rochford of the 3rd West York Militia. A wager of £50 was at stake and the task was to kill 15 birds each out of 20 birds, at 15 yards rise, to fall within a circumference of 40 yards, using a 16 bore gun, with a one ounce shot. A large number of spectators assembled and considerable speculation existed on the issue. The Lieutenant won, beating the Captain by 14 birds to 10.[85]

The following month there was a shameful act enacted by a militiaman who later claimed to be drunk at the time. Private James John Smith was charged with stabbing a worker with a bayonet. It appeared from the evidence that Caffrey, who was in the employment of Mr. Thomas Seery, paper manufacturer, was passing Richmond Barracks on his way home, when the soldier rushed out in a state of intoxication, and, advancing towards Caffrey, inquired if he were a Papist? I will here give the quote, as the reporting has a certain attraction in spite of its grim content:

Caffrey replied that he *was*, upon which the prisoner struck him a vigorous blow on the countenance, telling him to *'take that'* (meaning the eye-closer) for his candid admission- and the Papist (Caffrey) fell to the ground. Whilst he was down the prisoner, by way of finishing off his achievement, bestowed a few kicks on his ribs, and was about departing, when seeing Caffrey attempting to rise, he drew his bayonet and made a thrust at him, no doubt with the intention of letting the daylight through his body. Providentially, however, the weapon did not penetrate beyond the clothes of Caffrey, who started to his legs and chased the West Yorkshireman, who had retreated to his barrack in the belief that he had been the means of reducing the number of Irish Papists by one. [86]

A witness, who was in a house nearby, saw the prisoner running away and Caffrey following, the bayonet hanging from his clothes. The prisoner was arrested in the barrack and identified by Caffrey, and the case having being fully proved before the magistrates, he was committed for trial in the County Sessions. The West York Militia left Richmond Barracks in April 1855. It was originally envisaged that they would be deployed to do foreign garrison duties in places such as Gibraltar, but things did not go according to plan. About 300 of the men were allowed to return to their homes in the West Riding, Yorkshire having claimed their discharge under a new directive by Lord Panmure respecting militiamen who enlisted prior to the 12th May 1854. The rest of the militia headed for Waterford amid growing fears that more of them would avail of the same directive. However, we are next reminded by the New Zealand, *Daily Southern Cross*, 4th May 1855, of the 200 who had already volunteered and were then serving in the Crimea. Other militias at Richmond Barracks were the 109th County of Dublin Regt Militia (raised almost entirely in the metropolis) and the 93rd Roscommon Militia. Author and Police Magistrate, Frank Thorpe Porter remarked:

'The three regiments of militia embodied at the commencement of the Crimean war relieved us of several hundreds of loose, disorderly and dishonest fellows the riddance of whom produced a very desirable decrease in the convict cases of our police courts. On return there were fears but these were without grounds as the men had changed.' [87]

The 'She' Barracks

The Crimean War highlighted the woeful conditions of soldiers in camp and in barracks. A wave of public indignation at the sufferings of soldiers spearheaded a campaign against the demoralising environment in which the men were compelled to exist. *The Parliamentary Papers* for 1855-56 shows that a grant was made available for the provision of gas lighting at Richmond Barracks. More improvements were demanded and military surveys were carried out countrywide. The resultant reports showed that overcrowding was common, made worse by poor ventilation or in some cases no ventilation and poor sanitation. In fact, ventilation and sewage disposal were so bad in some barracks that they were almost uninhabitable. Fuel being in short supply for the fireplaces, the men would often stop up the vents and close the windows to keep in the heat. Wooden urine tubs were left in the rooms all night and in the morning merely rinsed out. By then the smell was overpowering. One sergeant describing how he found the morning air in the rooms under his supervision stated:

'...in a very thick and nasty state, especially if I come in out of the air. If I went in out of my own room sometime I would not bear it until I had ordered the windows opened to make a draught. I have often retired to the passage, and called to the orderly man to open the windows. The air was offensive both from the men's breath and from the urinal tubs in the room; and of course some soldiers do not keep their feet very clean, especially in summertime' [88]

For the married soldier and his family conditions were even worse. Separate married quarters were virtually non-existent in the forces. Instead wives were given a bed in the corner of the barracks, shielded from the view and attentions of others only by the protection of their husbands, and a blanket hung on a cord. The following report delivered with much sarcasm gives us a graphic picture:

The pleasures of a barrack-life are much increased when it happens that regiments are 'doubled up,' that is, two of them crammed into the building intended for one; the soldiers lie three and four in a bed, and every officer has a *chum,* the more delectable when one of them happens to be married and has children. I knew of a case of this kind in a Dublin barracks, where a field officer, who could not afford expensive lodgings in the town, was " doubled," or bundled, with a wife and eight children, into one room; which besides, served as his study and dormitory. [89]

For half rations the women cooked, washed, cleaned and 'mothered' the men in their barrack rooms. Children lived with their parents usually occupying a vacant bed or sleeping on whatever furniture was available. If a young daughter sent out as a servant lost her position she might return to stay with her parents until something else could be found. Small boys were treated by the men as a species of mascot or performing monkey and were soon taught to drink, smoke and swear like their elders.[90] Children were no longer permitted to live in barracks if their mother died. The truth is that the military did not want wives and children there at all and did everything to discourage it. Unlike most civilian employers, the army restricted the number of men who were permitted to marry. Under normal circumstances, a maximum of six men per company of 100 might received official permission. The families of soldiers married without permission had no security since the government refused to recognise them and made no provision for them. Instead of quarters in barracks they were forced to live in isolation in lodgings outside the base, their only means of support, the pittance their husband could spare them from his meagre pay and the small sum the wife could earn as a seamstress or a servant. When the regiment's turn for a transfer came, especially an overseas posting, transportation was provided only for some of the wives and children who were *'on strength'* (married with permission).[91] Although no figures were kept, it is thought that there were at least as many married *'off strength'* as there were officially. In some instances the regimental officers, at their own discretion, provided for the wives of soldiers during war and illness, but only for those whose marriages had been approved by the army. For those unapproved marriages, the wives and children had to rely on charity, such as 'The Central Association of Wives and Families' It is known that at the Royal Barracks, wives left abandoned by soldiers killed or serving lengthy periods overseas were so destitute that some of them turned to prostitution, starting a long tradition in Benburb street and the surrounding district. Again, the military took no responsibility for these women.

At Richmond Barracks there was accommodation rented for wives who were, for whatever reason, unwelcome in the barracks. Some idea of the location of this building was indicated in 1855, in an account by Robert Reynolds of the 83rd regiment in evidence to a committee reviewing the need for separate rooms for married soldiers. He was 23 years in service and was a colour-sergeant for the past 14 years:

Q. *Assuming then, it is your view, that each family ought to have a separate arrangement, what extent of accommodation do you think a married private ought to have?*
A. *One small room would be sufficient. If they were constructed as cottages, there could be four families dwelling on the ground floor with one entrance.*
Q. *Do you mean with no upper floor at all?*
A. *Of course, if they were built with two stories, every upper floor would have the same rooms.*
Q. *You think that one room is sufficient for a married private?*
A. *Quite sufficient.*
Q. *You would give him a fireplace in that room, in which his wife could cook the dinner?*
A. *Yes. I take my idea from the barracks, vulgarly called, in Dublin, the "She Barracks," where the married soldiers lodged, and paid a small weekly rent for the barrack utensils, which were supplied by the barrack-master, such as a wooden bedstead and table, and two, and in some cases three, ordinary sized stools.*
Q. *In the barrack you speak of, what was the size of the rooms?*
A. *I cannot say the actual size, but they were small-sized rooms; they varied in size, and there was a trifling variation in the rent.*
Q. *What was the average rent paid for one of those rooms?*
A. *From 5d. to 9d per week.*
Q. *Did that include furniture?*
A. *Everything,*
Q. *Fuel?*
A. *No, not fuel; they had to purchase their own fuel.*
Q. *Was that barrack at any distance from the men's barrack?*
A. *Just across, from the back gate of the men's barrack, about 40 or 50 yards, across a narrow street.*
Q. *What barrack was that near to?*
A. *Richmond Barracks.*
Q. *Do not you think it would be very desirable, if possible, to keep women of all descriptions, non-commissioned officers' wives and privates' wives, out of the building appropriated to unmarried men?*
A. *Entirely so.*[92]

The 83rd Regiment was stationed at Richmond Barracks for the year 1846-47 and presumably that was the time when the colour sergeant observed the special arrangement there. While the report was focussed on permitted marriages, it seems that what Reynolds witnessed may have been an innovative measure to deal with the problem of unapproved wives as well as those with permission. Furthermore, it appears that it also served the women from the neighbouring artillery barracks at Island-bridge. In any event, having a house full of women close to a barrack full of men was certain to promote activities which were not just outside the boundaries of the barracks but also outside the boundaries of marriage. This in turn would have led to angry exchanges between the women especially where alcohol was involved. Inevitably, some of the women found themselves in front of the police magistrate. Judge Thorpe Porter later recalled:

A person in the vicinity had a large building constructed through a speculative motive of a very extraordinary kind. He was aware that soldiers marrying without leave, or whose wives were dishonest, turbulent, quarrelsome, slovenly, or habitually intemperate, were not allowed to bring such objectionable characters into the regimental quarters. He consequently calculated that he would find no difficulty in having his premises occupied by tenants, to whose habits and morals he attached no importance, provided they paid the rent, and his expectations were not disappointed. His apartments were no sooner vacated by the incorrigible termagants of one regiment, than a succession of vixens was supplied from another to fill the unedifying edifice. The proprietor had not appropriated any particular name to the building, but it became speedily known in the district under the designation of 'The She Barracks.' In the southern division of the police district, there were five extensive military barracks, and I can unhesitatingly declare, that the cases supplied for police intervention or magisterial decision from them all, were completely outnumbered by those derived from the comparatively diminutive limits of the structure designed for the use and associated with the name of the softer sex. The details of the various charges and summonses in which inmates of these premises were compromised, would neither be instructive nor amusing, but I cannot ever forget a case in which two women, the wives of artillerymen, appeared, on summons and cross-summons, to swear against each other to the greatest extent of culpability. Each of them imputed to her adversary the inclination and avowed intention to commit every offence of a violent or malicious description, and neither came unprovided with witnesses ready to surmount the most elevated pinnacles of exaggeration. Whilst this auction of swearing was in progress, the husbands of the two inmates of the She Barracks were seated together, quietly listening to the proceedings, apparently on very friendly terms with each other, and not evincing any anxiety for the success of their respective consorts. At the close, I directed the informations of the parties to be engrossed, and stated that I would commit both for a month, unless they respectively found a surety in five pounds for their future good behaviour. I added, that as they were strangers, I did not suppose they could easily find bail amongst their neighbours, and that I was satisfied to take the husband of each as a surety for his wife. Immediately I was addressed by one of the artillerymen to the following purport: —

'May it please your honour, I'm only a private soldier, and where would I get five pounds in a day or two, when they begin again. Besides, if I was a fit bail, I would sooner be bound for his wife's behaviour than for my own wife's. 'Tis best to let them go." Then turning to his comrade, he added, "Come, Sam, we're likely to have a quiet month while they're both up.'

Nevertheless, he was disappointed, for the two viragoes, acting on the suggestion of an attorney who had been engaged in the case, came almost immediately to terms, and neither of them would make an information. They were consequently liberated, and instead of having a quiet month, I am sure that the artillerymen had, during that time, to undergo some heavy domestic bombardments. [93]

Often the military would requisition houses for barrack purposes. In regard to the 'She Barracks' it is likely that several houses, or perhaps one large house and a number of cottages were used. It is likely that the area which was later known as the Puck comprised these buildings. One large building in that area was Cambridge House and it is interesting to note that this was Major Kirkman, the barrack-master's house and that he was also barrack-master for Islandbridge. Locals say that there was a tunnel from there leading to Richmond Barracks. This too would fit with the details as there were very strict regulations regarding women entering and leaving barracks. Here is the standard order:

No soldier's wife will be allowed out or in to barracks after tattoo. Women not belonging to the regiment are never to be harboured in barracks, for the purpose of cooking or cleaning rooms, and if Commanding Officers permit any of their married soldiers to employ girls to look after children, these nurses are to be all seen every night out of barracks at drummers call.

As a result of the enquiry and the example cited by Colour Sergeant Reynolds the committee recommended a general adoption of the system of separate rooms for married privates. One of the beneficiaries of this was Richmond Barracks where married quarters were to be introduced within the confines of the barracks. In September 1856, an ordnance contract was issued for works connected with the erection of quarters for married soldiers including laundry, drill-sheds, privy, ash-pit and etc.; also, for drains, gas, and water piping and etc, and converting soldiers rooms into staff- sergeants' quarters.; the work to be completed by October 1857.

Further insight into the She Barracks at Golden-Bridge can be gleaned from a report of an identically named arrangement in the Curragh. The encampment at Kildare played a large part in the history of Richmond Barracks; whenever there was insufficient room at the barracks, detachments were posted to the Curragh; it was also used for training purposes. Knowledge of the fact that this 5,000 acre plain was the training ground of the legendary Fianna would have fuelled the young men's imaginations; and not just the Fianna:

> From the end of the sixteenth century onwards there are records of encampment there, and by 1804 the success of the annual summer mustering was confirmed when an extensive panorama by graphic artists of the encampment was put on public display in Dublin 'bringing to the eye, as a view, a body of 16,000 troops'. The camp was seen as a major military and social occasion, bringing together regular and volunteer soldiers from all parts of the country, and attracting thousands of spectators and camp followers. [94]

Conditions for the soldier were thought to be good there when the weather was dry, but after a day's rain the men would be ankle deep in mud (an appropriate preparation for Sebastopol!)

> Uncertainty as to the future of the encampment arose when the war in the Crimea ended, but from lessons learned on the battlefields it was decided that training camps should be established at which the three arms—infantry, cavalry and artillery—would train together. The Curragh was so designated, and henceforth it was to be the seasonal training ground for the army in Ireland. Each year thousands of men rotated there during the drill period, while the resident population of all ranks, their families and civilian employees numbered about 4,000. Regular and militia regiments met there on the squares and on the sward of the plain, and the major exercises which were held became important events in the social calendar of not alone the county, but of a wide area, including Dublin......The Curragh Camp was planned as a self-contained unit, a place where the soldier and his family, if he was on the married establishment, would be adequately provided for. There were hospitals, churches and schools, a bakery and an abattoir, canteens, recreation rooms and sports fields. A weekly market and visits from sutlers and travelling salesmen enabled the residents to purchase their necessaries locally, or they might venture into Newbridge for a wider range of goods. However as admission to the married establishment was limited many men elected to wed outside it, with the hope of being admitted in due course. Such brides found no support from the War Office, and the only accommodation they would find was in the cottages on the fringes of the plain, or in the back streets of the nearest towns. In Newbridge the area they occupied was known as the She Barracks. It was

not unusual for such women to be left behind by their husbands when a regiment moved to another station, or was despatched overseas. Then the plight of a family could be extreme as the mother sought to support her care, and it was not infrequent that such women fell into prostitution.'[95]

Some of these women lived on the open plains of the Curragh, with only the shelter of furze bushes to preserve them. They became known as the 'Curragh Wrens.' There they even gave birth and many of them died. Of course these matters led to public outrage, but the concern was not for the unfortunate women; rather, it was focussed on the health of the soldiers who were prone to venereal diseases, thereby rendering them unfit for duty.

The Puck

Golden-Bridge Village, an area to the west of Richmond Barracks, bordered by St. Vincent's street, Tram Terrace, the River Camac and the convent wall has for many years borne the colloquial name of 'The Puck.' Indeed, it was shown on a 1911 map of 'Dublin and its Environs' under that title. Local legend has it that at one time a regiment returned from India to Golden-Bridge and there being no room at the barracks a temporary accommodation was set up on nearby ground. They named it 'The Puck,' as that was a name they had heard used abroad for a similar type of arrangement. Apart from the reference to India, the story seems plausible enough, as Puk is the Serbian word for 'regiment.' The same word appears with identical translations in the languages of the Bosnians, Croatians and the Czechs. It would seem, however, that in some instances a Puk denotes a group who are somewhat less in character than the normal rank and file of a regiment. In 1918, the American periodical *Everybody's Magazine,* edited by the famous short story writer, O. Henry and the novelist, Frank Norris carried an account as follows:

> These men were a *puk* which had been drawn from the prisons and penitentiaries, and were in no way representative of the brave Serbian army. These mutineering renegades left desolation everywhere, plundering like drunken pirates. [96]

The above description would fit with the term 'She-Puck' a term which local historian Seosamh O' Broin has heard used in relation to the She barracks for unwelcome women and their equally undesirable spouses. Between 1911 and the 1950's about 70 houses in this area were demolished, including Gorman's buildings, two sets of cottages in a yard behind a large house. While most of the houses in the Puck were one storied, some had two floors with an outside stairway. This largely remained a rural area for the duration of its existence; sheep and pigs were kept by most of the inhabitants, who rarely, it is said, ventured into the city. A number of sources have commented on the presence of peculiar architectural features, including archways and steps which seemed out of place or of no evident purpose. These perhaps, once constituted the entrance to the spa of former days.

GOLDEN BRIDGE HOUSE, COUNTY DUBLIN,

Golden-Bridge Refuge

I mention the following only because of the association of the house with the history of the barracks. In 1855, Cardinal Cullen invited the Sisters of Mercy to provide a rehabilitation service to women who had been incarcerated in prisons by educating them and preparing them for final release. He originally rented Golden-Bridge House and lands and paid the rent for a five-year period. The convict refuge was opened in 1856. It was described as been very 'un-prison-like' in appearance and was a halfway house where women serving penal servitude spent the final part of their sentences. The house was by no means suited for the purpose, and immense pains, contrivance, and perseverance were needed to enable the Sisters to receive prisoners there at all; out-houses, lofts, and sheds were converted into dormitories and work rooms, while money was collected for the building of large laundries. A wooden gate originally led into the domain. It was claimed that no punishment regime existed, that prisoners were only locked in at night, and were allowed to dress as they pleased. Much was made of the fact that the women were not confined, but that was a nonsense; they had to earn a 'ticket -of –leave' from prison in order to be sent there and as the licence was exclusive to Golden-Bridge anyone found outside the refuge would be liable to be sent back to one of the main prisons.

The laundry would, in time, become its primary source of income and was in operation up until the 1950's. The main work of the establishment was washing and needlework but, in an attempt to alleviate the boredom, in 1866 the weaving of lindsey was introduced. There were no alternative manufacturers of this fabric in Ireland at that time; all lindsey, as well as most other articles of wear, was imported. Several looms were in operation at the Refuge.[97] The women also tended to pigs and poultry on the spacious surrounding grounds.

The necessity for an intermediate institution between the prison and the public for these women was mainly due to the fact that no one was prepared to take a female servant into his family fresh from a convict prison. There was a strong belief that women were harder to reform than men. Character was not important among tradesmen, as long as they were equal to the task. But a person who would be coming into your home, in close contact with your children and with ample opportunities to steal - that was a different matter. Women from some of the main prisons such as Dublin's Mountjoy and Galway Prison were sent here when they had about two years left of their sentence. Almost 1,500 convicts passed through the Catholic refuge and there is no doubt that, as well as finding work for some at home, the nuns ran a programme of assisted emigration through their network of convicts in America. Mother Mary Magdalene or Mrs Kirwan as she was generally known was the superintendent. Born at Tuam, Charlotte Kirwan was a descendent of one of the ancient 'Tribes of Galway' and a grand-daughter of the high sheriff of Galway. She was known to visit the workhouses and prisons and would personally select those whom she considered suitable to be transferred to Golden-Bridge. In addition, she wrote letters of complaint to the relevant boards about the appalling conditions in some of these places, especially when, as sometimes happened, she could find no one suitable for transfer. After 1883, the selection of inmates was taken over by the government.

The Reformatory

There is great confusion between the Convict Refuge and the Reformatory opened here in 1858, owing to the fact that both institutions are sometimes referred to as reformatories and because the Reformatory was later used as an extension of the Refuge. So successful was Mrs Kirwan that there were even calls in the House of Commons for a similar establishment for Protestant women on the same lines as Golden-Bridge Refuge. At the request of Sir Walter Crofton she then established a Reformatory for young offenders; girls supposed to be of a class who would not be taken by others. Named St. Vincent's Reformatory, it was located in the same grounds as the prison and was more or less a precursor to the industrial school of the 1880's. There would be an average of about 30-40 girls here at any one time. A report of 1863, lists the 'industrial' occupations of the girls as: washing, making up shirts, and general laundry work; needlework, cutting out shirts, and the use of the sewing machine. However, the report found that some of the girls here were more than twenty years old and as such would be a bad influence on the younger ones. At the other end of the scale, newspaper reports indicate that some very young children were sent here:

> Mary Neill, a little girl aged 11 years, was charged with stealing a cloth cape and bonnet from the shop of Mr. Eades. The magistrate sentenced her to be imprisoned for 14 days and at the expiration of that period to be sent to Golden-Bridge Reformatory for 4 years. [98]

The reports of Golden-Bridge being un-walled and unguarded gave the impression that the inmates were here of their own choice and belied the fact that anyone who disobeyed the rules faced harsh penalties:

> Three small girls named respectively, Margaret Lennon, Mary Anne Byrne, and Eliza Bennet, of the Reformatory school, Golden -Bridge, were brought up by constables 5G and 25G, charged by the mistress of the said Reformatory School, with obstinately refusing to abide by and conform to the rules of the Reformatory School. The prisoners were each sentenced to six months imprisonment, and after that term to be sent back to the Golden-Bridge Reformatory. [99]

Closure of the Reformatory & Expansion of the Refuge

Up to 1861 Mrs Kirwan took none but strong healthy women for whom work could be found in the Refuge. There was no room to classify, or employ any others.

Finding, however, that this had a bad effect on the women in the prison, she resolved to give up the reformatory school: it closed in 1865.[100] She was thus enabled to take from the prisons a considerable number of women not strictly able-bodied or calculated for rough farm or laundry work, but quite capable of undertaking remunerative work such as needlework, household service, and of getting through the recognised amount of industrial work in one shape or another. Those with an illegitimate child were allowed have the child with them, but life and twenty-year sentence servers were barred. It would appear that they occupied the old St. Vincent's Reformatory buildings. The juveniles were transferred to High Park and to Monaghan. In 1865, Mrs Kirwan was promoted to take charge of the Baggot Street Convent and of her Order in Dublin. Her successor at Golden-Bridge was a much younger lady. Laundry work continued to be their main occupation. A new laundry had been built and there was also a garden attached to the Convent. It was probably around this time that high walls (the remnants of which can still be seen today) were erected to contain the prisoners, as this much publicised press story from 1868 reveals:

Daring Escape from a Convent Reformatory

On Wed 9th Dec. 1868, a convict named Honora Burke made her escape from St. Vincent's reformatory, Golden-Bridge, Dublin, by means of a ladder which she placed against the yard wall of the prison. She ascended the ladder and leaped from the top of the wall to the ground- a height of seventeen feet- and strange to say, she accomplished the feat without injuring any part of her body. No trace of the daring fugitive could be found until Saturday night following, when she was arrested by Sub-constable Mc Nickel in Newbridge. She was subsequently brought before the Hon. W. Forbes. R.M. who remanded her until yesterday, when she was brought up again and identified by the Matron who was in attendance. [101]

In June 1875, another escape occurred that was widely reported upon in this country and in Britain. The escapees made it as far as Drogheda. This account is from *The Staffordshire Sentinel*:

Capture of Two Escaped Convicts at Drogheda

At 11 o' clock on Saturday a picket of the Drogheda Constabulary Sub-Inspector Carey and Constable Collum established a cordon round the town, and about one o'clock discovered the objects of their pursuit, to be Browne and Ryan, who on Monday last escaped the Refuge Sisters of Mercy, Golden-Bridge Female Convict Prison, Dublin, and who had since evaded the diligent search of the Metropolitan Force. They were taken before the Mayor and remanded. A part of the convict dress was found on them.[102]

126

—PILLOW LACEMAKING AT THE INDUSTRIAL SCHOOL CONDUCTED BY THE CONVENT OF MERCY, GOLDEN BRIDGE, DUBLIN.

The Industrial School

The expression 'Industrial school' means a school for the industrial training of children in which children are lodged, clothed and fed, as well as taught. The definition of a 'reformatory school' is defined in the same terms by section 44 of the 1908 act, but with the substitution of youthful offenders for children. The reformatories were for those guilty of offences and industrial schools were for those neglected, orphaned, but potentially exposed to crime. In 1881, an Industrial School was established at Golden-Bridge; in 1883 the convict refuge was also designated part of this industrial school, though there is evidence of convicts still here for some years after that. In 1890, the dexterity of the girls at lacemaking was even commented upon in the *English Magazine*. Some illustrations showed a group of the industrial school children engaged in making little pillow lace edgings and insertions generally, known as 'torchon' of which great quantities were more skilfully made in the Auvergne and other parts of France and in Belgium, by women and girls who were born lacemakers, and were the descendants of generations of lacemakers.[103] The Golden-Bridge industrial school was in existence up until recent times.

127

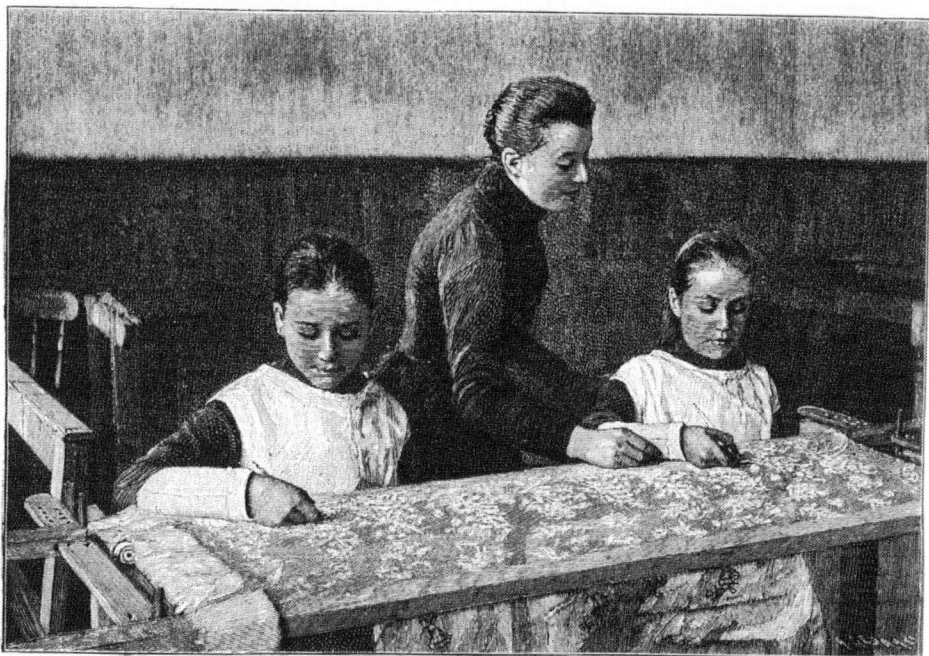

—LIMERICK LACEMAKING (TAMBOUR EMBROIDERY ON NET), INDUSTRIAL SCHOOL, CONVENT OF MERCY, GOLDEN BRIDGE, DUBLIN.

Former superintendent, Mrs. Kirwan, came to further notoriety during the times of the Phoenix Park Murders in 1882. The men assassinated were Lord Frederick Cavendish, newly appointed Chief Secretary for Ireland and Thomas Henry Burke, the Permanent Undersecretary who was also Mrs. Kirwan's first cousin. The two were stabbed to death by members of the Irish National Invincibles. One of those arrested, tried and sentenced to death, Joe Brady, could not bring himself to forgive the informer, though he did forgive the judge, jury, jailers and police for doing their job. The prison chaplain enlisted the aid of Sr. Magdalen, though it is unknown if he was aware of her relationship with Burke. Up to the time of her last visit on 13th May 1883 - the day before Brady's execution - her efforts to guide him to forgiveness had failed. As she left, she turned at the door and addressed him:

'The man you so barbarously killed without a moment's warning, and sent before the judgement of God, was a dear cousin of mine, and I came to tell you I have freely forgiven you and the others who took part in the deed, and so, if I forgive, why not you forgive the informers? Although they swore away your life they did not kill you, so will you now grant my request and forgive them?'

Brady became agitated, proclaiming that it was hard to do so. However, after a pause, he stated that he forgave them. His last wish was that Sr. Magdalen should meet his mother and console her following his execution the next morning.

Proof that prisoners were still here long after the refuge officially closed was the case of Galway woman, Brigid F. (No.3286). She was a 44 year old prostitute convicted of robbery and sent to Grangegorman for 5 years. She had 93 previous convictions. In 1887 she was transferred to the Golden-Bridge Refuge.

****

Sr. Magdalen Kirwan died at Golden-Bridge in February 1906 and was buried in the nuns' cemetery. After her death, John Spencer, 5th Earl Spencer, erected at his own expense a window memorial in memory of Mrs. Kirwan in the chapel of the Dominicans at Dominick Street, Dublin.

There followed another century, a different era and the events of more recent times have eclipsed the work of Mrs. Kirwan. During her years at Golden-Bridge there were many visits from the authorities, even a Royal Commission enquiry made on the running of such refuges and reformatories and to which Mrs. Kirwan was obliged to answer questions, which she did to their satisfaction. Ironically, it was the Irish Party in parliament that decided to exclude such surveys in the 20th century, on the grounds that religious bodies should be exempted from all such enquiries.

James Thomson

James Thomson (B.V.), Poet

In May 1858, James Thompson arrived with the Westmoreland Regiment at Richmond Barracks. Thomson was an acclaimed Scottish poet whose pessimistic masterpiece *The City of Dreadful Night* was described by Herman Melville as 'a modern book of Job.' Usually he wrote under the initials BV: from Bysshe (Shelley) and Vanolis, an anagram of the German poet and writer Novalis. In many details his sorrowful life can be compared with that of Edgar Allan Poe, and this is also reflected in his work. He was born in 1834 in Port Glasgow in Scotland. His father, a sailor, was semi-paralysed by a stroke when he was four, his baby sister died from measles which she caught from him, and his mother died of dropsy when he was nine. He was placed in an orphanage in London and then sent to a military academy. Not surprising that melancholia was to play a part in so much of his work. In 1854, about the time of the Crimean war, he joined the Army as a schoolmaster. In those days a schoolmaster in the English army was considered a soldier rather than a civilian and he wore the uniforms of the respective regiments to which he was attached. He taught children in the morning and the soldiers in the afternoon, besides additional instruction during the evening. On the whole, Thomson proved to be an efficient teacher, owing to his keen, clear intellect and to his methodical habits. Yet his heart was not in the work, which he described as *'Pumping muddy information into un-retentive sieves.'* It was in the army that he met and was greatly influenced by Charles Bradlaugh, then a trooper in a regiment of Dragoons in Ballincollig, Co. Cork. Bradlaugh was already the atheist republican who later founded *The National Reformer*.

In Ballincollig, Thomson fell in love with Matilda Weller the daughter of a regimental armourer; she was only thirteen, and was dead within eighteen months. Bradlaugh dismissed the suggestion that her loss destroyed Thompson's whole life though she certainly inspired some of his poetry. According to Bradlaugh, Thomson romanticised a memory after many years of very heavy drinking. He also suggested that Thomson made a habit of idealising women, without being close to them, throughout his short life:

'The armourer-sergeant's daughter ...was only a little child, playing with children's toys- a very pretty child, and it was not till long after her death, and in morbid times, that Thomson, little by little, built the poetical romance about her memory.'

Thomson spent three years 1856-59 in Dublin, two at Richmond Barracks with a year in the middle garrisoned at Ship Street. While stationed in the city he wrote more poems than at any other three-year period in his life   At Richmond Barracks, described by the poet, as his 'Castle hight of indolence,'[104] he was neither isolated or deprived of friendship. The 55th Foot had 158 non-commissioned officers and men from the regiment on the school roll. Average daily attendance was nineteen, ten boys and eleven girls. Tom Leonard, in his recent study of the poet, suggests there was likely to have been some resentment towards him on account of the army pay:

> A Third class schoolmaster was still paid well in comparison with the ordinary soldier. The former received an 8s 6d weekly 'lodging and fuel allowance' on top of his pay, and could earn extra money giving private lessons to officer's children. The infantryman who did the actual fighting in wars like the Crimea was paid 1s a day, less 4 and a half pence stoppages for meat and bread. This soldier was now confronted with young schoolmasters who not had never seen action, but had pay, privileges and rank such as they could never hope to attain. Attendance at school was compulsory for two hours after drill, a privilege for which the soldiers had to pay.[105]

Since the death of Matilda Weller, Thomson had again loved and lost a girl by the name of Helen Gray. She was betrothed to another, and so her parents, though fond of him, forbade him to correspond with her; as a concession they allowed him to write to her youngest sister Agnes, as a friend of the family. He wrote a number of letters to her and also some poems while stationed in Dublin. Of the poems, not all are fully dated, but it is thought that 'At Death's Door,' 'The Fadeless Bower,' 'A Happy Poet,' 'A Real Vision of Sin' and 'The Lord of the Castle of Indolence' were all written at Richmond Barracks. The letters are good- humoured banter and the haughty tone is artificial, though there is no doubt that he is talking down to the young girl in typical schoolteacher style in all of the correspondence:

Richmond Barracks April 8, 1859

'Dear Agnes, - I have just been re-reading your last letter, which plunged me deep into Christmas jollities again... I of course thoroughly despise your unprovoked attack upon my smoking. I have experience both in smoking and non-smoking, and so am entitled to pronounce which is the better. But you have no right to speak upon the question until you shall have smoked some scores of cigars and hundreds of pipes. To you ladies it may be even the fox's sour grapes- for I am told that abroad, where the ladies are graciously permitted by their lords to smoke, they are very fond of it; and I am told that never does a lady look more charming than when, reclining luxuriously, she inhales and exhales the fragrant ether from nargileh or cigarette. It

seems to me that the greater portion of the much speaking and writing against tobacco is blank nonsense. I think tobacco considerably less hurtful to us than our tea and coffee; and I think it is truly beneficial to men engaged in the fierce toil and struggle of modern business.' [106]

His sense of humour is more evident in another letter recalled by Agnes Gray in later years:

> At last he wrote that he was to have a fortnight's holiday and would pay us a visit. We were all excitement at his coming. I had previously informed him in one of my letters that Helen had become a Ragged School teacher, and in reply he had said he could not imagine a creature so bright, and, in his remembrance, so beautiful, being arrayed in sombre habiliments, and acting such a character.

However, when he did come to visit, the family noticed a change in the man: *'We thought him much altered in appearance and manners; indeed we were somewhat disappointed. He was by no means so manly-looking as when he left London, and was painfully silent and depressed.'* [107]

In Thomson's future life he managed to find despair at every turn. During 1862, when the regiment were at Portsmouth he went for a stroll with a group of his fellow schoolmasters and one of them out of bravado or for a wager swam out to a boat which was moored on a pond where bathing was prohibited. An officer demanded the names of all present and on this being refused and there being further altercation, he found himself subject to a court martial. It resulted in a reduction in rank and a dishonourable discharge from the Army on the basis of his disobeying an order and disrespectful conduct. Back in London, he moved in with Bradlaugh and his family and also went to work for him as secretary in the offices of 'The National Reformer.' However Bradlaugh was soon bankrupt. Various other career changes came to nought, though it is said that he spurned many golden opportunities along the way. Friends contrasted his personal wit and good company with the misery of much of his verse. Oddly for a heavy drinker, he was also an insomniac who spent entire nights till dawn pacing the dark streets of London. Inevitably, he ended up in all sorts of trouble, including drunken behaviour, arson and even robbery and a prison term of fourteen days for unpaid fines. His death was predictably pathetic: on a night in June 1882, a friend found him lying on a bed in the dark. He struck a match and saw the blood soaked pillow. *'I'm dying,'* Thomson told him; he had burst a blood vessel. He died in hospital a day or so later, aged forty-seven. It was the end to a strange, sad and brilliant life. Some critics claim that his prose was actually better than his poetry, with one exception: 'Only in The City of Dreadful

Night did he really find himself and write seriously and deeply about something he knew intimately and at first hand — his own inner being.' [108]

> The City is of Night; perchance of Death,
> But certainly of Night; for never there
> Can come the lucid morning's fragrant breath
> After the dewy dawning's cold grey air;
> The moon and stars may shine with scorn or pity;
> The sun has never visited that city,
> For it dissolveth in the daylight fair.

(Short extract from The City of Dreadful Night)

*****

Minden Day at Richmond Barracks
Lord Seaton and Viscount Geogh

In August, 1859 the ceremonial presentation of colours to the 2nd battalion of the 20th Regiment took place in the presence of Lord Seaton, Lord Viscount Geogh and a large number of nobility and gentry, including ladies in the grand square of Richmond Barracks. The day chosen was the centenary anniversary of the Battle of Minden, fought on the 1st August 1759, where the 20th Regiment distinguished themselves. The first battalion of the Regiment was at this time serving in India. The new battalion was all in the bloom of youth, full of hope and strength. According to the *Irish Times* they 'paraded to receive that charge so dear to every soldier- the colours that he hopes will precede him in the path of glory; and which he must be every ready to defend to the last extremity.' At 12 0'clock, about 600 officers and men of the new battalion, each of whom wore two laurel leaves in his cap with a rose in the centre, formed three sides of a square with the Elthorn Militia, under the command of Colonel Prior to the left. General Lord Seaton arrived at half-past twelve o'clock, accompanied by a numerous staff of officers, and attended by a troop of the 18th Light Dragoons. His Lordship was received with the usual military honours, and as he rode in front of the square the bands played, *See the conquering hero comes.'*

The ceremony took place in the centre of the square, where the colours were consecrated by the Rev. J.L. Parsons, Junior, Chaplain to the garrison. The colours were then placed in the hands of Lord Seaton, and the two senior ensigns of the regiment advanced in front of his Lordship and received them kneeling. The ensigns then marched back to the ranks with the colours unfurled. Lord Seaton briefly addressed the officers and men and alluded to the distinguished services of the Regiment in the Peninsula and elsewhere. After the presentation, the colours were trooped down the ranks. The troops then marched by Lord Seaton, in quick and slow time, saluting him as they passed. After the ceremony a celebration was provided in the officers mess room. A banquet was also provided for the men in honour of the occasion.

John Colborne- Lord Seaton

There was nothing particularly remarkable about this event apart from the presence of Lord Seaton (who became Field Marshal of the 20th East Devonshire Regiment in 1860), and also Lord Geogh who, it is said, commanded in more general actions than any other British officer of the 19th century except the Duke of Wellington. A statue erected to his honour in the Phoenix Park in 1880 would ensure that Dubliners would remember his name. The statue made of bronze, was cast from the metal of guns taken during the Sikh campaign. In the 20th century it was targeted a number of times by republicans and was eventually removed and sold.

Local Issues

The next item concerning the conditions of the roads and footpaths in Golden-Bridge was written 150 years ago, but it could easily have been written today regarding Dublin City Council's neglect of the St. Vincent street area; particularly apt is the comment that the situation would not be tolerated anywhere else.

Frightful Condition of the Roads, County of Dublin
To the Editor of the Irish Times

January 12th 1861

'Sir, allow me through your columns to direct public attention and the attention of the proper authorities, to the condition of the public roads in this locality, from the police-barrack at Kilmainham, along Richmond Barracks, Richmond Road, Golden-Bridge, and the road to Inchicore. These roads are continually in a very worse repair, but in wet weather they are almost impassable. It is a disgrace that, notwithstanding the very heavy rate at which the inhabitants are taxed, these roads are kept in a condition which would not be tolerated in any other part of Ireland. I understand that the contractors are well paid for keeping them in a proper state, but they neglect their duty, as the county inspector seldom or never comes near the place, reserving his visits for other and more classic neighbourhoods. The way in which the immediate neighbourhood of Richmond Barracks is surrounded by hillocks of mud and dirt is a disgrace to the authorities. . In the village of Richmond, the people are allowed to deposit heaps of dirt directly opposite their doors in the public view, and this within a few paces of a police barracks! I hope the inhabitants of this locality will arouse from their apathy and take proper steps to have this frightful state of things remedied, which is so hurtful to health and property, and prejudicial to the well-being of the neighbourhood. Indeed, I have heard that a meeting of the ratepayers is about to be summoned, to take measures to have the proper presentments ready for the kerbing of the roads, &c, and also to enquire into the cause of the negligence of the contractors, county inspectors, and the apathy of the police. This is a step in the right direction.-

Yours, Sir, respectfully,

SUBURBAN, '[109]

136

The meeting referred to took place on Feb 2nd of that year at the Parochial Schoolhouse, Golden-Bridge which was numerously attended by the ratepayers and inhabitants of the districts of Golden-Bridge, Richmond, New Kilmainham, and Islandbridge in order to adopt measures 'for the better repair of the public roads, footpaths, &c.' At half past seven o'clock, the chair was taken by Robert Smith, Esq., Rialto Lodge. The chairman, never straying too far from the sentiments expressed in the letter, stated that the inhabitants of the neighbourhood had much reason to complain of the unsatisfactory manner in which the public roads in the district were kept. In wet weather they were covered with mud, and so irregular and full of holes that it was almost unsafe to walk upon them. The district was also insufficiently lighted, particularly in the neighbourhood of Richmond Barracks, where sometimes, under cover of darkness, drunken soldiers committed many offences...It was a matter of grave importance to the inhabitants of the district that something should be done to have the roads repaired and a sufficient number of lamps provided.

The Rev. Thomas Mills, incumbent of the district, contributed to the debate, observing that the village of Golden-Bridge contained 1,200 inhabitants. This included a parish church, a reformatory and a cemetery, which drew to the neighbourhood daily a large number of visitors, which alone was a reason for having the roads properly repaired and the district properly lighted. At the meeting, resolutions were moved and passed on the matters aforementioned and also calling for the road leading from the Circular-road at the police station to Richmond Barracks to be lighted with gas. This road was the leading thoroughfare to the barrack and, as such, attracted prostitutes to the area. Despite its proximity to the police station, many females blatantly used to congregate there under cover of the darkness, where they would indulge in 'every description of immorality, much to the annoyance of the well-disposed.' They were further causing 'the demoralisation of society in general, and rendering person and property unsafe.' After some further discussion it was resolved, that a committee should be appointed to meet on another date to prepare a memorial on the subject. [110]

The Recreation Room

Often dinner parties and balls were given at the barracks. Up until 1863 the Sergeants Mess would the likely location for such events; in August of that year the sergeants of the 11th Foot gave a farewell banquet to the sergeants of the 19th Foot (2nd bn), on the eve of their departure for the East Indies. The following year, the opening of the newly built Recreation Room was marked with a celebratory Ball on the 10th May 1864 and a supplementary Ball two days later on the 12th

The Grand Ball of the 10th May 1864 was given by Colonel Stapleton and the officers of the 32nd Regiment. It was attended by the *elite* of the city.

> The new building which has recently been erected for the recreation of the men was decorated for the occasion with rare and artistic effect, and nothing was spared which could possibly secure greater *éclat* to the brilliant entertainment. The entire suite of rooms was hung with scarlet, blue and white cloth, and the apartment devoted to the torpsichore was brilliantly lighted by four large crystal gasalters, pendant from the ceiling, and a series of candelabra, with handsome reflectors, arranged around the walls. Three large full length mirrors gave the dancers an opportunity of viewing their movements in the stately quadrille and the bewitching valse. The orchestra was occupied by the band of the regiment (under the direction of Mr. Miller) and by Mr. Hanlon's string band... the drawing room was richly furnished with ottomans and loungers, and separated from the supper- room by scarlet cloth. The supper, which was of a *recherché* description, was supplied by Mr. Sproutt, and the wines, &c, were the oldest and choicest in the cellars of the mess. The guests, who numbered upwards of three hundred, began to arrive at a quarter to eleven o'clock, and shortly afterwards dancing commenced. [111]

In future years most events, including plays and lectures would be held here. An excellent library was provided: a reading room furnished with the leading newspapers and periodicals of the day. In the larger rooms there was bagatelle, dominoes, dice etc; in fact every amusement harmless in character calculated to 'elevate and develop the mind,' but really designed to keep the soldier to his barracks in his leisure hours and divert his mind from the aforementioned distractions which were to be had in the vicinity. The Parliamentary Papers of 1865 indicate that an additional recreation room was then occupied. A bread and meat store had also been erected here and in other barracks. [112] Talks and shows of religious themes were held in the large chapel school-room, which was a partitioned part of the garrison chapel.

Mutiny
The Planned Fenian Revolt

The escape of the Fenian leader, James Stephens from Richmond Penitentiary (on the South Circular Road) was one of the most daring acts in Irish history. The gaoler, Daniel Byrne, a sworn Fenian and the prison pharmacist, John Breslin were complicit in his escape. Keys were provided from beeswax impressions, but Stephens had still to scale an inner wall on a ladder balanced on two tables and then to climb a rope ladder to the summit of an 18 foot high outer wall. On reaching the top, he had no option but to drop to the ground, which he did, landing on two Fenians who had attempted to break his fall and who were each sent sprawling backwards into the mud.

With Stephens on the loose again the British establishment knew that rebellion would once more be imminent. On February 17th 1866, Prime Minister, Lord John Russell, suspended habeas corpus, rushing the bill through both houses during a single sitting and securing the Royal assent the same evening. The next morning police began mass arrests, including English, Scots and American Fenians who had gathered in Ireland in large numbers. John Devoy, chief lieutenant, was later to complain that had Stephens not previously ordered all revolvers to be given up and stored, many policemen and detectives would have met a bloody end. The arrests caused panic among Fenians and sympathisers, especially at Richmond Barracks where loyal supporters who had infiltrated the ranks were anxiously awaiting the word to revolt.

With still no word forthcoming from the leadership, a message was relayed to Devoy on the 19th February that the Fenian-men of the 61st and 60th Rifles, who were in the majority, were threatening to seize the barracks and start the fight at once. Details of this intended mutiny would later be revealed. On the night before the mutiny, a sworn member of the Fenian Society in each of the barrack rooms was to stuff a fine sponge into the chambers of all the rifles belonging to the men who were not Fenians, thereby rendering them useless. When the regiment was called out to meet the Fenians the men of the 61st who belonged to the Fenians would fire over their heads, and the others who were not loyal would not be able. Then the Fenians among the 61st would go over to their party, and at once fire on those who refused to join the society.[*]

---

[*] Mutiny-Trial of Private Cranston of the 61st Regiment, Richmond Barracks, Courts Martial at the Royal Barracks : *The Irish Times*, June 20th 1866

John Devoy donned the uniform of the 3rd Buffs

This greatly alarmed Devoy, for he knew that Richmond Barracks was central to the plan for rebellion. They would need those men to rise up and take the barracks, but not in isolation, only as part of an all-out rebellion. He determined that he must get to see the impatient men even if it meant going inside the barracks and risking his arrest. At the time when he received the message Devoy was in a back room of a public house at the corner of Camden Street and Long Lane. In another room were William Curry, of the 87th, in civilian clothes, and Fennessy of the 3rd Buffs in uniform and who was on furlough.

Fennessy and I were about the same size and build, and the buff facings of the Third could hardly be distinguished at night from the white ones of the Sixty-first. I put on Fennessy's uniform and he my clothes, and Curry, with a borrowed scissors, cut the beard off my chin (not then very much) so as to give me the regulation British side whiskers and moustache. Fennessy's shoes were too large for me, so I kept my elastic boots, which were wholly unmilitary, but would hardly be noticed in the night. As I had only been four years out of the

140

Foreign Legion and had been frequently drilling during the intervening time my appearance was not likely to attract attention.[113]

He took an outside car to Thomas Street and walked to James's Street, where he visited a number of public houses frequented by the soldiers, getting closer to Richmond Barracks as he went along. On his travels, he met a number of the soldiers of the 61st who assured him that the problem was confined to a few hot-heads, but that the situation was still dangerous. Despite their insistence that it would not be necessary for him to go into the barracks, at this stage he was still determined to do so. He knew that if he went in with a group of them he would escape notice and there would be no difficulty coming out, with the furlough and the forage cap of the 3rd Buffs; besides almost all of the guard at the gate that night were Fenians. When he reached the front gate of Richmond Barracks he walked past a few times and met about 50 of the men of the 61st and some of the 60th Rifles as they were returning to barracks. They promised to pass on the word to keep quiet until orders for action came. Satisfied with this, Devoy no longer felt it necessary to go inside the barracks (contrary to what you may have read elsewhere).

With more and more Fenian arrests however, it became clear that unless action was taken soon there would be no organisation left to run. Stephens's procrastination was mainly due to events in America where the movement was in disarray and also the failure to procure arms from Liverpool. However, he knew that Devoy and others were demanding answers. He summoned an unofficial war council of eight advisers who met on February 20th and 21st, 1866, across from the Kildare Street Club, Kildare Street in a house belonging to a Mrs. Butler, a society seamstress (later ruined when her association with the Fenians became known). Present at the meeting were Stephens, Devoy, Thomas Kelly- the American, a second American officer, and the head centres for Athlone, Cork, Limerick, and Ulster. Devoy presented to this meeting his plan for providing the necessary arms. His plan was to capture Richmond Barracks with the assistance of soldiers who were Fenians there, to seize the armoury and take possession of the arms and ammunition stored in it. However, he was unable to convince the council, and later ruefully reflected:

> With 900 Fenians out of the 1600 men of the Sixty-first and the Sixtieth Rifles in Richmond Barracks and a key of the back gate facing the canal in our possession, I was confident that we could surprise and capture it without difficulty.' The bank of the canal at the back of the barracks was closed to traffic between two bridges, was very dark on moonless nights because it was shaded with large elm trees and there were no lamps, and the grass was so thick and long that the tramp of men over it would make practically no noise.
> 'I proposed that our riflemen should be collected on the canal bank at an hour when the soldiers would all be in but before they would have gone to bed. Tom

Chambers, the Centre of the Sixty-first, then a deserter in Dublin, would pick out a small number of the best men of the regiment to remain out of barracks and form the vanguard of the attacking party. They would know every man of the guard and would serve as guides. Without giving any notice to our friends inside, so as to avoid loose talk, excitement or chance of betrayal, the gate would be suddenly opened and our men would march inside, move rapidly to the positions assigned them make prisoners of such officers as happened to be on duty, rally our friends to our support and capture the Englishmen. **We could have probably captured Richmond without firing a single shot.** If there was any fighting it would speedily be over. With Richmond in our possession, reinforced by 900 Fenian soldiers and probably several hundred others, with the balance of the rifles to arm another contingent of our men our next move would naturally be on Island-Bridge Barracks, which were near at hand, where the 10th Hussars were lying. With Richmond and Island-Bridge in our hands the south-western outlet of Dublin would be open to us, in case of defeat in the other parts of the city, and we could march out.[114]

Devoy's plan was favourably received by the meeting and would have been acceptable if 2,000 rifles expected from Liverpool had come to hand. The scarcity of rifles in the hands of the civilian forces was the deciding factor against its adoption, and furthermore, as most of the trained American officers had been arrested and lodged in Mountjoy Prison a few days previously, the majority of the eight men present at that meeting on the night of February 21st, 1866 saw no hope for a successful start. The result, said Devoy, was that 'the last chance for a Rising in that year was thrown away.' The most terrible military weapon, the mutiny of Irish troops in the British army, which even Smith O'Brien believed a virtual certainty in 1848, was never to be put to a test in Irish history.[115] The following day John Devoy was arrested and James Stephens fled the country to France en-route to America. By the end of the week three thousand Fenians were imprisoned. Stephens' failure to act cost him the leadership of the movement. By the year's end he would be stripped of his command in favour of Colonel Kelly.[*]

Isaac Butt

Today, Isaac Butt is quite rightly remembered as the founder of the Home Rule League and as a barrister and M.P; however, his personal life was an unhappy one. Throughout his years he amassed debts and was a womaniser. It was said that at

---

[*] Activity in Canada achieved little and attention again shifted to Ireland. Kelly, a veteran of the US Civil War was sent to Ireland in January 1867 with a group of Irish-Americans to plan the ill-fated rising of 1867.

meetings he was occasionally heckled by women with whom he had fathered children.[116] He was also involved in a financial scandal when it was revealed that he had taken money from several Indian princes to represent their interests in parliament. Just before the time in question, Butt was confined in the Four Courts Marshalsea, Debtors Prison, Thomas Street. However, he sought and was granted a transfer to Kilmainham. His desire to move was apparently to avoid another prisoner, some 'very important personage' who was bothering him. One day as he was sitting in the alcove of the prison window which overlooks, what we now call, Emmet Road the drowsiness of evening, following a hot summer's day was broken with a strange sound:

'All of a sudden there was borne along on the evening air, a weird, wailing cry, which caused a feeling of sadness...' [117]

Butt mechanically closed the book he was reading and appeared spellbound. The wail became more and more distinct. Standing up in the window recess and looking in the direction of Richmond Barracks, he at once saw what it was. It was simply a Highlander's funeral. The Scotch wail or dirge was played on the Highland pipes whilst the cortege was on its way to Bully's Acre, then used as a military burial-yard. The deceased was possibly a soldier of the 92nd Gordon Highlanders who were here until September 1866. After the procession had passed Butt dropped into a sad dreamy mood and began talking to a friend, who was visiting him, about his own death. He word-pictured the spot he wished for his grave, in the churchyard at Stranorlar, county Donegal, just beside the wall of the Manse, which separated it from the graveyard. He told how he had often crossed this wall and studied his lessons under the shade of a large tree which stood close to it. He also wished if possible that at the time of his interment a keen would be sung over his corpse, but he wished above all, that it should rain as he was being interred. Thirteen years later, when he died and the family were discussing where he should be buried, a fellow M.P., Dr. O' Leary produced a letter given to him by Butt some three years previously outlining in the same manner the location at Stranorlar.

If the expense would not be an inconvenience, I would wish to be buried in Stranorlar Graveyard, as close as may be to the south-eastern angle. The ground is - or was - a good deal lower than the rest of the churchyard. A very shallow grave would be enough, with a mound of earth or a tomb raised over it. Put no inscription over the grave, except the date of my birth and my death; and, wherever I am buried, let the funeral be perfectly private, with as few persons attending, and as little show and expense as possible.

Few people have the foresight or the motivation to make their own funeral arrangements and it would seem that memories of the poignant funeral procession

143

and the thoughts it inspired prompted Isaac Butt to leave that all important letter with Dr. O' Leary.

The Closure of Golden-Bridge Cemetery

The proximity of the cemetery to the Barracks was always considered a nuisance to the military authorities because of the frequency of funerals and the disruption they caused. By autumn 1866, there was further consternation when the military formed the opinion that the drainage from the burial ground was contaminated and a possible health hazard to the soldiers and the people in the locale. It seems that the military would not accept the fact that their own sewage and drainage systems were drastically inadequate and were willing instead to blame some other source for recent outbreaks of fever and other illnesses. The Catholic Cemeteries Committee was surprised to receive from the quarters of the 92nd Highlanders, the following letter:-

R.E. Office, Dublin Castle, 29th August, 1866
'Sir - Being given to understand that the Cemetery adjoining Richmond Barracks is under your jurisdiction, I have the honour to request you will inform me whether any and what steps you could take to render it less obnoxious to the troops quartered at the barracks - whether it can at least for the present be closed, or if not, that internments may be made as far from the barracks as the nature of the ground will admit of. I have the honour to be Sir,

F. Macbean, Major, 92nd. Highlanders,
President, Sanitary Committee. [118]

The Committee replied on 5th September 1866, as follows:-

Catholic Cemeteries Office, 7 Lower Ormond Quay,
'Sir - In reference to your communication of 29th ultimo, I have the honour to inform you that the Cemetery at Golden-Bridge cannot be closed as it is established under special Act of parliament, and that the governing body are not aware of any sanitary inconvenience that has arisen from it. I am to add, that the majority of the interments are made in the portion of the Cemetery most remote from Richmond Barracks, and that a sub-committee from this Board visit the Cemetery once a month, and take into consideration any complaints that may be made in connection with it. I have the honour to be, sir, &c

C. Coyle, Registrar [119]

This correspondence gave rise to a number of reports by sanitary inspectors and doctors to examine the condition of the Cemetery and report back to them whether any reasonable objections could be made. Meanwhile, however, the cholera epidemic of 1867 had occurred, resulting in an increased amount of funeral traffic and related commotion which greatly annoyed the military personnel. General Lord Longford, the War Secretary, in a letter dated August 10th, 1867, issued a bold statement. Writing to General Sir T. Larcom, who, in point of fact, was the Government of Ireland, he alleged:

'It is stated that this Cemetery is situated in the midst of a populous district, and is so overcharged with bodies that the surface is much raised above the level of the ground in the vicinity, and that, consequently, the drainage from it is liable to impregnate the water in the neighbouring tanks.[120]*'*

Sir Charles Cameron visited Golden-Bridge, and wrote a report, dated 24th March, 1868, in which he stated:

I have made a careful inspection of the Cemetery at Golden-Bridge. The grounds appeared to me to evidence great care on the part of those persons entrusted with the charge of them. The walks were very clean, and in no part of the Cemetery did I observe decomposing vegetable matter or filth of any kind - of course I refer to the surface of the ground. The soil is covered with grass, which, at the time of my visits, the 17th and 24th March, was healthy and luxuriant. I also observed numerous trees and shrubs, which exhibited all the appearances indicative of healthy vitality. The soil appeared to be dry, and I am informed that the drainage of the ground is secured by means of two deep cuts, which, after nearly encircling the Cemetery, meet near the entrance. So far as I could judge with the eye, the level, at the lowest part of the Cemetery, is not more than two feet below the level or surface of the highest portion.

A second opinion obtained by Dr. Mapother confirmed these findings. However, these reports from two esteemed medical examiners had little bearing on the outcome. They proved that that there was no legitimate reason to close Golden-Bridge Cemetery, but the decision was a foregone conclusion. Without further communication with the Committee, the Government, in the Gazette of June 9th 1868, announced its intention to close Golden-Bridge Cemetery. At a subsequent meeting, the Lord Chancellor Abraham Brewster restricted future interments to those who had acquired rights of burial by purchase, or had relatives already entombed at Golden-Bridge. This virtually caused the cemetery to cease functioning.

The Fenian Rising 1867

The 52nd Oxfordshire Light Infantry arrived at Richmond Barracks in April 1866, under the command of Major E.G. Curzon. In the spring of the following year Fenian activity was rife, and now there was a strong American dimension involved. As always, however, informers were intent on frustrating the Irish cause. In 1867, a certain Sergeant Talbot of the Royal Irish Constabulary attended Fenian meetings in disguise, and passed on details of proceedings to the military. It was Talbot who gave the startling information that March 7th of that year was the appointed date for a great rising to take place all over Ireland. He paid for his treachery with his life, not long afterwards, when the revolutionaries unmasked him.

As soon as Lord Strathnairn, who held the Irish Command, heard of the intended rising he ordered a heavy siege gun to be brought to the Royal Hospital and the superior officers had instructions that as soon as the gun was fired three times they were at once to occupy the posts assigned to them. Sources indicated that there was to be a large contingent of Fenians concentrated in Tallaght on the night of the 7th March, so a flying column under the command of Major Curzon was to be sent to Tallaght to meet them. A second column would set out from Newbridge in the opposite direction towards Tallaght, hoping by this means to fall upon the rebels from the front and rear. Major Curzon's column consisted of a wing of the 52nd from Richmond Barracks, two troops of the 9th Lancers and two field guns. All parties were awaiting the signal when a member of the metropolitan police arrived at the Royal Hospital that evening. He was running and panting for want of breath. He told Lord Stratnairn that the Fenians had risen, had attacked a metropolitan police barrack between Dublin and Tallaght and massacred the occupants. Col. Frederick Arthur Wellesley [*]was given command of the Lancers and told to send them at once to the Royal Hospital to await the guns and the infantry. He then rode to Richmond Barracks to inform Major Curzon personally of the revised plans before proceeding to the Royal Hospital, where the Lancers were already in waiting. Shortly afterwards the great doors opened to admit the guns, which in turn were followed by the infantry.

It was pitch dark when at about 10 p.m. the great ponderous gates of the Royal Hospital opened and the little column emerged, the cavalry leading, followed by the infantry and guns. I had received orders from Lord Strathnairn to throw out an advance guard, not, he said, according to the drill book, but in knots of twos and threes. Everybody was to be

---

[*] Colonel, Hon. Frederick Arthur Wellesley a nephew of the Duke of Wellington, gained the rank of Colonel in the service of the Coldstream Guards. He became a diplomat and held the office of First Secretary to Vienna and the office of Military Attaché at St. Petersburg.

challenged and anyone unable to account satisfactorily for his being out on such a night was to be made prisoner. We had not gone far before there was a scuffle ahead in the advance guard. They had challenged a little man who had run into their arms in the darkness of the night and in whose hands they found a loaded revolver. He made a great row, protested against his capture, and declared that he belonged to the Chief Secretary's office. He could not, however, give any reason for being abroad on a night when all well-disposed citizens should have remained at home. I sent him to the rear of the column, where an escort for prisoners had been told off. Shortly afterwards a sergeant was sent to tell me that they could not get him to walk, and that they had endeavoured to drag him, but to no purpose, as he threw himself on the ground. There was nothing for it but to have him tied to a gun. When it advanced he again threw himself down and was consequently dragged along like a minnow at the end of a trolling line. The gun plan was, however, completely successful, as the little creature soon found that walking was after all the best means of locomotion. As we cleared the Dublin suburbs we began to take any number of prisoners. Never was I out on a darker night. The darkness much facilitated the taking of prisoners by the advance guard. Those we captured were all returning to Dublin, some of them carrying pike-heads, some revolvers and others more primitive weapons such as scythe-blades, etc.[121]

The military could not believe their luck and were puzzled as to what was going on. It later emerged that the meeting of the Fenians was arranged to take place at a gorse covert near Tallaght. The rank and file had turned up faithfully, but the leaders failed to show up. The group despaired of waiting and eventually dispersed, most of them taking the route to Dublin, where they ran right into the advancing troops from Richmond Barracks. There were that many prisoners taken that Col. Wellesley sought help from Lord Stratnairn to strengthen the escort, fearing that he could be no longer responsible for their safe-keeping. Putting it bluntly, the guard was so weak that the prisoners could make their escape at any time if they chose, and the night being so dark it would be impossible to recapture all of them. Stratnairn was reluctant to reduce the fighting force, convinced he would need his men at some further point. However, he came up with a novel way of dealing with the problem: 'Return at once to the escort,' said his Lordship, 'and halt it. You will find that every prisoner wears either braces or a belt. Take these from all of them and then see that their trousers are cut down from between the buttons behind to the bottom of the seat. When this is done you will not find many escape.'

This somewhat comical operation was carried out to the letter, much to the indignation of the prisoners. Their ludicrous position was not noticeable at night-

147

time, but when morning dawned it was indescribably amusing to see these men, some of them respectable drapers' assistants with high hats and overcoats with velvet collars, marching along holding up their trousers.[122]

All the while, the one thing uppermost in the minds of the military was the plight of the constabulary in the R.I.C. barracks which they were told had fallen to the rebels. When they arrived there, however, they found that the occupants had not just fended off their attackers but had pursued them, making a great number of arrests. Here, the elderly Sub-Inspector Burke, known locally as 'Chief Burke,' had taken 14 well armed constables out onto the crossroads between Tallaght and Roundtown. They had knelt down and fired in volleys, leaving six Fenians bloodied on the ground. The remaining Fenians, according to Burke, had run away *'in the greatest disorder.'*

Searches were made of cottages along the way, but nothing was found except old women, some of them calmly sitting up in their beds smoking clay pipes. Further along the way more arrests were made nearer to Tallaght, including a convoy of 6 hay carts driven by women. On this occasion the soldiers found ammunition and firearms of various descriptions concealed under the hay. There was one more incident before they reached Tallaght.

> The sun had now risen, and we resumed our march towards the gorse covert. On our right was a wall some six feet high, and as we rode along we saw some half-dozen Fenians in the fields beyond. Lord Strathnairn at once ordered me to take some men and catch them, an order more easily given than executed. In the first place there was no gate in the wall, and secondly the men we were to capture had a very considerable start of us. I was riding a cob about 14.2, which I brought alongside of the wall and from which I was able to clamber over it, telling some of the men of the 52nd to follow me. We then commenced to run, although it was evident that we should never catch our men, so far were they ahead of us. I was at the bottom of the near ditch and was about to climb the bank when I heard *"Look out!"* just in time to duck my head as Lord Strathnairn, who by the way was riding his favourite hunter, topped the bank above me and landed safely on the other side. He then pursued the fugitive Fenians by himself and drove them back to us as a sheepdog rounds up sheep. We soon after arrived at the end of our journey, but alas there was no one to fight.

Still, our march had not been entirely fruitless, for although we found no enemy at Tallaght we had taken many prisoners and the covert was strewn with arms, ammunition, etc., which the Fenians had left behind them. The ammunition, copper caps, etc., we threw into a wet ditch, but the arms we

148

took to Dublin in carts we requisitioned for the purpose! It was about two o'clock in the afternoon when we reached Dublin on our return...In the Lower Castle Yard was a strong detachment of the Coldstream Guards under Captain S. Hall ready to convey the prisoners to Kilmainham Gaol, and I well remember their look of terror when, at Captain Hall's word of command, the men loaded their rifles with ball cartridge. Most of the prisoners evidently thought that they were about to be shot there and then without even a drumhead court-martial. The men were, of course, only ordered to load as a precaution against any attempt at rescue on the way from the Castle to the prison.'[123]

The Fenian conflict with the police under sub-inspector Burke at Tallaght

149

St. Jude's and the Rev. Thomas Mills

Rev. Mills
V Rev. Tudor Craig

The Church Row

In 1867, a case came before the Provincial Court of the Archbishop of Dublin, which, on account both of the novelty of the issue raised and the effect of the decision given, was regarded as one of the most famous cases of the nineteenth century. It concerned the Reverend Herbert Tudor Craig, who had succeeded the Rev. William Hare as chaplain of the garrison chapel at Richmond Barracks. He had followed his predecessor, in obedience to orders issued from the military in officiating regularly in the barrack chapel. He also placed himself towards the officers and soldiers and their families acting in the same way as a parish priest, administering the sacraments, visiting the sick, catechising the children, and preparing the young of both sexes for confirmation. As it proved, he had no authority whatever to do so, either from the incumbent of the parish (Rev. Mills) or from the bishop of the diocese. It was believed, both at the Horse Guards and in the War Office, that such authority was not necessary to a chaplain holding her Majesty's commission. Until the arrival of Mr. Craig, the military chaplains doing duty in Richmond Barracks had never been called in question for any act performed by them. The previous incumbents of St. Jude's had presumed that the military must have the law on their side. The Rev. Thomas Mills was under no such illusion, but when he found a chaplain already facilitating at Richmond Barracks he decided to let the matter stand. In fact, in 1865, he had given a lecture on *Scenes and Objects of Interest in the Holy Land*, illustrated by some 'splendid views in the magic lantern' in the partitioned part of the chapel used as a school.[124] When, however, he discovered that there was to be a change of military chaplain he decided it was time to act. It might also have been to do with his zeal to personally manage all parish finances.

The Rev. Thomas Mills had arrived as curate-assistant of St James's parish in 1857 and was given responsibility for developing the Kilmainham and Golden-Bridge areas where a school was used for Sunday services from the late 1820's. The area had seen a considerable growth since the establishment of the Great Southern and Western Railway works in Inchicore with a substantial influx of railway workers from England, many of whom were members of the established church. As well as the new local church population, there was also the contingent comprising the soldiers based in the Infantry barracks, who were under the care of the garrison chaplain. Mills set about renovating the school building as a more permanent place of worship. In the early 1860's this area of St James's parish was given parochial status as the parish of Kilmainham, and Mills put in hand plans for a new church. St Jude's church opened on 2nd. January 1864, consecrated by Richard Trench the day after his own consecration as archbishop of Dublin. As Mills had been responsible for the erection of the church, he considered that he also should have the complete running of the parish, and he handled all the financial business, as well as his duties as vicar. Consequently, at the first meeting of the select vestry in 1871, after disestablishment, he refused to give the vestry any authority over the finances of the parish. It was his weekly practice to take Sunday collections home with him and to pay all the bills, including those of the church officers. He continued with this practice, more or less until the day he died despite many objections from the select vestry.[125]

In December 1867, at a sitting of the provincial court, Judge Battersby presided over a case brought by The Rev. Thomas Mills, Incumbent of St Jude's against The Rev. Herbert Tudor Craig, Chaplain of Richmond Barracks. The Judge, summing up the case said it was a suit,

> Instituted to restrain the Rev. Mr. Craig from officiating or celebrating Divine service, or preaching in a chapel within the Richmond Barracks, or otherwise, without the assent of the Rev. Thomas Mills, incumbent of St. Jude's parish, within which Richmond Barracks are situated. The petition stated in substance that the respondent, under the pretence of authority from the Secretary at War, did officiate in a public building called the "Military Chapel," in the parish of St. Jude, by reading publicly the morning prayers to a congregation composed of soldiers and their wives, and others of the parishioners of the petitioner, and officiated otherwise, as set out in the petition; that the petitioner has been always ready and willing to discharge all the duties of the clergyman of Richmond Barracks, and that the respondent has no license from the Archbishop of Dublin. The answer of the respondent asserted that he is a priest in holy orders of the United Church; that by a commission bearing date in January, 1864, he was appointed by her Majesty to the chaplains' department of the British army, and commanded to follow such orders as he shall receive from his superior officers; that on reporting himself in Dublin he was ordered to perform all the duties the subject of the suit, and that he never performed them outside the barracks; that he does not know who the congregations were, but that he could not exclude them. [126]

Judge Battersby ruled in favour of the Rev. Mills and decreed that the Rev. Tudor Craig be admonished and inhibited from performing divine service, or administering the sacraments in the chapel or barracks attached to Richmond Barracks, or elsewhere in the parish of St Jude's, without the consent of the Rev. Mills; and also, that the Rev. Craig pay the costs of the suit. [127] The main effect of the judgement was to render all ministrations of military chaplains illegal. As a result of the case, the army moved to correct the situation. The War Office issued an 'Army Chaplains Bill' in the House of Lords, which included many amendments sought by the bishops. It was passed by the House of Commons in July 1868. [128]

Amateur Theatricals

Good use was being made of the large new recreation rooms. In October 1867, Superintendent Schoolmaster Newsome delivered a lecture on 'Astronomy.' This was followed in November by three successive evening presentations of a theatrical and musical show by the amateurs of the 63rd (West Suffolk) regiment. What is interesting here is the influence of Irish culture:

> The performances commenced with the old national drama of *'The Wren Boys,'* which, from the number of times it has been repeated in Glasgow, Aldershot, and other places, has now become the stock play- the *piece de resistance* of the company. Corporal J. Robinson and Private J McCabe gave a clog hornpipe and an Irish jig respectively, and with much taste and finish. The evening's amusement concluded with the burlesque of *Bombaste's Furioso.* The amateurs' experience of their 'three first nights' at Richmond Barracks has been such as to induce them to announce a series of such entertainments to extend over the winter months ...We may mention that while the regiment was lately stationed at Glasgow the amateurs gave upwards of fifty entertainments. The scenery and costumes were kindly supplied by T.G. Phillips, Brunswick Street. [129]

The Departure of the 74th Highlanders

A great spectacle was often the leaving of a regiment, especially one of the better known or most popular ones. So it was with the departure of the 74th Highlanders on the 2nd February, 1868. The Regiment had occupied Richmond Barracks since 26th Sept. 1867, having removed from Limerick, where they had been stationed for nearly thirteen months. While at Limerick, detachments had been told off to do duty at Clare Castle and Nenagh. In consequence of Fenian riots, flying columns were sent out on several occasions, of which various companies of the 74th formed a part. In December 1867, orders had been received to make ready to proceed to Gibraltar;

the depot companies, consisting of 92 men, under Captain Thackeray and 3 subalterns, having, on January 27, 1868, sailed for Greenock in order to proceed to Fort-George, where it was to be stationed.

THE SERGEANTS, 74TH HIGHLANDERS.—DUBLIN, 1867.

Before their departure the sergeants of the regiment posed for a photograph. As evidence of the popularity of the corps in Dublin, and of the esteem in which it was held by the several regiments in garrison there it was escorted from Richmond Barracks by large crowds and no fewer than seven bands, representing the Coldstream Guards, the 3rd Buffs, the 63rd (West Suffolk), the Carabiniers, the 12th Lancers, the 39th and 89th. The 74th left in two detachments for Westland Row station, the left wing commanded by Major Irby, and the headquarters, under command of Lieu. Colonel McLeod. The route was by James's Street, Thomas Street, Dame Street, Nassau Street, to the station; the bands playing 'Auld Lang Syne,' 'Scots Wha Hae,' 'The Girl I left Behind Me,' and other well known airs.

The following was the numerical strength of the regiment as it embarked:- two field officers, 9 captains, 19 subalterns, 3 staff, 8 staff sergeants, 39 sergeants, 27 drummers and pipers, 40 corporals and 628 privates. There also embarked 3 officers' wives, 8 officer's children, 1 officer's male servant, 9 officer's female servants, 81 women, 87 children, and seven horses.

The following were the officers accompanying the regiment (given here as they may be of interest to family researchers):- Lieu. Colonel William R. McLeod (commanding), Major L.H.L. Irby, Captains: Robert F. Martin, H.G.L Campbell, Abel Straghan, Robert E, Deare, Norman M. McLeod, Edward Bradby, Peter McLaren, Charles J. Rolleston, and Charles T. Wallace; Lieutenants: Thomas Colville, Simeon H. Hardy, Richard Leigh Conyngham, M. Mc Alpine, D.D. Mc Leod, George Farie, Evelyn John Hamilton, George A. B.Godbold, Charles Douglas Hay, Henry T.C. Hunt, and William F. Fairlie; Ensigns:-David Mailtland, Charles Hamilton Simpson, - Kettle, - Hay, - Kirwan, H.L. St. George Stewart, -Toler, and A.W.J. Stewart; Adjutant. Lieu. H.Curry; Paymaster, Capt. Roger Sheey: Quartermaster, John Cole; Surgeon, W.B.Wallis, and Assistant Surgeon, William R. Burkett.[130]

The regiment sailed from Kingstown on February 2d, on board H.M. ship "Himalaya," for Gibraltar, where it arrived on February 7th, disembarked on the 8th, and encamped on the North Front until the 13th, when it was removed to the South Barracks. The 74th remained there until February 1872, when headquarters and four companies under Colonel Macleod sailed for Malta. [131]

The Township of New Kilmainham

The Towns Improvement (Ireland) Act 1854, allowed the inhabitants of populous places to choose to establish town commissioners. This enabled many newer communities that had never had municipal status to gain local government bodies. In the nineteenth century many of the Dublin middle class left the city for the suburbs resulting in the formation of new town-lands. However, some of these areas took a different route to establish local authorities in their areas by having private acts passed in parliament. These acts established "townships" with defined boundaries, defined the powers of the commissioners, gave them powers to make rates, named the first members and provided a procedure for subsequent elections. A number of areas thrived after becoming townships.

Kilmainham was an area dominated by large institutions such as Kilmainham Gaol, Golden-Bridge Refuge and Reformatory, the Oblate religious house at

Inchicore, Richmond Barracks and the Great Southern and Western Railway. Many of the residents were connected with these institutions, a large number making the area their home for a period of time, including workers from England employed by the railway. Housing in the area was of the modest variety; in 1868 only sixteen houses were valued at more than £20. The initiative for the establishment of the township came from a number of industrialists such as Francis Moore Scott, the owner of Island Bridge Woollen Mills, David McBirney, a prominent city draper and textile producer and ex-member of Dublin Corporation, and Samuel Shelly, an Islandbridge flour miller. The district was under the supervision of the Grand Jury, whom many people believed were not providing adequate facilities. They were aware that the Towns Improvement Act 1854 to make better provision for paving, sewerage, lighting, etc. was available. To be considered for this, it was necessary for 21 or more of the £8 occupiers or householders in the district to apply to the Lord Lieutenant to have the Act of Parliament put into operation. In 1867 the people took this measure and the Lord Lieutenant replied by issuing a precept to Mr. Place, Governor of the Gaol, and himself to call a meeting to confirm the recommendations of the memorialists. Accordingly, a meeting was convened at Kilmainham Courthouse on 27th May 1867.

Dr. E. Kennedy, J.P., was chairman. Having lain before the meeting some facts connected with the town-ship, he reminded people of the improvements previously sought and which were still left undone. He claimed that there was no more neglected district, perhaps, in Ireland than this, in the precincts of a large town. They had no sewerage, no water, no lighting, and no access from that to Dublin. The only decent access they had to it was through the Park, and only a certain number would be permitted to past that way. The district was 'charmingly situated' to as to elevation, well protected by adjoining heights, and connected with that district of Dublin which required more especially villa residences for the trading population …But there were grievances of a serious nature. He alluded to the open sewer into which was discharged the sewage from Richmond Barracks. Within the last few years they had had three epidemics traceable to that nuisance—cholera, fever, and even lately some cases of 'black death.'

He realized that, owing to the small number of houses in the area and their low valuation, the revenue raised would be small. The total annual income derived from a rate on the 3,776 houses and other buildings in the area valued at £6,255, would amount to only £520 a year. Their first object would be to see after proper sewerage, the heavy part of which would be done by the Government, according to arrangement. They would next endeavour to obtain a supply of water, and then they would try to get a decent approach to the town. It was well known that in all large towns near which there were garrisons, the Government came forward to assist township proprietors in the improvement of the district, and very properly so in localities where there were large portions of the army existing.

The question was put as to the adoption of the Act of Parliament. The proposal was approved. The railway company originally opposed the establishment of the township and, when it failed in its opposition, had two of its staff elected to the board. Adoption of the 1854 Act was an interim measure while the commissioners applied for a special act giving further powers. [132]

Special Act of Parliament

New Kilmainham was one of only 14 townships to be formed as a result of special Acts of Parliament. When the Bill for the 'Improvement of the Township and District of New Kilmainham,' was printed in January 1868 it was found to have 51 clauses and 6 schedules. A number of debates followed in the House of Commons. On 12th June, the first meeting of the Select Committee of the House of Lords met. Present were: Lord Egerton, (chairman), Viscount Strathallan, the Marquis of Normanby, Lord Leigh and Lord Howe. Contributors to the debates who were examined by the Committee included: The Rev. Mills, David McBirney, Lord Cloncurry, Judge Frank Thorpe Porter, Mr. Barnewell, Mr. Francis Moore Scott, and Mr Price. There was also representation on behalf of the Great Southern and Western Railway Company in opposition to the Bill. The railway at Inchicore was very much a self-sufficient community. It covered 76 of the 534 acres within the boundaries of the proposed township. The company had invested over £228,000 in the works and on facilities for its workers, including housing. It had built 148 cottages housing 850 people. Its property was valued at £3,053, and although land actually under the railway lines was rated at a quarter of the usual rate, it faced a large rate bill. The works' complex also had its own water supply and gas lighting; the gas it produced was more than sufficient for its own needs, and it supplied the village of Kilmainham, contrary to the claims of the promoters of the township. [70] The railway company had no desire to be rated to pay for such facilities for the general area. In its opposition to the proposed township it claimed that it would be liable for two-fifths of the rates but, out of an electorate of around 110, it would control only five votes.

The Rev. Thomas Mills stated that he was incumbent of St Jude's and had been so for 10 or 11 years, the church cost £5000 to build, and there was a parsonage house next to it; it was he who first went to the parish at a time when the roads were impassable; the present condition of the footpaths was very bad, so much so, that a visitor coming into Dublin by them might suppose he was about to enter some uncivilized city. The board caused some improvement to be effected by having large quantities of rubbish removed. Before the township was formed there was not a glimmer of light on the roads, and at night it was common practice to carry matches in order to read the numbers of the houses; the Commissioners had since lighted the roads pretty well, and now the appearance of the township at night was agreeable. New Kilmainham had some admirable sites for building, and if this bill is passed, it might become as prosperous as any of those near Dublin; it was healthy because the land was high; some portion of it was on a level with the summit of the spire of St. Patrick's Cathedral, and the west wind reached it first. He once again drew attention to the fact that except for the Inchicore cottages, there was no water supply. The people had to go to Richmond Barracks for their water supply, and since the Fenian troubles, they were not very readily admitted within them, so that in many cases people had to go without. The puddles and streams were resorted to, but as there was no sewerage at all, sewage was perpetually flowing into the puddles and the drains.

There was, said the Rev Mills, a large omnibus traffic between Dublin and Kilmainham. He had a share in an omnibus, and he knew from their returns that some years ago the number of passengers was 155,600 in one year, and that it was increasing. He had traced an open drain running into the Liffey, just above the point where the water was taken from the Royal Hospital. That water had a strong smell of creosote about it, which the Railway Company used for their sleepers; in his opinion it was better that they should have local government by merchants than by an irresponsible body of men, residents like the Grand Jury; he did not know anyone outside the company, who was opposed to the bill.

Cross-examined by Mr. O'Malley (on behalf of the GSWR), he said that the lighting now had the effect of improving the morality of the neighbourhood; the omnibus stopped at Golden-Bridge, where some of the railway people resided; he did not know that the Grand Jury was composed of the most eminent persons in the county; he knew nothing of them, except that they were a most useless body- (laughter)- they had neglected their duties; the fountains were entirely out of repair; the Commissioners had officers, but they were honorary ones. (The area had previously been under the jurisdiction of the Grand Jury). Frank Thorpe Porter, examined, said that he remembered Kilmainham before the Courthouse or the Infantry barracks were built; he was old enough to remember when the River was clear (more laughter).

Lord Cloncurry was examined. He said he possessed manorial rights over the whole parish of Kilmainham, and he had some holdings there also; he paid much attention to county business, and for many years before succeeding to the peerage he had served on grand juries; county surveyors ought to be men of high professional standing, and grand juries generally endeavoured to secure the services of such men; he thought it would be unfair to the ratepayers of so limited a locality as Kilmainham to have to pay such a salary to a surveyor as would secure a man of eminence for the office; he doubted that the neighbourhood of Kilmainham was improving; the locality was not one which builders or private individuals had selected for houses. The increase of Dublin had been in the direction of the south and the east, and recently a little in the direction of the north; for the last year or so there had been a little building going on in the neighbourhood of Howth, where previously building speculation had been stagnant.

Council for The Great Southern and Western Railway Company claimed that they had 115 signed petitioners against the Bill, but on investigation it was found that these were all railway workers. Mr. Huthwaite, of the firm of Barrington, Jeffers, and Co., was then examined and read statistics of the population and rateable value of the township. He said the figures showed that in 1851 the population was 4,533 including 1,589 military; in 1861 it was 4,733 including 1,697 military; of the population in the latter year an increase of 128 was due to the residence of railway people so that there was a decrease in the general population; excluding the railway people, the military, and the inmates of the gaol and other public institutions, the population in 1861 was only about 2,100; the Great Southern and Western railway Company paid to within a few pounds of one half of the entire taxation of the township; there were only 46 residents who possessed a qualification for the office of town commissioner, and among these were some fine ladies, who, he presumed, would not be eligible; the whole valuation of the neighbourhood was £6171 -5s. of which £2,410 was the value of the property of the railway company. Cross examined, he said there was no comparison with the Township of Rathmines (as claimed by Mr. Mc Birney); that Kilmainham was more similar in size to Dalkey than Rathmines, but one might as well compare Shadwell to Belgravia, as Kilmainham to Dalkey; the neighbourhood of Kingstown and Dalkey were inhabited to a considerable extent by wealthy and respectable persons; in most districts there were houses valued at £1,000 a year; in Kilmainham very few premises were valued at more than £50 a year except those in possession of the railway company.

Mr. McBirney, Chairman of the Commissioners, Mr. Price, Governor of Kilmainham Prison, and Mr. Francis Moore Scott, a woollen manufacturer and commissioner of Kilmainham, all gave strong evidence in support of the Bill. Such was the zeal of David McBirney that, at one point, Mr. Davidson QC, addressing the Committee in opposition to the bill, said that while he did not wish to impute personal motives, the only person who appeared to him interested in the passing of the Bill was Mr. McBirney. Indeed the township might as well be called "The McBirney Township" as the township of Kilmainham.[133] The insinuation was that he (McBirney), in common with other wealthy businessmen, was motivated by an agenda of his own, perhaps a desire to avoid heavy City rates.

The New Kilmainham Township Improvement Bill (short title) was finally passed in July 1868. The area covered included Inchicore, Golden-Bridge, Islandbridge and the area of the Goal, as far as the Kilmainham crossroads. It limited the boards borrowing powers to £10,000, a very modest sum. Apart from the prominent businessmen who founded the township, and continued to play a prominent part in its administration, the railway company had a strong, if limited presence on the board. Some of its representatives were prominent in the history of Irish railway engineering, such as Alexander McDonnell, the Great Southern and Western's chief engineer.

The Township, in its short existence, never built a town hall, and its board met in Kilmainham courthouse. Its nine members set about their task of developing the area without delay. They immediately obtained a loan of £2,800 from the National Bank to cover the expenses of the enabling legislation and lay in mains pipes in preparation for the Vartry water. The water mains cost £1,200 and the rest went on legal expenses, which were high owing to the original opposition to the act by the railway company. The institution that caused the greatest problem to the township, Richmond Barracks, with its 1,600 inhabitants, including married women, continued to prove contentious. The matter rankled all the more as the military authorities were not obliged to pay rates; an *ex gratia* payment of £100 made by them to the township, was regarded by the board as "totally inadequate."

As the township was prevented from allowing its sewage to enter the Camac River, and a main drainage scheme was never undertaken, the area continued to harbour cesspools. Not surprisingly, the township was subject to only moderate population growth, and between 1861 and 1871, it grew by a total of only 224 persons. It remained an area different in character from the other townships and it never developed into an affluent residential quarter.[134]New Kilmainham only lasted until 1900 when it was amalgamated into the city, reversing the spread of these townships which the Corporation by then considered were responsible for stunting growth in the metropolis.

Gymnasium to be Built

In 1868, according to the *Parliamentary Papers*, a night ablution room was installed at the barracks. This was followed by the announcement of plans for the erection of a gymnasium. In 1869, a board of officers including, the District Commissioner Royal Engineer, Captain, and the Principal Medical Officer of the Dublin District, met to select a suitable site. It was found that the soldiers were fortunate in having ground to spare. They already had two splendid recreation rooms and would soon have a gymnasium. [135] We hear no more of the gymnasium until January 5th 1877, when Corporal D. Scollard of the 1st Battalion 7th Royal Fusiliers Regiment is appointed assistant instructor of the gymnasium. In 1879, Sergeant Nadin would be employed as an instructor of gymnastics and fencing. The three buildings now comprised:

North Recreation room:
Librarian's quarters; Billiards and Games room; Book room; Reading and Writing room.

Gymnasium:
Instruction room; dressing room; ventilation; glazed tower; ventilation.

South Recreation room:
Canteen and Soldiers' bar, Corporals' room and Serving bar; kitchen, beer cellar; coffee room.

Close to these buildings to the west were the women's wash room and the cook house. Behind these buildings were the obstacle course and the officers' block. Despite the new recreational and physical exercise facilities, the mental health of some soldiers continued to be tested at times. A harrowing account from this period recounts the case of Charles Rudle, a young private soldier belonging to the 15th Regiment who committed suicide in one of the water closets by cutting his throat from ear to ear with a razor. [136]

John Mackenzie Rogan

In 1867 a fresh-faced youth, four-foot seven in height and barely 15 years of age, enlisted as a band-boy with the 11th North Devonshire Regiment. His great-grandfather had fought under Marlborough, his grandfather was a soldier and his father joined the British army in the year before Waterloo. This boy would one day become a master musician of world renown. In his memoir *Fifty Years of Army Music*, the old soldier recalled his introduction to army life and music in Dublin:

In October 1870 we were ordered from the Curragh to Dublin. The band of the 70th Regiment met us and played us to Richmond Barracks, but soon after our arrival left and their place was taken by the 1st battalion, 9th Regiment (the "Holy Boys"- the nickname earned, tradition has it, over a century ago from the fact that the 9th always went into action each man carrying a Bible or a prayer book.) One of the staff officers at Dublin was known as "Mad Jack" or "Hell Fire Jack" (though his name was not Jack). He had his own rigid notions of parade discipline. When the bands were brigaded for a march past of the garrison troops in Phoenix Park, he would often gallop from the saluting point before we started to play, and, raising himself in the stirrups, address us fiercely in a tremendous voice something after the following manner:
"I saw some of you men moving just now! If I see this again, I'll have you all severely punished! Remember while you are on parade you stand like a stone

wall. No man is to move or fiddle about with instruments until the bands are required to play."

On one occasion he was walking in the street dressed in mufti, when a soldier, evidently not knowing him, passed him without saluting. He called the soldier back and asked him if he did not know who he was. When the soldier replied that he did not, "Mad Jack" told the soldier who he was and his position on the staff of the garrison, adding that the next time they met he doubtless would remember him. Then he ordered the soldier to march to and fro in front of him, saluting him each time till he was told to stop. The colonel of the regiment to which the soldier belonged wrote a strongly worded letter of protest to the G.O.C. We were none of us sorry when "Jack" shortly afterwards disappeared from the Dublin district.

The young Mackenzie Rogan was as fun-loving as any other lad of his age and he recalled how on one occasion his antics led to a ducking:

The bands of the 8th Royal Irish Hussars and the 11th Foot were engaged to play at Kingstown regatta, and the committee placed two or three boats at our disposal to row round the harbour, if we chose, during the intervals. In the boat in which I took an oar there were about a dozen of us, and we were well out in the harbour when some of my companions began larking and rocking the boat from side to side. The result was we were all thrown into the water, wearing our white tunics, forage-caps, belts and swords, and the Hussars their full dress tunics, overalls and spurs. Fortunately we could all swim, but it was difficult to keep afloat, especially for the Hussars in their tight, strapped down overalls. Boats came up from all parts of the harbour and took us ashore to the hotel, where we had to strip and sit in blankets while our clothes dried. It was not till early evening that we were able to rejoin our bands and take part in the performances. The next day we found our swords rusted in the scabbards and we had to take them to the armourer-sergeant to be put right again. It was an expensive lesson, for we had to pay out of our own pockets for new tunics, caps and trousers.

Being a bandsman had its advantages as Rogan found when he got to meet one of his heroes, W.G. Grace, 'the greatest batsmen of the day,' who brought a team over to Dublin and stayed for a week. It was a revelation to him to watch the great man and his side. The bands of the garrison took it in turn to play music while the visitors played cricket. To the delight of all "W.G" was in his best scoring form. More important, had he known it at the time, was Rogan's first meeting with musician, Dr. Robert Stewart (later Sir Robert). He was surely among the first to take an interest in the young man and he made a lasting impression on him, imparting a love of music which would endure throughout a lengthy career. They met when the band played a big concert that was held at the Exhibition Buildings in aid of the Drummond institution under Dr. Stewart's direction. Dr. Robert was then organist of St. Patrick's Cathedral and professor of music at Trinity College, Dublin. All the bands of the garrison took part and one soloist from each band was invited to play a special solo. In addition, they had special band pieces which were conducted by the different bandmasters. Then there were vocal choruses sung by a choir, accompanied by the combined bands and conducted by Dr. Stewart. Rogan was determined to meet the man personally and managed with the aid of a friend to get an introduction. Following that, Rogan played for him on several occasions. Dr Stewart would send the lad a message sometimes to go and see him at the Cathedral, generally during the service; then he would ask him to sit down beside him near the organ, and give him his instructions while accompanying some portion of the service. To Rogan it was a wonderful experience. He marvelled at how any man could extemporize on the organ so beautifully, especially during the Psalms, and at the same time carry on a conversation about a future concert.

In the summer of 1871 Rogan's old commanding officer retired and his place was taken by Major W. H .Crompton, who not long after, for a family reason added Stansfield to his surname. The farewell dinner to Colonel Jenner, given by the officers of the regiment, was a great function; it was held in the officers' mess-room, the band playing just outside. The windows were open and they could hear the speeches. The one which naturally appealed to them was the new Colonel's, especially the part of it which referred to the band. They gathered from his remarks that the band in future would be paid for all private engagements as other bands were. On hearing this they all felt inclined to give three cheers - in fact, three times three; but were too well disciplined to give way to their private feelings.

Major Crompton, according to Rogan, began building up a battalion which came to be regarded by general officers and others as second to none among line regiments. He was many years in advance of his time in his ideas of drill and organisation. He introduced developments then of which no one seemed to have thought. Apart from his keenness for drill and parade work, he also took great interest in how the men looked and even employed the services of a high class civilian tailor from London to act as master- tailor for the battalion.

The 11th regiment left Richmond barracks for the Curragh in August 1871. John Mackenzie Rogan later joined the Coldstream Guards as Bandmaster. He was the first bandmaster in the Brigade of Guards to be granted a substantive commission with the rank of 2nd Lieutenant and after passing through all the various ranks retired as a Lieutenant-Colonel. Never before had a serving bandmaster or director of music attained this rank. For 20 years he was the senior director of music of the

Brigade of Guards, and he was responsible for the massed bands of the Brigade at the funeral of Queen Victoria, the coronation and funeral of King Edward VII and the coronation of King George V.

Between 1896 and 1920 he made many gramophone records with the Guards. Few of these were his own compositions, but his march *The Bond of Friendship* was often played, as were his novelty selections *Festival of Empire* and *Church Parade*. Amongst the decorations and the many awards that he received were the Commander of the Royal Victorian Order, Officer (Knight) of the Order of the Crown of Belgium, Cavaliere of the Order of the Crown of Italy and Officer of the Black Star of Benin (France). His service medals consisted of the Silver Medal Queen Victoria's Jubilee, Silver Medal Royal Victorian Order, Long Service Medal, Burmah Medal and two clasps (1885-87 & 1887-1889), Victory Medal, General Service Medal and Coronation Medal (1911). In October 1904 he was elected an Honorary Member of the Royal Academy of Music, and in 1907 the Senate of the University of Toronto conferred an honorary Doctor of Music degree on him. He retired in 1920

John Mackenzie Rogan in later life pictured with his son.

The Sanitary Condition
of Kilmainham Township

The Courthouse was once again the scene for a meeting held in December 1871, before Captain Robinson, Poor Law Inspector. The occasion was for the purpose of an inquiry into charges contained in a memorial to the Lord Lieutenant regarding the sanitary condition of the township. The memorial was signed by Dr. Evory Kennedy, Clondalkin, Mr. Joseph Egan, Inchicore, Mr. Michael Kennedy, Golden-Bridge; Rev. Thomas Mills, Vicar of St. Jude's, and Captain Gresham, Queen's Royal Rifles. It was alleged by them that the Kilmainham Township Commissioners had not exercised the powers vested in them for the purpose of preserving the health of their district, inasmuch as they had not since the district was formed into a township in 1865 taken measures to construct sewers and other necessary works for the purpose of carrying off the sewage the area. The Lord Lieutenant had called on the Poor Law Commissioners to have an inquiry held in the matter.

Captain Robinson began by reading the memorial presented to the Lord Lieutenant, and then read the reply of the Kilmainham Town Commissioners. The reply stated in effect that until the Dublin Corporation gave them an outlet for their sewage under the provisions of the Dublin Main Drainage Bill, they were powerless to act in the matter; that the nuisance complained of was caused principally by the two Government institutions in the township-Richmond Barracks and Kilmainham Gaol; that it flowed into the Camac River, and from that into the Liffey, and that the necessary drainage works should be constructed under the provisions of the Main Drainage Act. Mr. Price, Governor, Kilmainham Gaol complained that by 'some extraordinary piece of legerdemain' those who had been complainants were turned into defendants, and said that the moment the Commissioners were prepared to give them a place in which to divert their drainage they would go to any expense to carry it out. After a couple of other similar objections the meeting was adjourned until the following week.[137]

Amongst those present at the next meeting were- Mr. F. M. Scott, Mr. Shelly, Very Rev. Dean Dickinson, Dr Evory Kennedy, Captain Gresham, Mr. Alexander McDonnell, Mr. Byrne, TC; Mr. Price; Mr. Hepburn, Mr. Richard Cook, Mr. Doran, Mr. Byrne.

Mr. Hepburn, Clerk of the South Dublin Union, stated that before it passed into the hands of the Commissioners an offer was made by the Government at that time of £1,000 towards the drainage, the rest was to be raised by a vote, but the guardians had not the power in their hands to do the necessary work. The district was not then under the Town's Improvement Act. He stated that the Richmond Barracks were in a very bad sanitary state at that time. Mr. Kennedy also gave evidence with regard to the state of the sewerage. He stated that he lived at Susan Vale, which was situated along the stream, and the exhalations from the River were most offensive, so much so that he used studiously to avoid passing close to it when on his rounds. Several cases of Black Death had taken place in Richmond Barracks about the year 1867, and he considered it was due to the sanitary condition of the district. He gave evidence at the Castle at this time relative to Richmond Barracks; and he also examined Golden-Bridge cemetery, and satisfied himself that the drainage was very defective. As to the remedy or the nuisance he would agree entirely with Mr. Neville about seeking the lowest possible level, and carrying the drainage in pipes below the Kilmainham Bridge.

The Very Rev. Dean Dickinson stated that he lived for two months of this year at Susan Vale, and was well acquainted with the mill stream from Golden-Bridge to Susan vale. When passing the stream the smell was so offensive as to cause him to feel quite sick, and hindered him from walking in the neighbourhood of it.

Mr. Boyle, C.E. sanitary inspector to the Corporation said that he knew the Camac River as far as McDonnell's Mills. The River ran out into the Liffey at Usher's Island. He made his first visit in '69, and found the River very foul, and also the mill stream. In consequence of a complaint made by the authorities in Stephen's Hospital he made a third visit in the summer of 1870. The weather was very warm, and the exhalations most offensive, more so than on any other occasion. There was not sufficient water in the bed of the River to carry off the sewage. He would recommend flushing as a means of carrying off the sewage, if there could be a reservoir constructed to supply the water, but he could not state how that was to be done, or where it was to be placed, but merely mentioned it as a suggestion.

Mr. Clay, solicitor acting on behalf of the mill owners, objected to the proposal contemplated by the memorialists. He said that it would be unpardonable if it was carried out: namely, to carry the sewage in pipes below Kilmainham Bridge, and then to empty it out into the River again, thereby stopping the proper course of the River, and hindering the operation of the mill owners. They had a perfect right to the free passage of the River, and should not be interfered with.[138]

And there, for the time being, we leave the sanitary problems of Kilmainham. It would take more than commissioners debating issues; rather, it would be an epidemic of fever with tragic consequences leading to a Commons enquiry and a lengthy surveyor's investigative report before any real progress would be made. Besides, the New Township had other problems to deal with: ones which were a lot easier to sort out. A number of "Rogue Traders" were hauled before the courts in 1873, having being caught overcharging or short changing their customers. The offences were very cunningly performed. It was all to do with weight measures: John Proctor, a butcher, was fined 10s. for using a 1lb weight measure that was a quarter of an ounce light and two ounce weights that were each a shade light. Michael J. McCarthy, a publican had 5 gills pint measures, each nearly a quarter of a gill short and one gill over a quarter of a gill short. He was fined 40s. Catherine Gregory, a provisions dealer, was fined 10s.for having 7 lbs weights a quarter of an ounce light and two quarter pounds each a shade light. Joseph Mc Loughlin, a provisions dealer, was using a bacon scales that was a quarter of an ounce against the buyer, for which he was fined £1. James Darby, a coal dealer, was found to have a 14lbs weight that was a half an ounce light, and was cautioned. Terence Gorman, a grocer, had a half lb weight a shade light, for which he was fined 5s. All of these unscrupulous merchants were operating in the Golden-Bridge area. [139]

100th (Prince of Wales's Royal Canadian) Regiment

Special mention is due of the arrival of what was perceived as an 'Irish Regiment.' The 100th Regiment of Foot (Prince Regent's County of Dublin Regiment) was raised in Ireland in 1804 for service in the Napoleonic Wars. It was disbanded after these wars and later (1858) raised as the 100th Prince of Wales Royal Canadian Regiment. On 7th May 1874, they arrived at Kingstown on board the *Euphrates*. They numbered, 19 Officers, 43 Staff Sergeants and Sergeants, 44 Corporals, 17 Drummers, 475 Privates, 65 Women, and 121 Children. Headquarters and the right wing marched to Richmond Barracks, followed the next day by the rest. During the summer they were broken up into detachments around the country, which characterized soldering in Ireland in those days. In September Headquarters and 4 companies were sent to Mullingar and detachments of one company to Sligo, Boyle, Navan and Trim. The depot of the 109th Regiment seems to have been still attached to the 100th at this time. At Mullingar the Regiment availed of the excellent hunting conditions together with the Westmeath Hounds.

In March 1875 notification was received from the Adjutant-General of the Force stating that Her Majesty the Queen had been pleased to approve the word "Niagara" being included in the regimental colours, as formerly granted to the old 100th, the Prince Regent's County of Dublin Regiment in commemoration of its distinguished conduct in the capture of Fort Niagara by assault on 13th February 1813. Effectively the regiment was now considered as the successor to the latter named regiment. In July, "non effectives," women and children moved to Kilkenny and the regiment spent a month in the Curragh for the drill season. The following June 1876, the whole regiment would depart for Kingstown and there board the *Orontes* taking them to Portsmouth and back to Aldershot. [140]

The Spink Theatre

Relations between the military and the Rev. Thomas Mills of St Jude's would seem to have improved by 1875 when he presided at a 'Service of Song, illustrative of *The Pilgrim's Progress,*' at the Recreation Room. It was held under the patronage of Colonel Hales Wilkie and officers of the 29th regiment. The readings selected were given by T. A. Jennings, T.C.D., and the music was selected by the united choirs of St. Jude's and the Richmond Barracks Chapel. R.J. Polden, Esq., MA., played the harmonium and Mr. A. Patterson, bandmaster of the 29th, conducted. The Rev. Mills then delivered a suitable opening address, on the author of *The Pilgrim's Progress* and his times. The several arrangements for the meeting were carried out in a "very satisfactory manner" by Mr. Edward Croker and Mr. J. Robinson.[141]

With the arrival of the 90th Perthshire Regiment one of the Recreation Rooms occasionally became a dramatic centre. The officers of this regiment seemed particularly interested in the arts and named the room 'The Spink Theatre' for nights when performances were held. Here is a report of one of those nights:

> The members of the Dramatic Club connected with the 90th Perthshire Volunteers, at present stationed at Richmond Barracks, gave an entertainment last evening in the "Sphinx Theatre" attached to Richmond Barracks, which afforded unalloyed pleasure to the large audience that had assembled on invitation. The piece of the evening was the operatic drama in three acts, entitled "Rob Roy" or "Auld Lang Syne," in which the *dramatis personae* acquitted themselves with much credit. The stage arrangements were most creditable to Colour-Sergeant J. Treadwell, and the general management of Sergeant -Major Tailor. J. Scott gave great satisfaction.[142]

*****

The Chapel of Ease at Golden-Bridge was at this time vacant and a decision was made to sell the property. This was originally leased to the military in 1827 as the 'General Male and Female Day and Evening Schools.' It ceased to be used as a school in 1857 when the much larger 'Model School' (1853) became the preferred choice. It was then enlarged and converted into a Church of Ireland church serving the local community until 1864 when St Jude's church on Inchicore road was built.

The Rev Mills moved his flock to the impressive new church and the chapel at Golden-Bridge had by 1878 become disused. The Chapel, 'held free of rent for ever, fully fitted as a place of worship, with pews, gallery, stove, etc, capable of accommodating from 300 to 310 people,' was then put on the market.

The vacant chapel was later acquired by the Catholic Archdiocese of Dublin and opened as a Chapel of Ease under the title of Our Lady of Mercy in 1885. The Methodist meeting-house referred to was also sold at this time and a new Methodist chapel and school was opened on Tyrconnell road. The vacant building would become the first Irish Christian Brothers school in the area.

Major Hans Garrett Moore
who won the First V.C. on South African Soil

While Garnet Wolseley was, without doubt, the most famous Irish born British soldier ever associated with the area of Golden-Bridge, he was not the only one. Hans Garrett Moore was born at Richmond Barracks, on 31st March 1834. He was the son of Captain Garrett Moore and Charlotte Butler of Drum, Co. Tipperary. The family could claim descent from Rory O' Moore, an Irish Chieftain who fought against Henry VIII and forced that Tudor monarch to sign a peace treaty. Garrett Jnr. was educated at the Royal School, Banagher and Trinity College, Dublin. Having volunteered for the army, he requested a commission without purchase on account of his father's military record. This was granted and he was gazetted to the 59th regiment as an ensign. At age 20, he transferred to the 88th Foot, his father's regiment, which had always been his ambition. Soon, Hans Garrett was promoted to the rank of Lieutenant. He was next involved in subduing the Indian Mutiny:

> The 88th Regiment moved to India late in 1857 to help quell the Indian Mutiny. Lieutenant Moore served with distinction at the siege of Lucknow, Siege of Calpee, Selimpore (where he was slightly wounded and the eights were shot off his cap), Jamoo and the storming and capture of the Birivah Forts. During the latter action his revolver broke, so armed with only his sword, he single-handedly attacked a house and accounted for three rebels. [143]

He later volunteered for, and was employed on special service in the Ashanti War 1873-74. Coincidentally, it was General Sir Garnet Wolseley who commanded an expedition into Ashanti and burnt the capital, Kumasi. For his services, Moore was made a brevet-major. Conflict in another part of Africa came just three years later. The Ninth Frontier War in the Cape began because of an argument at a wedding between the Galekas and the Fingoes who were under British protection. In August 1877, Kreli, Chief of the Gaelekas and paramount chief of the Xhosa nation, was joined by the Gaikas and invaded the Fingo territory with 12,000 warriors. Colonial troops could not cope with the situation so imperial troops were called in. The Connaught Rangers were sent to East London (an area in the East Cape) and Major Moore's detachment to Komgha. On December 6, 1877, Moore was second in command of the Frontier Armed and Mounted Police. He was joined by the main body of 88th under the command of Lieutenant-Colonel Lambert. After what appeared to be a rout (100 Galekas killed, the rest sent fleeing across the Umtata River), but which later turned out to be a strategic withdrawal, the two opposing sides were destined to meet at Draaibosch.

Major Hans Garrett Moore who was born at Richmond Barracks

At Draaibosch, four scouts of the police were sent ahead of the main force. They were Sergeant Dan Harber, Corporal John Markham Court and Privates Giese and Martindale. The patrol came up against a group of 300 Gaikas who advanced on them. The troop dismounted and fired a few shots. Private Giese who was 50 yards from a thickly wooded gully, out of which scores of shouting Gaikas were pouring, was unable to mount his frightened horse. The three other scouts seeing his difficulty charged to his rescue followed by Major Moore who was some 400 yards away with his detachment, but who dug his spurs in and raced to the scene. Major Moore helped by Corporal Court fought his way through the milling hoard to Giese's side. However Giese already had three assegais (short spears) protruding from his chest and died on the scene. The Major and the Corporal then fought their way back to safety repelling stabbing spears and clutching hands. An assegai tore through Moore's arm and although he wrenched it out the blade remained lodged in his bicep.

The Gaikas

Reunited with his detachment, Moore was satisfied that he had drawn the Gaikas away from a convoy of wagons which later reached Komgha without further mishap.

171

The following account from a short biography is the stuff of legend:

Moore sat on a tree stump smoking his black pipe while the unit's doctor cut the bent assegai blade out of his arm. When the doctor attempted to cut the sleeve from his patrol jacket, Moore calmly said, *"Hold on, this is my only coat, rip it up the seam."* It was no wonder that he was known as "Bold Moore" by the men of his regiment, the Connaught Rangers. [144]

The following day, in this same region, a battle was fought between 700 Gaikas and 40 inexperienced Connaught Rangers supported by 30 police and 6 burgher volunteers. Some of the young troops wavered as the natives charged, but Major Monore calmly sat on his horse and issued orders as if on a parade ground. Reassured, the young men, greatly assisted by the deadly accuracy of the police firing, won the day. During the ensuing hour and a half they completely broke the Gaikas with frequent bayonet charges. Moore was promoted to Major and recommended for the Victoria Cross. Police scouts, Sergeant Harber and Corporal Court were also commended and the Frontier Armed and Mounted Police was recognized and formed into a regular regiment of mounted riflemen: the Cape Mounted Riflemen, with Major Moore as its first commanding officer. He returned to England in 1879 and joined the 93rd Argyll and Sutherland Regiment. He retired in 1888.

There are some discrepancies concerning the circumstances of his death. Most reports suggest that he was drowned in Lough Derg attempting to save a man from drowning. The confusion may be related to an incident that occurred in the early part of his military career in India, while on a shooting expedition in the Oudh province; fully clothed, he had plunged into the flooded Goomti River to save a native beater. The following, however, is Mr. Ian S. Uys's account of his last moments:

'On October 6th 1889, Moore was drowned at Dromineer Bay (on the Eastern shores of Lough Derg). He rowed into the bay during a tremendous gale in order to secure his steam launch *Foam* to a buoy. He found that he could not row back to land against the wind. The boat drifted in the gale and was swamped.'

He was buried in Mount Jerome cemetery Dublin. In South Africa, a fitting memorial, shaped into a cairn, was erected beside the road between King William's Town and Komgha. It bears a plaque on which the following words are inscribed:

'It was near here during the first battle of Draaibosch on the 29th December, 1877 at the beginning of the Ninth Kaffir War of 1877-1878 that Major Hans Garrett Moore (Connaught Rangers) while commanding a patrol of the Frontier Armed Mounted

172

Police, and courageously assisted by Sgt. D. Harber and Corporal J. Court of that force, performed the deed of bravery which won him the first Victoria Cross to be earned on South African soil.'

The memorial to Major Moore at Komgha, South Africa

Zulu War

Zululand had become a strong kingdom under the rule of the warlord king Shaka in the early 19th century, but by 1870 European colonial expansion was starting to encroach on their territory. The British were expanding from the south in Natal and the Boers were expanding from the west in the area known as the Transvaal which the British annexed in 1877. The British had seized their South African colonies during the Napoleonic Wars, but these acquisitions had been plagued with trouble due to violence between the British, the Boers and local African kingdoms. The British plan was to unite black and white under their rule, but first the Zulu kingdom had to be removed. General Lord Chelmsford decided that war with the Zulus was unavoidable. Using the delay in communications between London and themselves they set in motion what they hoped would be a small quick war. Using a minor border incident as justification, Zulu representatives were summoned to a meeting of the Border Commission where a condition was imposed that the Zulus would have to give up their military system; this was key to their culture and a condition King Cetshwayo could never accept.

King Cetshwayo

Lord Chelmsford then decided to invade Zululand with 3 columns leaving 2 more to protect Natal and the Transvaal. He expected the Zulus to behave like the other African Armies he had fought and prove elusive and unwilling to fight pitched battles. This was to prove a serious mistake. The British Army suffered one of its few defeats by native tribes at the Battle of Isandlwana on 22 January 1879, followed the next day by the gallant defence of the mission station of Rorke's Drift, under the command of Lieutenant John Chard of the Royal Engineers together with the 24th regiment. Just over 150 British and colonial troops successfully defended the garrison against an intense assault by 3,000 to 4,000 Zulu warriors. 17 British soldiers perished and some 500 Zulus. A fair number of the 24th Regiment (renamed the South Wales Borderers) were Irishmen, later reunited at Richmond Barracks.

In February the detachment of the 77th Regiment at Richmond Barracks was called into action to strengthen the regiment on its arrival in South Africa from Ceylon. They left on board the steamship 'Countess of Dublin' from the North Wall, on the 19th February. The men were in the charge of Captain Henderson, Lieutenants Westmacott and Wodehouse, of the 77th Regiment, and Second-Lieutenant Litton of the 57th, with which regiment the 77th was a linked battalion. A number of men under punishment for petty offences were brought down by an escort, but were released from arrest when they reached the steamship. The troops, who were nearly all Londoners, disembarked at Portsmouth, remaining there for a short time before and sailing on board the 'China' from Southampton to the Cape.[s145]

In March 1879 the second phase of the war began. After a number of fierce encounters, fortunes eventually turned in favour of the British as a Zulu attack on the British camp at Kambula was repulsed on 29th March. In the aftermath of the battle it was clear that the Zulu Impi would never take to the battlefield with such confidence again. As fresh British troops started to arrive the final invasion of Zululand (May to July 1879) began. King Cetshwayo sent messengers to the British asking for terms of surrender but the British demanded unconditional surrender and Cetshwayo made his last stand at the battle of Ulundi (4 July 1879).

Garnet Wolseley was Commander in Chief at this time, but it was Lord Chelmsford and Sir Redvers Henry Buller who led the men at this decisive battle. The British, having learned a bitter lesson at Isandlwana, did not meet the Zulu army in the open with their normal line of battle. They instead formed the infantry into a large hollow square, with mounted troops covering the sides and rear. The leading face was made up of five companies of the 80th Regiment. Also taking part were the 2nd Battalion, 21st Royal Scots Fusiliers, 58th, 90th, and 94th Regiments and the 17th Lancers. Within the square were headquarters staff, No. 5 company of the Royal Engineers led again by Lieutenant John Chard, (of Rorke's Drift fame), the 2nd Native Natal Contingent, fifty wagons and carts with reserve ammunition and hospital wagons, two 7-pounder and two 9- pounder cannons and two Gatling guns.

Rushes were made by the Zulus, in an attempt to get within stabbing range, but neither their courage and determination nor their belief in tokoloshe and their cowhide shields prevailed against the torrent of bullet and shell. The Zulu force finally yielded and fled with the 17th Lancers at their heels. The pursuit continued until not a live Zulu remained on the Mahlabatini plain. The Zulu wounded were slaughtered in revenge for the slaughter at Isandlwana. After half an hour of concentrated fire from the artillery, the Gatling Guns and the thousands of British rifles, Zulu military power was broken. The British casualties were 3 officers and 79 men. Zulu casualties were said to be 1,500. Chelmsford ordered the Royal Kraal of Ulundi to be torched. The capital of Zululand burned for days.

The *Orontes* troopship arrived back at Kingstown in May 1880 with the battle-worn 80th Regiment directly from Natal. They disembarked and were marched to Richmond Barracks.

After the defeat at Ulundi the Zulu nation was smashed and split up into 13 kingdoms which were given to pro British Africans, only for it to dissolve into civil war a few years later. The British pulled out of Zululand soon after and Cetshwayo was hunted down and exiled. After a brief return to try and halt the civil war Cetshwayo was defeated and later died in 1884.

The burning of Ulundi.

The Phoenix Park Murders

Charles à Court Repington

Charles à Court Repington was the son of a Conservative Party Member of Parliament. He was educated at Eton and Sandhurst, and in 1878 entered the army as a junior officer with the 4th battalion of the Rifle Brigade. Having returned from service in the Khyber Pass in India he then transferred to the 3rd battalion in 1880. They were at this time stationed at Richmond Barracks together with the 2nd Battalion of the Coldstream Guards. It was an eventful time for the young soldier as this was the era of Parnell, and the Land League struggle was at its height. The 'uncrowned King of Ireland' made his speech at Ennis, on September 19th, advocating a moral Coventry for all men who owned farms from which another man had been evicted. The most important person to be thus treated was Captain Boycott of Galway, and after that the practice became known as boycotting, a word that has remained with us ever since. William Edward Forster, dubbed "Buckshot" by the Nationalist press, on the supposition that he had ordered its use by the police when firing on a crowd was the Chief Secretary for Ireland. When it seemed that agrarian agitation had paralysed the country he decided to use the military to support the police at evictions. The 3rd Battalion was sent on this unpleasant business. Mr. Repington, while giving us his recollections, shows little regard for the plight of the Irish peasant.

> The Lord Lieutenant's policy, insofar as concerned us soldiers, was, in case of serious trouble, to show such force that open resistance to authority should be manifestly impossible. We proceeded to various districts by train and became better acquainted with the people. Often- times affairs looked threatening, but Irish humour on one side, and the perfect discipline of the Royal Irish Constabulary and of the troops on the other, prevented, on numerous occasions, a serious outbreak. But things were very bad indeed, and agrarian outrages went up by leaps and bounds.[146]

I can not imagine what Irish humour there was to be had at the scene of an eviction, but he continues…

The disaffection in the West in 1880 caused most of our companies to be moved in the autumn into Galway, Connemara, and Mayo, and here we remained for the best part of a year. The 3rd R.B. companies were at Galway, Headford, Tuam, Oughterard, Ballinakill, and other places, and in turn I was at three of these stations, and found much to interest me in Irish life. I marched into Tuam first. We did not have a particularly cordial reception there, and on our gates in the morning we found painted *'Down with the Black Rifles*, with a drawing of a rifle underneath. But my mastiff Leo, who still accompanied me on my travels, was the terror of the town, and alarmed the Tuamites even more than the Black Rifles.

From Tuam I moved to Oughterard, where we occupied an old barrack near the shore of Lough Corrib, and here I spent the exceedingly hard winter of 1880-1. Near by, some of the worst outrages of this period occurred, notably the murder of Lord Mountmorres and of the Huddys (two bailiffs); and things were so bad that many of the landlords left the country and the tenants refused to pay their rents, secured in their holdings, as they thought, by the boycott decree of Parnell. All sorts of scares were current, and the police used to send to us two or three times a week for a night patrol, when we walked sometimes for sixteen or twenty miles to search for men drilling and to impress the people. It was bitterly cold work, and in our barracks we only had peat fires which gave out little heat. In these various detachments the people only behaved badly to us on one occasion at Galway town, but we got our own back and with something to spare. The corner- boys of the town had waylaid a couple of our men returning to barracks one night, and had beaten them so unmercifully that they were almost killed. Corporal West, a stout fellow of my company, organised a counter-attack, and laid an ambuscade. Two of our men played the part of the men returning, and presently the corner-boys came out and began to attack them. A whistle was then heard, and from various dark corners there appeared riflemen armed with shillelaghs, and the corner-boys were soon pounded into a jelly. Twenty- four of them were admitted to hospital with severe contusions, and after that night our men were let alone. We had spoken in the Galway dialect. [147]

The struggle between Gladstone's Government and Parnell had grown more bitter than ever, and with daily incidents of violence against landlords and the police Gladstone had been compelled to take drastic measures to preserve order. Finally, on October 12, 1881, Parnell was arrested and lodged in Kilmainham Gaol. This only strengthened Parnell's popularity. He issued a manifesto telling the tenants to pay no rent until their leaders were released, and the Government countered by declaring the Land League an illegal association. A branch of the I. R. B., known as the Invincibles, had taken an oath to remove all tyrants from the country, and had made unsuccessful attempts to assassinate both Lord Cowper and 'Buckshot' Forster. The Kilmainham Treaty, which had effected an accommodation between the

Government and Parnell, led to the release of the latter on May 2, 1882, but Cowper and Forster resigned. Repington was actually on the guard of honour which paid the last honours to the departing Viceroy as he left Kingstown amidst the complete indifference of the people. Lord Frederick Cavendish became Chief Secretary.

The Invincibles had received orders from the secret head of their association, known as No. 1, to kill Mr. Thomas Henry Burke, the Under-Secretary to the Lord-Lieutenant. The man who would lead the assassination was Dubliner, Joe Brady, aged 26, who was second of 20 sons and five daughters of Thomas Brady, a Dublin Corporation employee. Joe was a stonecutter and was powerfully built; he was known as 'Bulldog Brady.' On the afternoon of May 6th, 1882, Burke and the new chief secretary, Lord Frederick Cavendish were walking home along Chesterfield Avenue in the Phoenix Park, Dublin, when a group of seven men approached. Armed with long surgical knives and revolvers concealed in their pockets, they walked towards Burke and Cavendish in three groups – Daniel Curley, Joe Hanlon, and Michael Fagan in front; Brady and Tim Kelly a few steps behind, and Patrick Delaney and Thomas Caffrey at the rear. After their targets had passed, Brady and Kelly wheeled about rapidly and Brady stabbed Burke from behind. Brady was then struck in the face with an umbrella by Cavendish and turned on him, stabbing him several times, while Kelly is alleged to have attacked Burke; as Burke lay on the ground, Brady cut his throat before fleeing. He later told a colleague that he did not know the identity of the man who struck him, '*and only for himself . . . he would not be where he is.*'

They then jumped into cars that were in waiting; the cab carrying the assassins actually passed Richmond Barracks, a very short distance from the scene of the murder, and turned up Richmond Hill towards Dolphin's Barn. This crime made a tremendous stir among the men stationed there. The soldiers there were very bitter against Parnell, and contemptuous of the Government, which they considered culpably weak. As Repington remarked:

> We often walked up to the scene of the murder. There I discovered the reason why grass never grows on the spot where a murder has been committed: so many come to see the ground that they wear away the turf. [148]

The 3rd battalion Rifle Brigade now looked forward to hearing of a move away from the gloom that had descended on the country in the wake of the affair. They were hoping to be sent to Egypt where Wolseley was engaged in the battle of Tel-el-Kebir and the rapid conquest of the lower region of that country. However, to their disappointment, they were ordered back to England. In later years Colonel Repington became a military correspondent. Although considered the finest writer in the field, his life was plagued with further scandals which were of his own making. He lost many friends because of his willingness to publish private conversations.

179

Most notable among these was his publication of confidential information in 1915, which led the 'Shell Scandal', exposing the lack of shells available to the military; an episode which greatly compromised the war minister Lord Kitchiner and Sir John French, eventually leading to the resignation of the latter.

The arrival of Joe Brady at Kilmainham

Preliminary hearings were held in Kilmainham Courthouse in February 1883, when James Carey and Joe Brady and a group of six others were put forward and charged with the Phoenix Park murders. Evidence was given and an adjournment followed and one informer gave evidence; but on the 17th February, there was consternation in the dock when it was seen that one figure was absent and when James Carey was finally led forward to the witness chair. Joe Brady glared at him and stretched forward towards him, as though he would have liked to tear him to pieces.

The trial of Brady was referred to Green Street Court and was opened before Judge William O'Brien on the 14th of April. Few trials had ever attracted anything approaching the almost feverish excitement which centred upon this case. The Judge was known as "hatchet-face," because of his cadaverous appearance. As the case for

180

the prosecution was presented Brady listened with apparent unconcern, occupying himself at intervals picking his teeth with the stump of a pencil. The calling of Carey as a witness created a sensation, even more than it had at Kilmainham previously. Knowing him, as nearly everyone in Court had done as a Town Councillor and a citizen of repute, every head was stretched forward for a better look. During his evidence he had occasion to look straight at Brady, and their eyes met, and there was nothing but contempt and hatred in Brady's piercing eyes. The informer outlined fully the preparations for the murder of Mr. Burke, the arrival in the Park of the conspirators, some on a car driven by Kavanagh and others in a cab driven by Fitzharris, the arrangements for the signal to be given by him (Carey) and the lurid details of the flashing knives, the brief struggle of the victims, and the final fatal blows. When sentence of death was pronounced on him, Brady, bowing to his counsel, thanked them. Brady's father was in court and was deeply afflicted, and a pathetic figure in the front of the gallery was a gentle-faced young girl, said to be his sweetheart, and whose tearful eyes were riveted upon him to the end. Lady Lucy Cavendish, the chief secretary's widow is said to have given Brady an ivory cross.

The execution of the Invincibles caused more excitement a month later. We have already heard how the redoubtable Mrs Kirwan of Golden-Bridge Prison sought and eventually obtained Brady's forgiveness of the informer. She was also called upon to give religious ministrations to Tim Kelly, who was extremely youthful and simple-looking, and had an air of 'bewildered anxiety.' He was in fact only 19 years old and there was great doubt about the evidence presented against him. Since 1868, executions had been brought out of public view under the 'Capital Punishment within Prisons Act,' and in Kilmainham Gaol a temporary gallows was re-assembled as required in one of the exercise yards. On this occasion prisoners from Mountjoy Jail built the gallows to execute the Invincibles.

The executioner was William Marwood, who is the man of whom it is often claimed, invented the long-drop system of hanging. The terrible sentence of the law was carried out on Brady on the morning of 14th May 1883. Elaborate preparations were made by the authorities to meet the possibility of a demonstration of popular sympathy or disturbance. Almost the whole of the 3rd battalion Grenadier Guards from Richmond Barracks were under arms in the Courthouse, and in the grounds of the Royal Hospital. Also present were the police in great numbers (50 outside the gate of the jail alone) and members of the marines force. All five of the condemned, the others being Michael Fagan, Thomas Caffrey, Dan Curley and Tim Kelly were hanged between May 14th and June 4th 1883.

The crowd outside the prison numbered far in excess of 3,000 sympathisers and reached as far as Islandbridge where the largest group of people were assembled. Women and children knelt on the road praying and there were many remarks made against the Government. There were cries of: *'Pity his poor mother now"* and *'a curse on that villain Carey who swore away his life.'* [149]

Tim Kelly's demise attracted a crowd of about 1,000 persons. There was no disturbance and no incident beyond the hoisting of a black flag. Three other members of the Invincibles, including James Fitzharris (*Skin-the-Goat*) were sentenced to life in penal servitude. He had an ability to make ballad poetry and while in jail he composed a number of ballads. In August 1899, having served 15 years, he was released from Maryborough Prison. Accompanied by a prison warden he arrived by train at Inchicore and made his way to James Mullet's pub in Bridge Street, where he spent the night. He then went to America, but was deported by the United States Government. During the latter years of his life Fitzharris had a small appointment as night watchman under the Dublin Corporation. He died in 1910.

James Carey with the help of the authorities was spirited away to South Africa under a false name, but the Invincibles had discovered the secret, and had sent an emissary to avenge them. Carey was killed, and the avenger, Pat Mc Donnell, was hanged in December without disclosing the names of his associates.

Richmond House Licensed Premises

There are numerous incidents of robbery in the course of the long history of Richmond Barracks, usually the theft of silver plate, cutlery, jewellery and even army boots. I have chosen to relate the details of one that gives a lot of colour to an establishment well known to local people.

You can be sure that the soldiers availed of the various public houses in the area. Mrs Shaw, a grocer and spirits merchant, traded from a shop on the second lock, at the rear of the barracks (the previous supplier from here was Patrick Tighe). The nearest public-house was the Richmond House, situated directly opposite the barracks. As far as I can ascertain the Richmond House, not to be confused with the Richmond Tavern, was established in 1868 and the first name associated with the premises was a Mr. James Raymond, grocer and wine merchant. We are fortunate that this house has survived to the present day and with many of its original features thanks to the care of its respective owners. For a short period recently the name was painted over, but I am glad to say that the original title can now be seen again, with the additional information as to the year, as suggested by me to the present owner. It is a semi detached building and it would appear that the two houses were originally under the same ownership. Though sold separately throughout its history they are again today owned jointly and trading under the one name.

By 1885 the Richmond House licensed premises was under the new management of Mr. M. O'Reilly. In October, three members of the Scots Guards, named James Lomas, Wm. White, and James McNab were charged in custody with having stolen a gold watch and chain, value £10 from Christian Jacobsen, captain of a Norwegian barque. Mr. O'Reilly, stated that on the evening in question, White, accompanied by the prosecutor, came into the tap-room of his house and had some drink. Shortly afterwards, Lomas and McNabb came in and had a drink also. They went into the tap-room and got into a conversation with others. In a few minutes Mr. White came out and said the gentleman's watch had been taken and that he ought to see after it.

Mr. O' Reilly went in and asked who had the watch? Lomas replied that he had and that it would be all right. O'Reilly, however, sent across for the guard at Richmond Barracks in order to have the affair settled. When the guard came over, Lomas took a *silver* watch from his pocket and gave it up. O' Reilly then asked for the chain and Lomas took the gold chain out of his pocket. The guard took the three soldiers into the barracks and the publican acquainted the police of the affair. The Captain who was under the influence of drink went off with a constable. Samuel Wilson, an officer's servant in Richmond Barracks produced the gold watch and stated that it had been handed to him the previous day by McNab, who asked him to take charge of it, as he was going on guard. Subsequently, however, he had given the watch to a Sergeant Major on account of something he heard during the day.

Christian Jacobsen, stated that on Wednesday he met the prisoner and drove with him in a cab to the public-house, where they had some drink. He became stupefied by the wine he drank, and forgot everything else that happened. He was wearing the gold watch and chain when he met White, but missed it the next day. The prisoners made various statements. It would appear that the silver watch that Lomas gave up to the guard belonged to McNab. The latter stated that Jacobsen was drunk and was throwing his clothes about, and he took the watch merely to mind it. That, of course, did not explain why he had later produced a silver watch with a gold chain while the gold watch was in safe keeping at the barracks. The prisoners were sent for trial at the Commission. [150]

183

The Crawford Divorce Case

Sir Charles Wentworth Dilke

In 1886 a sensational divorce case developed into one of the biggest scandals of the 19th century. The Dilke Case was the Profumo Affair of the Victorian era. Novelist, Thomas Hardy sat in the courtroom throughout some of the hearings at the time when he was writing *Jude The Obscure* and he referred to it later in his autobiography, the *Life*.

Many believe that the fallout from this case had repercussions for Charles Stewart Parnell when his private life came under the spotlight in 1890, especially as it was the same newspaper journalist, William Thomas Stead who was a key player in both cases.

The casualty in this instance was a very promising politician, Sir Charles Wentworth Dilke, the elected MP for Chelsea in 1868.

By 1883 he had secured a seat in the Cabinet, as President of the Local Government Board, a position he retained until Gladstone's election defeat of 1885. He was seen as a potential leader of the Liberal Party and as a future Prime Minister, but that was before he fell foul of a certain Mrs Crawford and her scheming lover, Captain Henry Forster of Richmond Barracks, an officer of the Duke of Cornwall's Light Infantry.

In July 1885 Dilke was named co-respondent in the case of Crawford v Crawford. Dilke was no saint, but he strenuously denied any involvement with Mrs Crawford.

Virginia Crawford was related to Dilke by marriage: his deceased brother's widow was one of her sisters. She herself had been forced into the marriage to Donald Crawford, a man almost twice her age. To compensate for her husband's shortcomings she was known to have hung about with medical students from a nearby hospital. She and another sister, Helen, also frequented a Knightsbridge brothel where both women had been conducting an affair with Captain Forster.

Eventually Mr. Crawford, who had been in receipt of anonymous letters alluding to the affair, confronted his wife and she said that her only lover had been Dilke.

Mrs Virginia Crawford

The affair had begun six weeks after her marriage, when she was just 19 years old, and had continued for the next three and a half years. They had met secretly at his home in Sloane Street and in a love nest he had rented for the purpose at Tottenham Court Road. Mr. Crawford petitioned for divorce and his legal team named a long list of people with whom Dilke was alleged to have been intimate. In addition to Mrs Crawford, they mentioned a maid named Sarah Grey and her sister Fanny Grey- a buxom serving girl who supposedly engaged in three-in-a-bed romps, Mrs Rogerson his old friend and neighbour, and most damning of all, Mrs Eustace Smith- Virginia Crawford's mother! This last allegation was true. In a statement, Virginia Crawford later claimed that, tucked up in bed with Fanny and herself, *'The MP taught me every French vice ...He used to say that I knew more than most women of 30.'*

When the case first came to court in February 1886, neither Dilke nor Mrs Crawford appeared in court and the witness Fanny Grey could not be found. This led to some newspaper headlines that seem hilarious to us today: 'THE MISSING FANNY' and 'THE SEARCH FOR FANNY.' Justice Butt found that the case against Dilke was unsubstantiated as there was only Mrs Crawford's confession, in support of which there was not a shred of evidence. He therefore ruled that there was no case for Dilke to answer. However, he then controversially granted the *decree nisi* on the grounds that by her own admission Mrs Crawford had committed adultery with Sir Charles Dilke even though there was no evidence of his having committed adultery with her. Still, the judge maintained, Dilke could leave the court without a stain on his character. That was not the perception of the Victorian public however, nor, unfortunately for Dilke, did the matter end there. It was at this stage that investigative journalist William Thomas Stead, editor of *Pall Mall* launched a public campaign calling on the politician to clear his name if he was sure of his innocence. The late British politician and author Roy Jenkins commentating on Stead's obsession with the case remarked:

> It is impossible to read the files of (Stead's) paper for the weeks after the February trial without believing that his main interest was to print anything which would keep the case alive, and enable him to go on exploiting its sensationalism for some time to come. *The Pall Mall's* circulation had been dropping … and it badly needed to attract new readers… (Stead) became seized with an abiding but self-righteous vindictiveness towards Dilke. He saw himself as the chosen instrument of public morality… protecting the innocent citizens of Britain against the impudent attempts of a shameless adulterer to climb back into their favour.[151]

In April 1886, Dilke sought to re-open the case making the Queen's Proctor a party to the case and opposing the decree absolute. He had reason to be optimistic after his legal team had found the elusive Fanny Grey who denied that any threesome had taken place involving her. Mrs. Rogerson (a personal friend of Dilke) and the soldiers at Richmond Barracks had given evidence of the relations that existed between Mrs. Crawford and Captain Foster. However, Dilke was subjected to severe scrutiny in the witness box (5 hours in total) and proved an unconvincing witness. His habit of physically cutting pieces out of his diary with scissors was held up to particular ridicule, as it created the impression that he had cut out evidence of potentially embarrassing appointments. It was remembered that he had not testified at the original hearing.

Although Mrs Crawford was forced to admit her adultery with Captain Forster, she stuck resolutely to her claim that Dilke had been her main lover. The jury found that Virginia had presented the true version of the facts, and that the *decree absolute* should be granted. Although Dilke had not been found guilty of adultery as he was not on trial, it was almost as though he had. Before leaving the court he was heard to say to Captain Forster that he would meet him in Paris the following week, intimating a duel. There was history between these two. Dilke did not like Forster and had tried to prevent him from seeing Mrs Crawford. When Forster persisted, Dilke had reported him to the War Office. Forster then accused him of attempting to 'blast' his career and demanded satisfaction by way of a fight or duel. Dilke declined on that occasion. There is no trace that I can find of any duel having taken place.

Following the court proceedings fresh rumours of previous affairs and impropriety emerged: most notably, Jennie Jerome Churchill (mother of Sir Winston, and wife of Lord Randolph Churchill) openly spoke of how Dilke had once approached her for a liaison. On the other hand, new findings gathered by Dilke's supporters were published in a pamphlet in 1891. It showed that Mrs Crawford's affair with Captain Forster was much more involved than she admitted at the second trial. As regards the evidence of other lovers, they served to establish strong alibis for Dilke on three of the nights she had claimed to have spent with him. But it was all too late to save him. He had lost his Chelsea seat and Gladstone dropped him from further consideration of being his successor.

In 1892, Gladstone was elected Prime Minister for the fourth time. Although Dilke had been re-elected by the burghers of the Forest of Dean, this gifted politician was never again rewarded with public office. He held his seat until his death in 1911.Virginia herself was by no means finished. She survived until 1948, becoming a public figure in her own right: as a writer and thinker (actually writing for W. T. Stead's *Pall Mall*), a Labour councillor, and so ferocious a campaigner against fascism that Mussolini blacklisted her.[152]

William Johnson, Quartermaster of the Coldstream Guards, who fought at Rourke's Drift, was later stationed at Richmond Barracks in 1888. Pictured here in civilian clothes

Typhoid Fever
Troops evacuated to the Phoenix Park

According to naturopathy, typhoid fever can hit only that body in which there is accumulation of toxic waste and other putrefying materials in the intestines. It is transmitted by the ingestion of food or water contaminated with the faeces of an infected person, which contain the bacterium *Salmonella enterica*, serovar Typhi. For this reason it is most prevalent in developing countries where sanitary water and sewage systems are lacking. As previously mentioned these were precisely the grievances in need of redress at Richmond Barracks. In January 1886 a question was put in the House of Commons by Sir James Fergusson. He asked whether attention had been called to the unsanitary state of Richmond Barracks and whether any special reports had been made upon the drainage and other circumstances of the barracks, and in that case whether any early steps would be taken to remedy the defects. Mr. Northcote in reply said that the attention of the War Dept had been drawn to the issue, but that the problem was believed to be attributable to the conditions of the neighbourhood generally than to any special deficit in the drainage or ventilation of the barracks themselves. [153]

In June 1889 the following letter first informed the public how this serious neglect of the situation had led to fatalities among the soldiers:

The Richmond Barracks, June 10th, 1889

To the Editor of the Times
'Sir, The public have heard much and read more of the state of the Royal Barracks, Dublin. They are now notorious. Little, however, is known of the Richmond Barracks, which are nearly, if not quite, as unhealthy. The 1st. South Wales Borderers (24th Regiment) has now been stationed there for about 18 months. They have had six officers and six non-commissioned officers and men already down with typhoid Fever. One of the latter has lately died. The barracks are known to be unhealthy and the drains are known to be defective. Instead of at once removing these troops, thoroughly overhauling the whole barracks, and putting the drains to rights, the authorities, apparently callous of the sickness that is going on, are content with half measures. They are examining and patching up just those drains within reach, and this, too, while officers and men are daily exposed to the germs of*

189

fever. By kindly making this known and calling public attention to what is really going on, you will greatly oblige,-   The Brother of a Victim.'

A photograph of a group of the South Wales Borderers and Coldstream Guards in 1888 taken by James H. McLean, Inchicore, bears the words "SS Clyde 1879." It is extraordinary to think that these were the very men who had withstood the onslaught of 4,500 Zulu's at Rourke's Drift in 1879 and who were now threatened by Typhoid in barracks. Major Gonville Bromhead had already died in India of the same disease in 1891. (The part of Bromhead was played by actor Michael Caine in the popular film *Zulu*).

Left, Elijah Dredge and Right, William Johnson, Quartermaster, Coldstream Guards.
Middle seated is Lt-Colonel Farquhar Glennie, who at the time of the photograph was taken, was commanding the 1st. Battalion South Wales Borderers in Dublin.

The matter was raised again in the Commons on the 21st June 1889 by Mr. Lowther, who asked the Secretary of State for War whether the details as stated in a 'public journal,' were true, that six officers and six non commissioned officers of the 24th regiment were down with typhoid fever and whether one of the non commissioned officers had died!; On this occasion, Mr. Edward Stanhope, Secretary of State for War, confirmed the story and named the deceased soldier as a Private Jones. He mentioned that Mr. Rogers Field, an eminent sanitary civil engineer, of London was making a careful inspection of all the sanitary arrangements of the barracks, including the drainage, and preparing a report. Already Mr. Field had discovered certain defects in the drainage, which had been immediately remedied. One great difficulty in connection with Richmond Barracks was that there was no outfall and until the local authority provided an outfall it would be difficult to do what was required. But there was also the necessity for considerable improvement in the subsoil drainage. There was much evidence to show that the illness in these and other barracks had been largely due to the unsanitary condition of guard rooms outside and this was confirmed by the fact that it was especially prevalent among subalterns.[154]

The Report of Mr Rogers Field

In a previous General Report presented to Parliament in 1861 from the 'Commissioners for improving the Conditions of the Barracks and Hospitals,' a number of recommendations had been given as to the improvements required. These related chiefly to the reduction of men so as to prevent overcrowding, the abolition of cess-pits, the reconstruction of privies as water latrines, improvements in the ventilation and lighting of the barrack rooms and improvements in scavenging. Mr. Field found that most of the recommendations had been addressed over the intervening 20 years. His main remit now was to find the possible source of the recurring bouts of enteric fever at these barracks.

In 1881, the Commanding Royal Engineer in Ireland had called special attention to the offensive arrangement of carrying away the 'night soil' from the latrines, and said that it had been reported on several times but nothing had been done in hopes the Dublin Corporation would carry out a new system of sewers into which the sewage of the barracks would be discharged. However no action was taken on this or in relation to the large masonry culvert (5 ft. high by 3 ft. wide) on the west side of the barracks which had been built by the War Department but claimed by the Commissioners under the Public Health Act. It was suggested that the sewer which was too large for its purpose should be obliterated and a new pipe sewer be constructed by the commissioners to serve as an outfall for the barrack drainage. Kilmainham Commissioners objected as they believed it was part of a plan to introduce a water closet system which would discharge soil into the River Camac. As this was not done it was suggested that the latrines should be converted into earth closets. The earth closet or composting toilet was invented by the Reverend Henry Moule. It was found that dry earth mixed with human waste produced clean compost in just a few weeks and the compost could be sold to market gardeners. Queen Victoria used an earth-closet at Windsor Castle, although many types of water-closet were available. However the introduction of the earth closet system at Richmond Barracks created other problems as Mr Field reported:

> When I examined these earth closets I found that the pails almost invariably contained nothing but faecal matter, without any signs of earth over it so that the smell was very offensive. As there was generally earth in the boxes I was first inclined to attribute the failure to apply the earth to the fact that the scoops were generally missing, but on examination of the closets used by the Guards, I found that in there the scoops were generally attached to the boxes, but that the earth was no better applied. From this it is, clear that the cause of the earth not being used was that the men would not take the trouble to apply it. The pails from the earth-closets are removed daily in carts to some land on the east side of the barracks; and as there were originally complaints about the disposal of the night soil, I made a special examination of the locality where the contents of the pails are now deposited. I found that the pails were carted by the contractor to a large manure heap a quarter of a mile from the nearest point of the barracks. The contents of the pails were emptied on the side of the heap furthest from the barracks, were then mixed with spent hops, stable manure, and ashes, and left to consolidate for a considerable time (the foreman said for six months or more) before they were spread about the field. There was a very offensive smell on the near side of the heap perceptible quite 200 yards away, but on investigation this smell was found to come entirely from the portion of the heap where the pails had been recently emptied, which was a filthy semi-fluid mass, and that the portion of the heap from which manure was taken to spread on the land was quite inoffensive, in fact, only a black mould. The conclusion I arrived at was that though it was possible that under certain circumstances the smell from the emptying of the pails might reach the barracks, the manure spread about the fields was quite inoffensive.[155]

His investigations were somewhat impeded by a pervasive smell, which might easily have been mistaken for sewage but which in fact was sulphuretted hydrogen, emanating from a cement factory on the east side of the barracks. It was also discovered that old disused drains were not properly blocked off, allowing for possible emissions of odours into the ventilation system. Mr. Field examined everything, including the subsoil water, part of which he found to be polluted and even the milk supply which had been grossly adulterated with water. At the end of the 5 month study, although minor defects were detected, he was unable positively to trace the disease to its cause. The findings of Mr Field's lengthy and comprehensive report were presented to Mr. Stanhope on 23rd July 1889. On the drainage, which was the main issue he had this to say:

> The conclusion I have arrived at, after careful consideration of all the details, is that the drainage of the barracks is decidedly bad— in fact, so bad that I do not see how anything short of radical alterations, amounting virtually to reconstruction will suffice to meet the necessity of the case. [156]

Under Canvas

In August 1889, it was made known to the House of Commons that there had been a fresh outbreak of fever in July and as a result the whole of Richmond Barracks and Royal and Palatine-squares in the Royal Barracks had been evacuated. The works of improvement were being carried on, as well as the subsoil drainage which had been recommended.

Mr. Mac Neill- *'Are not the troops who have been removed from these barracks now under canvas in the Phoenix Park and suffering great hardship?'*
Mr Stanhope- *'This is the first time I have heard it suggested that in the summer months the troops of the British Army consider it a grievance to be under canvas.'* (cheers)[157]

As a result of Mr Field's report, what was described as 'the largest drainage job hitherto attempted at any barracks in Ireland' was commenced in October 1889. It was carried out on the most approved principles, covering some fifteen acres of ground. The work was done under the personal direction of Major Dickenson, of the Royal Engineers, and there were contracts for two complete systems, one for foul drainage and the other for subsoil drainage. Part of the foul drainage was undertaken by (sappers) the corps of the Royal Engineers and a working party of 150 men from all the infantry regiments in garrison, who were paid for their labour. The drains were of great depth, averaging ten feet. The sewage of Richmond Barracks would be carried by pipes to the Camac River running underneath the wall at Kilmainham Prison. Important renovations were also made in the Barrack rooms where sanitary plans were redesigned on more modern principles than those heretofore prevailing. Great attention was paid to ventilation, and particularly on the staircases, which were supplied with louver ventilators running through the roof. This system of foul and subsoil drainage was virtually the same recommendation advised by Colonel Slack, of the Royal Engineers several years earlier and which was ignored, despite the fact that he was regarded as one of the highest authorities in the Kingdom on the subject of drainage. Finally, under Major Dickenson's directions extensive disinfecting operations were carried out throughout the barracks and grounds. It was remarked at the time that even if their drainage search for the cause of enteric fever should not result in its discovery, they would at least have "gone a long way towards rendering the extensive barracks in the neighbourhood of Inchicore one of the healthiest in the United Kingdom."[158] Indeed it would appear to have worked, as I can find little further mention of fever at these barracks

Mr. Stanhope's remark about the British soldier under canvas, which raised laughter in the Commons, proved regrettable when the weather turned inclement at the close of September and the beginning of October. To his way of thinking, the uncertainty of Irish weather was nothing to what the soldier might expect when abroad on active service. But here in full view of the public and the Press it was clear that the men could not be kept in such conditions for the winter months. In what was quite an innovative arrangement, the Royal Lancaster Regiment and the South Wales Borderers were removed to 'snug quarters' in the secure shelter of the Royal Dublin Society's premises at Ball's Bridge. This was to be their accommodation for the winter and the following spring. The 680 officers and men, of the Lancaster Regiment occupied two buildings comprising the new hall in which canine shows were usually held, and the large one specially built for the accommodation of ponies and cobs at August Horse Shows.

The men of the South Wales Borderers occupied the lesser of the two large main halls- the one occupied by cattle at spring shows. This room was no way near as suitable for the men's purposes. It was far too large and of peculiar construction. The roof was high, and as it opened onto the grounds outside by a large gateway it was subject to draughts on occasions. However, within about three weeks the whole place began to take on a barrack-like appearance, although on a much larger scale than was to be found in any other part of the United Kingdom. The temperature which was low owing to the vast spaces had been rendered more tolerable by the introduction of huge coke stoves. Six rows of cots ran the whole length of the building, ample space being obtained between for the tables on which the men took their meals. In addition, each of the halls was fitted with a complete system of shelving on which the troops could store their kits and accoutrements.

Outside the main hall on the side next to Simmons-court Road an extensive system of wash-houses was constructed, and opposite the ring enclosure bathrooms were provided. These were placed next to the cooking houses, which enabled the baths to be provided with hot water when required. In the cook-houses which were placed in

194

the range of sheds facing the ring enclosures, Soyer's stoves were built in, and a number of gas stoves were also added, some of them large enough to bake and roast for 120 men. Drains had been laid on to the boxes in which the officers' horses were stabled, and in others of the boxes which were used as shops for tailors, armourers, and shoemakers, stoves and windows had been introduced. The officers of both battalions were accommodated in separate marquees on the galleries of the Central Hall, those of the Lancaster Regiment on the right hand side of the main entrance at Ball's Bridge and the officers of the South Wales Borderers on the opposite gallery. They shared a mess-room in the place known as the third-class bar, everything required for them being cooked there. The first class refreshments bar became the officers' canteen:

> Not the least wonderful of the many transformations effected at Ball's Bridge within the last three or four days is the change in the class of customers attending the first-class refreshment bar and room, this portion of the building being now employed for the purposes of the garrison canteen, and judging by the briskness of the business carried on there yesterday, a profitable business for those interested in its success was being done. The postal and telegraph offices and cloak-rooms at the front entrance are employed by the orderly sergeants and their assistants, and only a short time will elapse until all the available accommodation that can be discovered at Ball's Bridge will have been utilized by the troops.[159]

The married women belonging to the two regiments were not at Ball's Bridge, quarters being retained for them at Arbour Hill and Richmond Barracks. Another disadvantage for the soldiers was that they had to travel great distances when supplying guards for the Viceregal Lodge and other far-away places. On Sundays, religious services for Protestants were held in the main hall, but the Wesleyan soldiers had to travel to Sandymount, and the Roman Catholics to Irishtown Chapel. The troops took the opportunity of their new surroundings to stage a number of theatrical and musical shows which were numerously attended by the residents of the Pembroke Township and by ladies and gentlemen of the city. The South Wales Borderers were surprised to find that along with the stage-scenery their baggage was also forwarded from Richmond Barracks, an indication that they would not be returning to Inchicore when the drainage works were completed.

By 1890, the whole episode of enteric fever at Richmond Barracks was a thing of the past, and no event signalled this more than the arrival here of the Commander of the Forces, General, his Serene Highness Prince Edward of Saxe-Weimar, G.C.B., and the Princess, on 29th September. Prince Edward was a British military officer of German parents, Prince Bernhard of Saxe-Weimar-Eisenach and Princess Ida of Saxe-Meiningen (whose sister Adelaide was King William IV's wife.) He had served

195

with much distinction in the Crimean War, became colonel of the 1st Life Guards, and later a British Field Marshal. His wife was Lady Augusta Katherine Gordon-Lennox, (a daughter of Charles Lennox, 5th Duke of Richmond), who was created Countess of Dornburg. The royal couple had come from the camp in the Curragh. A farewell military display was given there by the Gordon Highlanders and other regiments before the Prince's party were escorted to a saloon car specially placed at their disposal by the Great Southern and Western Railway. They travelled to Kingsbridge, and from there they drove to Kilmainham. Subsequently, his Serene Highness honoured the officers of the Grenadier Guards with his company at luncheon at Richmond Barracks.[160] The Prince died within two years of this visit.

Prince Edward of Saxe-Weimar

Fire at Golden-Bridge Convent

On the evening of 6th December 1893, at about 6 o' clock the Fire Brigade received an alarm of a fire at Golden-Bridge Convent. The message was conveyed from the tramway offices at Inchicore. Lieutenant Byrne proceeded at once to the institution with a number of men and with a steam engine and a hose carriage. It was found that the fire had originated in the centre of the laundry attached to the institution. The brigade who were soon joined by Captain Purcell and his men, laid a line of hose 1,000 feet long, and water was played on the burning building from the Grand

196

Canal by means of the fire engine. A body of the Grenadier Guards, from the Richmond Barracks, under the command of Colonel Harten, also gave valuable assistance, and brought their fire engine into requisition. At one time it looked as if the fire would be a serious one, for the portion of the building attacked was full of woodwork, and there was strong breeze blowing at the time. The Sisters of Mercy and the other inmates were naturally very much alarmed. However, owing to the energy displayed by the brigade and the military, the flames were contained within a space of 100 feet on either side of the portion of the house where the fire broke out. A boiler and engine were saved. Considerable damage was, however, done before the fire was completely got under control.[161]

Enlargement of Richmond Barracks

Richmond Barracks were originally intended for the accommodation of two infantry regiments, but were built at a time when there was little idea of the requirements of sanitary science, and when military activities were carried on outside more than within the barracks square. For many years past it was found impossible to accommodate the full strength of two regiments there and some companies of the other regiment stationed there had to be put up in one of the other city barracks. This arrangement was of the greatest inconvenience to the military authorities and the heads of the battalion. It seemed absurd to have one battalion split up into two divisions, located in different barracks, and drilled on different parade grounds. Yet the arrangement was necessary to the health of the forces that two whole regiments should not be huddled within the Richmond Barracks.

Richmond barracks stood on an area 130 yards by 240. However the barracks square, in which the drilling and manoeuvres were carried out, was only 120 yards by 40 yards. The utter inadequacy of this space for any regimental evolution was manifest to everyone who understood anything on the subject. It was suited for no more than company drill, and it was to that purpose that it was mainly applied. The battalions had to be drilled in sections, which was a great encroachment on the hours of the men. After the necessary offices, canteen, etc, were provided for, the space available for sleeping quarters for the men was entirely inadequate, and they had to occupy a close and confined space. In consequence of this it had been found necessary for the health of the men to remove portion of one of the battalions elsewhere. Three essentials, sufficient accommodation for the men, drill space, and the health of the forces, compelled the military authorities to either seek to enlarge the barracks or abandon it to one regiment. They decided upon the former course. In August 1895, a Bill granting permission for the purchase of lands for this purpose was passed. The Royal Engineer Dept. recommended the acquisition of 10 acres and 25 perches of ground adjoining the Kilmainham Road. The advantage of this site

197

was that it did not encroach on any residential plots, which made its purchase all the cheaper. The lands were known as Golden-Bridge north, and they lay between the Grand Canal and the Kilmainham Road, extending down to nearly opposite Kilmainham Jail. [162] The land, known locally as the Barrack Field was used for recreation, exercise and practice. This is the site of some of the present Bulfin housing estate.

The 1st Battalion Durham Light Infantry were here at this time and posed for some photographs at the recreation rooms and elsewhere. While here, Lieutenant Colonel William Gordon, commanding the battalion announced his retirement on 30th October 1896.

Lieutenant Colonel William Gordon of the Durham Regiment

The Durham Regiment 1st Battalion.

Baden Baden Powell

In 1897, another famous name was to be found at Richmond Barracks. Most people will have heard of Baron Robert Baden-Powell, founder of the Boy Scouts, and hero of Mafeking, but his lesser known younger brother, Baden Fletcher Smyth Baden-Powell had a distinguished career in his own right.

The Scots Guards marching through Lord Edward Street en route to Richmond Barracks.

The unusual circumstance of his identical forename and surname came from the fact that he was named after his father, the Rev. Baden Powell and later, on the demise of his father, his mother changed the family name from Powell to Baden-Powell. She did so as a tribute to his father and to set her own children apart from their half-siblings from a previous marriage. Like his brother, he was later an army officer and served with the Scots Guards, one of England's most distinguished regiments, but his passion was for aviation. In 1880 he joined the Royal Aeronautical Society and soon decided they were too much talk, not enough action. He bought his own balloon and learned to fly it. Within a year of joining the army, he was lecturing on military uses of lighter-than-air flight. He would become a pioneering thinker in the use of military aviation and a Fellow and later President of the Royal Aeronautical Society as well as a Fellow of the Royal Geographical Society. Baden-Powell was the author of '*In Savage Isles and Settled Lands,*' published in 1892. It recounts his journey of some 50,000 miles extending over three years as he travelled around the world to his duties as Aide-de-Camp and Military Secretary to the Governor of Queensland, Australia, and home via the Pacific, America and across the Atlantic. He was at the forefront in balloon, kite and then powered aircraft in the very earliest days of manned flight. In 1897, then honorary secretary of the Aeronautical Society of Great Britain, he was also serving with the Scots Guards at Richmond Barracks.

Percy Pilcher's flying machine at Stanford Hill

He wrote from there to Ella Pilcher in March 1897 concerning illustrations used in a lecture given by Percy Pilcher, British inventor and pioneer aviator who was his country's foremost experimenter in un-powered flight. Ella was a staunch supporter of her brother's experiments in flying machines. She used to sew the wings for his gliders and helped generally with all of the gliders that he invented. Baden-Powell wrote for the Aeronautical Journal and wished to publish the lecture, *"Experiments in Flying Machines"* which was given to the Military Society of Ireland in the Royal

University Buildings, Dublin, on the 21st January 1897. The letter, which he wrote from Richmond Barracks, still exists and has recently appeared at auction.

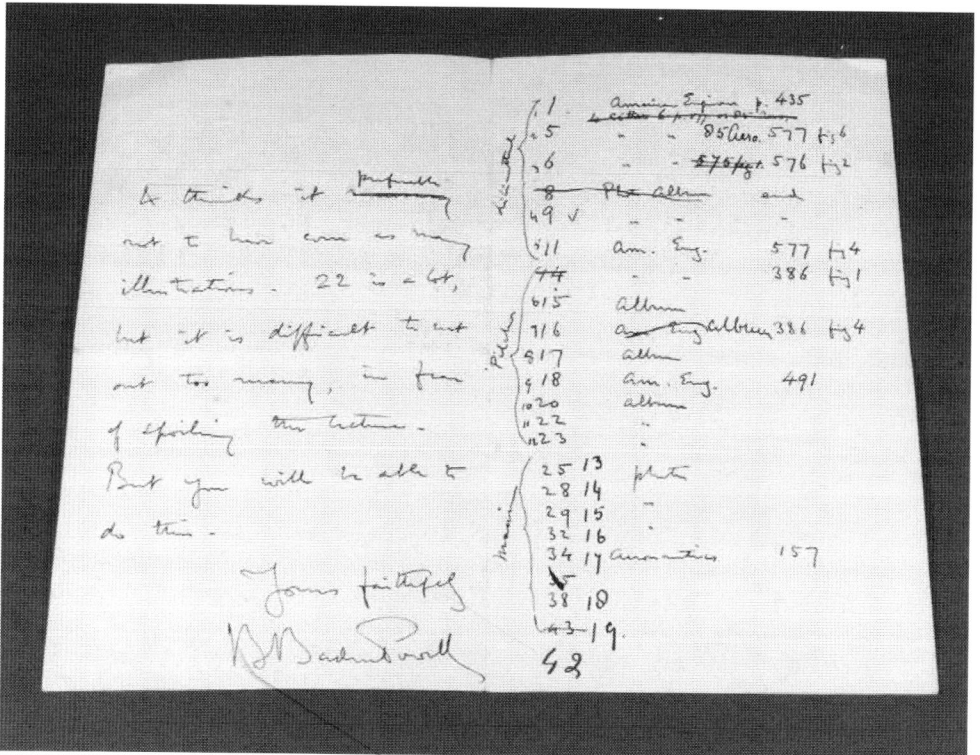

An ALS by Baden-Powell addressed to 'Miss Pilcher, dated March 8th. 1897

Percy Pilcher was later involved in a fatal accident in 1899. Baden-Powell and Ella were among the crowd present as Percy gave his last demonstration on Stanford Hill. Baden-Powell reported the crash in the Aeronautical Journal. It is thought the wings had become too wet in the pouring rain and, as a result, too heavy. The height of the fall was judged by him to be 30 or 40 feet. [163] It was apparently, to those of poetic bent, like the fall of the mythical 'Icarus,' who had flown too close to the sun.

Having attained the rank of Major, Baden Baden Powell's duties in the army led him to travel to even more countries than his more illustrious older brother. They were, though, both in South Africa during the Boer War, resulting in an amazing coincidence at the relief of Mafeking on May 17th, 1900. He entered Mafeking with the Relief forces and reportedly woke his brother from his slumbers to tell him that Mafeking had been relieved!

The Second Boer War

The defeat of the Zulus and the Pedi inevitably led to further conflict in South Africa. There followed what became known as the First Anglo-Boer War, a short lived series of encounters from 16th December 1880 until 23rd March 1881. The Transvaal Boers, always wary of the Zulu threat, were then able to give voice to the growing resentment against the 1877 British annexation of the Transvaal. They complained that it had been a violation of the Sand River Convention of 1852, which recognized the independence of the Transvaal Republic, and the Bloemfontein Convention of 1854, which recognized the independence of the Orange Free State. The discovery of diamonds in 1867 near the Vaal River, some 550 miles northeast of Cape Town, ended all that. The subsequent "diamond rush" attracted people from all over the world turning Kimberley into a town of 50,000 within five years, and drawing the attention of British imperial interests. In 1877, Sir Theophilus Shepstone, the British Secretary for Native Affairs in Natal, annexed the South African Republic .

On 16 December 1880, the Boers revolted and took action at Bronkhorstspruit against a British column of the 94th Foot. Lieutenant-Colonel Anstruther and 120 men of the 94th Foot (Connaught Rangers) were dead or wounded by Boer fire within minutes of the first shots. A number of other victories followed for the Boers, culminating in the Battle of Majuba Hill on 27 February 1881, the greatest humiliation for the British. Major-General Sir George Pomeroy Colley, who lost his own life, was posthumously blamed on this calamity. He had attacked while hostilities were suspended, awaiting the outcome of peace negotiations initiated by an offer from Kruger. He had sought to attack again with a view to enabling the British government to negotiate from a position of strength, but he underestimated the fighting ability of the Boers, their expertise with horses and their marksmanship. In a peace treaty on 23 March 1881, the British agreed to Boer self-government in the Transvaal.

The uneasy peace that followed was broken by the discovery of gold in the South African Republic in 1886. The Transvaal became the richest and potentially the most powerful nation in southern Africa; however the country had neither the manpower nor the industrial base to develop the resource on its own. As a result, the Transvaal reluctantly allowed immigrant *uitlanders* (foreigners), mainly from Britain, to come and seek their fortune. It was not long before the number of uitlanders in the Transvaal exceeded the number of Boers. This led to confrontations between the old and the new settlers. In 1895, Dr Leander Starr Jameson, the Administrator in southern Rhodesia of the Chartered Company, led an uprising which he thought would be supported by the uitlanders in Johannesburg. However, the uitlanders in Johannesburg did not take up arms to support the raid, and Transvaal government forces surrounded the column and captured Jameson's men before they could reach Johannesburg. This embarrassing episode became known as the "The Jameson Raid."[164] As demands for voting rights for the uitlanders continued to be made and with more and more new arrivals of white immigrants, the Boers realised that their future was under threat. Negotiations began with a view to finding a compromise, but these failed and in September 1899, Joseph Chamberlain (the British Colonial Secretary) sent an ultimatum to the Boers, demanding full equality for those uitlanders resident in the Transvaal. President Kruger issued his own ultimatum, giving the British 48 hours to withdraw all their troops from the border of the Transvaal, failing which the Transvaal, allied with the Orange Free State, would declare war against the British. Both sides rejected the others' ultimatums, and the Transvaal and Orange Free State governments declared war.

Lord Roberts at Richmond Barracks

On 25th October 1899, at Richmond Barracks, Field Marshal Lord Roberts, Commander of the Forces in Ireland, inspected the 1st. Battalion Argyll and Sutherland Highlanders prior to their departure for South Africa. The battalion mustered 1,100 of all ranks including a large number of Reservists and the men, who were dressed in their Foreign Service uniforms, looked "extremely fit and cheerful." Colonel G. L. Goff [f] was in command, and the other officers were about 30 in number. Lord Roberts was accompanied by Major-General Gossett, commanding the Dublin district, and by a number of staff officers. At the conclusion of the inspection, Lord Roberts addressing the men, said:

'Lieutenant Col. Goff, officers, non- commissioned officers, and men of the 1st Battalion Argyll and Sutherland Highlanders, I thought I should like to inspect you before you left Dublin, and I am glad I have been able to do so, for it has given me great pleasure to see the battalion so fit and ready in all respects for active service. The manner in which the Reservists of the regiment have responded to the call of duty is eminently satisfactory, and with the 548 old soldiers who have joined your ranks the battalion will embark at Queenstown over 1,100 strong. Many fine

---

[f] Killed in action at Magersfontein, December 1900

battalions have already gone to the seat of war, and others are preparing to start, but I am confident there is not one that will do better service, or be a greater credit to Her Majesty's army than the 1ˢᵗ Battalion of the Argyll and Sutherland Highlanders.

The first Highland regiment, with which I was associated on service, was the 93ʳᵈ, now your 2ⁿᵈ. Battalion. It came to India during the Mutiny, and quite captivated me by the splendid courage officers and men displayed at the storming of the Sikandar Bagh in November, 1857; it was a sight I shall never forget, the way in which they raced with the Sikhs to see who should be the first to reach the deadly beach. South Africa is no new field to the regiment. It is very nearly a century ago since the 93ʳᵈ Highlanders sailed from Cork with the force under the command of Major General Sir David Baird, to take possession of the Cape of Good Hope. On three subsequent occasions your own battalion did good service in South Africa, in campaigns which, however important they may have appeared at the time, dwindle into insignificance in comparison with the great event in which you are now about to take part, the establishment of British supremacy throughout that portion of the country where the suzerainty of the Crown has been denied, and the blood of so many English, Irish, and Scotch soldiers has already been spent. Everyone throughout the length and breadth of this vast Empire watches eagerly for news from South Africa.

All hearts have been stirred by the accounts of the splendid manner in which the King's Royal Rifles, the Royal Irish Fusiliers, and the Royal Dublin Fusiliers behaved at the battle fought last Friday near Dundee, where my gallant friend Lieutenant General Sir William Symons received his dangerous (not mortal, I sincerely thrust) wound. I am glad to see Col. Clements and some of the South Wales Borderers here, for that was the regiment in which General Symons rose, and it was as a Major in the battalion stationed in the Madras Presidency seventeen years ago I was attracted by his soldierly bearing. A day or two later we heard of the successful fight under another friend and comrade, Lieutenant General Sir George White, near Elandslaagte where the old 92ⁿᵈ Foot, a regiment I know so well, and to which I am so deeply indebted showed the enemy how Highland soldiers can fight. I wish you one and all, officers, non commissioned officers, and men, God- speed, and I pray that every success may attend you. As the 91ˢᵗ foot you have a grand record, and as the 1ˢᵗ Battalion of the Argyll and Sutherland Highlanders I know that you will maintain your glorious reputation, and do all that soldiers can do to uphold the honour and dignity of the country to which we are all so proud of belonging.'[165]

The Field Marshal's hopes for Major-General Symons were in vain. He had been mortally wounded at Talana Hill (also known as the Battle of Dundee) and died three days later. The inspection by Lord Roberts was witnessed by a large gathering of the citizens of Dublin, who cheered frequently and enthusiastically during the course of the proceedings. The men remained the following day at the barracks while the baggage party was send ahead by train. Then, at half past four o clock on the morning of the 27th October eight companies of the 1st battalion Argyll and Sutherland assembled for the last time in the barrack square. A photograph was taken, the original of which can be seen at Stirling castle in Scotland.

Despite the early hour and heavy rain the road outside the gates was crowded with people. Officers and men were in fighting 'trim,' wearing kharki service dress, the mounted infantry being distinguished by their "putties." The scene in the semi-darkness of the morning was a most impressive one, as the men in their light brown tunics and kilts, and bearing their full 'kit,' assembled in front of the Lieutenant Colonel. Precisely at five o' clock the gates of Richmond Barracks swung open and the band of the Royal Dragoon guards issued out in front of the first division, Companies E, G, and H, Lieutenant Colonel Goff riding in front of his charge. Cheers were sent up by the **thousands of people on the roadway**, and the regiment headed for the Royal Hospital, through which the route to the station lay. Almost all the spectators joined in the march, and along the entire way there was witnessed a scene of the greatest enthusiasm. The men sang to the music of the band, and the civilians cheered continuously. The bands of the Bedfordshire Regiment, the pipers and drummers of the King's Own Borderers, the 4th Rifle Brigade, and the fife and drum band of the South Wales Borderers took part in the march and played in turn. At the Royal Hospital the old veterans of the Institution turned out in force, and gave a rousing cheer, and waved Union Jacks as the troops passed.

The distance between Richmond Barracks and Kingsbridge is comparatively short, and was accomplished quickly, the men being received there by another considerable crowd, who cheered again and again as the regiment poured in though the gates on St. John's Road. When the full division had arrived it was paraded on the departure platform, and then entrained within an incredibly short space of time, eight men being placed in each carriage. Once in the compartments helmets were exchanged for caps, and pipes were lighted, while the Dragoon band played lively airs on the platform. Apparently there were few relatives of the men present, but those who had assembled evinced the greatest eagerness to give the soldiers a cordial send-off. Many of those who had been forbidden entrance to the station climbed to the top of the high wall to see the train as it steamed away, and it was only with difficulty that the Dublin Metropolitan and Military Police prevented the crowd forcing its way into the platform. The band played 'Soldiers of the Queen,' and 'Rule Britannia,' and the men leaning from the carriage windows joined lustily in both, and their cheers were answered by the cheers of the populace.

At a quarter to six Field-Marshal Lord Roberts arrived, and after a few minutes' chat with the Lieutenant-Colonel passed along the train, casting a keen glance into each carriage as he went by. Colonel Kelly, Deputy-Adjutant General and other members of the Headquarter and Personal Staff accompanied the hero of Kandahar, who a few minutes later, was joined by Major-General Gossett, C.B., Commanding Dublin District, Colonel Farrant, Chief Staff Officer; Colonel Courtenay, Major Cavendish, and other officers. Several of the officers of the King's Own Scottish Borderers and South Wales Borderers were also present to bid their comrades adieu. The battalion consisted of eight companies, comprising 1,082 non-commissioned officers and men, with 29 officers, and 548 of the battalion wore decorations gained in previous campaigns. Two special trains were provided to take the men to Queenstown, where the troopship 'Orcana' awaited to convey them to South Africa. All the bands except the Dragoon Guards, at once returned to Richmond Barracks to play down the second division.

The men had apparently done their leave-taking overnight, and sat quietly in the carriages while the Field-Marshal passed along, but when the bugle sounded at ten minutes past six, and the word was given, 'Officers in,' every window was packed tightly with heads and face to reciprocate the final good-bye. The officers entered a first-class saloon carriage; the Field-Marshal shook hands with the Lieutenant Colonel, the whistle sounded, and the strains of the National Anthem, joined in by the men, the train steamed out of the station. From one carriage a fine "brawny" young Scotchman shouted *'Let 'em all come.'* Four hundred men left by the first train, and immediately it had disappeared beneath Kilmainham Bridge, another train was shunted into position. The strains of the bag-pipes announced the approach of the second division of 500 men under Major Wilson. The National Anthem was again played, and was joined in by the men, and, amid, cheering from those on the platform, the train steamed out of the station at seven o'clock. Mr. Colhoun, manager of the railway company, was present, also Mr. J. Neville, district superintendent.[166]

Vonolel

Earlier that year, in June 1899, Lord Roberts' famous horse, 'Vonolel' had passed away and was buried in the rose gardens of the Royal Hospital Kilmainham. Roberts was said to be heartbroken, 'Vonolel' was twenty-nine years old on passing. It is perhaps with the Battle of Kandahar, the last serious engagement of the Anglo-Afghan war, that Roberts (and by extension Vonolel) is most closely associated. For victory in the Battle of Kandahar, Roberts received the thanks of Parliament. When the Queen awarded medals to her officers and men who had taken part in the Afghan campaign and in the expedition to Kandahar, she did not forget Vonolel. Lord Roberts hung round the animal's neck the Kabul medal, with four clasps, and the bronze Kandahar star. The gallant horse wore these medals on that day in June 1897, when the nation celebrated the Queen's Diamond Jubilee. Included on the headstone are the lines:

'There are men both good and wise
Who hold that in a future state
Dumb creatures we have cherished here below
Shall give us joyous greeting when
We pass the golden gate
Is it folly that I hope it may be so?

Lord Roberts and his famous white Arab charger, Vonolel.

The war had three distinct phases. First, the Boers mounted pre-emptive strikes into British-held territory in Natal and the Cape Colony, besieging the British garrisons of Ladysmith, Mafeking and Kimberley. The Boers then won a series of tactical victories at Colenso, Magersfontein and Spionkop against a failed British counteroffensive to relieve the three sieges. Second, after the introduction of greatly increased British troop numbers under the command of Lord Roberts, another, and this time successful, British offensive was launched in 1900 to relieve the sieges. The Siege of Mafeking was the most famous incident in the Second Boer War. It took place over a period of 217 days, from October 1899 to May 1900, and Robert Baden-Powell with a small body of men held out in what seemed to be a hopeless situation, turning him into a national hero. It emerged that he had trained a cadet corps of boys aged between 12-15 as messengers and orderlies and this freed up some of the men, increasing the number of available troops. It is thought that this later inspired the formation of the scouting movement. After Natal and the Cape Colony were secure, the British were able to invade the Transvaal. Here, the British were met by the Transvaal Brigade led by Irishman, **Major John Mac Bride (pictured here on the right, holding a sight from a British cannon captured at Colenso).**

At the Siege of Ladysmith, they serviced the famous Boer artillery piece, called Long Tom, and they fought at the Battle of Colenso. Having worked in the gold mines, they had a reputation as demolition experts and it was they who delayed the British advance on Pretoria by blowing up bridges. The capital was eventually captured in June 1900.

In the third and final phase, beginning in March 1900, the Boers launched a protracted guerrilla war against the British forces, lasting a further two years, during which the Boers raided targets such as British troop columns, telegraph sites, railways and storage depots. In an effort to cut off supplies

209

to the raiders, the British, now under the leadership of Lord Kitchener, responded with a scorched earth policy of destroying Boer farms and moving civilians into concentration camps.[167] Some parts of the British Press and British government expected the campaign to be over within months, and the protracted war gradually became less popular, especially after revelations about the conditions in the concentration camps (where tens of thousands of women and children died of disease and malnutrition). The Boer forces finally surrendered on Saturday 31 May 1902, with 54 of the 60 delegates from the Transvaal and Orange Free State voting to accept the terms of the peace treaty.[168] This was known as the Treaty of Vereeniging, and under its provisions, the two republics were absorbed into the British Empire, with the promise of limited self-government in the future. For Britain, the Second Boer War was the longest, the most expensive (over £200 million), and the bloodiest conflict between 1815 and 1914, lasting three months longer and resulting in higher British casualties than the earlier Crimean War.[169]

King Edward VII and the Irish Guards

Queen Victoria paid her last visit to Ireland on 1st April 1900, in the course of which she visited the Royal Hospital Kilmainham. Coinciding with her visit, the Irish Guards were raised as a Regiment on the same date. Queen Victoria, wished to honour the Irishmen who fought in the British Army's South African Campaigns. The creation of The Irish Guards was ordered by Her Majesty following a suggestion in 1900 from Lord Wolseley that the Irish Regiments of the British Army should wear the shamrock in their headdress on 17th March (St. Patrick's Day) each year as a mark of The Crown's appreciation of their exceptional gallantry at Ladysmith, South Africa during the Boer War. During the battles at Ladysmith and Bloemfontein the Irishmen of The Inniskilling Fusiliers, The Dublin Fusiliers and The Connaught Rangers had particularly distinguished themselves by their bravery. An Irish M.P. then suggested in Parliament that as there were already regiments of Scots Guards and English Guards, a regiment of Irish Guards should be created. The Irish Guards' first Commanding Officer was Irishman Field Marshal Lord Roberts. Queen Victoria died in January 1901 and was succeeded by her son, King Edward VII., who had survived an assassination attempt the previous year when Jean-Baptiste Sipido shot at him in protest over the Boer War. The Regiment received its first colours from His Majesty at a parade held on Horse Guards Parade, London in May 1902. From that year, the Irish Guards adopted as its official mascot a pedigree Irish Wolfhound, and one of that breed has taken part in its formal parades ever since, wearing a specially embroidered coat of livery.

Queen Victoria at the Royal Hospital Kilmainham

In July 1903 Edward VII, accompanied by the Irish Guards paid another royal visit to Ireland. A newspaper report set the scene for the King's arrival:

> All public and very many private buildings are hidden in gay buntings, and great patches of crimson are supplied at frequent intervals by the carpeting of the stands which have been erected at every point of vantage along the twelve miles of the Royal route. The sunshine and the excitement of next week's great event combined to bring all Dublin into the streets today. They were filled with gay masses of spectators and in Grafton Street, which is a blaze of colour, at the Bank of Ireland, where a wonderful scheme of illumination is being completed, at Leeson- street-bridge, where the "ancient" gate through which their Majesties will enter the city is rapidly taking shape. At there and other points of particular interest it was difficult to force a passage through the crowds.[170]

But the great centre of attraction to the people of Dublin was the line of quays along which the Irish Guards and the two squadrons of Horse Guards which left London the previous night were to march shortly after noon to their barracks at the other side of the city. Everyone was keen to see the King's new regiment set foot for the very first time on Irish soil. The guards numbering about 400 men, under the command of Lieutenant-Colonel Cooper M.V.O., were headed by their own band and by the band of the Royal Irish Rifles. They set out at quick march, followed by an enormous crowd, which gained in size as they went through Westmoreland Street and Dame Street. The Officers of the Irish Guards were to be guests of the messes of the Royal Irish Rifles and the Seaforth Highlanders at Richmond Barracks.

Billie the Bulldog

Although often referred to as a bulldog, 'Billie of South Africa' was in fact a brindled bull-terrier, and a very famous one. He was hardly a handsome canine, but what he lacked in beauty he made up for in courage. The dog was found in September 1900, when No.2 Company, The Royal Irish Rifles Mounted Infantry, was making raids from the Cape-Transvaal Railway on small parties of Boers. One of these expeditions took them to a deserted farm of Commandant Botha, a brother of General Louis Botha in Doorberg, where the only survivor was the bull terrier. He was adopted by the unit and became Billie of The Royal Irish Rifles. Billie went into battle with the men, and in January 1901, near Transvaal, Orange Free State, the dog was wounded in the leg. From that time until the end of the war he trekked from Griqualand to the west to Basutoland and was with General French's column in Cape Colony. He tried valiantly to keep up with the company, covering as much as sixty miles a day on three legs, holding up the other paw pathetically, but eventually

Billie needed a lift. He accompanied his regiment when it returned to Dublin in January 1903, and was decorated by a British General at a full battalion parade. Billie regularly attended ceremonial parades in Dublin and wore a specially made rifle coat with the medals presented by the commander. For his services in the war he was awarded the Queen's South Africa Medal with three bars and the King's South Africa Medal with two bars.

In December 1903 Billie attained further notoriety when he appeared as a witness in the Dublin Police-court. The case, involving cruelty, was brought against a man named Ernest Warmingham, employed in the canteen kept at Richmond Barracks, where Billie was stationed with his regiment. The dog, though not at all savage-looking was muzzled as he was led into court, decorated with the honours of war attached to his coat. He was conducted to the witness box untroubled about the evidence which might be given in the case. Colour-Sergeant Edwards gave evidence to the effect that the dog was his property. On the day in question he missed the dog from the Barracks, and after searching for him he found the animal in a bad state, bleeding from wounds in his legs and from a cut on the head. Edwards mentioned how the dog had become a pet of the regiment and of the expense incurred in bringing him home. Other witnesses deposed that they had seen Warmingham thrashing the dog with a stick outside the canteen at Richmond Barracks. The defendant broke the stick in the course of the beating and then kicked the dog. When told to desist he had retorted that the dog ought to be *'damned well shot.'*

In his defence, Warmingham deposed that he was canteen manager at the Richmond Barracks. On the 2nd inst while proceeding to the canteen with an Irish terrier the bull dog attacked the smaller dog, and in order to separate them witness had to use the stick. He admitted he broke the stick on the dog, but denied having kicked the animal. The dog, he asserted, had been twice sentenced to be shot for worrying other dogs. However, Colour Sergeant Edwards denied that the dog had been sentenced to be shot. The dog, he claimed, was a most inoffensive animal. Mr Drury, presiding, was most impressed with Billie's medals and said he was the most distinguished dog in the country. He found that there was clear evidence that gross and unnecessary violence had been used, and he fined the defendant £1 with £1 costs. [171]

The only blip in Billie's distinguished career was in 1911, when he was 'in the doghouse,' or in disgrace, having bitten a boy; a fact that is noted on an old Player Wills cigarette card.[172] He was later to serve in Ireland throughout the First World War (with the 3rd battalion), passing away in Ireland in 1915, of nothing more sinister than old age and rheumatism. So well loved was this old dog that his body was preserved after his death in 1915. Today he takes pride of place, exhibited at the Royal Ulster Rifles Museum in Belfast, in a glass-case which was made for the Regiment in Armagh in the 1930s.

Royal Berkshire Regiment, 1st. Bn. Richmond Barracks 1905.

Officers of 1st Bn., Royal Berkshire Regiment beside the garrison church Richmond Barracks, Dublin in 1905, showing, in the rear row from left to right, Lieutenant A.J. Fraser, Captain A.S. Turner, Lieutenant and Quartermaster Mr. J.H. Redstone, Lieutenant B.G. Bromhead, Lieutenant H.M.L. Hunter, Captain W.R.E. Annersley and Captain E.H. Blunt; in the middle row are Captain A.G. Macdonald, Captain F.J. Gossett, Major A.J.W. Dowell, Lieutenant Colonel W.K. McClintock, Major H.E. Taylor, Captain W.R.P.K. Betty and Captain J.G.R. Walsh. In the front row are 2nd Lieutenant A.H. Perrott, 2nd Lieutenant E.A.B. Orr and Lieutenant G.W. Hopton.

A Time of Transition

The Formation of Police and Cavalry Depots

Following the end of the Boer War there began a period of relative inactivity at Richmond Barracks and at Head Quarters in Britain. This was shown clearly from 1903-1909, when regiments were stationed here for longer periods— from 2 to 4 years, instead of the usual twelve months. Also, regiments spent as much time in training at the Curragh as they did in barracks. The Royal Berkshire 1st bn. (Sepember 1904) and the 56th Royal Essex Regt 2nd bn. (April 1907), joining the Royal Irish Fusiliers 4th bn., present since October 1904, were the only troops here in a 5 year period and the last infantry regiments before the barracks would undergo a significant change of personnel.

The Prince of Wales in Dublin

The Prince of Wales, who was the future King George V, and grandfather of the present Queen Elizabeth II, visited Dublin in February 1905. He was Colonel in Chief of two regiments which he inspected in the course of his stay. At 11 o' clock on the morning of 3rd February, he drove in an open topped carriage from the castle to the Richmond Barracks, the quarters of the 4th. Battalion of the Royal Fusiliers. All along the line of route through Christ Church-place, Cornmarket, Thomas Street, James's Street, and from there to Kilmainham, small knots of people gathered and respectfully saluted the Prince as he drove by attended by an escort of Inniskilling Dragoons and members of the mounted force of the Dublin Metropolitan Police. The battalion of Fusiliers was drawn up 500 strong on the square of Richmond Barracks in command of Lieutenant Colonel R.J. Pinney. The Prince was received by General Lord Grenfell, commanding the forces in Ireland, Field Marshal Lord Roberts, Major General Sir G. De C Morton, Major General Vetch, and members of Headquarters staff, and the wives and families of Officers and men watched the ceremony from the side of the square. The general public were not admitted. The inspection was brief. After a short stay in the Officers' mess the Prince walked to the saluting base, where the troops were drawn in a line and saluted his Royal Highness. Then he passed down the ranks from right to left and made a critical inspection of the men and their accoutrements. He expressed satisfaction at the turnout and praised the efficiency of the men, as they marched past. After the parade was dismissed, His Royal Highness visited some of the barracks and regimental institutions, and at 12.20 o clock, drove to the Royal Barracks by way of the Royal Hospital, Kilmainham. [173]

The Fire at Mountshannon Mills

In January 1906, a 'destructive' fire occurred at the Mount Shannon Mills owned by the Irish Peat Industry Company. Fires were always described as such in those days, as if to suggest that a fire could be in any way creative. However, the description was particularly apt in this case. The premises were for many years previously a floor mills owned by J. A. & F Journeaux, but at this time held in storage about 30 tons of peat litter in bales, which provided fuel for the blaze. At ten minutes past six o'clock that morning, information was received at Chatham Street fire station that the buildings were on fire. Captain Purcell of the Dublin Fire Brigade and a number of his men, with a steam engine, two hose carriages, and a section of the brigade from Winetavern Street, arrived promptly on the scene. The premises, which were situated almost at the rear of Richmond Barracks were six storeys high, with frontage of 40 feet on the Grand Canal, and extended backwards about 100 feet. The sentries on duty from the 1st Battalion of the Royal Berkshire Regiment were the first to make the discovery. The alarm was sounded by the bugler, and with 'commendable promptitude' the troops, under the command of Captain Gossett, Captain Redstone, and officers, manned two manual engines. Despite the rainfall, most of the men appeared coatless on the scene, and worked hard to prevent the spread of the fire to adjoining buildings, the property of the company, which included a factory, stores, and workmen's cottages.

When Captain Purcell arrived he found that the military were working energetically to save the minor buildings and stores as there was no possibility of saving the main building. The Dublin Fire Brigade laid down two lines of hose, and with the steam engine obtained a water supply from the canal. The flames from the main building lit up the sky, and the glow could be observed for miles around. The roof of the building soon collapsed, and carried the machinery from one floor on to those beneath, causing masses of flame and myriads of sparks, resembling 'a pyrotechnic display,' to ascend. Owing to the intense heat the machinery and ironwork were twisted into the most fantastic shapes. The factory was completely gutted; the loss of the machinery was the most serious concern in the calamity. The fire was not got under until half past eight o'clock, and it was two o'clock in the afternoon before the Brigade were enabled to leave. Owing to the early arrival of the men of the Royal Berkshire Regiment on the scene much property was saved. The origin of the fire was unknown. The damage to the machinery was estimated at about £3000. It was

216

said that this was partly or wholly covered by insurance.[174] The buildings were restored and later acquired by Thomas Parsons and Sons, Ltd., a branch of an old English manufacturer of varnish, enamel and colour.

The Coming of the Royal Irish Constabulary

For almost a hundred years Richmond Barracks was used exclusively as an infantry barracks, but in September, 1907 a change in personnel was evinced with the arrival of the Royal Irish Constabulary. The men who were led by County Inspector, W. de. R. Shoveller, Barrack Master and Assistant Storekeeper, Head Constable Horan took charge of a wing at the Barracks, where the 1st Berkshire Regiment was stationed. The congested state of the Phoenix Park Depot rendered this sub-depot necessary, as their numbers, including reserve and recruits in training, exceeded 600. The new premises and squad rooms at Richmond Barracks accommodated upwards of 400 recruits. Several instructors were added to the drill staff to meet the emergency.[175]

The combined presence of the military and police did not dissuade a certain private of the Berkshire Regiment, who was under arrest on a charge of desertion, from attempting an escape. He was confined in the guardroom at the front of the Barracks where he was awaiting court-martial. When an opportunity fortuitously arose, he dashed past the guard, eluded the sentry at the barrack gate, and ran towards Kilmainham. The guard immediately pursued, but he outstripped them, and seemed likely to get away until one of the pursuers, who was mounted on a bicycle, overtook him. With some difficulty (after running for half a mile along the Inchicore road) the fugitive was again taken in charge, marched back to barracks and placed in the guardroom.[176]

In February 1908, the police staff and recruits were inspected by Colonel Sir Neville Chamberlain, KCB, Inspector-General (a former British soldier and inventor of the game of Snooker) accompanied by Assistant-Inspector-general, W. Reeves and District inspector J.E. St. George. Private Secretary. The force present on parade, numbering 400 men, was under the command of District Inspector J. M. Poer O'Shee, Assistant Commandant who received the Inspector-General on arrival with a Grand Salute. The inspector then closely inspected the ranks, which were drawn up in line, after which they marched past in columns and quarter columns and went through various evolutions. The Sub-Depot officers were examined in their knowledge of Company Drill, after which the recruits were dismissed. Subsequently, the inspecting officer visited the School and Gymnasium, etc., and expressed himself highly pleased with the whole days' proceedings. The RIC band from the

Depot, Phoenix Park, under the command of Sergeant T. Kinsley was present. The following were the Sub-Depot officers present: District inspector G.D. Rodwell, I.M.; C.C. Robinson-Glasgow, G.A. Morant and R.F.R. Cruise.[177]

At a session in the House of Commons on 6th April 1908, Mr. Longsdale asked the Chief Secretary to the Lord-Lieutenant of Ireland whether the auxiliary training depot for the Royal Irish Constabulary at Richmond Barracks was to be discontinued; and, if so whether he would state the reasons for this step and the nature of the arrangements to be made for the accommodation of the recruits in training. Mr. Cherry replied that the loan of quarters at Richmond Barracks was obtained in order to provide for the training of constabulary recruits specially enrolled for the purpose of augmenting the force in proclaimed counties, and as such training had been completed the quarters would shortly be given up to the military authorities. There was, he said, sufficient accommodation at the constabulary depot for the training of recruits ordinarily enrolled. [178]

R.I.C. Sub. Depot, Richmond Barracks 1908.

In September of that year two hundred recruits were drafted from the sub-depot to R.I.C. Depot for their final course of training in police duties and drill. Owing to the

218

unusual demand for accommodation at the Depot of so many men at one time it was a difficult matter to provide for their personal comforts. Mr. Heard, instructor of Musketry, who was acting Commandant, superintended all detail and in a marvellously short time saw all arrangements completed, and none too soon as the last man was of the detachment was scarcely under cover when the rain came down in torrents. Recruiting continued until the following year, when in February 1909, the sub-depot was abolished. The R.I.C were said to be glad as they were not at home in the 'gloomy old military barracks.' Remaining at the barracks were the 56th Royal Essex Regiment, 2nd Battalion, who had arrived in April 1907 replacing the 1st Royal Berkshire Regiment.

56th Royal Essex Regiment, 2nd Battalion at Richmond Barracks 1910.

Assault on a Boy

While the Essex Regiment was stationed at Richmond Barracks a Private soldier brought embarrassment on his fellow soldiers when he threw a boy into the Grand Canal at Golden-Bridge, landing himself in 'hot water.' Private Ezra Thomas Brown, a native of Essex, was charged with the attempted murder of ten year old James O' Reilly. A witness in the case, Michael Farrell, of 2 Golden-Bridge deposed that on the evening of 29th July 1909, at Cemetery Lane, Golden-Bridge, near the canal bank, he heard a soldier asking James O'Reilly, *'Do you know how to swim?'*

and the boy said he did not. The soldier then caught O'Reilly by the leg and arm, and threw him into the canal. The soldier then laughed and went off towards the back gate of the barracks. There was another soldier with him, who did not do anything to the boy. O'Reilly scrambled out and went home with his mother who arrived on the scene. Patrick O' Reilly, brother of James O'Reilly stated that when he went to see what had happened to his brother he met the accused and other soldiers. As he was endeavouring to pass them to look for a policeman the soldier made a blow at him. Witness drew back, and the blow missed him. The soldier followed him along the bank in a fighting attitude. Witness, with his clenched fist, struck him between the eyes and knocked him over. The soldier got his arm round witness's neck, and they both fell. They struggled for about ten minutes. Then the soldier wanted to shake hands with him, and have no more about it. Witness went away, and the soldier went into the barracks.

Inspector Ennis read a statement, which the prisoner subsequently made, in which he said, *'I saw a boy playing in the water in the canal. I touched him for a joke, when he fell in. I pulled him out and he then went home and told his mother that he was thrown in. There was no other soldier with me, he had gone away.'*

The injured party, James O'Reilly then gave evidence. He said that two soldiers came up, and that the prisoner asked him whether he could swim, and when he replied that he could not, the prisoner threw him into the water. His back struck the bottom, and on reaching the surface again he grasped some weeds and pulled himself to the bank. The prisoner and two other soldiers were standing by laughing, and did not attempt to save him.

It was suggested at this stage by Mr. Tobias for the defendant, that the only charge could be one of aggravated assault. The prisoner denied the charge and was returned to the City Commission on bail of £100. At the Commission hearing on August 1st, the details were again related of how the boy's elder brother came onto the scene, and how in an encounter that followed the soldier did not at all come off victorious (laughter in court). Evidence as to the exemplary nature of the accused was given by the officer in charge of the battalion. It was claimed that the accused was simply playing with the boy on the bank, and the latter fell into the water. Mr. Justice Dodd said the assault was one of wanton character. The jury found Private Browne guilty of a common assault, and suggested that he should pay compensation to the boy. He was bound to the peace for two years and ordered to give compensation to the extent of £5 to the little boy.

The 56th Essex Regiment moved to the Curragh in September 1909 and although officially listed as being based at Richmond Barracks remained there until the arrival of the 1st battalion Rifle Brigade to replace them at the Barracks in January 1910

Private Fred Peters

1st Battalion Rifle Brigade
The Letters of Rifleman Peters

Rifleman Peters has left us a fascinating insight into the lives and times of the 1st battalion while they were in Dublin. Frederick George Peters, born in Folkestone, was the son of Robert and Sarah Peters. The family are shown on the 1901 Census as living at 20 Hillside Road, Dover (Parish of Buckland St. Andrew). His father's occupation was that of a Railway Locomotive Driver. Frederick enlisted in Dover in 1910 and would have been posted to the 1st Battalion depot at Colchester. In February 1911 he was drafted to Richmond Barracks where the battalion was already stationed. Fred, as he was known, wrote over 50 letters to his parents, a few of which were from Dublin. They are difficult to read. This first one is dated 10th February:

'Dear mother and father I got your letter safely. I am over in Ireland now. We got

here at 8 o'clock this morning. We had a good journey but could not sleep much. We started from Winchester at 6 o'clock and reached Waterloo at 7:30. Then we were driven in buses to Euston Station, we went through the Shand, over Waterloo Bridge and past the Hotel Cecil. It looked very pretty passing over the Thames with all the lights shining on the water. We had a good supper at Euston, ham, cheese and pickles, and tarts and mince-pies. We left Euston at 10:05 and got to Holyhead at 3:20, a 230 mile journey. We only stopped once, at Crewe. When we got round the corner of the platform at Holyhead, we saw the boat waiting for us. We started off after all the mails and baggage was stowed away. Most of us sat up in seats on deck, and all except me and another one were seasick. It was very rough and cold going across, the boat kept dipping down in the water and rising up again, with the propellers out of the water. It was as bad as the mountain railway. One boy had his khaki hat blow overboard, so he had to put on his best one. We were over four hours on the water.

We got to Dublin at a quarter to eight this morning. We got ashore and walked a mile [sic] along by the River Liffey past dozens of breweries and distilleries. That is the chief work in Dublin. We got on a tramcar at Sackville Street, the widest street in the world. Then we had a four mile ride to the barracks for 2d. Directly we got here, we had breakfast. Then we were separated and sent off to different companies. Another chap is with me. We have done nothing all day except unpack and get our fresh equipment and bedding out. We have been fitted out with our busbies. The barracks here are alright, but not so good as the Winchester ones. They are old ones. I shall be able to tell you more about the place when I get used to it. I think this is all I can say at present. If you write again before I do, my address is Rifleman Peters G Company Richmond Barracks Dublin.

    Goodbye all from
    Fred, 1st battalion, G Company.'

Fred soon acquainted himself with Dublin and its many attractions. He was also doing well in his training:

'*March 1911*
I am glad to tell you I was passed off the square yesterday, and dismissed drills. So I am not a recruit now, but a duty-man and only do about two parades a week. I shall be able to get a permanent pass now which allows you to stay out any night you like after 9:30 till midnight. We start company training next week so we shall be route-marching, scouting, tent pitching, trench digging, and goodness knows what. I did two guards last week, one at the quarters, and the other at the Vice-regal Lodge. I was on sentry go for two hours each turn with four hours off, or eight hours on out of twenty-four. We have to learn map-reading, or how to find our way about by a

map. It is nothing to do with the first class certificate. I have not started school again yet, but I think I shall before long. I was the only one in our squad of 24 that had a 2nd class certificate. I shall be firing my course very soon. I shall finish the gyms in two weeks time. We are learning bayonet fighting now, and when I have learnt that I shall be finished everything.

We get very good grub here, extras every morning, such as Quaker oats, sausage and mashed, or liver and onions. We only have to pay 3d a week extra. We get two plates every dinner time, always pudding of some sort to finish up, and butter and jam for tea. We can always save something for supper. I have been too busy to have my photo taken yet, but I will send you them before long. I haven't had any money to spare, as I have bought a new razor and a strop, and some more kit. I hope you get the box of shamrock alright, it is real Irish, from the Wicklow Mountains. I don't think I can find any more to say now, so goodbye all.'

1st BATTALION.

PARADING IN RICHMOND BARRACKS, DUBLIN, 12 JULY, 1911, WITH THE COLONEL-IN-CHIEF, F.M. H.R.H. THE DUKE OF CONNAUGHT, AT ITS HEAD.

223

In July 1911, the King George V and Queen Mary of England came on a royal visit to Ireland. As the 1st battalion would be part of a review scheduled for the Phoenix Park they were inspected by the Duke of Connaught in the square of Richmond barracks. Fred Peters was among those reviewed and mentioned it in the next letter to his parents.

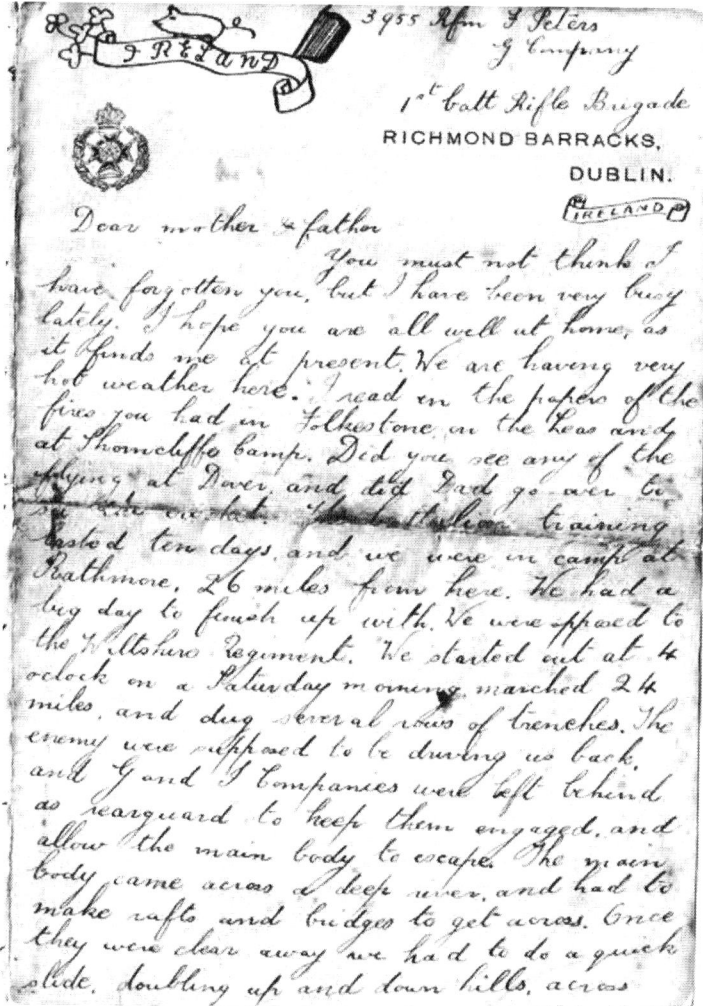

'The battalion training lasted ten days and we were in camp at Rathmore, 26 miles from here. We had a big day to finish up with. We were opposed to the Wiltshire Regiment. We started out at 4 o'clock on Saturday morning, marched 24 miles and dug several rows of trenches. The enemy were supposed to be driving us back, and G and I Companies were left behind as rearguard to keep them engaged and allow the main body to escape. The main body came across a deep River and had to make rafts and bridges to get across. Once they were clear away we had to do a quick slide, doubling up and down hills, across ditches, and through hedges and gorse, turning round now and again to fire at the enemy and keep them at a distance. We reached camp again at 11 o'clock on Sunday morning, after *fighting all the time. It was very warm, especially with a full pack and rifle to lug about.*

In the afternoon, the officers of both regiments gave a tea to the farmers and their tenants whose land we had been over. There were about 500 people came in and I think the bands amused them more than the tea. I don't suppose they hear much music in these parts. The next day we marched back to Dublin and we didn't get much rest for we were up in Phoenix Park rehearsing for the review. We had a holiday on Coronation Day. We had plenty to do while the King was here, and I saw the Royal Family face to face four or five times. The King is a small man, not more than five foot four, but the Queen is a big woman. The Prince of Wales and Princess Mary are very goodlooking, and didn't seem a bit stuck up or proud. They were made a terrible fuss over here, even more than they are in London. I also saw Lord Kitchener, the Duke of Connaught, Lords Aberdeen, Shaftesbury, and Iveagh, Mr. Redmond and Mr. Birrell.

There were 27 battleships at Kingstown when the King landed, and the route to the Castle, nine miles long, was lined by soldiers, sailors and marines. We were placed between the Royal Fusiliers and the Essex Regiment with the 5th Lancers drawn across a side street at the back. The King had an escort of Life Guards with him. The Duke of Connaught is our Colonel-in Chief and he dined along with our officers on the Saturday night. I was one of a guard of honour, 100 strong, which he inspected. On the day of the review he led us from the barracks to the Park, giving us Form Fours, Right Turn etc. The review took place in the centre of the Park a flat place about four times as big as the Dover Athletic Ground.

The salute of 21 guns was given by some naval 12 pounders, and we knew that the Royal Family were leaving the Vice-regal Lodge. We could hear the cheering a half hour before they arrived, and it kept getting louder as they came nearer. At last, after waiting about four hours, we saw the Life Guards coming through the trees, followed by the Royal Family in an open carriage. The order was given, "Royal Salute, Present Arms", the massed bands played the National Anthem, and some sailors unfurled the Royal Standard at the saluting base. There were over 20,000 soldiers and sailors on the ground, and we were the only regiment that didn't wear red, except the cavalry and artillery.

We were drawn up in quarter column, and the King passed along the ranks and inspected us, afterwards returning to the saluting base. The march past lasted an hour and a half. First came the sailors and marines, drawing along their heavy guns. They wore straw hats, white jumpers, and brown leggings. Then came the infantry. Next, the Rifle Brigade, led by the Duke of Connaught, the Wilts, Buffs, Essex, Manchester's, Kings Own Scottish Borderers, Royal Fusiliers, R Welsh Fusiliers with their white goat, Dublin Fusiliers, Munsters, Connaught Rangers, and

225

South Lancs. We differed from the others in that we marched at the trail instead of the slope, and never fixed swords or carried colours, because we have none, being light infantry. Last of all came the Field Artillery, Hussars, Dragoons and Lancers, who charged past the saluting base like lightning. You couldn't see them for dust. We lined up outside the station when the King left for Wales and he inspected us, marching along the lines, followed by the Prince of Wales and the Duke.

We begin field firing this week and finish up at the Curragh, where the Rifle Meeting takes place. I have entered for this and may stand a chance of winning something. This meeting takes the place of a summer furlough and it is a nice little holiday there, better than staying behind here. The sports take place at the end of August and then we shall begin getting ready to shift to Colchester. We are sending a big draft to the 2nd battalion at Calcutta beforehand, but of course I shant go yet.'

This was the last letter sent by rifleman Peters from Richmond Barracks. The next letter detailing his final days in Dublin was sent from Colchester. Some of the information is interesting as he talks about the railway strike that occurred two years before the general strike of 1913. In 1911 William Martin Murphy defeated the unions in the Great Southern and Western Railway, a victory so comprehensive that, while British rail workers took limited solidarity action with Dublin during the lockout, local railway employees remained quiescent.

'Meeanee Barracks
...The training did not last the full fortnight, only 3 days, as on the 12th of Sept. we were all ordered back to Dublin owing to the outbreak of the Irish railway strike, where all the men came out in sympathy with two who fancied they had a grievance over something. The Buffs and Wilts had gone overnight and at 4 am we were aroused, packed up, and left for Dublin at 8 o'clock by the only line running, the Dublin and South Eastern. We were in barracks by 2 o'clock, and immediately 2 companies were sent out on strike duty, while 2 stood by ready to turn out at a minute's notice. All the garrison were confined to barracks. Matters kept getting worse, and to crown it all, the bakers all came out as well, and over half the people were starving. Those who could, lived on potatoes, but hundreds had to go without. It didn't affect us, for the Army Service Corp bake our bread and they also supplied the hospitals. The Rifle Brigade were on guard at Kingsbridge Station and Inchicore Junction & Railway Works, with sentries placed all along the line and in the signal boxes. The Buffs and Wilts were at the other stations and along the quays. G Coy did three days duty at Inchicore Railway Works, where the 4000 employees were locked out. The company allowed us to sleep in carriages, waiting rooms, offices, etc., and supplied us with suppers and fires. We were only on guard to protect the property, and for the sake of precaution, for the strikers were quiet enough, and used to come

in the railway institute and chat with us. It was the hooligans who caused the disturbances, for they thought it a good chance to set about the policemen, whom they hate like poison. Some of the Royal Engineers came over from Aldershot to work the railways and one of the sergeants made a start by driving the mail train from Dublin to Athlone. He wore the blue overalls over his khaki, and carried his rifle and ammunition in the cab. His mates performed the duties of stokers, platelayers, & signalmen, and they managed to keep a good bit of the traffic going between them.

We left Dublin on Oct 3rd. In the morning we cleared up all ready for the West Kents to take over...The boat left at 3 o'clock and as it steamed out of the River Liffey into the open sea, those on the quay were waving hands and handkerchiefs, while our band were upon the upper deck playing Auld Lang Syne. We were on the water an hour and a half before Ireland faded out of sight.'

Rifleman Peters third from the right pictured here cleaning rifles at Rushmoor Camp, Aldershot 1912.

There ends the connection of Frederick Peters with Richmond Barracks. He travelled out to India in December 1912, joining the 2nd Battalion in the January.

227

The Battalion arrived back in England on 22nd October 1914 and made its way by train down to Winchester from where it marched to Hursley Park where the 8th Division was being assembled. It arrived in France on 7th November 1914.

Frederick was killed on 9th May 1915 at Rouges-Bancs, Fromelles during the northern attack of the Battle of Aubers Ridge. According to a soldier friend, death was instantaneous, *'the poor lad he never spoke a word, the bullet passed through his forehead.'* He was twenty-five years old. Fifteen officers and two hundred and forty-seven of his comrades were killed alongside him. At 5.00 a.m. on 10th May, and out of a battalion which had gone into action twenty-four hours earlier with twenty-four officers and something in the region of a thousand men, only two officers and approximately one hundred and ninety-five men marched back to their billets in Sailly. The 2nd Rifle Battalion suffered the highest casualties for any unit involved that day - from either the northern or southern attack. Only two of the officers and fourteen of the men have known graves, the rest being commemorated on the Ploegsteert Memorial to the Missing.

The Cavalry Depot

It was while the Rifle Brigade was here that another great change would take place, with the formation of a Cavalry depot. Previous to this, cavalry recruits began their training as soon as they had enlisted, with their regiments, which were organised in four squadrons, one of which was a reserve squadron, consisting principally of the band and men on staff duties. In 1910 the regiments were reorganised into three service squadrons and from then on recruits were trained for three months at the depot before being posted to them. Six cavalry depots were established, each one catering for four regiments. Richmond Barracks was designated Cavalry Depot No 2. The depot of the 11th Hussars was moved from Canterbury to Dublin, and was combined with the depots of the 4th, 8th, and 13th Hussars. Two of the four regiments were serving abroad, and so recruits were sent from the depot only to the two regiments stationed at home, who supplied their linked regiments overseas with trained men. The 5th Lancers were also in depot here. The 11th were destined to remain until the First World War. Even after the war and the 1916 Rising some cavalry recruits (the 13th and 4th Hussars) were still to be found here, and up until 1921 (15th and 8th Hussars).[179]

Incidents of suicide at Richmond Barracks were sadly all too frequent and too numerous to record; also, it was often impossible to understand what had driven an individual to take such a drastic action. In one case, however, we know exactly why and because of that I have included the following.

On the 2nd January 1911, the city coroner held an inquest on the body of Private H. Gardner, aged 21 years of the 11th Hussars, who was found hanging in a bathroom of the barracks and was dead when taken down. Sergeant Ethridge, in evidence, stated that he had missed the man from roll call on the previous night and again on the morning in question, but thought it nothing unusual. Gardner was not known to be depressed, and had sung at a concert on Christmas Eve. Private Hemsworth deposed that he found the deceased man hanging in the bathroom. He was suspended by a lanyard worn by soldiers of his regiment. He obtained assistance, and the man was cut down, but he appeared to be dead already, the body being cold. A Sergeant of the D.M.P., deposed to having found a letter in the pocket of the deceased man's tunic. It read as follows:

'Spon Lane. West Bromwich
Staffordshire, Dec 30th 1910

My Dear Harry,
I dare say you will think I am a long time in answering your letter but I did not want to spoil your Christmas, or else you ought to have had this for Christmas morning. I did not think I should have had to tell you such sad news to tell you about the Hill Top people, but I am very sorry to have to tell you so sad news that poor Florrie has passed away on December 23rd and was buried on the 30th. She will never but no more trouble to you (sic); her suffering must have been terrible, as I did not know her myself. I was more than glad you were away from home on such a job as this, or else I think you would have fared very bad with some of the people, as I heard some rather strong talk about you in the cemetery. Her mother and father are very much cut up about her, as you must; that your father and me sent a wreath and cross and they put mine in the centre of the coffin, just where yours ought to have been. They made a very decent burial of her, but you must know what a time they have had to go about collecting, if I had not given them the £2 you left. I think they are looking for you to pay the funeral expenses, but if you will say whether you intend to or not let me know by return, then I shall know what to do. You will be surprised to know that the child is alive- a lovely little thing, I would have it myself, but they say they will not part with it for no money. Mind you, do not get a furlough yet awhile 'til it's all died away. Your father is sending you a new purse, as yours is very shabby. I think I have told you all this time. Am pleased to know you are keeping steady. With best love from all at home,
              From your loving Father and Mother.'

The coroner said he had very little doubt that the letter which had been read had unhinged the young fellow's mind. The jury returned a verdict of suicide during temporary insanity.

A Hussar Wedding

On a happier note, a double wedding of the 11th Hussars was recorded at St James's Church on the 15th April 1912. One couple was identified as Maria Margaret Farrelly and Harry Jones, 11th Hussars, Richmond Barracks where they lived after the marriage. A remarkable photograph of the event was taken in a meadow behind the bride's parents' house at Old Kilmainham.

Double Wedding of 11th Hussars at Old Kilmainham

Thomas W. Mitchell

INCHICORE DUBLIN.

The 5th Lancers

Architect's drawings from 1912

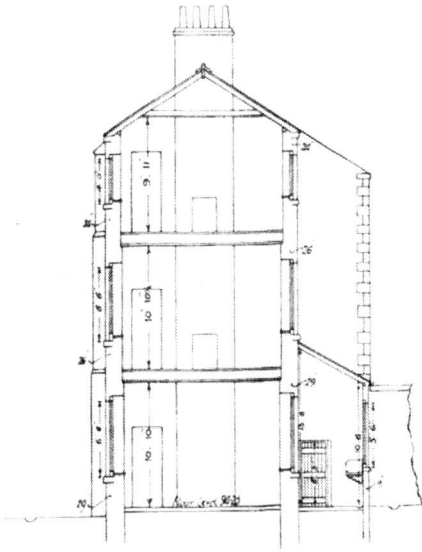

- Section U.V. -
- Hospital -

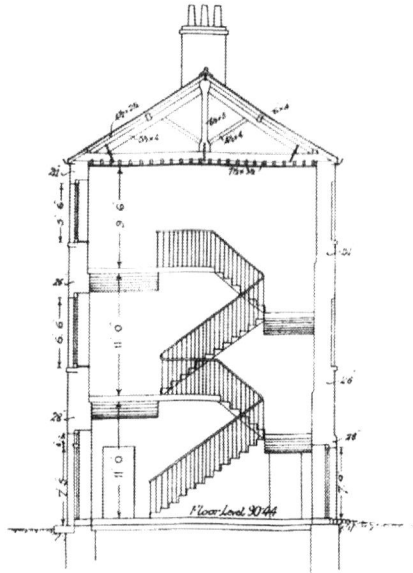

- Section Y.Z -
- Officers Block South -

Sergeants Mess.

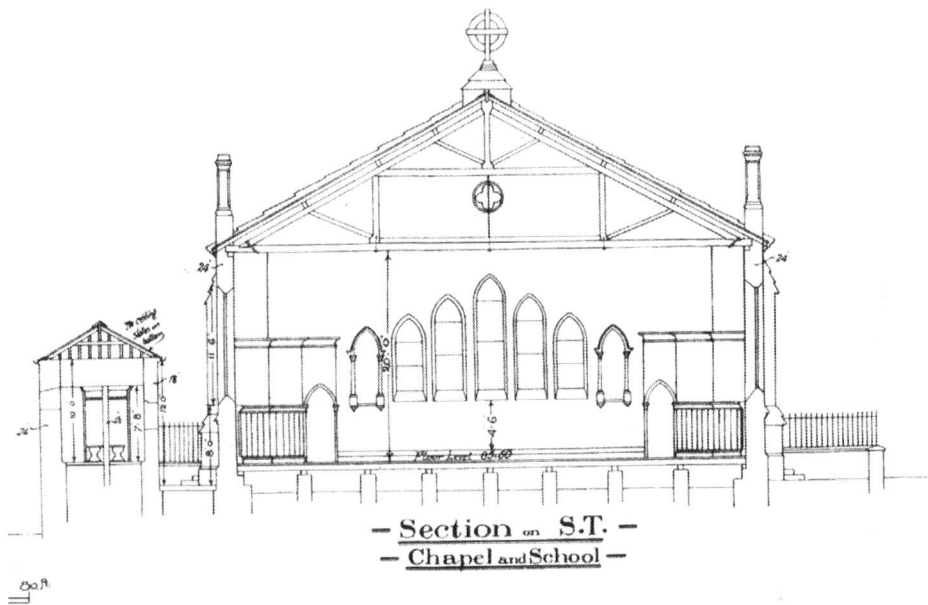

Section on S.T.
Chapel and School

The Garrison Chapel.

233

Emmet Hall today.

The West Kent Regiment at the training field near the officers' block.

1913 - 1915
The Dublin Lockout

The Royal West Kent Regiment spent three years at Richmond Barracks, from 1911-1914. During that time their fortunes were mixed; two suicides in the space of 11 months and some light relief with their success over Bohemians in the Leinster League in March 1913. While celebrating the latter, little did they know of what fate had in store for them. Soon, they would be in France embroiled in the business of the First World War; but first, they would have to deal with an unpleasant situation on their own doorstep. Having built up good community relations they were called upon to assist in policing matters, with inevitable consequences to their reputation.

The village of Inchicore featured strongly in the Dublin strike, owing to the presence of a prominent trade union quarters at Emmet Hall, Emmet Road, and the D.U.T.C. depot at Spa Road. The Emmet Hall premises were first purchased in 1912 by Jim Larkin, founder of the I.T.G.W.U. He appointed William P. Partridge as manager of the hall in 1913. Sligo born Partridge, was reared in Ballaghadereen, County Roscommon. He was the son of an English Protestant father and an Irish Catholic mother. Having been elected to Dublin City Council in 1904 he fought for better housing and health facilities for the working people. He was successful in getting workers' houses built near the Oblate Church in Inchicore in an area commonly referred to as 'The Bungalow.' He was also treasurer of the Inchicore branch of Conradh na Gaeilge. Partridge sought to have Council meetings held in the evenings so that working people could play a bigger part in local government. While serving his time as a city councillor, Partridge was still employed at Inchicore Works. However, the railway company objected to Partridge's absences from work to attend City Hall and he was forced to resign his seat on Dublin Corporation in 1906. He continued to work for the G.S. & W.R. at Inchicore until 1912. In that year he publicly attacked the policy of religious discrimination and nepotism which openly operated at the Works. He was ordered by the Railway Company to retract his accusations. When he refused to withdraw them he was dismissed after thirteen years service with the Company. In response Partridge wrote a pamphlet entitled *My Crime* in which he reiterated his accusations of sectarianism and nepotism against the company. He attacked the way in which men with less experience and lower qualifications were promoted over their Catholic fellow workers and also the disparity between Irish workers' wages and those of workers imported from Britain. When Larkin appointed Partridge- his most loyal and faithful lieutenant- to Emmet Hall in 1913, the latter organised I.T.G.W.U. meetings and activities in the Hall and he travelled extensively around Ireland organising the activities of the union.[180] This great, though often overlooked, local hero would distinguish himself even further in the few remaining years of his life.

William Martin Murphy was a founding shareholder of the Dublin United Tramways Company. He was also owner of Clerys department store and the Imperial Hotel. Murphy controlled the Irish Independent, Evening Herald and Irish Catholic newspapers. Worried that the trade unions would destroy his Dublin tram system, he led Dublin employers against the trade unions led by James Larkin. On 19th July 1913, he told his workers that if they continued to be members of the union they would be fired. When he was ignored, he wrote on 21st August a letter to just under two hundred workers in the parcels office of the Tramway Company:

'As the directors understand that you are a member of the Irish Transport Union, whose methods are disorganising the trade and business of the city, they do not further require your services. The parcels traffic will be temporarily suspended. If you are not a member of the Union when traffic is resumed your application for re-employment will be favourably considered.'

So then even those who were not in the Union were sacked. Five days later a strike began. It was the first day of the Dublin Horse Show on August 26th, a very busy time in Dublin. That morning at ten o'clock nearly seven hundred of the tram drivers took out their union badges and pinned them onto their jackets. Then they left the trams including the bemused passengers where they stood and walked off the job. The Union wanted the reinstatement of all parcels staff and the same hours and wages for the Dublin workers that those in Belfast received. Two days later James Larkin, William O' Brien, P.T. Daly, William Partridge and Thomas Lawlor were arrested, charged with libel and conspiracy, and then released on bail. When Larkin organised a meeting for 31st August a proclamation was issued banning the rally. Larkin publicly burnt this proclamation. The following day, Partridge was re-arrested along with Connolly, but Larkin went into hiding at Surrey House, the home of Countess Mickiewicz. A warrant was issued for his arrest.

Riots ensued in Ringsend, Beresford Place, and Eden Quay, during which the police baton-charged the crowds and injured many protestors. A labourer called James Nolan was one of the first casualties of the Lockout. The brutal force used by the police was condemned by many. Nolan, who was not involved in the conflict, was struck by a policeman when leaving a pub at the scene of the riot.

Thousands of locked-out workers turned up for the meeting in Sackville Street the following day. At the Imperial Hotel a room was booked in the name of Reverend Donnelly and his niece. The hotel is now part of Clerys in O'Connell Street. Larkin was heavily disguised in a long black robe and beard when he appeared on the balcony, but he only spoke a few words before the police grabbed him and he was arrested. Fighting broke out between the crowds and the police. Forty five police and four hundred and thirty three men women and children were injured. The force escorting Mr. Larkin to the College Street police station was repeatedly attacked and in the evening, after the labour leader had been removed to the Bridewell, the station itself was assailed by a furious crowd, which was only dispersed after repeated charges had been made by the police who were guarding it.

Meanwhile, at Inchicore there was another significant episode. Thirty four of the forty three tramway men at the D.U.T.C depot had joined the strike, the largest number in any part of the city. They now had the premises blockaded, with the support of a large crowd of local people. At between 5 and 6 o'clock on Sunday evening a crowd of about 150 persons assembled at Spa Road and were hissing and booing at the driver and conductor of one of the cars. One of the men in the crowd, Michael Costello, assuming a leader's role was warned to go away, but refused to do so, and called upon the crowd to wreck the car. He was then arrested by Sergeant Kincaid who, with two constables, was on duty at the terminus of the tramway. The man resisted arrest, but was secured with the assistance of the constables, and was then taken in the direction of the Kilmainham Police Station. However this meant having to pass the Emmet Hall and as fortune would have it, a large crowd was also collected outside these premises. As the three policemen with their prisoner approached the Emmet Hall a crowd of people came out of the Hall and, with the people already in the street, came towards and confronted them. They demanded the release of the prisoner. The crowd then commenced to throw stones, and bricks, and other missiles. The sergeant ordered his two men to draw their batons, and keeping the prisoner between them, with the sergeant behind them, they tried to get their prisoner past the crowd. The crowd closed in on them; the prisoner was rescued, and the police got separated. Sergeant Kincaid was surrounded, knocked down, kicked, and left unconscious on the ground. He was brought into a neighbouring house by a woman and her family, and only regained consciousness after two hours. He was one month in hospital. His two constables fled: one, Constable Cawley found refuge in Richmond Barracks, and the other, though badly beaten, managed to escape the mob by running through a house. With no reinforcements available, Mr. Harrel, the Assistant Commissioner of the D.M.P. contacted General Capper who agreed to turn out the West Kent Regiment. [181]

A little later at about 6.30 Councillor Carroll addressed a crowd of about 400 from a window of Emmet Hall. Mr. Carroll made some references to the police, and he said to the crowd that the women and children should go away, and that the men would look after themselves, and also that the police who had arrested a man that evening were now sorry. At this point most of the women and children departed leaving a gathering of about 300. While the meeting was going on two trams came along and were held up. There were police escorting the trams and they appeared to have had a rough time. Nearly all the glass of the trams was broken; in fact, the trams had been under siege the whole of the route from College green. Some of the policemen had had to abandon the cars at Thomas Street to take refuge in the Parochial House. The crowd became determinedly hostile and did not make any attempt to clear the way, and the police drew their batons. Stones were thrown from all directions and struck the tram. Many of the crowd, allegedly from the country, were armed with sticks, and stones were coming freely from all directions, some of them from the windows of the Emmet Hall. In these circumstances, a number of police entered the Hall and cleared it out, resulting in a lot of terrified people there having to come rushing out by the back.[182] It later emerged that the police had badly beaten Partridge and Carroll. At the same time the detachment of the West Kent Regiment, who had been sent to the assistance of the police escorted the tram cars to the Depot, and the police were able to disperse the crowd. The police aided by the military now raided homes in Emmet Road and its side streets, repeating on a smaller scale the havoc wrought on Corporation Buildings earlier in the day when many atrocities were enacted. Among the casualties was another Labour councillor for Inchicore, Thomas O'Hanlon. It was after midnight before peace was restored to the city. The Tramway depot at Inchicore was shut down on 1st September ending activity in the area.

Michael Costello, the escaped prisoner who had created the scene at Inchicore was not rearrested until 9 days later in Clondalkin. He and two others, Patrick Power and Patrick Stymes were charged with riot and of assaulting Constable Crawley. All three were convicted in January 1914. After the failure of the General Strike, Partridge became a member, along with Larkin, P.T. Daly, Thomas Foran and Sean O'Casey, of the first Provisional Council of the Irish Citizen Army, set up in November 1913 to protect the workers from police brutality. It is said that it was on the suggestion of Councillor Partridge that the I.C.A. Council resolved to hoist the green flag of Ireland over Liberty Hall. When he became National Organiser for the Union he was replaced at Emmet Hall by Irish Citizen Army leader Michael Mallin. The Mallin family moved to rooms above the hall in 1915.

The Mallin family moved into Emmet Hall Inchicore.

The First Deserter of World War One

Following the Strike and its unsatisfactory conclusion many Dubliners were left impoverished and without a job or any realistic prospect of finding new employment. To these people the outbreak of the First World War seemed like providence. Many enlisted for economic reasons. This is why three cheers were raised for Jim Larkin in the trenches before the Second Battle of Ypres. Richmond Barracks once again became a hive of activity preparing men for active service overseas.

Thomas Highgate was born in Shoreham near Sevenoaks, Kent and was the son of a farm labourer at Oxbourne Farm. He was just 17 years and 5 months old when he joined the Royal West Surrey Regiment at London on 1st October 1912. Four months later, on 4 February 1913, he transferred to the 1st Battalion, Royal West Kent Regiment, Richmond Barracks. On arrival there he claimed to have been a seaman before joining the army and that he had been shipwrecked twice; he had a tattoo of a ship on his arm. If true, then he was a very young sailor. Most sources list him as a farm labourer like his father. Highgate was constantly in trouble while at Inchicore. Offences ranged from being unprepared on parade (with a rusty rifle); absent from military tattoo (several times); and one very significant case of desertion. It would appear that in February 1914 he absconded to England and was only found out when he tried to re-enlist at Woolwich three months later. He was charged with absenting himself from the corps and of attempting to fraudulently enlist by wilfully making a false answer on attestation. He signed a full confession and was sentenced to 40 days detention back at Richmond Barracks.

There was concern among the officers and they had him examined by a doctor who reported that his patient was complaining of periodic memory loss and claimed that it originated from a bout of yellow fever contracted on foreign service (presumably with the West Surrey Regiment, who were in East Africa the previous year). The Doctor could not rule this out as a possible explanation for Highgate's behaviour. With this background he was not fit to be sent away. However, when the First World War began he was sent with his regiment to France. It later emerged that on the day after Britain declared war, August 5th, he had written a will on the back of his army pay book naming his 18 year old Irish sweetheart as his beneficiary:

'If I get killed, all I have to come for my services I leave to Miss Mary McNulty, 3, Leinster Street, Phibsborough, Dublin.' [183]

Highgate's regiment took part in the Battle of Mons, Belgium in which 8,000 men died, and the subsequent retreat to Tournan, 20 miles east of Paris, a 200 mile slog in merciless heat. They were forced to march as hard as they could because they were never out of reach of German fire. The retreat lasted from August 24th to September 5th. On the morning of September 6th, a gamekeeper found Thomas Highgate hiding in a barn on Baron Edward Rothschild's estate at Tournan, dressed in civilian clothes and his army uniform concealed nearby. To Highgate's misfortune, the gamekeeper was an Englishman and ex soldier. He handed Highgate over to the Gendarmes, who in turn gave him over to the British Military Authorities. Private Highgate was tried that same day by Field General Court Martial on a charge of desertion. He was unassisted in his defence although entitled to have an officer speak on his behalf. It was claimed by General Sir Horace Smith-Dorrien, who authorised the trial, that because of the proximity of the enemy, it was impossible to allow adequate time to prepare a case and that he would have to defend himself. His defence was weak. He claimed that he had left the bivouac that morning with his regiment. They had halted on the side of the road and he had become detached from them when he went to relieve himself. He went into a barn to rest. However, he could not account for why he was found wearing civilian clothes. Damning evidence was provided by the gamekeeper who alleged that Highgate had told him *'I want to get out of it and this is how I am doing it.'* [184] He was sentenced to be shot at dawn. His alleged offence, trial and confirmation of death sentence all took place on the 6th September 1914.

Highgate's execution was almost as hasty and Commander-in-Chief Sir John French gave orders that the execution be carried out 'At once, and as publicly as possible.' Highgate was informed of his fate at 6.22am on 8th September in the presence of a Church of England clergyman. An officer then ordered a burial party and a firing squad to prepare, and Highgate was shot, aged 19, at 7.07am in front of men from the First Battalion Dorset Regiment and First Battalion Cheshire Regiment. News of his fate was also distributed to the remainder of the British Expeditionary Force via Army Routine Orders, as a lesson to all. Thomas Highgate became the first solder of the First World War to be shot for desertion. Another 305 executions would follow including that of 26 Irishmen. Mary McNulty may never have known the truth of Thomas Highgate's fate as the initial communication to his relatives (with Lord Kitchener's note of sympathy omitted) was that he was killed. His name became taboo in his home village of Shoreham and it is believed his parents left in shame for the relative anonymity of the suburbs. It is a tragic irony that three of their sons later died in action and two other brothers survived the war.

In August 2006, the Ministry of Defense, following a vigorous petition on behalf of the relatives of Private Harry Farr, announced a pardon for all 306 servicemen executed during 1914-1918. The subject of desertion, however, continues to be a contentious issue. Although villagers voted in the year 2000 to have Highgate's name added to the war memorial there and despite the pardon in 2006, the eight-member Parish Council of Shoreham, Kent recently denied him a place on the Roll of Honour.

No. 1006 Private Thomas Highgate has no known grave, but his name features on the La Ferte-sous-Jarre British military memorial to the missing and the encyclopaedic memorial publication, 'Soldiers Died in the Great War' refers to him having 'Died of Wounds.'

Private Thomas Highgate

241

Major Matthew Perceval Buckle

In contrast to Thomas Highgate, who is today sadly remembered mostly for what was deemed an act of cowardice, another soldier of the Queen's West Kents, is today commemorated in his native Lincolnshire for his bravery. Major Matthew Perceval Buckle, D.S.O., was born on September 29th, 1869, the son of Vice Admiral C.E. Buckle, of Raithby, Lincolnshire. He passed through Sandhurst, and in 1899 joined a battalion of the Royal West Kent Regiment, of which he afterwards became Adjutant. He fought in South Africa from 1900 to 1902, being severely wounded at Thabanchu. He received the D.S.O. for his services and was twice mentioned in despatches. On his return to England he entered the Staff College and passing out with distinction, was appointed in 1904 to the General Staff, War Office. Subsequently he served as Brigade-Major of the 2nd Infantry Brigade at Aldershot, and from 1909 to 1913 as instructor at the Indian Staff College, Quetta.

On 31st May 1914, a son, Peter, Charles, Matthew was born to Major Perceval and his wife Marjorie while he was stationed at Richmond Barracks as second in command of the 1st Battalion. One can imagine his jubilant celebrations, not knowing that he himself would be dead in just five months. In July 1914 he was ordered to Albania to take up a staff appointment at Scutari, but on the outbreak of war these orders were cancelled. Instead he sailed for France with his regiment on the 13th August 1914. Like Highgate, Buckle was present at the Retreat from Mons and the Battles of the Marne and the Aisne. Early on the morning of October 27th, a German patrol, trying to work down a dry ditch leading into the battalion's line was met and repulsed by Major Buckle, the Major himself accounting for six Germans with his revolver.[185] However, later that day he was killed in action while holding the line in command of his battalion near Neuve Chapelle. At this time the Royal West Kents, though greatly outnumbered, inspired by his leadership held their position for eight days without losing a trench.

Major Buckle's son, Peter, born at Richmond Barracks would later join the army and eventually command the 1st Battalion.

****

The Irish Volunteers 'F' Company Inchicore

In 1914, shortly after the Howth gun-running incident of 26th July, a branch of the Irish Volunteers was started in Inchicore. Both Con Colbert and Robert Holland were in command of the Inchicore Sluagh of the Fianna and when Colbert took charge of one section of the Volunteers there, Holland assisted him in the drilling and scouting of the men. That September, 1914 John Redmond made his well known speech at Woodenbridge calling for the Volunteers to join in the War. This was followed by a general mobilisation of the Irish Volunteers of the Inchicore area in the fifteen acres site of the Phoenix Park. Many speakers were in favour of the Redmond proposal, but William Partridge spoke against it, saying that we should at least have our own freedom first before we fought for anyone else. Tom Clarke and Thomas MacDonagh were in attendance and also spoke. Only a fraction, 40-50, out of approximately 800 of the men present joined what afterwards made up 'F' Company of the 4th Battalion of the Irish Volunteers. Robert Holland commented:

> The Inchicore area was very much a garrison district and in addition a large number of the instructors were ex- British Army men. This explains the high percentage of men who remained on the Redmondite side. After that our numbers got smaller as everything tended to favour the Redmondites who had the use of the Courthouse at Kilmainham as their headquarters and being pro-British had much greater facilities than those who went over to the Irish Volunteers. Another enticement to these men was that they were offered half pay from their employers, principally the Great Southern Railway and Guinness's, and were promised their jobs as well if they joined the British Army. In this way the Irish Volunteer were only a skeleton of their original number... 'F' Company trained at the back of the Workman's Club, Inchicore (of which, Peadar Doyle was secretary) and did its indoor training in Emmet Hall Inchicore. [186]

Only a high wall separated the Emmet Hall building from the Barracks enclosure. The hall was used as a training centre by the Irish Volunteers and by the I.C.A. The Citizen Army needed to build up a supply of arms and had secured the help of a sympathetic Irishman who was a member of the British army. By this contact they were able to increase their stores of up-to-date rifles. These could only be kept in the hall for a very short period as the premises were liable to be raided at any time. A tight schedule of delivery and collection of the weapons was in operation. On one occasion in the winter of 1915, it fell to the lot of Frank Robbins of the Citizen Army to be detailed to visit Inchicore at 9 pm. His instructions were to get there sharp on time. His journey to Inchicore was accomplished on a bicycle. On his way up Lord Edward Street, just at Christ Church Cathedral, a member of the D.M.P stepped out and held him up because he had no light. His bicycle was not in perfect condition, the chain was defective, and he had no alternative but to halt. He was questioned by the D.M.P man, who asked for his name and address and was given a fictitious one. During all the questioning Robbins was in a state of panic having to be at the collection place on time. This could allow of very little further delay. He tried to impress on the police officer that he was on a very important mission of mercy, seeking a doctor for his mother who was very ill. The D.M.P man became suspicious and it seemed that little would have made him decide to take Robbins to the nearest police barracks. His mind was made up that this must not be allowed to happen, and just when it seemed certain that he must use his revolver, the policeman decided to let him pass on, with instruction that he must not ride the bicycle without a light. This instruction was immediately ignored, for he immediately hopped on the bicycle and set off for Inchicore. He arrived there on time, and a Lee Enfield rifle was quickly strapped to his bicycle and he set off again to the city. Less than 4 minutes had elapsed from the time he had entered the premises in Inchicore. Other members of the Citizen Army and the Irish Volunteers made similar visits from time to time. [187]

Murder by Bayonet

Incidences of suicide and murder continued to pepper the history of Richmond Barracks. Mental illness, presumably brought about by the strict army code and harrowing experiences on active service, was the root cause in so many of the cases. A particularly grisly affair took place in December 1915. The accused, Patrick Conway, a private in C Company, 3rd Battalion Royal Irish Regiment, was convinced that his own life was under threat from Lance Corporal Michael McEvoy, the man he had killed. He testified as follows:

'He had his eye on me, and said he would shoot me the first chance he would get... when he would not get me in the square he came up to the room to try and get me there."

A witness gave evidence that on the night of December 29th, the deceased was sitting in front of the fire in room No. 4, Richmond Barracks talking with Conway about India. There was no quarrelling. Witness saw deceased suddenly fall forward toward the fire. Witness's bayonet was sticking in McEvoy's back, and a rifle to which it was attached was in Conway's hands. Deceased said nothing, and died in about half an hour. Witness brought a guard and arrested Conway, who had some drink taken. The accused was at that time confined in the guardroom. When he was arrested the accused said,

'He deserved it, I would do the same with any non-com in the army. I would do the same with the Commander of the Forces. I don't care if I had the rope round me. That is the way with me, if you get a bad non-com.'

The prisoner was then removed to Kilmainham Police Station. On the 4th February 1916 Patrick Conway tried and was found guilty, but declared insane and ordered to be sent to an asylum.

Lance Corporal Francis Ledwidge

Francis Ledwidge

On the 3rd February 1914 the Meath poet and protégé of Lord Dunsany wrote to a friend to say that he had recently been hospitalised with neurasthenia (manifest in a general nervous disposition): *'I am not quite right and can't stop long in any place.'* This may have been brought about by the abrupt ending of his relationship with local girl, Ellie Vaughey. However, he soon found plenty in World events to distract him from personal woes. It is astonishing that someone who suffered with his nerves should have forsaken the comforts of 'sleepy Slane' for the pandemonium of the battlefield. Ledwidge was a Home Ruler and a founding member of the Slane branch of the Irish Volunteers. The Volunteers were formed in 1913 to enforce Home Rule, if necessary in opposition to the Ulster Volunteer Force.

When war broke out in Europe in August 1914, John Redmond and the Irish Volunteers were faced with a difficult challenge. The widespread view was that the war would only last a few months and the Ulster Volunteer Force had volunteered en masse to enlist in the army while Home Rule was put on the back burner. Redmond in turn offered the services of the Volunteers to prevent the Ulstermen gaining any political advantage, and in so doing split the Volunteer movement. It was, of course, an uneven split with 175,000 of the Volunteers siding with Redmond as against 13,500 who did not. The 5th Royal Inniskilling Fusiliers arrived at Richmond Barracks in September 1914 and began the recruitment of men for service.

At a number of meetings in Meath to discuss the Redmond Proposal Ledwidge was keen to make a point of principle that the decision to enlist should be for those who believed in the cause and not have anything to do with Home Rule. He still believed that the latter could only come after a violent confrontation with the Ulster Volunteers. This was evident in two statements he gave: *'Home Rule is as far off now as ever,'* and *'Ireland will need her Volunteers when the war is over.'*

At the meetings at the Navan Board of Guardians he was branded a Sinn Feiner, a coward, and even a pro-German. A week later the same board, composed largely of members who were themselves too old or unfit to be considered for active service, offered their congratulations to him, in his absence, on learning of his decision to enlist. We are fortunate to have, in his own hand, his reason for joining the army. However, this is often taken out of context. His biographer, Alice Curtayne, quite cleverly and skillfully used a lengthy autobiographical letter as a framework for her *Life of the Poet.* In doing so she broke up the letter in segments of his life upon which to build. When dealing with his decision to join the army she quoted him as saying:

'Some of the people who know me least imagine that I joined the army because I knew men were struggling for higher ideals and great emprises, and I could not sit idle to watch them make for me a more beautiful world. They are mistaken.

I joined the British Army because she stood between Ireland and an enemy common to our civilization, and I would not have her say that she defended us while we did nothing at home but pass resolutions.'

This unfortunately has led most commentators to assume that this was some sort of Press release given in 1914, and some have even tried to suggest that he later regretted saying it, having had 'a change of heart.' The original quote however, comes from the aforementioned letter written from the trenches on 6th June 1917, less than two months before his death, and should therefore be regarded as his final and considered words on the subject; one which he knew would be quoted far and wide.

On the 24th October 1914, Francis Ledwidge cycled to Dublin, where he enlisted in the Royal Inniskillings. From there he wrote to his schoolteacher friend, Paddy Healy:

'I was waiting a few days to see how I would like a soldier's life before writing to you. I am having a royal fine time. I only parade one hour per day, the other six I spend in the quartermaster's store as clerk, for which I receive extra pay and mess with clerks, in a place specially allotted to them. For breakfast we get tea, bread, butter, fish sometimes, or steak, always something; for dinner beef, vegetables, and afterwards rice; for tea, again and usually pineapple. You can see I am not so badly off after all. I see Lord Dunsany every day, and in the evenings we meet in his quarters and discuss poetry, the thing that matters. Dunsany saw to it that I was not sent to Tralee, as he brought forward the fact of my being an Irish Volunteer and therefore had a certain amount of training. At the recreation rooms on Saturday I am giving a reading from some of my embryo books.'

Ledwidge's appearance at Richmond Barracks would have created a bit of a stir. He was something of a celebrity owing to news reports of his discovery by Lord Dunsany, his introduction to the National Literary Society and his much anticipated first poetry collection. Captain (Lord) Dunsany, himself a writer of great renown, was already at these barracks and was less than pleased when Frank tuned up: he was concerned that some would accuse him of influencing the young man; further, that he might be blamed if anything should befall him. Frank's brother, Joseph later did his best to exonerate his Lordship, saying that the decision to join the army was entirely his own.

Captain Edward Dunsany

Frank soon earned a Lance-Corporal's stripe and was assigned clerical duties in the orderly rooms of the officers' quarters (this ironically was the same block later used for the courts martial of the leaders of the 1916 Easter Rising). Having access to a typewriter, his leisure time was spent typing new poems. Army notepaper was in short supply; however he also had use of the YMCA hut which was available as a reading and writing centre for all troops and where free stationery was handed out. Here, he wrote in his own hand, on YMCA headed notepaper, a series of love letters to his new girlfriend, Elizabeth Healy.

Y·M·C·A·
With H.M Forces
on Active Service

FOR GOD — AND — FOR COUNTRY
FOR KING

Patron of National Council of Y.M.C.A.'s:
HIS MAJESTY THE KING
Patron Military Camp Department
H.R.H. THE DUKE OF CONNAUGHT.

Reply to "D" Co. 5th Batt. Inniskillings
Stationed at Richmond Berks.
Dublin

Feb 16th 1915

My dear Lizzie :—
I suppose you think I have
been to France and got shot since you didn't
recieve the letter I promised you. I am not
looking for an excuse when I say I have been
very busy. I apoligize for the photograph I send you.
It is rugged but has sweet memories. I will
send you a good one when I find a photographer
who is capable of the task.
I often wonder if I will ever be home again
for altogether, and I often wonder if you ever
think of me in the peace of Wilkinstown.
Do you?
When you have a minute to spare drop
me a few lines as I watch and watch

for something from the old place every day. I hope the little lad is very well. I saw Jerry on duty yesterday - We were sending the Lord Lieutenant away and Jerry was just opposite me. I winked at him and he winked back and I made a gesture which he must have understood. I was thinking of Fleming's Gramophone and the "little grey home in the West."

Best love.

Frank

The Y.M.C.A Hut, Richmond Barracks.

250

Frank wrote many poems in Dublin for the entertainment of the soldiers. One of these was 'Billy the Bulldog,' set to the tune of the *Ballad of John Moore*. This was outrageous! Here was an Irishman in a British regiment 'sending up' one of their most revered heroes. A lot of the lads at the Richmond Barracks were Irish and you may be sure they howled with laughter on recognising the air. The subject of the poem was a pet of (A) company, the 5th (S) Battalion, Royal Inniskilling Fusiliers, rather than a mascot, and is not to be confused with the famous Billie the Bull-terrier-dog of the Royal Irish Rifles, mentioned earlier in this book. The poem tells us of what became of Billy:

The Departure of Billy the Bulldog

Not a bark was heard nor a sigh nor moan
When they put the chain around him,
But quiet he munched a cow's thigh-bone
By the side of the man who found him.
He broke the rules and he had to go,
Let he who may lament him,
The Army orders would have it so
And silently we sent him.
Say, have we loved his twisted face?
Have we loved his sly cold manner?
Say, is there soldier in the place
Would sell him twice for a tanner?
Ask at the cook-house door today
Will they miss his noon day calls there?
Ask of the Transport, what do they say?
There! Nought but sighs and brawls there.
He bit the horses and chased the mules,
So they gave him a court martial
And despite the strictness of the rules
Was the jurisdiction partial.
His transfer papers we made out
Tho' it's many the tear that wet them
And he went away to the feeble shout
Of the few who won't forget him.

Among the letters of writer George Russell (AE) is a record of an interview with the military authorities at Dublin Castle. They asked him if he could suggest people in the literary world who might be used to spread propaganda on the war effort. He proffered the names of Patrick Mac Gill and Francis Ledwidge. There is no evidence that they ever approached Ledwidge, but he did write a couple of poems that would fall into that category. One of these was 'The Call' which dealt with the plight of the Belgians. Another significant poem written by Ledwidge at this time was '*The Call to Ireland,*' in which he echoed Redmond's call to his fellow Irishmen to follow him into the army. It was published in *The Irish Times.*

The Call to Ireland

It's time to be up and be doing,
To be up and be doing now;
For, lo, anywhere around you,
From the vale to the mountains brow,
The grass grows up through the harrow,
And the weather rusts on the plough.
Oh, let us be up and be doing
The work that is calling us now.

We have fought so much for the nation
In the tents we helped to divide;
Shall the cause of our common fathers
On our hearthstones lie denied?
For the price of a field we have wrangled
While the weather rusted the plough,
'Twas yours and 'twas mine, but 'tis ours yet
And it's time to be fencing it now.

There is gall in the cups of our children,
But ours is the goblet of wine.
They are crying away in the future:
Is their cause neither yours nor mine?
Better they die in their mothers
Than our shame be writ on their brow,
If we will not be up and be doing
The work that is calling us now

Unusually, the entire regiment of the 5th Royal Inniskilling Fusiliers gathered at Richmond Barracks in May 1915 and marched to the transport ships which would convey them to Basingstoke en-route to Gallipoli. Ledwidge survived this encounter and two other major military engagements at Serbia and Salonika before being lifted to a hospital in Cairo suffering from inflammation of the gall bladder. From there he was moved to a hospital in Manchester, and it was here that he first heard of the events of the 1916 Easter Rising. He was particularly saddened on learning of the execution of fellow poets Padraig Pearse and Thomas MacDonagh whom he referred to as *'two of my best friends shot by England'* and wrote his famous elegy:

Thomas MacDonagh

He shall not hear the bittern cry
In the wild sky, where he is lain,
Nor voices of the sweeter birds
Above the wailing of the rain.

Nor shall he know when loud March blows
Thro' slanting snows her fanfare shrill,
Blowing to flame the golden cup
Of many an upset daffodil.

But when the Dark Cow leaves the moor,
And pastures poor with greedy weeds,
Perhaps he'll hear her low at morn
Lifting her horn in pleasant meads.

Ledwidge was sent back to Ireland to recover and told to report at Ebrington Barracks in Derry, as the Inniskilling had of course vacated Richmond Barracks. He first visited his home in Slane. He was clearly moved by the executions of the 1916 leaders and in a brief moment of despair, mingled with frustration at the slow progress of the war, told his brother that if the Germans were coming over the back wall he would not stop them, they could come. In the final 12 months of his life he would go on to write a score of poems dedicated to the Rising and the executed Irish patriots. However, in doing so he refused to accept that his role in the British Army was any different to that of the men who had occupied the G.P.O:

'For am I not of those who reared
The banner of old Ireland high,
From Dublin town to Turkey's shores,
And where the Vardar loudly roars?'

In little more than 6 months he was on his way again to the front in France and Belgium. In June 1917, on receiving news of the death of Willie Redmond, he wrote a glowing tribute to him which was published in the *Irish Independent*. His own death came soon after, on the 31st July 1917, when he was killed at Pilchem in Belgium. In what may have been his final and certainly his most frequently quoted letter to American professor, Lewis N Chase, he had made the following statement:

'I am sorry that Party Politics should ever divide our own tents but am not without hope that a new Ireland will arise from her ashes in the ruins of Dublin, like the Phoenix, with one purpose, one aim and one ambition. I tell you this in order that you may know what it is to me to be called a British soldier, while my own country has no place amongst the nations, but the place of Cinderella.'

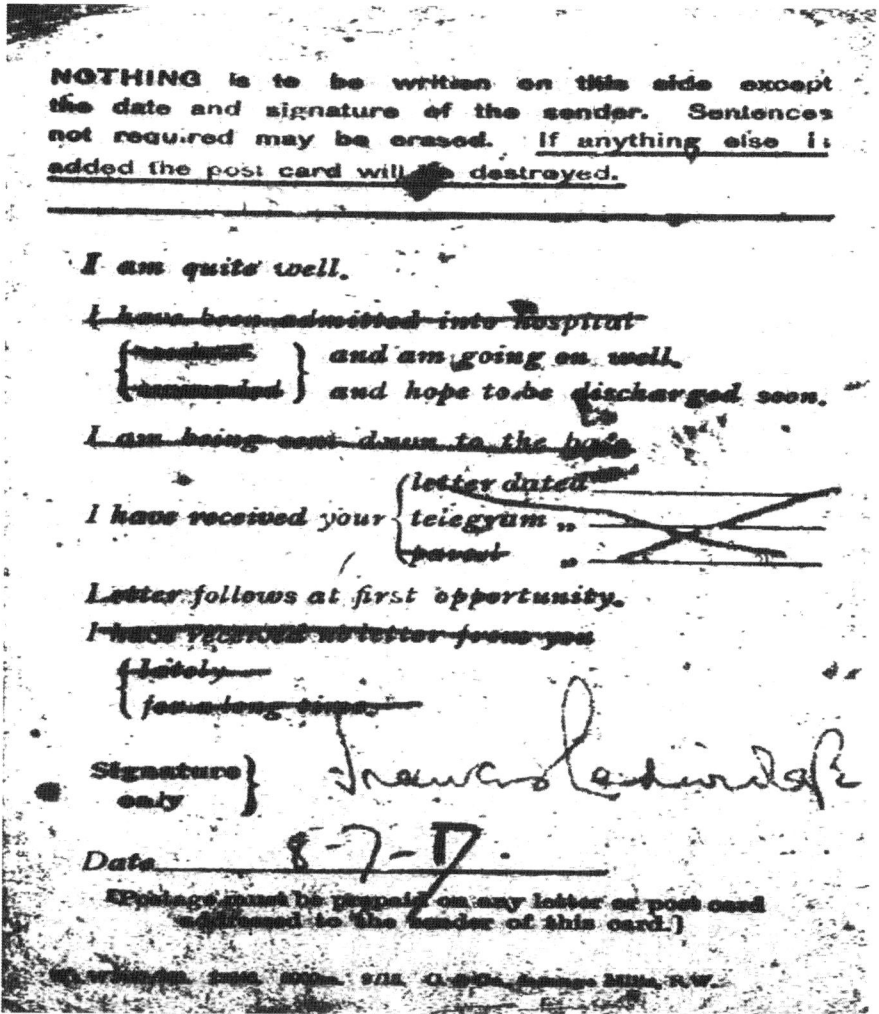

Field Card signed by Francis Ledwidge, 8/7/14 indicating that he was well.

Richmond Barracks, 1915. (Last 3 Images, courtesy of the National Library of Ireland.)

The Assault on Michael Mallin

Shortly after a great mobilization of the Irish Volunteers on 17th March 1916, James O' Shea, of the Irish Citizen Army received orders to go to Emmet Hall to collect rifles which Michael Mallin had arranged to be smuggled out of Richmond Barracks. He and Mallin had sat on many an evening under the wall awaiting "friendlies to hand over the stuff." The hall lay in close proximity to the barracks. O'Shea described how he entered the hall and walked about 30 feet to where there was a small room used for the committees. Immediately to the right was the entrance to a yard and opposite this door at the far side of the yard was the entrance to the kitchen of the Mallin family. At the rear of the yard were a neglected garden and the wall of the barracks. O'Shea waited in the small room for about ten minutes. It was 9 pm and very dark with just a fire lighting. Seamus Mallin, a lad of about 8 or 9 years came in and informed him that his daddy had gone up the path to the garden and that he was to wait. This seemed like good news to O'Shea as it suggested that Mallin was in the process of acquiring the rifles.

As time elapsed however, it was evident that something had gone wrong. O'Shea was reluctant to move from where he was as Mallin's instructions were always exact. He then heard a groan and reached for something for protection. He was fortunate to be able to identify in the firelight Mallin's scabbard and sword. Clutching the sword he ran out to the yard and saw two dark objects making for the wall. He gave chase, but tripped over something on the ground. It was Michael Mallin and he was in a bad way: he was unconscious, having being hit on the head with a bar. When he was able, Mallin told him that it was a machine-gun he was after, but that he had been the victim of an official attack worked from high command in barracks. O'Shea was in no doubt that the attack was intended 'as a way of putting him (Mallin) out for good.' Shortly before the attack, Mallin, a former British soldier himself had been approached by the military and asked to rejoin. He had refused. O'Shea was in no doubt that the assault was carried out as a consequence of that decision.[188]

Michael Mallin

257

STANDING. Wm. PEARSE. T. MᶜDONAGH. SEAN HEUSTON. M. MALLIN. SEAN MᶜDEIRMAD. M. OHANRAHAN. CAPT. DALY CORNELIS COLBERT
SITTING. P.H. PEARSE. MAJOR MᶜBRIDE. TOM CLARKE. EAMON CEANNT. JAMES CONNOLLY. JOSEPH PLUNKETT

The 1916 Easter Rising

At precisely five minutes past nine on the morning of Easter Monday, 24th March 1916, Irish Volunteer Captain Con Colbert knocked on the door of 159 Emmet Road, Inchicore, which ironically was situated directly opposite Richmond Barracks. The occupant of the house, fellow Volunteer, Peadar Doyle was reading the *Daily Independent* when he heard the knock and the voice enquiring for him. He immediately dressed and bade what at the time he thought was a last farewell to his wife and family. He walked along past Golden-Bridge on the Grand Canal and continued until he came to Emerald Square, Dolphin's Barn, where the 4th Battalion of the Irish Volunteers had arranged to assemble under the leadership of Eamonn Ceannt. Doyle found that he was the first to arrive and had to wait around, 'dressed in a semi-military uniform, fully armed with 500 rounds of ammunition, etc.,' and the only person in sight was a policeman on duty!

Shortly after ten-thirty a.m., he was detailed to take up a position in the convent area of the South Dublin Union. On entering the convent one of the nuns who opened the door asked if they had come to read the gas meters. He politely replied: *'No, sister, but we are in a hurry.'* [189]

Apart from Ceannt, other notable Volunteers posted at the South Dublin Union included, Cathal Brugha and William T. Cosgrave. As the men were filing in and taking their stations at various parts of the Union, the strains of the military band at Richmond Barracks were carried on the air. This caused Brugha to remark:

'They don't know we're here yet.' But then the music died in the middle of a phrase. *'They know now,'* Ceannt muttered.

****

On Easter Monday the fighting strength of the Royal Irish Regiment battalion at Richmond Barracks under Lieut. Colonel R.L. Owens, stood at 18 officers and 385 men. Shortly after noon a message was received from the Adjutant of the Dublin Garrison ordering all available troops to proceed to Dublin Castle which had come under attack by a unit of the Irish Citizen Army commanded by Captain Sean Connolly. The picket, commanded by Major Holmes, moved from the barracks by the most direct route to the castle. On marching down to the end of Emmet Road they encountered an outpost of Eamonn Ceannt's force under Section-Commander John Joyce in Mount Brown.

The entrance to the South Dublin Union

From the crossroads at Kilmainham the group of Irish Volunteers could be clearly seen leaning over a wall at McCaffrey's Estate. Major Holmes advance guard consisting of one sergeant and five soldiers, who were 150 yards ahead of the column, were allowed to pass by the Volunteers unscathed and continue towards the city. Lieutenant Malone was then ordered to proceed with a party of 20 men on the same route as the advance guard. This party was fired on by the Irish Volunteers and three were wounded in the first volley. The soldiers sought cover in a tan-yard opposite, but as they broke open a door one soldier went down and in attempting to assist him Lieutenant Malone was himself hit. The British then took up positions and in the return fire one Volunteer was mortally wounded while two others were injured. The remainder of the picket was soon joined by the main body of troops from the barracks commanded by Lieutenant Colonel R. L. Owens. A company was also sent to The Royal Hospital Kilmainham, then the residence of the commander-in-chief of the British armed forces in Ireland. From there the military took up firing positions in the windows overlooking McCaffrey's Estate. A Lewis machine-gun was set up on the roof to provide enfilading fire. Meanwhile, Lieutenant Owens ordered an attack on the western and southern flanks of the Union via Brookfield Road, Patriotic Terrace to the

Rialto Gate and the Grand Canal. Two experienced officers, Captain Warmington and Lieutenant Alan Ramsey assisted Major Milner in this encounter. Cover here was provided by soldiers occupying the Rialto buildings and the upper floors of other houses in the area as well as on the road outside the Rialto gate.

After a lull in the action, the Lewis gun shattered the silence as it opened fire on the volunteers at McCaffrey's Estate. Quickly realising their vulnerable position the men there retreated into the open fields ducking to avoid being hit as the bullets hit the ground in front of them. Volunteer Richard O' Reilly was killed in the attempt to reach safety. At the Rialto gate and the canal the Volunteers also came under fire. Patients within the hospital had to cower for cover and one member of staff was slightly injured. Volunteer, John Traynor, was mortally wounded. He was 17 years old. A party led by Lieut. Alan Ramsey then broke open a small door next to the Rialto gate, but he was immediately shot. He staggered a little way and dropped dead in front of the chapel. The Volunteers allowed a brief ceasefire to enable a stretcher party to remove the body of the fallen officer. Ramsey was from a well known family living at 'The Nurseries,' Ballsbridge. He had been stationed intermittently at Richmond Barracks since August 1914 and at 26 years of age was already a war veteran. He was the first Dublin born British officer to die in the Rebellion.

Another wave of attack led by Captain Warmington charged the door but Warmington, too, was killed. A second truce was allowed so that he could be laid alongside his fellow officer. When news of Ramsey's death reached the rest of Ceannt's men it was hailed as a minor victory, however the Volunteers at the canal end were in a hopeless position: the tin hut which they occupied was riddled with bullet-holes and several of the men carried injuries. Eventually the superior numbers and firepower of the British were decisive. Volunteer Captain Irvine was issued with an ultimatum to either surrender or the hut would be blown up. Irvine had no option but to comply and the men at this end of the Union were taken under armed guard to Kilmainham police station and from there to Richmond Barracks.[190]

The fight for the South Dublin Union however, was far from over; it would continue for the whole of Easter week The Volunteers were ensconced in various other buildings within the Union and often were able to retreat from one location to another. The British found themselves in a labyrinth of buildings, not knowing from where the next shot might come. Reinforcements from the Marrowbone Lane area were cut off by the Volunteers holding Jameson's distillery; in particular, Robert (Bob) Holland, the unsung hero of the Rebellion who, from his rooftop tower, inflicted heavy casualties on the British soldiers. Holland, from Silverdale Terrace Inchicore, had just turned 19, but was already a good marksman. He was using one of the Howth rifles:

'It was a bad weapon for street fighting. Flame about three feet long came out through the top of the barrel when it was fired, and a shower of soot and smoke came back in one's face. After three shots were fired from it, it would have to be thrown away to let it cool and the concussion of it was so severe it drove me back along the floor several feet.' - Robert Holland.

Con Colbert's outpost of the South Dublin Union garrison at Marrowbone Lane.

An unexpected break in the fighting occurred on Tuesday when the Royal Irish Regiment was reluctantly withdrawn from within the complex and moved to Kingsbridge and other areas. Wednesday was uneventful at the Union and by Thursday morning the Volunteers were able to wash and shave and even stretch their legs in the small garden behind the rear of the Nurses' home. A semblance of normality could be observed, with civilians venturing outdoors to resume their daily routines. The Hospital staff took advantage of the situation to move patients to the Rialto end of the complex for their own safety.

Meanwhile a convoy of supplies and ammunition led by a battalion of the Sherwood Forester Regiment was proceeding from Ballsbridge to the Royal Hospital. An advance guard had crossed the Rialto bridge unscathed the previous day, however as the main body of soldiers neared the bridge on Thursday they came under sniper fire. Although they had some veterans among the officers, the rank and file were young and inexperienced men. As the firing intensified, the Foresters, depleted in number and suffering the effects of Wednesday's gruelling encounter at Mount Street Bridge, were in great distress. Relief came from Portobello Barracks: fifty or so, men of the Royal Irish Rifles and others mustered under the able command of Major (Sir Francis) Fletcher Vane of the Royal Munster Fusiliers. They were soon joined by Lieutenant Monk Gibbon who had arrived from Kingsbridge with a number of men. The military had abandoned the South Dublin Union to concentrate on events in the city, but now they realised that no progress could be made until the root source of the sniper fire was dealt with. They would either have to take the Union or at least distract the Volunteers until the transport had passed over the bridge.

The Nurses' Home, the scene of a lot of the fighting.

A fierce encounter followed in the region of the Nurses' home. The Volunteers put up a strong defence, but eventually were pushed back availing of openings they had created through adjoining buildings. This process continued until the fight was concentrated at the Boardroom near the front of the institution. They fortified this building as best they could with official ledgers and other large books being piled through the windows as part of the defences. Apart from bullet perforation in the windows and some loose tiles on the roof, the frontage at James's street was not badly damaged. The presence of patients and staff within the Union deterred the British from using heavy artillery which meant that much of the fighting was at close quarters. Dublin born, Major Fletcher Vane who was a very fair-minded man later described the fighting in a letter to his wife:

'Well I have been in some fights but never in such an odd one as this, for we commenced by open fight in fields and so far as right flank was concerned fought up to literally three feet of the enemy. But everything was bizarre on that day for we advanced through a convent where the nuns were all praying and expecting to be shot, poor creatures, then through the wards of imbeciles who were all shrieking — and through one of poor old people. To get from one door to another was a gymnastic feat because you had to run the gauntlet of the snipers.' [191]

Patrick Pearse

The battle at the South Dublin Union was eventually brought to a close by events elsewhere. The principal position occupied by the Volunteers was the General Post Office on Sackville (now O'Connell) Street. This was designated as the headquarters of the Provisional Government and five of its members were among the garrison there: Pearse, Connolly, Clarke, MacDiarmada and Plunkett, all signatories to the Proclamation. By Friday evening 28th April, owing to the constant bombardment, the G.PO. was on fire, at which point it was decided to evacuate the garrison. Sean McLoughlin led the Volunteers across to Moore Street where they occupied a number of houses. McLoughlin initially proposed that they fight their way via Henry Street and Capel Street to link up with Commandant Daly's 1st Battalion in the Four Courts area. However, on learning that Daly was in difficulty and also of the slaughter on the streets, they agreed on a surrender in order to avoid further casualties among the citizens of Dublin. At 2.30pm, Saturday 29th April, Patrick Pearse accompanied by Cumman na mBan nurse Elizabeth O'Farrell arranged a meeting with Brigadier General W. H. M Lowe, the British G.O.C., at the corner of Moore Street. Pearse gave a handwritten note to Lowe confirming the unconditional surrender and was then driven to Irish Command Headquarters at Parkgate Street. General Sir John Grenfell Maxwell was there to receive him. Maxwell had arrived from London the previous day having received orders from the British Minister for War, Lord Kitchener to quell the Rising and pacify Ireland operating under martial law. Pearse was relieved of his personal possessions and told to type out copies of his written surrender statement for conveyance to the other Volunteer positions. He was then taken to Arbour Hill detention barracks where fellow Irish leader Sean Houston was also confined. Meanwhile the garrison, formerly of the G.P.O., were taken from the Moore street location to the gardens outside the Rotunda Maternity Hospital, where they were joined by the garrison from the Four Courts. They spent a cold night huddled together and surrounded by British soldiers with fixed bayonets. Here the old Fenian, Tom Clarke and his brother-in law, Ned Daly were stripped naked and publicly degraded by Captain Lee Wilson, in charge. The next morning at 9am they were marched to Richmond Barracks. Sean MacDiarmada, who was disabled, suffered greatly during this journey as the British soldiers had deprived him of his walking stick.

The battalion of the Royal Irish Regiment from Richmond Barracks that was removed from The South Dublin Union had been involved in the action at the northern end of O'Connell Street. On the morning of 27th April, a party commanded by Major John. D. Morrogh had taken up rooftop positions on the east side of O'Connell Street and had opened fire on the General Post Office. Other units were involved in holding positions in the Moore Street area to prevent a breakout from the rear of the building. One of Morrogh's sharpshooters wounded James Connolly in the arm as he supervised a barricade in Prince's Street. He was subsequently wounded more severely by shrapnel while observing Sean McLoughlin lead a party of Volunteers in the Independent Offices in Abbey Street. The R.I.R Regimental History also records that: 'On the morning of the 28th April, a party under Major Morrogh and Company Sergeant Major Banks, succeeded in capturing the republican flag.'

Irish Rebellion_May 1916.
A group of Officers with the captured rebel flag.

A well known photograph was taken at the Parnell monument showing Morrogh and his fellow soldiers holding the Irish flag. This man had some sense of the value of a good photograph, as a short anecdote from his past will reveal:

John Morrogh was from a well-to-do Cork family whose wealth derived from a woollen mills and a share in De Beers diamonds. In 1912 he witnessed the *R.M.S Titanic* leaving Queenstown, whereupon he hastily set up a tripod and took a photograph as the ship was nearing Red Bay, Crosshaven. The photograph was published in the *Castleknock Chronicle*, a yearbook for Castleknock College, on the west side of Dublin. It did not appear anywhere else and only came to light in 2001. It is today considered to be the last known photograph of the *Titanic*. Morrogh enlisted in the 18th Royal Irish Regiment and was wounded, together with Alan Livingstone Ramsey, in Flanders in the First World War. Both men were returned home to the reserves at Richmond Barracks. Eight of his brothers also joined the British army. John Morrogh and his family fearing for their safety left Ireland for Uruguay during 'The Troubles' and never returned.

In the immediate aftermath of the Easter Rising the 3rd Battalion R.I.R. was involved in guard duties at Richmond Barracks.

By 3p.m. on 30th April 707 prisoners had been taken into custody. In the course of the day this figure rose to 1,000 as Pearse's order was relayed to the various positions in the City. The men at the South Dublin Union were determined to fight to the death; they had held their positions for the whole week and only surrendered on receiving the directive from headquarters. On Sunday 30th April, Commandant Thomas MacDonagh, accompanied by Fr. Aloysius and Fr. Albert were admitted to the South Dublin Union where they informed Ceannt of the situation. There was still ample opportunity for any of the men to evade capture if they so wished, but they chose to stay together. The order was complied with and that day the men assembled in the square of the Union under Lieutenant Cosgrave. A British Officer having arrived to take charge was surprised at the small number of just forty-one Volunteers: *'You had a fine position here,'* he said.

Ceannt replied: *'Yes, and we made full use of it. Not only did we hold your army for six days but shook it to its foundation.'*

The fighting had resulted in seven British Army fatalities including Captain Livingstone Ramsey and fellow Dubliner, Lieutenant Warmington and seven wounded among the 3rd Battalion, Royal Irish Regiment. Major Fletcher Vane later wrote: *'I am sorry for our poor fellows who were killed. They fought splendidly. So did the enemy.* [192]

The Irish Volunteers had lost William Francis (Frank) Burke, who was killed while in command of a section that had gone to intercept British Troops attempting to leave Richmond Barracks. In addition the Irish had lost: Brendan Donelan, William McDowell, Richard O' Reilly, John Owens, James Quinn and John Traynor. Most notable among the injured was Vice-Commandant Cathal Brugha, having sustained twenty-five wounds from a hand grenade blast and a number of bullet wounds; it was assumed that Brugha would not recover, but he lived to fight another day in another great conflict. In addition, there were some civilians killed, including, Nurse Margaret Keogh (accidentally shot inside the Union while discharging her duties), and two young children at Dolphin's Barn.

The prisoners were then marched to Marrowbone Lane with the distinctive figure of Eamonn Ceannt leading the way. Jameson's Distillery in Marrowbone Lane was one of three outposts of the South Dublin Union, the others being Roe's Distillery and Watkins' Brewery. Soon into the battle, it became clear that only the position at Jameson's Distillery had any strategic significance. Captain Con Colbert and Captain McCarthy had moved their men to Marrowbone Lane to reinforce Captain Seamus Murphy's men. The men and women there had been well provided for thanks to Rose McNamara, Vice Commandant of the Cumann na Mban contingent. A local farmer was said to be not too pleased at the disappearance of some of his stock, as Ms. McNamara's accounts later revealed:

'Wednesday April 26th: 19 chickens captured from messenger boy. Quiet day; we cooked the chickens for dinner, having to take them out of the pots with bayonets, not having any fork or utensil for cooking. Dinner was very successful.'

Thursday 27th: Three live calves captured; one was killed by a Volunteer who was a butcher (Bob Holland) for dinner on Friday (God forgive us).

Friday 28th: Up early for breakfast; we fried veal cutlets and gave the men a good feed. We had a meat dinner, potatoes, etc., 9 chickens commandeered.'

The men at Marrowbone Lane were equally dismayed at having to end the fight. Colbert could hardly speak and reacted to the news with tears running down his cheeks. He managed to calm the men and assembled them in a dignified fashion ready for departure. Rose McNamara presented herself and 21 other women to the British. They marched down four deep in uniform along with the men. An attempt was made to get them to sign a statement recanting their stand, but this failed. Miss McNamara went to the British OC and explained they were part of the rebel contingent and were surrendering with the rest. Recalling these events, McNamara said:

"The men gave each of us their small arms to do as we liked with, thinking we were going to go home, but we were not going to leave the men we were with all the week

to their fate; we decided to go along with them and be with them to the end, whatever our fate might be.[193]

Both garrisons comprising the 4th Battalion were then marched to St Patrick's Park near the Cathedral, where they were joined by the 2nd Battalion from Jacobs biscuit Factory, including Thomas MacDonagh and Major John Mac Bride. Once the weapons had been loaded onto army lorries the men were all marched under British military escort to Richmond Barracks. At Kilmainham they were jeered as they passed Murray's Lane. F. Company, which comprised mainly men from the Inchicore area, heard all their names called out by the bystanders. They were subjected to the most disgusting comments from the 'separation women,' wives of British soldiers who were paid separation money. Local Volunteer, Peadar Doyle was a prime target. The female prisoners also, suffered great humiliation. On a more humorous note, Holland remembered two drunks near the Coombe Hospital who insisted on falling in with the men and, despite being ejected several times, eventually joined in at the rear. About two months later he saw the two in Knutsford Prison taking their daily exercise. The excessive zeal of the British military authorities eventually resulted in the arrest of some 3240 men and 79 women almost all of whom eventually passed through Richmond Barracks; it is estimated that approximately 1600 persons were actively involved in the Rising.

It was to these barracks that the prisoners from all of the Volunteers positions were taken. Those from the city positions had to run the gauntlet of a longer route then those of the 4th Battalion. Frank Robbins of the Irish Citizen Army who was posted at the College of Surgeons recalled the journey proceeding from Dublin Castle by Ship Street Gate, to Christ Church Place and then by High Street, Thomas Street and James's Street, finally to Inchicore.

'At the head of the column were Commandant Michael Mallin and Madame Markievicz...Throughout this journey we were left in no doubt as to the opinion of the vast majority of the citizens of Dublin....The cheering and waving of hats and Union Jacks for the Staffordshire Regiment, particularly at Inchicore as they marched us into Richmond Barracks; the cries of encouragement to the young Englishmen in that regiment; the shouts of "Good old Staffords" "Shoot the traitors," and "Bayonet the bastards." seem now almost incredible. - Were the British army to have withdrawn at that moment there would have been no need for court martials or prisons, as the mob would have relieved them of such necessities.'[194]

Sinn Fein Rebellion 1916.
D.B.C. Sackville Street, Dublin.

Devastation caused by the British shelling of Dublin

The prisoners were brought to Richmond Barracks.

As Robbins said, Countess Markievicz and Michael Mallin arrived at the head of their company, which also included William Partridge. The Countess would later recall how Partridge had saved the life of her friend Margaret Skinnider, the only woman casualty in the ranks. Skinnider had enlisted as a private in the ICA. She wore a uniform and carried a rifle. She and Partridge were of a party ordered to set fire to a shop behind Russell's Hotel. The English opened fire on them from the ground floor of a house just opposite and she was badly wounded. Partridge carried her away under fire and back to the College. [195]

Markievicz was not destined to stay long at Richmond Barracks; she was spotted talking to some of her fellow female prisoners and the commanding officer immediately had her removed to Kilmainham Jail. The last garrison to surrender was the one at Boland's Mills where Commandant Eamon de Valera was in charge. There had been little engagement at this location although the men were involved in the Mount Street Bridge assault on the Sherwood Foresters resulting in the greatest number of casualties inflicted on British forces in the entire week... After surrendering at Boland's Mills, 117 volunteers were herded into horse boxes at the Ballsbridge Show Grounds; de Valera himself was treated as an officer and placed under guard in the weights and measures office of Pembroke Town Hall. They were detained at the R.D.S for the whole of the next day and were not marched to Richmond Barracks until Tuesday, 2nd May.

On arrival at Richmond Barracks the prisoners from all Irish garrisons came under close scrutiny by the British troops and the G- men of the Dublin Metropolitan Police who immediately began to sort out those whom they considered should be subjected to courts martial and those who should be deported or released. Having been the first to arrive, the men from the GPO and the Four Courts were dealt with first. It was a hot summer's day and they were fatigued, hungry and thirsty, with many needing to relieve themselves; for some it all too much. Thomas Doyle recalled:

'We stood for about two hours on the square in Richmond Barracks, men continually falling down from exhaustion.' [196]

Among those who collapsed was Joseph Plunkett. They were told to deposit their personal effects such as, watches, money, rosary beads and other possessions into buckets; few ever saw those articles again. Pails of water were also provided for the prisoners, but as no drinking vessels were supplied it was necessary to put one's head into the bucket in order to drink. The British military then began processing the prisoners through an archway where they were subjected to a thorough search. Those found in possession of incriminating documents or photographs were sent to join the leading suspects in the gymnasium.

Prisoners in a barrack room and below, visiting relatives being searched.

Relatives and friends bringing food and news to the prisoners.

At that time the rectangular hall bore a number of characteristics that have since disappeared. It had a glass-sided octagonal turret topped by a conical roof, a tall chimney to the front elevation and two roof lights. There was an upstairs gallery (which remains) behind a wood and glass partition just inside the entrance. The latter was made good use of by the G-men to scrutinise the prisoners, who were led in singly and told to stand on the right hand side of the gymnasium. Inspector Love, Johnny Barton and Detective Hoey were chief among the many investigators who picked out the men as they passed among them: Barton with an ashplant walking stick and Hoey with an umbrella, *'You, and you and you.'* [197]

Those selected by the detectives were put sitting down in the left hand corner at the far end. Those not for courts martial were that same evening escorted via Emmet Road to the North Wall for deportation to prison camps in Britain. The others spent Sunday night in the Gymnasium and the next day were divided into groups and kept in various rooms within the barracks. Piaras Beaslai, who was Vice-Commandant of the First Battalion, wrote:

The gymnasium with the glass octagon boarded up- this is from a later date.

'On Sunday morning the prisoners were brought to Richmond Barracks. They were placed sitting on the floor of the Gymnasium and the political detectives of the "G" division of the Dublin Police came like a flock of carrion crows to pick out "suspects" as victims for court martial. I was one of the first picked out, and for the rest of the day could watch the detectives passing to and fro among the prisoners studying their faces for victims for the firing squad. Anybody who had seen that sight may be pardoned if he felt little compunction at the subsequent shooting of those same "G" men. Michael Collins, seated in a prominent position, was unknown to the "G" men, and passed by a hundred times without special notice. They little thought that this young man was soon to smash up their espionage system and end it forever. When about a hundred victims had been picked out about 300 more were marched off to the boat for deportation to England. Collins was among them. They were brought under military escort to Stafford Jail, where they were kept prisoners for two months, and then they were removed to an internment camp at Frongoch in North Wales.'[198]

Prisoners being deported to prison camps in Britain

When the others had gone, a few sergeants came into the Gymnasium carrying vessels containing food. The men, some of whom had not eaten for two days formed up in two or three long lines and a sergeant passed along handing each man his portion from the dixie. The ration consisted of a tin of bully beef and some hard army biscuits. Night came and darkness. A soldier on guard stood in the centre of the hall with a lighted lantern at his feet. Huddled in one corner of the Gymnasium lay Joseph Plunkett, Tom Clarke, Sean MacDiarmada, and Willie Pearse; a smuggled cigar was passed surreptitiously among them. Being unable to sleep they discussed in whispers the events of the week. All the others lay stretched on the floor with their heads to the wall. When sleep eventually came it was broken, as the men seemed to be dreaming of recent events in the G.P.O. Sean MacDiarmada called out in the sleep, *'The Fire, The Fire, Get the men out'* and was reassured by Tom Clarke, who said "Quiet Sean we're in the barracks now. We're prisoners now Sean". Likewise Willie Pearse, on a few occasions cried out, *'The Fire, The Fire.'* Soldiers came in quietly every hour or so to relieve the sentry. Whatever about the other rebels, Tom Clarke had no illusions about his fate. Expecting to be shot, even before his trial, he hastily wrote a last goodbye to his wife:

'Dear K., I am in better health and more satisfied than for many a day - all will be well eventually - but this is my good-bye and now you are ever before me to cheer me - God bless you and the boys. Let them be proud to follow the same path - Sean (MacDiarmada) is with me and McG (Sean McGarry), all well - all heroes - I'm full of pride my love.

> *Yours,*
> *Tom'.[199]*

Michael O' Hanrahan under guard at Richmond Barracks

A handful of Volunteers were prisoners at the Barracks since the 24th April. These were the men who surrendered after the first battle at the South Dublin Union and included among them, Gerald Doyle of Cambridge House, Golden-Bridge, a young plasterer by trade. They were initially kept in a large cell attached to the guardroom and later moved to the blacksmith's forge at the far end of the barracks. Locals will remember this building from its later use as a grocery shop in Keogh Square (Finnerty's). The rest of the 4th Battalion, having arrived at 8pm on Sunday 30th April, spent that night packed into rooms, 30-60 men to each room, with no furniture and with little ventilation. A large bucket in a corner served for sanitary use. Breakfast consisted of tea distributed in buckets and a basket containing hard biscuits. The biscuits were spilled out onto the floor and empty bully beef tins were used for tea containers. The next morning they and the other garrisons were examined and dealt with in the same way as the members of the 1st and 2nd battalions. They were held on the second and third stories, while troops occupied the ground-floor. Guards were posted at the doors and on all landings and the whole buildings were enclosed with barbed wire barricades guarded again by soldiers. The prisoners were each given a single blanket, and slept on the floor. The nights were so bitterly cold that they slept in twos together for warmth

Over 200 women, mostly from the Cumann na mBan participated in the Rising and 79 of them were eventually brought to Inchicore. Some had suffered greatly en-route, having been held in the louse infested rooms of Ship Street Barracks. On arrival at Richmond Barracks they spent the night in the married quarters and the next day were removed to Kilmainham. By May 22nd, all but 12 were released and eventually only 5 were deported to Lewes Prison in East Sussex.: Nell Ryan, Helena Maloney, Brighid Foley, Marie Perolz and Winnie Carney. All were released by Christmas 1916. The Countess Markievicz was the only woman of the Easter Rising to be sent for courts martial.

While awaiting his court martial at Richmond Barracks, Thomas MacDonagh presented to the officer in charge a list of prisoners' demands. The list read:

    1. Visits to prisoners;
    2. Treatment of officers;
    3. Dependents and relations;
    4. Blankets;
    5. Books;
    6. The wearing [of] Red Cross badge who were not combatants;
    7. Washing arrangements.'

It was signed, ***Thomas MacDonagh, Jacobs Factory.***

The officer in charge wrote on the bottom of the list: 'No 7 will be allowed. Other complaints cannot be dealt with here, -.Louis Ramsey I.C. 1/5/16 '. [200]

Above, the arrival of a prisoner. Below, Dr. Brigid -Lyons Thornton, one of the many women prisoners here, pictured later in Nice in 1925 with W.T. Cosgrave, another former internee.

Courts Martial

Maj.-Gen. Lord Cheylesmore, president and Kenneth Marshall, Judge Advocate arrive at Court.
(Image courtesy of the National Library of Ireland.)

On Monday 1st May 'preliminary investigations' began on the people selected by the G men and as early as May 2nd, just three days after the surrender, the trials began. The prisoners might reasonably have expected to be tried in accordance with the newly introduced wartime legislation 'DORA,' the Defence of the Realm Act, which at least would have allowed for a full court of thirteen members, a professional judge, legal advocate and a public presence. Instead, General Maxwell, who had overseen a state of Martial Law in his previous campaigns in Pretoria and the Sudan, implemented Field General Court Martial, which was trial without defence or jury and in camera. Most of the prisoners awaiting court martial were held in the officers' block opposite the gymnasium. This building was divided into units denoted as L, M and N. Unit L, room 4 is mentioned a lot in the witnesses statements. It is also apparent from witnesses that the courts martial of the prisoners took place in this block in two adjacent rooms on either side of the stairs on the first floor.

The Officers' Block where the courts martial took place.
(Image courtesy of the National Library of Ireland.)

On Tuesday morning May 2nd Piaras Beaslai, Eamonn Duggan and Joseph McGuinness were taken from their room. They were kept waiting for a long time on the grass plot in front of the building in which the court was to sit. Then Patrick Pearse, Thomas MacDonagh and Tom Clarke came along. The six men were taken into the hall of the building. Beaslai, Duggan and McGuinness were taken into a room on the right hand side of the hall; the other three men were taken into a room on the left hand side. On the previous day they had all received written copies of the charges against them. The room in which Beaslai and his companions were courts martialled was small and barely accommodated those present. Together with the three prisoners were the three officers who acted as judges, the officer who acted as prosecutor - there was no counsel for the defence - two witnesses, the soldiers forming the escort party and a few detectives.

Piaras Beaslai gives us this account of the proceedings:

'Each prisoner was tried separately, Eamonn first, I next, and then Joe McGuinness.

In each case the prosecutor spoke first and presented his case, and then he called on the two officers who had been prisoners in our hands during the week's fighting, to identify the "prisoner" and to testify that he bore arms. Then a detective was called to testify as to the prisoners "loyalty". Then the prisoner was asked if he had anything to say in his defence. As regards law, or right, or justice it was a mock trial but I must admit that the officers treated us with the greatest courtesy and politeness. They appeared to be Englishmen, elderly and they had no knowledge of Ireland. They had no means of recording the proceedings except notes taken in longhand, and they wrote all what the prisoners said, which took a considerable time. Then the proceedings closed we were taken out on to the grass plot again, and we waited there for the other three. No judgement was pronounced at the close of the proceedings, which is normal practice at a British court martial.[201]

On the other side of the corridor the trial of Patrick Pearse was in progress. His fate was sealed even before the court martial. General Sir John Maxwell had sent a memorandum to the then British Prime Minister, Herbert Asquith, with the following information:

> This man was a member of the Irish Bar and was Principal of a college for boys at Rathfarnham, Co Dublin. He had taken an active part in the volunteer movement from its inception, and joined the Sinn Fein or Irish Volunteers when that body became a separate organisation. He was a member of the Central Council of the Irish Volunteers and a regular attendant at the meetings of that body. He was one of the signatories to the Declaration of Irish Independence which document contains the following passage *"... She now seizes that moment and fully supported by her exiled children in America and by gallant allies in Europe ... she strikes in the full confidence of victory."* He was *"Commandant General of the Army of the Irish Republic"* and *"President of the Provisional Government,"* and as such, issued a Proclamation to the people of Ireland which was printed and distributed in Dublin and elsewhere.

The members of the court were Brigadier-General Charles. G. Blackader (President), Lieutenant-Colonels G. German and W.J. Kent. The charge against Pearse (similar to that which would be put to most of the prisoners) was as follows:

> **Did an act to wit, did take part in an armed rebellion and in the waging of war against His Majesty the King, such act being of such a nature as to be calculated to be prejudicial to the Defence of the Realm and being done with the intension and for the purpose of assisting the enemy.**

Pearse pleaded not guilty.

A witness from the 12th Royal Inniskilling Fusiliers identified the accused as the one who had surrendered to General Lowe wearing the same uniform as he appeared with in court, complete with belt, sword and revolver. Lieutenant King had earlier seen Pearse appearing from the position where the rebels were firing on the troops. A member of the D.M.P also identified him as a member of the Irish Volunteers who had gone about the city with groups of men and acting as an officer.

Patrick Pearse did not call any witnesses in his defence but made the following statement:

'My sole object in surrendering unconditionally was to save the slaughter of the civil population and to save the lives of our followers who had been led into this thing by us. It is my hope that the British Government who has shown its strength will also be magnanimous and spare the lives and give an amnesty to my followers, as I am one of the persons chiefly responsible, have acted as C-in-C and President of the Provisional Government. I am prepared to take the consequences of my act, but I should like my followers to receive an amnesty. I went down on my knees as a child and told God that I would work all my life to gain the freedom of Ireland. I have deemed it my duty as an Irishman to fight for the freedom of my country. I admit I have organised men to fight against Britain. I admit having opened negotiations with Germany. We have kept our word with her and as far as I can see she did her best to help us. She sent a ship with men. Germany has not sent us gold.'[202]

After the courts martial, Pearse, Clarke and MacDonagh were brought out and joined the other three back in the Gymnasium. Although accompanied by soldiers they were free to speak to one another. Pearse was silent. He sat on the floor, deep in thought and spoke only once, when he complained to a soldier about not having got something he had asked for. That evening the six were taken to Kilmainham Jail on foot. Beaslai recalled how he was put into an empty cell where he stretched on the ground and fell asleep having been without sleep for more than a week. He was awakened in the morning by the sound of shots. Thinking the shots were fired by some of the Volunteers who were still holding out he went to sleep again. Some hours later he was told that his three friends had been shot.[203]

The three had been attended by Fr. Aloysius, Fr. Columbus and Fr. Tom O' Ryan, the latter a curate of Goldenbridge, who persuaded Tom Clarke who had at first refused to see a priest. Following the executions, when it was discovered that Holy oils to anoint the bodies had been overlooked, Fr. Ryan sent for them to be obtained from his Chapel of Ease nearby. However, the military would not allow the priests to remain for the executions, so these were not administered. A priest named Fr. Farrington later described the burials of Pearse, MacDonagh and Clarke. The military sent a lorry at 3 o' clock in the morning to bring the priest from his house at

Aughrim Street to Arbour Hill Barracks. At 3.30 he heard from there the volley of shots at Kilmainham. The remains were brought at once to the military prison; he remembered seeing their arrival in pools of blood, still warm and limp, eyes bandaged and mouths open. They were buried, unconfined, in a trench 60 feet long. Those who brought them back told him that Pearse, in particular, had died like a soldier and a man.[204]

The courage of Commandant Pearse was also commented upon by General Blackader, who later remarked to his dining companion, Elizabeth, Countess of Fingal:

'I have just done one of the hardest tasks I have ever had to do. I have had to condemn to death one of the finest characters I have ever come across. There must be something very wrong in the state of things that makes a man like that a rebel. I don't wonder that his pupils adored him.' [205]

On the same day that the three were executed, May 3rd, at Richmond Barracks the trials were stepped up. 22 prisoners were tried, all of whom were sentenced to death, but only 4 confirmed by General Maxwell: Joseph Plunkett, Edward Daly, Michael O' Hanrahan and William Pearse. It was hardly a time for romance, and yet one of the greatest love stories in modern Irish history was due to unfold at this juncture. Joseph Mary Plunkett, a lifelong victim of tuberculosis had left a hospital bed to participate in the rising; indeed he still wore bandages from an operation performed on his neck glands only days previously. Despite this, the turmoil of a week's fighting, and his present perilous situation he was still determined to marry his beloved Grace Gifford. He had already named her as his heir in a will made on the 23rd April 1916, and he now wrote the following letter on the back of that document:

'Richmond Barracks,
Tuesday May 2nd 1916

My darling child,
This is my first chance of sending you a line since we were taken. I have no notion of what they intend to do with me but I have heard a rumour that I am to be sent to England. The only thing I care about is that I am not with you- everything else is cheerful. I am told that Thomas was brought in yesterday. George and Jack (Plun) (sic) are both here and are well. We have not had one word of news from outside since Monday 24th April except wild rumours. Listen- if I live it might be possible to get the church to marry us by proxy - there is such a thing but it is very difficult I am told. You know how I love you. That is all I have time to say. I know you love me and so I am very happy.
Your own Joe'

At about 5pm on Wednesday 3rd May 1916, Miss Gifford drove up to a jeweller's shop in Grafton Street. The jeweller, Mr Stoker had put his stock away for the night, and was about to shut the shop. She asked for any kind of wedding ring. The jeweller went over his stock, and gave her a ring. Despite her veil, he could see that her eyes were red from crying and then she began sobbing. He was curious to know the nature of her dilemma, whereupon Grace told him who she was and what was about to happen. The story was a fascination to the media (no doubt tipped off by the same gentleman). It was erroneously reported in *Pall Mall* and other papers that the marriage had taken place at Richmond Barracks, and that the couple were allowed to be alone for a while. It was Grace Gifford herself who set the record straight in a letter written years later and now kept at Kilmainham Jail.

At 1.30am in the morning of 4th May 1916, she was led into the small chapel of Kilmainham Jail and stood waiting until the handcuffed Joseph Plunkett was brought in, and led up the aisle to stand beside her at the chapel's altar. As there was no electricity available, the marriage ceremony was conducted by Reverend Eugene MacCarthy, using candles for light. Twenty British soldiers, with fixed bayonets, lined the walls of the chapel. Immediately after the conclusion of the ceremony Joseph Plunkett was taken away. They were not allowed to be alone for any period. Before Plunkett's execution by firing squad, Grace was allowed to see him for a further ten minutes. During this time, 15 soldiers stood guard in the cell, and the duration of the meeting was timed by a soldier with a watch. One hour after this last meeting, Joseph Plunkett, together with Edward Daly, Michael O'Hanrahan and Willie Pearse (the only one who pleaded guilty) were executed by firing squad in the former stonebreakers' yard at the Jail.

To add even more poignancy to the story, Grace was the sister of Muriel, wife of executed leader Thomas MacDonagh. Both sisters were now widows. Muriel was drowned in a swimming accident at Skerries just a year later.

In Richmond Barracks on the 4th May 1916, Joseph's two brothers, George and Jack Plunkett were courts martialled and sentenced to death, but their sentences were commuted to 10 years penal servitude. George Oliver Plunkett was somewhat overshadowed by his elder brother Joseph and even by his father, Count Plunkett who was also arrested after the Rising. However, George Plunkett was an important figure, not just in the Easter Rising, but later in the Irish War of Independence, the Irish Civil War; and as IRA Chief of Staff during World War II. One incident during Easter week in which he was involved will live on in legend. He was a Captain in command of the Kimmage Garrison. On Easter Monday he waved down a tram with his revolver at Harold's Cross and boarded it with his men armed with shotguns, pikes and homemade bombs. He then took out his wallet and said with an upper-class English accent (he was educated at Stonyhurst College), *'Fifty-two tuppenny tickets to the city centre please.'* Arriving at Liberty Hall in style they were organised into four companies under George's command and were almost as large as some of the IRA battalions.[206]

Second from left, Peadar Doyle, Tom Hunter, Jack and George Plunkett and John Byrne.
(Image courtesy of the National Library of Ireland.)

Major John MacBride (Image courtesy of The National Library of Ireland.)

Prisoners being brought to the wash room.

Eamonn Ceannt

Countess Markievicz brought by ambulance from Kilmaimham to court martial,
(Image courtesy of the National Library of Ireland.)

A total of 35 prisoners were tried on 4th May, including Con Colbert, Sean Heuston, Eamonn Ceannt (continued from 3rd May), John MacBride and Countess Markievicz. Major Mac Bride was perhaps the most experienced soldier of all of those executed, having fought against the British forces in the Second Anglo Boer War, where he had raised the Irish Transvaal Brigade. Ironically, his involvement in the insurrection on Easter Monday 1916 was accidental. Early that morning he had walked up Grafton Street on his way to his brother's wedding when he met Thomas MacDonagh in full uniform. He had offered his services and was appointed second-in-command at the Jacob's factory. Nonetheless, he was under no illusions: he knew that because of his past exploits he had no chance of a reprieve. On his way back to the gymnasium after court martial he saw a fellow prisoner with whom he was acquainted, Thomas Foran, (President of the I.T.G.W.U) and drew his finger around his heart indicating that he expected to be shot. One can imagine that General

289

Maxwell, himself a veteran commandant of the Boer War, was only too ready to exact the ultimate punishment on his old adversary. Maxwell had to leave urgently for England at this time, but he made sure to confirm the death sentence on MacBride before leaving.

W.T. Cosgrave, who was also court martialled and sentenced to death, was imprisoned in the cell next to MacBride in Kilmainham Jail. At daybreak on Friday morning, May 5th, he heard a slight movement and whisperings in the Major's cell:
'After a few minutes there was a tap on his cell door. I heard the word 'Sergeant,' a few more whispers, a move towards the door of the cell, then steps down the corridor, down the central stairs. Through a chink in the door I could barely discern the receding figures; silence for a time; then the sharp crack of rifle fire; then silence again. I thought my turn would come next and waited for a rap on the door, but the firing squad had no further duty that morning.' [207]

That afternoon, however, Cosgrave learned from a priest that his own death sentence had been commuted. It later emerged that Major MacBride when facing the firing squad had refused a blindfold saying: *'I have looked down the muzzles of too many guns in the South African war to fear death and now please carry out your sentence.'*

At her trial on the 4th May, Countess Constance Markievicz pleaded not guilty to "taking part in an armed rebellion...for the purpose of assisting the enemy," but pleaded guilty to having attempted "to cause disaffection among the civil population of His Majesty. There is some controversy concerning her behaviour in court. The prosecuting counsel, William Wylie, later to be appointed a High Court judge in 1924, wrote to his daughter and alleged that she said *'I am only a woman, you cannot shoot a woman'* and that she had "never stopped moaning the whole time she was in court".[208] Irish commentators have rubbished this account as it was at variance to the general perception of her character. There is another account, however, from the British side that I have not seen quoted in this regard. It comes from Sir Alfred Bucknill, the deputy judge advocate who also gave us the much quoted word picture of how the Countess looked on arrival at Richmond Barracks:
'When I first saw her she was standing gnawing an orange in the barrack square with a number of young prisoners standing behind her. She was dressed in dark green knickerbockers and puttees and tunic and had a green hat with cock's feathers in it.'

Elsewhere in his witness statement Bucknill commented on the trial and was a lot kinder than Wylie to the Countess. His account is deserving of merit as it gives details we now know of the court martial, but which were not available at that time.

'I saw her again on another day when she was brought to Richmond Barracks from Kilmainham for a summary of evidence to be taken. She was taken over in a Motor-ambulance attended by a wardress and a guard of soldiers. Evidence against her was a page boy from a hotel facing onto Stephen's Green. It appeared he saw her fire her revolver at a window in the hotel from which an officer in uniform was looking out. The bullet hit the window sill. When asked if she had anything she wished to say, she said: 'We dreamed of an Irish Republic and thought we had a fighting chance.' Then for a few moments she broke down and sobbed.' [209]

What she actually said, according to the court martial report was:
'I went out to fight for Ireland's freedom, and it doesn't matter what happens to me. I did what I thought was right and I stand by it.'

There is no evidence in Bucknill's statement or in the court record of any plea by the defendant. She was sentenced to be shot, but with a recommendation to mercy 'solely and only on account of her sex'. The sentence was commuted to penal servitude for life.

Even William Wylie had to concede (twenty years later)[210] that Eamonn Ceannt whose trial ran to two days 3 - 4th May was, *'a brave man who showed no sign whatsoever of nervousness before the court… in fact that he was the most dignified of any of the accused.'* Ceannt had instructed the men under his command to make the best possible defence and he led by example. His case was built mainly on the fact that he had not been in command of the garrison at Jacob's, an assumption made on the basis that he was seen leading those men to Richmond Barracks. He was allowed to be advised by a barrister, Ronayne and he was also able to call 3 witnesses; unfortunately his other key witness, Thomas MacDonagh had already been executed. John Mac Bride had given evidence on the 3rd May, before his own execution. Ceannt's efforts, however, were futile. There would be no reprieve either, Maxwell having determined that all signatories to the Proclamation were to die. He was removed to Kilmainham and returned the following day to Richmond Barracks. Gerald Doyle recalled the occasion:

'On the morning of the 5th May about 25 prisoners were brought to Richmond Barracks and included were Con Colbert, Eamonn Ceannt, Michael Mallin, Sean Houston, William Corrigan, James O Sullivan, J. J Burke, John O Brien, John Downey, James Morrissey and myself. We were placed in the blacksmiths forge,' (Finnerty's). [211]

At 4pm Eamonn Ceannt wrote to his wife:

291

Aine, (my wife)
Trial closed. I expect the death sentence which better men have already suffered. I only regret that I have no longer an opportunity of showing how I think of you now that the chance of seeing you again is so remote. I shall die like a man for Ireland's sake.   Eamonn Ceannt.'[212]

Later on the 5th May, Michael Mallin's trial got underway. He put up a rigorous defence in a desperate attempt to preserve his life for the sake of his young family. He denied that he had any commission in the Citizen Army and stated that Countess Markievicz was in command; it was she, he claimed who had commanded him to take charge of the men on Easter Monday. In shifting the responsibility to Markievicz he calculated that the authorities would not shoot a woman. He was nevertheless convicted and sentenced to death.

Michael Mallin was a former drummer boy in the Royal Scots Guards. His regiment was sent to India in 1896 where he had witnessed several uprisings by the native tribes. He returned to Ireland after 14 years service greatly disillusioned by the activities of the British army. His family had a newsagents shop in Meath Street in Dublin, but they were forced to close following the 1913 strike. In 1914 he had joined the Irish Transport & General Workers Union. Later that year, James Connolly appointed him Chief of Staff of the Irish Citizen Army. Having taken over the running of the Emmet Fife and Drum Band, which was based in the union's premises at Emmet Hall in Inchicore he moved his family to rooms above the hall. During 1915 and the spring of 1916 Mallin continued to train and drill the Citizen Army, and he also continued to conduct the Workers' Orchestra, who regularly gave performances at Liberty Hall. After a final performance of the Workers' Orchestra on Easter Sunday evening, on Monday, Mallin led a contingent of a few dozen men and women from Liberty Hall to take St Stephen's Green. On their arrival the Tricolour was raised above the Royal College of Surgeons.

Following the court martial, as Mallin was being brought to Kilmainham Jail he hoped that he might see his wife or one of his children as he passed Emmet Hall, but it was not to be. All he saw was his faithful dog "Prinnie" sitting outside. He was, however, allowed a visit by her and the family. She was pregnant with their fifth child. The scene was said to be harrowing with much sobbing that could be heard in the adjoining cells. Even the British soldier on guard was reduced to tears. That night, just hours before his execution, he wrote a parting letter to his Agnes:

'My darling Wife, pulse of my heart, this is the end of all things earthly; sentence of death has been passed, and at a quarter to four tomorrow the sentence will be

carried out by shooting and so must Irishmen pay for making Ireland a free nation... I find no fault with the soldiers or police. I forgive them from the bottom of my heart. Pray for all the souls that fell in this fight, Irish and English...'

'Una my little one be a nun. Joseph my little man, be a priest if you can. James and John to you the care of your mother, make yourselves good strong men for her sake and remember Ireland. Good bye my wife, my darling. Remember me, God again bless and protect yours and our children. I must now prepare, the last few hours must be spent with God alone. - Your loving husband,
Michael Mallin, Commander-Stephens Green Command. *[213]*

On the morning of 8th May 1916, Michael Mallin, Sean Heuston, Eamonn Ceannt and Con Colbert were taken to the old stonebreakers yard where they were shot. Eamonn Ceannt was executed sitting on a soap box clutching a crucifix and rosary beads given to him by Fr. Augustine who had attended him. He was still showing signs of movement after the volley and a *coup de grace* (revolver shot to the head) was necessary. The rosary beads were later returned to the priest who noted that 6 or 7 of the beads were missing, having been shot from the chain.

Eamon de Valera had spent his time from 2nd. ‾ 5th. May in detention at Richmond Barracks. On Friday morning, 5th May he was moved to the gymnasium, where he remained until Saturday afternoon 6th May. From 6‾8th May he was lodged, one of 30, in Room 4 (L block). In that room with him was Count Plunkett, Thomas Foran, Sean T. O'Kelly (later to be President of Ireland), John O' Mahony, Batt O' Connor (future Fine Gael TD) and Larry O'Neill (a future Lord Mayor of Dublin). Batt O'Connor later recalled:

> There was no bedding, or furniture. The weather continued very cold and we had great difficulty in getting any sleep. We took off our boots and used them as pillows, and anyone who an overcoat was able to use it as a blanket. We all felt great pity for the aged Count Plunkett, both on account of the execution of his son, of which he had not yet heard, and because he must have felt the hardship of the place more than any of us who had had to rough it from time to time. He could not sleep at all lying on the floor and never lay down. We managed to get an empty orange box from one of the soldiers, and, putting it against the wall, he sat on it throughout the night. One young man insisted on spreading his overcoat around his knees to keep him warm, and another wrapped his around the Count's shoulders...One day Count Plunkett had to go to the dispensary to see the doctor. When he gave his name he was asked, *'Are you the father of Joseph who was shot?'* That is how he heard the news of the death of his son, which he bore with great fortitude.[214]

293

The prisoners were expected to keep the latrines clean; a task they did not mind and they took it in turns. However, when they were then asked to clean the latrines being used by British soldiers, Gearoid O'Sullivan, whose turn it was, defied the order. He said he was prepared to take his turn in attending to the requirements of his comrades, but that nothing would induce him to do so for the English soldiers. The Sergeant of the Guard hurried off to report the matter to Major Orr. The Major arrived immediately in a towering rage. O'Sullivan repeated his refusal. Saying he would give him two minutes to obey, the Major walked back five paces, and, drawing his revolver, he took his watch in his other hand…When the two minutes were up Major Orr repeated his challenge, but already he knew he was beaten, and calling some of his men to arrest them, he ordered O'Sullivan and the five men with him to be taken to solitary confinement, preparatory to being courts martialled for disobeying a military order. The trial was held the next day. The military authorities decided that it was not the duty of the prisoners to clean the latrines of the soldiers and O'Sullivan and the other men were released. His courageous act freed the rest of the prisoners from what would have been an extremely unpleasant addition to their labours.[215]

To pass the time they bribed the guard to sell them the occasional bottle of whiskey at an inflated price. They also, engaged in a most bizarre and morbid game involving Eamon de Valera; it was literally, 'gallows humour:'

> With death but a short distance away, a mock trial does not appear to be the most happy of pastimes, but the irrepressible John O' Mahony insisted. The bearded Count acted as a sombre judge and Larry O'Neill was advocate for the defence. Sean T. O'Kelly prosecuted, since none of the others relished this task, and de Valera was charged with being a pretender to the throne of the Muglins, the rocky island on which a lighthouse stood off Dalkey Island. The verdict, as expected, was against the commandant. But the judge stopped short at pronouncing the frightening sentence, despite the urgings of one of the prisoners who had a black cap ready for the occasion. None of this gave de Valera much comfort and the grim game almost unnerved Larry O'Neill. Quietly that night, as they lay on the floor hoping for the oblivion of sleep, he moved over to the man whose doom appeared to be sealed, and whispered, *'This is terrible,'* and pressed a crucifix into de Valera's hand.[216]

Eamon de Valera at Richmond Barracks

On Monday 8th May, Eamon de Valera was sent to trial. Before leaving he gave his pen as a keepsake to Sean T. O' Kelly. It was subsequently stolen from O' Kelly while he was still in the barracks. Batt O' Connor was the last to shake his hand:

'Good-bye Batt,' he said, *'we may not meet again. You know I am expecting ----that!'* imitating with his hand the firing of a gun.[217]

On his way to the court martial an iconic photograph, one of his personal favourite photographs was taken. His grandson, Mr Justice Eamon de Valera, to whom he related the story, tells how this came about. *'Conscious that he was dirty and unkempt, he deliberately glared at the photographer trying to look as unrepentant as possible, knowing that the British would seek to make propaganda from an apparently cowed and beaten enemy.'* [218]

The court martial was short and businesslike:

'De Valera did not deny his identity or make any such difficulties. His wife had, a few days before, approached the American Consul in Dublin to make representations that he was an American citizen and the Consul had written to the Under Secretary, Sir Mathew Nathan, on the point. At his court martial, however, he did not make any claim on this basis. When questioned, he stated that he understood that he was born in New York, but he could not say whether his father was a Spanish subject or a naturalised American citizen. On one point he was firm. He said that he always regarded himself as an Irishman and not a British subject.'[219]

De Valera was sentenced to death, but this was commuted to life in prison. He would later strenuously deny that his American citizenship had any bearing on his case, reminding people that Thomas Ashe, commander of the Fingal battalion at Ashbourne where 11 R.I.C members were killed, was also spared.

Confidential.

RICHMOND BARRACKS
DUBLIN

From   Officer i/c Prisoners
To   178th Inf. Bde

1.   I have carried out the sentences ordered on the bodies of the prisoners named in the margin, at the time and place and in the Manner specified

JAMES CONOLLY.
JOHN McDERMOTT.

2.   I attach :—
        (a) certificate of death.
        (b)   "   "   burial.

C. Harold Heathcote.
Major.
Officer i/c Prisoners.

12/5/16.

Prime Minister Asquith at Richmond Barracks.
(Image courtesy of the National Library of Ireland.)

In the House of Commons on the evening of the 11th May, John Dillon made a remarkable speech in which he spoke of 'horrible rumours' in Dublin, and read a letter from Hanna Sheehy Skeffington concerning the murder of her husband. He called for a cessation of the executions. In his reply, Prime Minister Asquith said that unfortunately there would be two more executions. The last of the leaders to meet their fate were Sean MacDiarmada and James Connolly. The latter, who had been badly injured, was court martialled at Dublin Castle on 9th May. MacDiarmada was well known to the G men in Dublin, and easily identifiable because of a lameness (poliomyelitis) in one leg. However, he was not identified in the Gymnasium on Sunday 30th April, and he had escaped detection until a very late hour. He had been classed as one of those to be deported and interned. As fate would have it, on the evening that he was being paraded in the Barrack Square with other prisoners, before their departure for the boat, he was picked out by a detective who was moving through the ranks making a final scrutiny. After court martial, he was sentenced to death and was executed with James Connolly on May 12th. Connolly arrived in an ambulance and from a stretcher he was put onto a chair. He was shot in the chest while seated and the volley blew out the back of the chair.[220]

297

That same day Asquith arrived in Dublin giving rise to much speculation. At first it was thought that he came over for first- hand information, with a view to modifying martial law, excessive punishments, arrests, etc., and also to compensate those who lost property in the quelling of the revolt; but it was also thought he was contemplating creating a mixed Nationalist and Unionist Irish Council to govern the country during the war. On the morning of the 12th May he visited Richmond Barracks to see for himself the conditions under which the prisoners were being held. On arrival, he found that they were 'for the most part, men and lads from the country, who had taken no part in the Dublin rising.' Asquith mixed with the rebels and demanded they be given the 'best food possible,' much to the annoyance of the troops guarding them. Engaging one youthful Volunteer in conversation the Prime Minister asked him, what he thought of the outcome of the Rising. The young man replied that he thought it was a success. Asquith was incredulous, and asked him how such a conclusion was possible. The prisoner replied, *'Well, if no, what are you here for?'*

Asquith's visit brought an end to the executions; the British having carried out fifteen of the ninety death sentences. It also brought about a general improvement in the welfare of the prisoners. An immediate result was the release, that day, of several boy internees, one of whom was Vincent Byrne.

Vincent (Vinny) Byrne had fought in E Company, 2nd Battalion at Jacobs Biscuit Factory, seeing for the first time a man killed by gunfire. At one point armed with a .22 rifle the 15 year old Byrne held 2 policemen prisoner. He fought alongside men such as Thomas MacDonagh, John McBride and Mick McDonnell (later leader of the Squad). After the surrender order he escaped and was arrested in a British Army sweep on the following Saturday when his house was raided. He was among a group of the younger rebels, including Tom Kehoe, who were then held in Richmond Barracks. One of the DMP men who fingerprinted him was Detective Johnny Barton, who had led the raid on his home the Saturday after the Rising. Due to their youth they were released the following Friday evening:

'We were told to "come on, get ready," and we all thought we were going to be deported. We paraded on the square, about twelve or fourteen young lads. We were given the command: "Right turn quick march." We kept marching until we came to a big gate; the gate was opened for us and closed behind us. Someone of the party remarked: "Oh God, lads, we are out, see the tramlines." We proceeded down Emmet road to James's street and on into the city.' [221]

Strangely enough, in later years he was to find himself as officer commanding the same barracks where he was held prisoner (then renamed Kehoe Barracks after his fellow internee Tom Kehoe).

298

Young boys detained at the Barracks.

Robert C. Barton

On 17th May 1916, two officers, Lieutenants, Grant and Barton of the 10th Royal Dublin Fusiliers were sent up from the Royal Barracks to assist the military in clerical duties. Grant was put in charge of post office or prisoners' mail and Robert C. Barton in charge of prisoners' effects, a duty he hated. By this time, the buckets had been pillaged by his fellow soldiers and in some cases the name tags had been removed so that he could not identify the owners. Being a 2nd Lieutenant his authority was limited and nobody paid any attention to his enquiries. He was eventually relieved of total responsibility and put under Major Charles Harold Heathcote of the 2/6/th. Battalion Sherwood Foresters (the officer who had presided over the firing squads in most of the executions). As Barton wryly remarked, *'They were more likely to take heed of you if you had the word "Major" in front of your name'.* Heathcote even travelled to Frongoch to interview the detainees about their belongings and continued his investigations until 1919.

Barton continued at this work until May 1918, when he was allowed to quit the British Army. The English had decided to take out of the army the principal leaders of farming in all districts: *'There came a time when the provision of food was as important as fighting.'* [222]

He later joined the Republican movement and became an important figure in Irish politics. As for Major Heathcote, his nephew, Bernard Heathcote remembers his father telling him of his uncle Harold:

'I have very vague memories from my childhood of my then elderly father telling me that the terrible duty of being the officer in charge of the firing squad affected Harold (his eldest brother) for the rest of his life. Unlike my father, who's Sherwood Forrester battalion went to France in Feb 1915, Harold's battalion first 'blooding' was being sent to help put down the 1916 Easter Rising. His horrific and unwanted role in overseeing the prisoner executions would most likely have been his first experience of being involved with any shooting.'

Eoin MacNeill

General Byrne of the British Forces in Ireland was quoted by the *Irish Times* of 24th May 1916, as saying that the trial by Field general courts martial (FGCM) was concluded and that all further trials would be by General courts martial (GCM), where prisoners had the right to be assisted by council. Among those tried under this system was Eoin (John) MacNeill.

MacNeill was co founder of the Gaelic League and went on to establish the Irish Volunteers. He was Chief-of-Staff of the Volunteers at the time of the Easter Rising, but he took no role in it or its planning, and even went so far as to try to prevent it. He nevertheless had twelve charges levelled against him: eight were charges of attempting to cause disaffection among the civil population in Ireland, and four were of acting in a way likely to prejudice recruiting. He was tried on the 22nd May 1916. Unusually, the trial was held in the Gymnasium, signalling the fact that it was to be a much bigger hearing than the previous ones.

MacNeill had suffered greatly with his nerves since his arrest and imprisonment at Arbour Hill. He told Fr. Farrington that while he was exercising he had to pass, at regular intervals, soldiers who fired blank cartridges at him. Soldiers with fixed bayonets paraded him in front of the mass grave being dug for the executed leaders. Then he was visited in his cell by Major Price who offered him his life and good terms if he would implicate John Dillon and Joe Devlin in the Rising. On the night prior to his trial he had spent the night in the King George V hospital. At 10 am the judges were summoned into the Gymnasium followed immediately by the witnesses. There were about 10 or 11 military judges. They sat at a long table at the side opposite the entrance and windows. Facing them to the right of the entrance with their backs to the window were MacNeill and his council on the left and the military prosecutor Lieutenant J.E. Wylie (later Judge Wylie) with his solicitor on his right. Three shorthand writers sat at a small table between the Judges and accused. They included one R.I.C and one 'G' Division detective.

Wylie's prosecution speech took about one hour and included charges of indictment to sedition, based on articles in the 'Irish Volunteer' and on speeches made at Volunteer meetings. There was also an attempt made to prove that comments by MacNeill showed him to be pro- German.   During the break for lunch, Mrs. MacNeill was allowed to be with her husband for the full duration of the hour. The trial went over to the following day, May 23rd. which was the turn of the Defence, including input by Creed-Meredith, Captain Tom Kettle M.P., and Colonel Moore who gave evidence on the formation and history of the Volunteer movement. Evidence was also given on a note of Patrick Pearse acknowledging on Easter Sunday the receipt of John MacNeill's countermanding order, saying he did his best to have them obeyed and that he had added his own (Pearse's) name without which the leading men in the country would not have acted. (This was the first definitive evidence outsiders had of the existence of an inner I.R.B circle independent of John MacNeill.)[223]

It was noted at this time that the words of the 'Hail Mary;' in large Gaelic characters, had been written on the barracks wall by one of the Volunteers; an action which would have impressed the next witness. Fr. Michael Curran, Secretary to Archbishop Walsh, repudiated the allegation that MacNeill was Pro-German or belonging (in his opinion) to any secret society (I.R.B). He testified that the two factors which had influenced MacNeill were the threatened disarmament of the Volunteers and the failed attempt to land arms in Kerry. The latter, Curran claimed, was Mac Neill's first inkling of the true nature of 'the conspiracy' and he had thereupon courageously tried to stop the whole Easter mobilisation or parades to avoid all danger of bloodshed. The verdict of the court martial was not made known until the 30th May. Despite his role in trying to avert the Rising and his comparatively fair trial he was sentenced to penal servitude for life and sent to Dartmoor Convict Prison. There he was reunited with some notable figures, such as William Partridge (tried 17th. May) and Eamon de Valera.

While at Dartmoor, one day as some guards were leading Mac Neill into a courtyard de Valera called the Volunteers to attention and ordered them to salute their Chief of Staff; the men complied though many of them could not forgive him for the part he had played.[224]

Lizzie Mulhall

Local woman, Lizzie Mulhall, was an enthusiastic nationalist who had a draper's shop on 137, Emmet Road directly opposite the Barracks. In open defiance she hung a tricolour on the roof of her premises from time to time. In 1916 immediately after the Rising she was arrested and held for several days. It is said that she insisted in bringing her parrot with her![225] She was released on 22nd May 1916. Her shop is today the lounge of Mc Dowells, The Richmond House.

The Tullamore Prisoners

An amusing anecdote related by Brian Maye (biographer of Arthur Griffith) concerns two British soldiers discussing their prisoners:
'They are not as bad as we were told,' said one. The other replied: 'These are only the city blokes. The hill tribes haven't come in yet.'

People tend to view the Rising as a Dublin happening. But Volunteer prisoners from numerous other counties passed through Richmond Barracks, including those from Galway, Clare, Wexford, Tipperary and Limerick. The next trial was that of the Tullamore prisoners. They had been in custody since 20th March 1916, following a series of incidents which resulted in the serious injury of a police sergeant. At a time when the First World War was at a critical stage and the British were struggling to make any progress there was a lot of ill feeling towards the Volunteer movement. This was accentuated by recent public displays by the Volunteers, notably on St. Patrick's Day, 1916 when the Dublin battalions of the Volunteers numbering about 2,000 men had marched with full gear. There was bound to be resentment by relatives of Irishmen serving in the British army and members of the Volunteers. This was manifested at a hurling match in Tullamore, County Offaly in aid of the Wolfe Tone memorial on 19th March, when a spectator attempted to remove a flag from one of the men, who, it was alleged, retaliated by drawing a revolver. Later that day at the local railway station, the Volunteers demonstrated against an Irish regiment leaving for France. As a reprisal for this, an anti-Sinn Fein demonstration took place near a Sinn Fein venue in William Street, Tullamore, on 20th March. Fourteen Irish Volunteers were besieged by a hostile mob. Amid the booing and chanting, stones were thrown and windows smashed. Believing they were inadequately protected by the police the Volunteers fired revolvers to keep the mob away, and when the police moved in to disarm them resisted arrest, seriously wounding a Sergeant Ahern.
Twelve of the men were arrested and held initially at Tullamore, but were later transferred to Richmond Barracks where they were tried by General courts martial on 26th May 1916. They were fortunate to have the benefit of a proper defence council. T.M Healy, K.C., M.P., (later 1st Governor of the Irish Free State) successfully argued that the men had not been legally transferred from the civil to the military authorities. The General Officer Commander-in-Chief had not confirmed the proceedings, and ordered their release from military custody. They were discharged on 22nd June 1916.[226]

Captain J.C. Bowen-Colthurst

One of the most dreadful episodes of Easter week was the murderous campaign of Captain Bowen Colthurst, lasting two days 25-26th April 1916, during which he accounted for the deaths of at least five people (some claim it was as many as seven). Among them was a well known and respected suffragist, pacifist and writer, Francis Sheehy Skeffington. The Commander of Portobello Barracks, Major Sir Francis Fletcher Vane was absent at the time and was horrified on his return when confronted with the facts.

He ordered Bowen-Colthurst placed under arrest and informed his superiors. When General Maxwell, who was so diligently prosecuting the leaders of the rebellion, was notified he refused to act. As a result, Colthurst was left free to terrorise Skeffington's widow, Hanna, whose home was ransacked twice. A whitewash commenced: Royal Engineers were dispatched to fix the bullet holes in the Barracks courtyard and the bodies buried. However, Major Vane was a man of principle and took his evidence to London and the highest levels of the Military and the Government. His persistence finally resulted in Colthurst being put on trial on 6th June at Richmond Barracks.

Capt. J.C. Bowen-Colthurst, Royal Irish Rifles, was charged in connection with the shooting of three non-combatant Dublin citizens, Francis Sheehy-Skeffington, Thomas Dickson, and Patrick MacIntyre at Portobello Barracks, Dublin. We can reasonably assume that this trial was also held in the Gymnasium as there was no other room big enough to accommodate such a large assembly. Admission to the court was by ticket, and at the opening of the proceedings there were about 100 civilians present, including the widow of Francis Sheehy Skeffington and a number of other ladies. Dr. Skeffington (father of the deceased) was also present. The court was presided over by the distinguished figure of Lord Cheylesmore and twelve senior officers and staff. All the witnesses were military.

The court heard how, on the Tuesday of the Easter Rising, 25th April, a young officer named Lieutenant M. C. Morris of the East Surrey Regiment was put in command of a picket at Portobello Bridge, occupying premises at the corner known as Davy's public-house. His orders were to keep the roadway clear. The young officer was very apprehensive owing to the gunfire coming from the Jacob's factory and feared that an assault on Portobello Barracks could be imminent. He heard people in the street shouting out Mr. Sheehy Skeffington's name and decided as a precaution to detain him. He sent him under escort to Portobello Barracks. On being interviewed by the Adjutant, Lieutenant Morgan R.I.R., Mr. Skeffington explained that he was a pacifist and had been engaged in an attempt to organise a citizens' militia to prevent the looting of damaged shops; a document found on his person confirmed this. The officer wrote 'no charge' on the charge sheet and was respectful to him. The Adjutant's orders, however, were that Skeffington was to be further detained in the guardroom.

Captain Bowen Colthurst

Later in the evening Captain Bowen Colthurst, invalided home from service on the Western Front, received notice to occupy the premises of Mr. James Kelly, a tobacconist shop at the corner of Camden Street. Mr. Kelly was an Alderman of the City and a conservative loyalist whom the military had confused with Alderman Tom Kelly, a Sinn Feiner. Colthurst adopted the extraordinary measure of taking Skeffington along as a hostage; the raiding party had instructions that he was to be shot if it was attacked. He was brought with his hands tied behind his back and was asked to say his prayers. When he refused, Colthurst told his men to take off their hats and he himself uttered a prayer: *'O Lord God, if it shall please Thee to take the life of this man forgive him for Christ's sake.'*

As they went towards their destination Colthurst periodically fired his rifle in the air and at houses along the way. When they arrived at Kelly's shop, he threw a grenade into the premises and the soldiers then rushed in. They took captive two pro-British journalists who were in the shop -Thomas Dickson and Patrick MacIntyre. They were taken together with Skeffington back to Portobello Barracks. The court learned that Mr. Dickson was the editor of a paper called *The Eye Opener*. Mr McIntyre was the editor of another paper called *The Searchlight*. Neither had any connection with the Rising and the only reason for their arrest was the circumstance of their being found on Mr. Kelly's premises. The men spent the night in the detention room, while Skeffington, because of his superior social position was put into a separate cell and made as comfortable as possible.

The following morning 26th April, Colthurst arrived and ordered the prisoners to be taken out to the yard. He told the officer on duty that he was taking them out to shoot them as he thought it was 'the right thing to do.' The prisoners were told that he wanted to talk to them. The yard in question was reached from the guardroom, just a few paces away and comprised a space less than 40 ft. in length and some 25 ft. in width. It was surrounded by high walls. Colthurst further, ordered seven of the guard out into the yard with rifles. While the soldiers were entering the yard, Colthurst ordered the prisoners to walk to the wall at the other end. As they were doing so the soldiers arrived and fell into line. They received a command to fire on the prisoners who had only just turned to face them. Caught completely by surprise they fell without uttering a sound. Skeffington was still showing movement and Colthurst asked four of the guard to reload and fire into him again as he lay on the ground.

A number of witnesses in court testified as to the defendant's recent strange behaviour. Capt. Bowen-Colthurst successfully pleaded insanity arising from shellshock as a means of escaping a potential murder conviction. His court martial became a *cause celebre* and provoked a political furore which culminated in a Royal Commission of Enquiry at the Four Courts on 23rd August 1916. At this enquiry it was first learnt that a fourth person had been killed that night by Colthurst. A 17 year old boy named J.J. Coady was out after curfew, returning home from a church service with two friends when he was struck on the jaw with the butt end of a rifle by one of Colthurst's party and then shot by him. Colthurst fully believed that he was empowered to do this under the rules of martial law. Mention was made of a fifth victim, but there was no supporting evidence (possibly a reference to Sinn Fein's, Robert O'Carroll.) A statement by the defendant, who was already in custody, was read to the court. In it, he claimed that he shot the three men because he feared they would escape or that there would be an attempt to free them. He referred to them as 'dangerous men,' also 'rebels' and even 'ringleaders.'

He was sent to Broadmoor Hospital briefly and then to a hospital in Canada. He was deemed 'cured' 20 months later and was eventually released with a pension at the age of 40. Sheehy-Skeffington's wife was offered financial compensation by the British government of the day, but she refused this. Vane was dishonourably discharged from the army in the summer of 1916 owing to his actions in the murder case.[227]

The Louth Volunteers

The next trial by General court martial took place on the 9th and 10th June 1916 and involved the prisoners from Dundalk. They were, John MacEntee, Francis Martin, Denis Leahy and James Sally. The court heard that on Easter Monday a group of Louth Volunteers under Seán MacEntee mobilised in Dundalk and set off towards Dublin. At Castlebellingham they encountered a number of policemen and captured them, along with an army officer. In a confusing incident a Volunteer discharged a shot which wounded the officer, Lieutenant Dunville of the Grenadier Guards and killed Constable Charles Magee of the R.I.C. The verdict of the court martial was made known on 19th June. They were each sentenced to death, commuted to 10 years penal servitude.

Murder at Guinness's Brewery

Capt. Colthurst was not the only British soldier to appear before a General court martial at Richmond Barracks on charges of murder. On 12th June 1916, the bizarre case of Company Quartermaster Sergeant Robert Flood of the Royal Dublin Fusiliers was heard.

On the night of 29th April 1916, a picket of the 5th Battalion, Royal Dublin Fusiliers was stationed at the Malt House within the Guinness Brewery. Tension was high as the Volunteers were ensconced nearby at the South Dublin Union and at Marrowbone Lane. Orders had been given that no windows were to be opened. Lieutenant Lucas, however, opened a window causing Flood to believe that he was a rebel spy in the camp. He also believed that William Rice, a night-watchman carrying a lamp was giving signals to Lucas. He had both arrested and shot dead. That same night, in a separate incident, another officer, Lieutenant Basil Worswick and another worker Cecil Dockeray were shot. Lucas and Worswick were officers in the King Edward's Horse; Dockeray and Rice were employees at the brewery. The four men were killed while carrying out routine inspections of the premises. CQMS Robert Flood, commander of the picket and who ordered the executions was court-martialled, charged with the murders of Rice and Lucas but was acquitted, claiming in his defence that he believed the four to be members of Sinn Fein and that his picket was too small to guard the four prisoners.[228]

Summary

A total of 3,430 men and 79 women were arrested in the aftermath of the Rising. 1,841 of these were sent to internment camps in England. 2,700 of the total involved were released by August 1916. Those thought to have organised the Rising, 190 men and one woman were held back in Ireland for trial. In 90 of these cases the sentence was 'Death by being shot.' Maxwell confirmed the sentence for each of 15 of these, who were executed between 3rd-12th May 1916, and but for Prime Minister Asquith's intervention might have executed many more.

The last words on this chapter belong to Darrell Figgis. He was not directly involved in the Rising, but was arrested on 11th May because of his part (along with Erskine Childers and Roger Casement) in the Kilcoole gun-running episode, when 1,500 German Mauser rifles were successfully transported to Ireland in two yachts. His house at Achill Island was battered in by 20 armed policemen. He was first held in Castlebar Gaol and was a late arrival at Richmond Barracks (he would be further sent to Stafford and then to Reading Gaols). It was after the Prime Minister's visit and the executions had ceased.

In Dublin we were taken to Richmond Barracks...It was a university in which the doctrines, methods, and hopes of the men of Easter Week were folded into the life of men from every part of Ireland... **Nearly every man who took any kind of part in the events of the years to follow passed through Richmond Barracks**, and there for the first time many of them met... Nothing, I think, more surprised our guards than the unfailing hilarity of our company. In every room it was the same, and when we met in the drill-yards it was the same. That was the oddest experience of all. **Men had been arrested for drilling, yet at Richmond Barracks we were led out, in companies of fifty and sixty at a time, and drilled under some of the best instructors in the world**. Men were drilled there who had never drilled before in their lives, and had even, a year before, mocked at the manoeuvres of Volunteers. Many of them afterwards remembered their tuition, as they remembered the company in which that tuition had been received.'[229]

The return of the prisoners in 1917.
(Image courtesy of the National Library of Ireland.)

1917-1922

The years following the Easter Rising would see a great shift in public opinion. There were a number of reasons for this change, famously referred to by the poet, W.B. Yeats as the birth of a 'Terrible Beauty.' The Irish had already endured the 1913 Lockout and the brutality of the combined forces of police and military in support of the employers against the workers. Then there was the Bachelors Walk incident when the army had opened fire on civilians. Next came the shelving of the Home Rule Bill. In 1916, the excessive military might deployed in putting down the Easter Rising magnified the scale of the event internationally: after a week of resistance by the rebels the capital city resembled a bombed out city at the centre of the Great War. Atrocities enacted by the British at North King Street and again under Capt. Bowen-Colthurst at Portobello would be long remembered and contrasted against the bravery of the rebel leaders who offered surrender in order to avoid civilian bloodshed. If the Rising was a failure, then the response by the British was a military blunder, epitomised by the appointment of General Maxwell to deal with the situation. The mock trials, the death sentences for so many and the harshness of the prison terms for others all added to the grievance of the public. Their anger would turn to action when, in 1917, the prisoners returned under a general amnesty. For William Partridge, however, who had fought alongside Mallin and Markievicz at the Royal College of Surgeons, it was too late; the conditions at Dartmoor Prison (prior to Lewes) had caused irreparable damage to his health. After his release, he went briefly to his house at 3 Patriotic Terrace, Kilmainham and then returned to the home of his brothers and sisters at Ballaghaderreen where he died on 26th July 1917. Constance Markievicz delivered his funeral oration, in which she described Partridge as *'The purest-souled and noblest patriot Ireland ever had.'* She then fired a salute over the grave with her own pistol.

Sinn Fein, a party previously associated with radical nationalism, but not with the Rising was at this time taken over by Republicans and veterans of the Rising and won by-elections in North Roscommon and South Longford and East Clare. The fallout from the Rising was damaging to John Redmond's Irish Parliamentary Party and contributed to the rise of Sinn Fein. An attempt by the British to introduce conscription further alienated the Irish electorate, particularly as it was linked to the Home Rule Bill. Mass demonstrations followed. The British government reacted by falsely arresting 73 Sinn Fein members, including de Valera and Arthur Griffith on charges of plotting with the German's. The conscription law, though passed, was never enacted owing to the end of the First World War, but the damage had already been done and the popularity of the Sinn Fein party had grown to immense proportions. They won a landslide victory in the December general election of that year, at the expense (annihilation) of The Irish Parliamentary Party.

On 21st January 1919, they set up their first parliament or Dáil in the Mansion House, Dublin and there reaffirmed the 1916 Declaration of Independence, together with a message to the free nations of the world that there was an existing state of war between Ireland and England. That same day Daniel Breen took part in an ambush at Soloheadbeg in which two members of the R.I.C, who were escorting explosives to a quarry, were fatally shot. Thus began a guerrilla war which would be become known as the Irish War of Independence. The Irish Volunteers were reconstituted as the Irish Republican Army. Their cause was bolstered by an influx of fully trained Irishman returning from service in the First World War. Tom Barry was one of these men, and he went on to become one of Ireland's most prominent guerrilla fighters.

In November 1919, the first anniversary of Armistice Day was celebrated by a victory parade in Dublin. Troops from the various barracks were in attendance. The men from Richmond Barracks alone numbered over one thousand. The 'Golikell' ("Go like Hell"), a Whippet or small tank usually kept at Richmond Barracks featured in the parade. Because of the nature of the Irish War of Independence (guerrilla warfare) such tanks were of little use to the British beyond these occasional displays of military power.

The authorities were becoming increasingly uneasy with the Irish situation and continued to make rash decisions. In August 1919, a number of policemen and military visited the village of Fox and Geese, Co. Dublin and searched some houses, presumably for arms. They afterwards searched houses in Inchicore, but nothing was found. Then one night in September a group of soldiers gathered on Ring Street, Inchicore and discharged as many as 20 revolver shots. There has been friction between the soldiers and some of the inhabitants prior to this. The soldiers had received a bonus of £10 the day before and having enjoyed themselves in the city they thought that by firing revolvers they would frighten some of those who had been annoying them. While, 'It was not alleged they had fired deliberately at anyone,' several youths who were in the neighbourhood at the time were stated to have received injuries. One young fellow named O' Connor, was shot in the thigh. Another named Cannon, in the ankle, and a third boy on the hand; a bullet passed up the coat-sleeve of a fourth grazing his arm. The boys stated that after having fired the shots the soldiers broke into two parties and disappeared. The police investigated the incident, but no charges were brought.[230]

...

November 1919, Armistice Day victory parade in Dublin featuring the 'Golikell and a thousand men from Richmond Barracks.

The funeral of Sean Doyle passing down Emmet Road.

In February 1920 the soldiers from Richmond Barracks raided Emmet Hall and the apartments above it. While the raid was in progress Mrs. Mallin (widow of Michael) and her children were kept prisoners in the kitchen. The soldiers removed a deposit receipt which she needed to buy food and she was later forced to write to the military requesting its return. On 19th September 1920, Volunteer Sean Doyle, the nineteen year old son of Peadar Doyle (future TD and Lord Mayor) was killed by the Black and Tans at Kilmashogue Mountain in the Dublin Mountains. His funeral was one of the largest ever seen in Inchicore. Another casualty at that time was Sean Treacy. On 13th October 1920, he was involved in a shoot-out with British troops at Drumcondra. Making his way to the Holland home in Inchicore, he stayed the night there and continued on his way by bicycle the next morning. He was soon spotted, however, and shot dead during another exchange of fire at Talbot Street.

Sunday, November 21st, 1920 (Bloody Sunday) was a day that will always be remembered in Irish History. The Dublin football team was scheduled to play Tipperary, in Croke Park, all the proceeds to be donated to the Irish Republican Prisoners Fund. The night before, Michael Collins sent his 'Squad,' a group of specially trained hit-men out to assassinate undercover British agents known as the "Cairo Gang." A series of shootings took place throughout the night which left 14 members of the British Forces dead. The only IRA man captured during the operation was Frank Teeling. In reprisal, the Black and Tans invaded the pitch at Croke Park and fired on the crowd, killing 14 civilians including one of the players, Michael Hogan, and wounding 68. The incident shocked both the Irish and the British public. In January 1921 Teeling was sentenced to hang. However, he made an audacious escape from Kilmainham Gaol together with Ernie O'Malley and Simon Donnelly.

Corps of Drums 1st Battalion, King's Own, Richmond Barracks 1920.

The King's Own Regiment

The King's Own Royal Lancaster Regt 3rd. battalion arrived at Richmond Barracks in April 1919. In July of that year they were absorbed into the 1st battalion, King's Own Regiment. They were to remain here until the handover of the barracks in December 1922. The men were encouraged to take an interest in drama and music as some of the photographs show.

313

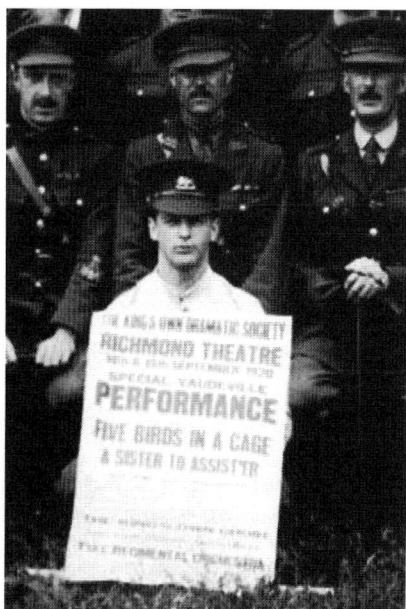

The above was the Dramatic Society of the 1st Battalion, King's Own, Dublin, September 1920, posing outside one of the recreation rooms. The poster read:

'Richmond Theatre, special vaudeville performance, 5 Birds in a Cage "A Sister to Assist'er," with full regimental orchestra.'

Ambush

On 17th May 1921 a Crossley tender was ambushed by a group of men of the Irish Republican Army who had been concealed behind a wall in Grattan Crescent, Inchicore. At that time it was partly a rural road with shrubberies at each side. Bombs were thrown and fire opened. Seven or eight IRA men were in the ambushing group. One soldier, Bandsman Mark Percival, of the 1st Battalion, Kings Own Royal Regiment, was killed and another injured. The soldiers returned fire, with unknown results. There was great military activity in the neighbourhood after the ambush. A young boy named Gray was arrested when standing at the door of his house. A military officer watched the passengers alighting from a tramcar at the terminus. Amongst them was a fourteen year old school girl, Mai Guilfoyle, who was carrying a parcel. This officer approached her and asked her what was in the parcel. This girl became frightened, and ran away, with the officer in pursuit. An armoured car and a lorry joined in the chase, but the frightened girl succeeded in reaching the Goldenbridge convent. On examining the parcel the officer found it contained the schoolgirl's lunch.

A party of the deceased's fellow soldiers from Richmond Barracks later held a small commemoration close to the spot where he was killed and fired a volley of shots in his honour. Percival was buried in Widnes Cemetery, Lancashire.

A firing party at the funeral of Mark Percival shot in Inchicore 1921

Barrack room group, 1st Battalion, King's Own, Dublin, including: Abner, Foster, J C Jones, Joe Canty, Corporal Claridge, Jimmy Hollin, Johnson, Ormerod, Pinder and Clark.

Soldiers marching out to an investiture at the Viceregal Lodge, Phoenix Park, 14/2/1920.

Finally, on 11th July 1921, a truce was called that signalled the end of active hostilities in the Anglo-Irish war, having been agreed two days earlier. It brought to an end two and a half years of conflict between the Crown and Republican forces and the beginning of five months of negotiations between representatives of the British and Dáil Cabinets. On 6th December 1921, the Anglo-Irish Treaty was signed in London. One of the Irish delegates at the negotiations was Robert Barton. This was the former British officer who had once been in charge of prisoners' effects at Richmond Barracks at the time of the 1916 Rising. After Barton was sent home from the British Army in 1918 to concentrate on farm produce, he was asked by Sinn Fein to stand for election as a Dáil candidate for West Wicklow. It was during the campaign that his election agent, Tom Fleming was arrested for distributing a 'seditious' leaflet depicting an executed prisoner. Barton advertised two protest meetings in February 1919 and these were proclaimed. He held them anyway and made comments at one that if anything were to happen to Fleming there would be a reprisal against Lord French. He was arrested two days later and sent to Mountjoy Jail. In March 1919 he made a daring rope-ladder escape with the aid of Richard Mulcahy and Rory O Connor. When he dropped to the other side of the wall Michael Collins was there to greet him. Finally, he was rearrested and sent to Portland Convict Prison in England on 15th February 1920. He spent 15 months at Portland and a further two months at Portsmouth Prison to where he was transferred having led a strike for prisoners' rights. He was released in July 1921 to help with the truce negotiations, along with Arthur Griffith and Eoin Mac Neill, who had both been arrested and held at Kilmainham.

Though the Treaty ended the Irish War of Independence and gave the Irish dominion status within the British Commonwealth as the Irish Free State, it led to a bloody civil war. As Collins predicted in a letter to his friend John O'Kane:

'When you have sweated, toiled, had mad dreams, hopeless nightmares, you find yourself in London's streets, cold and dank in the night air. Think—what have I got for Ireland? Something which she has wanted these past seven hundred years. Will anyone be satisfied at the bargain? Will anyone? I tell you this; early this morning I signed my death warrant. I thought at the time how odd, how ridiculous —a bullet may just as well have done the job five years ago.'

On the opening day of the Irish Civil War, 28th June 1922, Volunteer, John Monks of Nash Street Inchicore, a soldier of F coy, 4th Battalion IRA was killed in action during an ambush on Free State troops near Red Cow, Clondalkin. Later a woman drove up in a horse and car, and claimed the remains, which were handed over to her.[231] Earlier that day the new Provisional Government had shelled the Four Courts buildings where members of the Anti-Treaty forces were ensconced. Among those manning the artillery was Brigade Sergeant- Major William Fitzgerald of the Dublin Guard unit, formerly of the Glasgow Brigade. He was my maternal grandfather. He claimed that on the 30th June, Sean (Seaghan) Mac Bride (son of Major John Mac Bride) surrendered to him and handed over his Sam Browne belt. There was a long association between the families and the two men were well acquainted. Mac Bride is alleged to have said to him, '*Keep it* (the belt) *safe; don't let those so-and-sos get their hands on it, it was worn by my father.*' The belt is still in the possession of the family and has the word 'Seaghan' written on the inside.

William Fitzgerald was photographed speaking to Michael Collins, Commander-in chief of the National Army, at the funeral of Arthur Griffith, who died of natural causes on 12th August 1922. Just 10 days later, it was his sad duty to attend the funeral of Collins, who had met his fate in an ambush at Béal Na Bláth, Co. Cork. Although without their great leader the National Army continued the fight. In Thomas Kehoe, they still had a formidable champion, but he too, would meet his end the following month.

Gen. Michael Collins and the author's grandfather, Brigade Serg- Maj. Wm. Fitzgerald at the funeral of Arthur Griffith. Right foreground is Kate Mallon, sister of Michael Mallon.

Tom Kehoe- The Irish D'Artagnan

Thomas Kehoe (Tom, as he was always known) was born in Rathduffmore, near Knockananna, Co. Wicklow in 1899. At the age of 14 he left home to find work in Dublin and was apprenticed as a fitter on the Great Northern Railway. While in Dublin, Tom stayed with his half brother Mick McDonnell. It was through McDonnell that the young boy was indoctrinated into the cause of Irish republicanism. In 1915, only two years after his arrival in Dublin, he joined the 2nd Battalion, Dublin Brigade, of the Irish Volunteers. At the time of the 1916 Easter Rising the 17 year old Kehoe was part of the garrison at Jacobs and there met Vincent Byrne. McDonnell was there also, along with Mac Bride and MacDonagh who were in command. All of these men were eventually taken as prisoners to Richmond Barracks where, after a brief spell, Kehoe and Byrne were released owing to their age. In 1917, Tom set up an Ordnance Factory under cover of a bicycle shop in Aungier Street:

> There with a lathe and mandrill he manufactured weapons and hand grenades. Later on, he was involved in setting up a similar operation in Parnell Street, this time adding a small foundry where grenades were cast, including the famous "number 9" and the 'GHQ Grenade.' With Matt Furlong from Wexford he established a workshop in Luke Street where they developed mortars. [232]

When Michael Collins formed his special 'Squad,' Tom was one of the first to be selected. They were also known as 'The Twelve Apostles,' although they eventually numbered more than twelve. Their grim duty was the eradication of British agents and police touts. Tom Keogh was involved in the unsuccessful attempt on the Viceroy, Lord French at Ashtown. In response, the British authorities appointed Resident Magistrate, Alan Bell to assist the Secret Service at Dublin Castle to investigate the attack. Bell was causing a lot of bother for the Squad and had to be dealt with. Keogh, on his bicycle, followed him from his home in Monkstown on the morning of his execution. Bell took a tram, but on reaching Ailesbury Road, Tom, who was behind signalled to his comrades with a handkerchief and the unfortunate Magistrate was dragged from the vehicle. He was summarily dispatched by McDonnell and other members of the squad.

The most sensational event involving The Squad was Bloody Sunday 21st November 1920 when members of the Cairo Gang were targeted. Kehoe's part was mainly in the killing of Lieutenant Henry James Angliss, who operated under the cover name of Mc Mahon. Angliss, although a married man, was naked and sharing a bed with another man when the assassination team arrived. *'Where are your guns Mocker?'* Tom Kehoe asked while colourfully wielding a cut-throat razor. Angliss was found to have two loaded guns inside a portmanteau. He was ordered to lie face down on the bed. He was then shot in the buttocks and in the head.

> With a housemaid screaming for help from an upstairs window, two lorry loads of Auxiliaries screeched to a halt outside the house as the eleven Volunteers split into two groups. Ice cool in a crisis, in a hail of gunfire Tom Kehoe led the first group out saying, *'The best method of defence is attack. We're leaving by the front door.'* Upon entry, Kehoe had made a date with a house-maid. *'I will have to keep that date,'* he joked, as coolly he kept the Auxiliaries at a respectable distance with the two handed gun-play of his Peter the Painter and Long Parabellum while his unit withdrew down Grattan Street...In the midst of the battle, when changing weapons Kehoe dropped one of his guns on the roadway. Calmly he walked back in the midst of the gun-fire to pick it up... ...Later that afternoon he attended the football match at Croke Park, where we had a lucky escape from death when the spectators were machine gunned by Auxiliaries, Black and Tans and British forces.'[233]

'Long Tom' became renowned for his reckless bravery and his *uncanny* marksmanship with a revolver or automatic. When Mick McDonnell fell into bad health, he took over as Commanding officer of the Squad, a position he held until his arrest and internment in Kilmainham Jail following the burning of the Custom House on 25th May 1921. The attack on the Custom House was successful in terms of propaganda value, but it was a heavy blow in terms of the numbers lost, both killed and arrested. The Squad and Active Service Units were amalgamated thereafter into the Dublin Guard. The armed conflict was brought to an end on 11th July 1921 and negotiations were opened which would produce the Anglo-Irish Treaty in December of that year.

In the Irish Civil War that followed, Col. Comdt. Kehoe was sent on the 6th July 1922 with a Free State expeditionary force to County Wexford to re-take the towns there. It comprised 230 men under his control, with one field gun and four armoured vehicles. On the 8th July the Republicans in Wexford abandoned Enniscorthy and New Ross. Kehoe's deeds of bravado continued. A newspaper journalist later recalled:

> I met the late Col. Kehoe less than a month ago when travelling with the Dublin Guards in Kerry. He had just returned to Tralee, his head swathed in bandages; his clothes torn and dusty, and his appearance generally being that of a man who had just come through the wars. Brigadier O'Daly was standing in Ballymullan barrack square as the wounded officer was driven in.
> *'What's the matter, Tom, ambushed?'* he shouted, running to the assistance of his friend.

'No' replied Col. Kehoe dejectedly, *'Not so lucky as that. The car ran into a trench and I was out over the windscreen.'*

I was then introduced by the Brigadier as the Freeman's Journal representative with the Guards, and Col. Kehoe gave me a queer, imploring look which he followed up with a request that I felt must be respected. *'Never say that I came to a miserable end like this,'* he remarked. *'If I'm shot, all right, but don't let it be said that Tom Keogh ended up in a motor accident.'*

A few days in hospital and the patient told the doctors he must be off again. He wanted to report back in Limerick, and with another officer in the First Western Division decided to make the trip. They travelled on a Ford car, and got as far as Castleisland without incident. Here, however they were informed that a big party of irregulars was up the road lying in wait for any cars passing to or from Limerick. The two officers discussed the prospect ahead. What would they do? Neither wanted to turn back, and both felt it was madness to proceed. *'Let's decide the thing with a toss of the coin'* said Col. Kehoe and the penny coming down "head" the officers told the driver to fill the petrol tank and drive sixty miles an hour if the car would do it. Off they started, the Ford at times turning a bend on two wheels, as Col. Kehoe's fellow traveller told, and just as forewarned, when going up a little incline, fire was opened on the car from both sides of the road. The driver got speed up to fifty miles an hour. One of the gunmen, more daring than the others, stood on top of a ditch as the car approached and Col. Kehoe got his Peter-The Painter into action on the instant. Despite the speed and the excitement he shot the irregular through the stomach and the man died, following an operation, a few days later. Courage and daring were again rewarded for Col. Kehoe and his companions got through the ambush unscathed.' [234]

On September 16th 1922, a Free State column with several officers left Macroom to remove road obstructions which barred the main road between there and Ballymakeera. In the vicinity of Carrigaphooka Bridge large trees were felled and the military discovered a land mine, which they then proceeded to shift. Unknown to them, a secondary device was attached with the pin removed, so that the slightest movement would cause it to detonate. It was a deadly trap; when the large stone that lay on top of it was removed, a terrific explosion followed with catastrophic results. Heads, hands, legs and body parts were hurled across ditches and fields; the torso of one soldier was found five fields from the scene. Eight soldiers of the National Army were killed in the blast. The others died instantly, but Commandant Kehoe survived the explosion. He had, however, sustained horrific injuries; both of his legs were shattered and one foot severed. He fought hard to live having being brought to Cork City hospital. The nuns, a few of his old comrades from the Dublin Guards, and Michael Collins' sister, Mary Collins Powell were present when he died. The latter, cut a lock of his hair and a piece of his uniform which she sent to his mother with a letter in which she said:

'He died like a tired child going to sleep, just closed his mouth and his eyes and it was all over.'

Col. Tom Kehoe.

His remains were brought to Portobello Barracks, Dublin where requiem mass was celebrated, and from there to his native birth place. The coffin, which was draped with the Tricolour, was conveyed on a gun carriage to the outskirts of the city, and then transferred to a motor hearse. A firing party in Crossley tenders accompanied the funeral to Knockananna, county Wicklow. Two years later, on the 6th November 1924 three thousand people would gather in the Graveyard at Knockananna, to witness the unveiling, by Major General Liam Tobin, of a memorial to Col. Comdt. Kehoe. It would be followed by an oration by General Beaslai. This highly ornate and decorated Celtic High Cross cost £600, a small fortune in 1924. It remains one of the most outstanding memorials to any Irishman.

Members of the Squad: Vincent Byrne standing with his hand on Tom Kehoe's shoulder.

Kehoe Barracks
& Keogh Square

The Handover of Richmond Barracks

On 14th December 1922, a large crowd assembled outside the main gates of Richmond Barracks from where they could hear the band of the Kings Shropshire Light Infantry playing regimental tunes and Irish airs. Inside, the three British regiments, who for some time had formed the garrison, were drawn up in massed formation on the barrack square. The men totalled 55 officers and 912 other ranks. The officers in charge of the regiments were:

1st Battalion Kings Own- Capt. Boyce
2nd Battalion Welsh Regiment-Capt Derry
2nd Battalion Shropshire Light Infantry-Captain Fitzgerald.

The British forces marching out and the Irish Army marching in.

325

(Both images courtesy of the National Library of Ireland.)

After the unfurled colours of the three regiments had been borne into the ranks, the drums of the King's Own sounded the warning, and the regiments formed in column of route for the 'march out.' Then came the order to '*March!,*' and the three regiments, headed by officers with naked swords a-shoulder, started on their march to the point of embarkation at the North Wall. A small guard of National troops who had taken over the guardroom turned out to give 'a last salute' to the departing British troops. As the officers heading the regiment passed the new guard of the National Army, the latter presented colours and remained at the salute while the colours of the regiment were borne past. Eventful colours, those bearing such titles as Namur, 1695; Gibraltar, 1704-5; Guadaloupe, 1759; Corunna, Badajoz, Salamanca, and the rest of the Peninsular war; with Waterloo, Alma, Inkerman, Sevastapol, and the two South African wars, including the relief of Ladysmith.

And so passed out what was nearing the last remnant of the British garrison in Ireland. The National army under Commandant Coughlan marched in at the same time. The Tricolour was then hoisted in place of the Union Jack. The crowd outside the gate greeted the British troops as they left, particularly the Welsh Regiment, who emerged into the street to a loud burst of cheering.

At approximately the same time similar proceedings were being enacted at Islandbridge Barracks and the Remount Ordnance Department and the Chief Secretary's Lodge. Some 2,000 British soldiers marched to the city centre en route to the North Wall. The Word of their departure seemed to have reached a large section of the public, for there was a big crowd at O'Connell Bridge long before the advance guard arrived there coming down the North Quays. The rollicking music of the regimental bands announced their arrival and the crowd responded some with derisory cries of '*Up the rebels*' and others with handkerchiefs waved and "God Speeds" shouted. (The newspapers carried a notice to the Legion of Irish Ex-Servicemen that a parade would be held at Beresford Place on the 17th December to bid farewell to the last contingent of British troops; about 500 men attended). Finally the troops reached the Alexandra Basin and the troopship, *Menavia*, a steamer of the London and North-Western Company, which bore them off to Holyhead. The Slieve Gallion and the Slieve Donard, of the same company, carried the baggage, horses, and vehicles of the regiments; and all were accompanied by the T.B.D. (Torpedo Boat Destroyer) Venomous, well known in Kingstown. Their destinations were: King's Own to Shorncliffe; Kings Shropshire Light Infantry to Tidworth; and the Welsh Regiment to Colchester.

Richmond Barracks was renamed Kehoe Barracks after the late General Commandant Tom Kehoe. It accommodated the 1st Battalion and the 55th Battalion.

The Execution of Sylvester Heaney

Around this time, Padraig O'Connor, an officer of the National Army was sent with a group of men on a sweep of the area of Blessington where there had been an increase in I.R.A activity. He was thereafter sent to Richmond Barracks, where he received word that he had been promoted to Colonel in charge of operations and Second in Command at Waterford. O'Connor was originally from Nash Street, Inchicore, where his family had moved in Holy Week 1916. The family were known republicans and the home was often raided by the Black and Tans during 1921. His nephew later recounted how guns which used to be stored in the house had to be hidden in the grotto at the Oblate Church. O'Connor was particularly active in the Inchicore and Bluebell areas. During the Civil War he was the officer in charge of the execution of Erskine Childers at Beggars Bush on 24th November 1922. At Kehoe Barracks, a young man awaited a similar fate. Some of the details of his story have never been told until now.

On 1st December 1922, an attack had been carried out on an army supply lorry which had broken down in the townland of Collinstown on the Maynooth road. The occupants of the lorry, about 18 men were forced to surrender and were taken as prisoners to Grangewilliam House. The lorry was then set on fire. In follow up searches carried out by the Free State army a number of confrontations occurred with insurgents resulting in over twenty insurgents being arrested. During the battles three insurgents were wounded and a Free State soldier killed. Twenty one rifles, a Thompson sub-machine gun, six revolvers, a Lewis sub-machine gun, grenades and a substantial amount of ammunition were recovered. Along with the Irregulars arrested were five Free State soldiers who had deserted a few days earlier. The five, Laurence Sheehy, Terence Brady, Leo Dowling, Sylvester Heaney and Anthony O'Reilly were brought to Kilmainham Jail and Court Marshalled on 11th December 1922. They were charged with two counts of treachery:

(1) Assisting 'certain armed persons in using force against the National Army.'
(2) 'Communicating and consorting with armed persons mentioned in first charge.'

While in prison, Heaney did not seem to have any idea of the gravity of his situation, as this letter written to his mother from Kilmainham Jail shows:[235]

Kilmainham Jail

Dear Mother,
Just a few lines to let you know that I am in prison as you see on the address. I was caught on Friday last along with some more of my chums. I hope all are well at home and tell them all I was asking for them. Please send me a shirt if you've got one and tell some of the boys to send me some cigarettes as we get very little of them so far. Thinking this is all for the time been, and hoping to hear from you soon,
I remain your fond son
Sylvester Heaney. (Write soon)

All five were found guilty of both charges and sentenced to death. There is a great deal of confusion surrounding the execution of these men, with some sources giving Portobello as the location of the executions, while others give Kilmainham. In a letter in 2005 from the Military Archives (OIC) to the relatives of Sylvester Heaney it was stated that the five were executed and buried at Kehoe Barracks. With regard to Sylvester Heaney at any rate, a mass card held by the family names Kehoe Barracks. Also, there is the following account told by Padraig O'Connor.

On a morning in January 1923, not long after his arrival, O'Connor was still in his underwear when he heard the firing squad preparing for an execution. He then heard a young man cry for his "Mammy" just before the shots rang out. O'Connor was having eggs for breakfast and according to his brother he never ate eggs again for the remainder of his life. One officer, at the time, remonstrated with him saying: *'This is wrong... we should not be doing this.'* O'Connor put that officer in charge of

the next execution. [*]

In Loving Memory of our dear son Sylvester Heaney, Dillonstown, Irish Republican Army, who was Executed by the Free State at Kehoe Barracks, 8th January, 1923, in the 18th Year of his Age.

It may well be that Sylvester Heaney was dealt with discreetly at Kehoe Barracks away from the public glare. He was only a boy of 18 years, a similar age to Kevin Barry, executed by the British in 1920. The confusion over the location of the event could be due to deliberate obstructionist policy. As we know, most records of executions were ordered be burned by the Free State Army. On 28th October 1924 the remains of Heaney and others would be exhumed from Arbour Hill and repatriated back to their own individual localities; Heaney to his native Co Louth.

There were other Republican prisoners held at Kehoe Barracks. We know this from

---

[*] Told to me By Diarmuid O' Connor

a letter from Michael Behan on 5th Sept. 1923 to his mother in Killeshin, Co. Laois, with deletions by the official censor. [236]

On St. Patrick's Day, 1923, a grand parade of troops took place. Fr. R.J. Casey, Chaplain, blessed the garrison chapel as a Catholic Church. The troops then presented themselves under Capt. S. Byrne as they attended mass. At noon, a new flag was hoisted by Col. McDonnell, while the buglers sounded the general salute and the regimental band played the 'Soldier's Song.' The officers taking part in the parade and ceremony included Comdt. Saurian, Comdt. Vincent Byrne O.C 1st Battalion; Comdt. J Curley, O.C. 55th Battalion; Capt Donnelly.[237] That same evening as Col. McDonnell was motoring along St. John's Road he was shot in the stomach when the driver of his car failed to hear the challenge of a sentry above the noise of the engine.

The troops spent Spy Wednesday in an 'edifying and enjoyable' manner, as they were treated to a "most interesting" lantern slide show on the Passion Play at Oberammergau by the Rev. Francis A. Gleeson, Command Chaplain, Dublin command. The spacious accommodation provided in the gymnasium made a comfortable setting for over 400 soldiers and their friends. Sacred music was rendered by the regimental band under Bandmaster Flahive. [238] In April, one of the buildings adjacent to the gymnasium, comprising the soldiers' recreation rooms, was re-opened for use of the National Army. The Rev. Casey formally declared the reading, games and writing rooms open. Mr. John O' Neill, Chairman Cumann Sugraidh an Airm, opened the new billiard room, and played the first game on the new table given by the committee, to the great satisfaction and applause of the assembled troops. Amongst those present were Comdt. J.K.Curley, O.C. Kehoe Barracks; Comdt. Coughlan, Dublin District Staff; Wm Walsh, Quartermaster Kehoe Barracks; Dr. Doherty, M.O. 1st. Infantry Battalion; Capt Austin X Lawlor, Adjutant 55th Infantry Battalion; Capt. S. Roche, Chief of Staff Department and Capt. Donnelly, A Company 1st Battalion. [239]

The Irish Civil War had continued, particularly in the south of Ireland, for nearly another six months after the takeover. Republican operations degenerated into a campaign of sporadic sabotage. Both sides committed atrocities that would generate bitterness that has lasted to this day. The Irish government passed an Emergency Powers Bill allowing the execution of Republican prisoners, of which seventy-seven were killed (more than were executed by British authorities during the War of Independence). Following the death of Liam Lynch, his successor, Comdt. Frank Aiken, finally ordered his men to dump arms and to return home. On 24th May 1923, Eamon de Valera supported the order, adding that: *'Further sacrifice on your part would now be in vain.'* This effectively brought an end to the war. There was one last incident at Kehoe Barracks, however, where sniper fire was a daily hazard. On

May 25th rifle and revolver fire came from three points resulting in the wounding of one soldier. The fire was answered and patrols sent out, both from the barracks and the Railway Protection Corps at the railway works. This was the last action of the Civil War in this district.

Captain James Grey at Kehoe Barracks.

September 16th 1923, was the first anniversary the death of Colonel Comdt. Kehoe. Commemorations were held at Macroom, where a memorial cross was erected, and Knockananna, county Wicklow where mass was held with his family. In Dublin, many of his old friends and companions were present at Kehoe Barracks to pay their respects. All the troops stationed there turned out for parade and an anniversary mass. After the mass, full military honours were rendered by the troops under Comdt. R. Daly, O.G. 16th Battalion; Captain Mooney and Lieu. J Maguire.

Among those who took part were: Col. R. McDonnell O.C. Dublin District (who had made a full recovery from the shooting); Col. Mc Corley, Comdt. C. Saurin, Comdt. McNulty, O.C. 24th Battalion; Capt Carroll, Capt. J. Byrne, Capt. Walsh Q.M Kehoe Barracks; Capt S Byrne, **Capt. J. Grey**, Capt. J. Switzer, Capt. J. McNaily, Capt. Stack late A.S.U.; Capt J.K.Carley, Capts. Cassidy, Milligan and Maguire; Lieuts. T. Lynch, and J. Delaney.[240]

From 1st April 1924, a large number of ranks were reduced, and men either resigned, rather than accept the particular (lower) position that was offered to them, or were demobilised At this time the Government decided to dispose of Kehoe Barracks and other State property for the purpose of providing for housing needs. On the 18th June, W.T. Cosgrave, then President of the Executive Council received a notification at Dáil Eireann that two ex Officers, namely ex-Comdt. Vincent Byrne and ex- Capt. William Walsh were still residing in the Barracks with their families and were now given until 25th June to give up possession of their quarters. The two men however, reported that they were finding it difficult to find suitable accommodation. An extension of time was granted to the men. Vincent Byrne later resided at Errigal Road in Drimnagh.

The disposal of military barracks was discussed in the Seanad on 28th July, which marked the second stage of the State Lands Bill. Senator Col. Moore was against the idea; he thought it was a very serious matter to dispose of those barracks. If the Government was going to keep troops in Dublin, they ought to be placed in such a position where they could be trained. Senator Thomas Foran, however, said that as a citizen he would be delighted tomorrow if every military establishment in Dublin and Ireland was given over for the purpose of housing accommodation for the people that required it. Foran, a former prisoner at Richmond Barracks in 1916, said that they had had enough of soldiers and everything that appertained to soldiers. President Cosgrave said that they had at present in the city a number of military establishments, which more than provided for the number of troops that they needed to accommodate in them…the particular scheme with relation to housing accommodation at Kehoe Barracks had been put forward by experts in the matter of housing. He understood it would be possible to accommodate a large number of families at a price which was more closely approximate to an economic experiment of the kind than anything he had seen.[241]

Daring Raid on Kehoe Barracks

Following the passing of the State Lands Bill, it was decided to dispose only of Kehoe Barracks. Accordingly, the barracks was evacuated by the Free State Army, and just four sentries were retained at the main gate while the blocks of buildings were being converted into flats. On the night of Saturday, 29th November, 1924, four masked men, carrying revolvers, entered the Barracks. It was a simple matter to gain admission as the boundary wall had tumbled down in a few places. They overpowered the guard and then removed four service rifles and 250 rounds of ammunition. What happened is not quite clear, but the story is that the soldier in the sentry box was suddenly pounced upon and disarmed, and the three other men who were resting in the guardroom were surprised. The raiders, who looked to be little more than boys, snatched up the four rifles and ammunition, and also the keys of the main gate. The alarm was quickly raised, but they got clear away. Not surprisingly, the military authorities were reticent about the whole affair.[242]

Workers dismantling the gate of the former Richmond/Kehoe Barracks, 1926.

Keogh Square

By December 1924, 20 families were already housed in the converted army blocks. Then, in 1925 the rest of the units began to be filled. In 1926 it was formally proposed that the new development be called Kehoe Square. In media reportage the spelling 'Kehoe' was given as 'Keogh,' a variant of the name and one which Tom himself had sometimes used. Some still referred to it as 'Keogh Barracks' and the inhabitants as "Barrackers," a moniker that stuck. This area was particularly associated with a perceived betrayal of the forefathers of the new state. Somewhere in folk memory this betrayal was never forgiven and would attach itself to anyone who went on to live there. They became known locally as Barrackers.

With the growth of the population of St. James's Parish it had become necessary to find church accommodation for the increasing number of people in the Parish. Our Lady of Mercy Chapel Goldenbridge (Fr. Tom Ryan's) was closed down in April 1926 and taken over by the nuns for use as an infants' school. What was formerly the garrison chapel then became the chapel of ease. It was renamed the church of St. Michael of the Angels, and opened for public worship by the Rev. Dr. Byrne, Archbishop of Dublin, on Sunday 25th April 1926. A large statue of St. Michael slaying the Devil was a notable feature in the porch of the church for many years, but this was removed in more recent times because it caused some distress to younger children. Large numbers of people assembled to welcome the Archbishop to Inchicore and there was a lavish selection of decorations, mainly with Papal colours the entire length of Emmet Road. The new bell, which had been installed in the building, was blessed by the Archbishop.[243] There were those, however, who objected to going to mass in the "garrison chapel." as they continued to call it.

By August 1928, a total of 248 families were housed in the barrack buildings and 218 families in houses built on a thirteen acre field to the east of the square. The latter, was the former training ground for the British troops. The names of the new streets in the Kehoe Square area were announced. They were: 'Bothar Bulfin' (Bulfin Rd), 'Ascal O Conghaile' (Connolly Ave.), 'Ardan an Droichid Ordha' (Goldenbridge Tce.) and 'Gairdini an Droichid Ordha' (Goldenbridge Gds). Other houses would be added over the years to form what is today collectively known as the Bulfin Estate.

In addition, the Corporation renovated military stores as cottages which ran behind the newly built Connolly Avenue, a few facing St. Vincent's street and some behind them again. The Officers' Mess was rented to the City of Dublin Child Welfare Committee for use as a milk depot. There was a military mortuary chapel outside the wall at the rear of the barracks (the reason it was built outside was that it was considered bad for the morale of the soldiers to have it inside the walls). The ESB used this for a sub-station for a while and it was thereafter abandoned on open ground to be used by workmen to store their tools and often where rubbish was dumped. It fell into disrepair and there was also a problem of drainage in the area surrounding it. The occupier of No.1, Connolly Avenue faced with this unsightly problem bought the land and the building from the E.S.B. Today, Mr. Samuel Kydd uses the old mortuary chapel as a garden shed. The Christian Brothers' school based in the recreation rooms either side of the gymnasium was opened in 1929. The gymnasium itself, which was originally intended to be utilised as a public hall, was also given over to the Brothers to be used by the pupils for physical exercise. It still contained a pommel horse in good shape, which was literally worn out by the pupils over the years. In times of overcrowding some classes were held in the gymnasium.

The Mortuary Chapel

The area of Inchicore was still part of the parish of Saint James, but in 1933 was constituted as the separate parish of Saint Michael. On 7th October 1934, Archbishop Byrne returned, this time to lay the corner stone of an extension. The population had increased and many people were now living in Keogh Square. The Bulfin Estate too, had grown in terms of population. The church was originally built to hold 600; the new extension would accommodate a further 450 persons.

When Dublin Corporation took over Kehoe Barracks the buildings were in good shape and when converted into flats were considered to be among the finest in Dublin. In the main, families lived off hallways; there were six flats in each hall, two on each floor. A typical flat consisted of two or three bedrooms, a large living room with open fire often used for cooking, and a small kitchen and toilet. The rooms were about 30 feet square, with double doors and high ceilings. They were, of course, hard to heat and the stone stairs and plain block stone front were not attractive. Many took flats there as a stepping stone to getting a house in the Bulfin Estate. Railwaymen drivers and firemen did this as they had to be in easy reach of the railway works. In those early days the Square was a pleasant place. There was a band recital, for instance, at the band-stand every Sunday. A lot of those tenants remained until the end, despite the problems that followed through the years and the terrible reputation it had acquired. As early as the 1930's, Dublin Corporation had a policy of moving people into Keogh Square who had been evicted elsewhere for not paying their rent. Most of the tenants were decent people, widows, the unemployed, and those unfit for work owing to ill health.

Eucharistic congress 1932.

In a filmed interview, Labour Councillor Joe Deasy from Inchicore recalled that in 1945 there were 21,000 people on the Dublin housing waiting list and that during the War (Emergency) years no new houses were being built. It meant that people living in Keogh Square, for instance, had no option but to remain there. Joe worked alongside Jim Larkin during the latter's final years. Larkin and his son James rented a flat in Keogh Square in which union meetings were held and the needs of the tenants assessed. In 1948, Deasy pursued the City Manager, to say *'When the tenants of Keogh Square can expect to have electric light functioning in their flats.'*

336

Peter Johnston, bottom left with arm around Joe Weaver. Little man with hat, Paddy Smith. They all used to play handball against this wall. Paddy O' Hara, first left on top row; 1950s.

Josie's shop, Finnerty's: Mick Smith Snr, Jack Dempsey, Peter Bean, Terry Spider Mc Carty, Tommy Mc Carty, George Fitzpatrick, Michael Timmons, Pat Caulfield. Building on the right was the cork-maker's outlet.

Bros. Sullivan and Druin; two of the best, but capable of dishing out 6 of the best.

Confirmation class CBS 1966 wth Mr. Campbell.

Women of the huts group- left to right: Mrs White, Mrs Elliott, Mrs McMahon, bottom: Mrs Larkin & Mrs Bates, 1963.

The people who lived there up until the early 1960's were generally poor with large families, but it was a stable community with a strong sense of identity with close social ties within the Square. There were a number of quaint characters too, including 'the woman who walked backwards.' This unfortunate person used to have difficulty walking. It seemed her Achilles tendons were so tight that she walked on the balls of her feet and would take a few steps forward, then turn around and take a few steps backwards. Her name was Jane Fitzpatrick. She was full of fun and could often be found joining in the kids games. She passed into folklore and is still spoken of today, always with great affection.

However, after that time came another group of people who seemed determined to make life miserable for everyone:

'What destroyed Keogh Square was the putting of about 30 criminal families into it; families in which father, mother and the children were all criminals. These people materially affected Keogh Square by stripping the lead off all the roofs and all the copper water-fittings, etc. The Corporation never carried out

343

more than patchwork repairs and the buildings deteriorated rapidly. For the last few years the top stories were unoccupied (presumably because of leaks). Then these people made Keogh Square notorious as a criminal centre.'[244]

By 1962, Keogh Square was hitting the headlines for all the wrong reasons. It had become a slum and a no-go area for outsiders. Terrible stories were circulated, such as the account of one unfortunate man who was stabbed in the back with a pitchfork; the handle had to be sawn off before he could be fitted into the ambulance. The enormous grey walls, dilapidated tenement blocks and poor lighting (by gas until 1969!) gave the place a sinister appearance.

Dr. John O'Connell, later referring to Keogh Square in a Dáil Eireann debate on squatting remarked:

I know of one case of squatting in which the father of three children was involved. This man broke into an empty flat in Keogh Square. To break into Keogh Square is similar to going into a rat hole, but the man did this because he wanted to have a roof over his children. Rent was accepted from him for some time, but eventually he was evicted forcibly. However, he was put on a list for housing and some time later he was sent back to the flat in Keogh Square from which he had been evicted. [245]

Radio presenter, Joe Duffy's grandmother lived in Keogh square. Joe recalled: *'We seldom visited, but when we did, having the dark stairs smelling of urine, we only stayed long enough for the novelty of a heel of batch loaf crisply toasted on an open fire.'*[246]

The funeral of William T. Cosgrave at Goldenbridge cemetery, 1965.

One notable event occurred on the 18th November 1965 that diverted attention from domestic worries, if only for a brief spell. On that miserable rainy day, the State Funeral of William T. Cosgrave, former President of the Executive Council of the Irish Free State, took place. Following mass at the Church of the Annunciation, Rathfarnham, the remains were brought to Goldenbridge Cemetery. The chief mourners at the graveside were Mr. Liam Cosgrave T.D. and family, and Eugene

345

Timmons T.D., Lord Mayor of Dublin. To the elder inhabitants of the area the occasion would have brought back echoes of former times.

Fr. Peter Lemass, the globetrotter, reporter of 'Radharc' fame speaking in October 1967 at the annual meeting of the Irish Society for the Prevention of Cruelty to Children, said:

'I have never seen, in any part of the world to which I have travelled, conditions more degrading, an atmosphere depressing, or an environment more hopeless, than in Keogh Square'-

Author, T.P. Kifeather, went to interview the tenants and reported back to the Sunday Independent that it was a health black spot. They told him that they were afraid of the rats; they told him that a hall-way was used a lavatory and that the walls were so damp, pools of water formed on the floor. It was, he said, now one of the most foetid slums in Europe, housing scores of families. The three remaining sides of the huge barracks were still standing at that time. The contrast was startling between busy, neatly-kept Inchicore and that island of squalor and dirt. Most Dubliners, he asserted, would have been shocked to find that there was a slum in their city which, in many respects, was worst than those which existed in 1913. Keogh Square was a flash-point from which could spread an epidemic. Children swarmed there. Eighty per cent of them had no hope of growing into healthy manhood or womanhood. The dice of environment and neglect were loaded against them. They are, mostly, the victims of the parents who had brought them into the life of Keogh Square.

He spoke to a mother of nine boys and two girls. The boys were grown-up and all of them had employment. This family lived in two rooms. Rent-11/6 a week. But they did not want to leave Keogh Square. He asked: *'Have you ever been offered a house by the Corporation?'* They had -twice. But they did not want to move to Cherry Orchard Estate. That was the answer of another mother who lived in two rooms with her two children: *'I've lived here for years and I don't want to leave the Square.'* A high proportion of those who lived in the former barracks had been evicted not only once but twice from Corporation houses for non payment of rent. The Square was a place where the flotsam of the city found accommodation. Here too, were itinerants, families who had given up the existence of life on the road. Kilfeather reported:

> 'If you want to find examples of a quiet heroism of a kind that never get into the headlines you should visit Keogh Square. You will find it behind the windows in the gaunt and grim buildings which have neat and colourful curtains. There are not too many of these-but they are the outward sign of a mother who is fighting a battle of quiet desperation to the make the home she dreamed of on her wedding day. The odds against her are fantastically high.'[247]

He looked out onto the barracks square where sergeant-majors had once shouted their orders and it was easy to pick out the children of these mothers. The children were well-dressed and well- nourished. Not all of Keogh Square was a slum. Some of the single-storey buildings (military stores) which had been converted into dwellings were brightly painted and were well-kept homes. By contrast, they showed how slum-like were the other buildings.

The P.P. Rev. Fr. Meleady made frequent visits to the Corporation urging them to demolish the barrack blocks and to build houses on the site. Some blocks were demolished in stages between 1962 -67 and the rest left, making the place look even worse. Then in 1967 it was suddenly decided to demolish the remainder of the blocks at once and to build houses in 5 years time. Due to pressure from the shop-keepers, who were not willing to have a loss of income for the sake of houses, the Corporation opted for high rise flats instead. A similar development, though on a larger scale, had begun at Ballymun in 1966. Ironically, each flat would cost £1000 more than the current cost of a house, but they could be constructed immediately, whereas in another 5 years the flats would cost more.

Fr. Ryan's Chapel of Ease can be seen inside the walls of the convent.

Keogh Square partly demolished.

The Youth Club

Father Brian Power was a highly intellectual young curate sent to the working class parish of St. Michael's in 1968, more or less, as a punishment for getting the wrong side of Archbishop Mc Quaid. His 'sin' was that he said mass for clerical students at Newman House, without the Archbishop's permission and with no altar stone. He had tried to argue his case, but Mc Quaid had risen from his high chair and stood by the door with his arms stiffly by his side, signalling the ultimate insult to Fr. Power that he was not allowed to kiss the Episcopal ring. Notice of his exile to Inchicore came immediately after.[248] On arrival he visited the local priest, Fr. Tadhg McCarthy and in the course of the meeting this amusing exchange took place:

Fr. McCarthy: *'I must warn you, this is a tough area.'*
Fr. Power: *'Really?'*
Fr. Mc Carthy: *'Last night they burned down the Youth Club.'*
Fr. Power: *'Goodness, who burned it down?'*
Fr. Mc Carthy: *'Why, the youths of course!'* [249]

Allegedly, the fire was started by just one young man with a grievance and it was a great loss to the other boys in the area. St. Vincent's Boys Club was founded in 1958 by Gerry O'Sullivan (later a Legion of Mary envoy in South America) and Noel Clear. It was under the care of a St. Vincent de Paul youth conference and from it spawned other groups, such as: the Keogh Square Tenants Association; also, two girls' clubs, namely, Goldenbridge- run by the nuns, and St. Bridget's. After the fire they were left without a permanent venue and were forced to use a room in the old Dublin Health Authority dispensary in Keogh Square, described as 'an eyesore' awaiting demolition.

The Youth Club, Keogh Square.

Fr. Power visited them there and spoke to Mr. Tom Gilmore, a holy ghost seminarian at the club told him that when a boy went for a job, the fact that he lived in Keogh Square was a barrier against him. There was plenty of employment for girls, but when the boys left school at 14 there was little for them but to become messengers. Then at 18, the strong ones got labouring work, but if they are not strong enough for heavy work they would be idle for a very long time. Out of 100 club members, only 3 had attended Vocational school and none went to Secondary school. The introduction of free education had made little difference; there was no tradition of post-primary education there and a boy who went on for it would be the odd man out; he would not have the few shillings to spend at the weekend. Then his family would not be able to afford to buy books and could not do without the few pounds he could earn. Mr. Terry Kelly of the St Vincent de Paul conference said:

'Since the beginning of the year several hundred boys from Inchicore area have gone to Letterfrack, Daingean, and St. Patrick's and we visited them there. The club has done much to divert them from crime to constructive activity. We try to get jobs for them when they come out of these institutions. It is good for them, too, to find themselves accepted back with the club.'

They were trying to talk against high-powered céilí music from a gramophone, as a swirl of pretty young girls performed four-handed reels and polkas. They had not much room to dance: they were in the small central space in the dispensary; its other rooms were locked up. Some of them came over to Fr. Power and spoke to him. Chrissie Carroll, (16) was a hairdresser and enjoyed going to plays; Kathleen O'Keefe, (19) a worker in Jacob's came from a family of 15 and was determined that she was not going to marry young; Celia Russell, (15), was employed in a stocking factory folding tights; Noeleen Donovan, (13) had moved to Crumlin and wished she were back in the Square; Marie Hyland who had moved to Sean Mac Dermott Street thought the same.

Then there was a flutter of chat and giggling as the *Irish Times* photographer arrived. They were all then anxious to give their names, which may be of curiosity to their families now. They included:
Bernadette Moran, Catherine Russell, Catherine Bernie, Eileen and Katherine Moran, Tina Kennedy, Ann Nolan, Imelda Mc Guinness, Pauline Ashmore, Maria Archibold, Ann Cannon, Catherine O'Reilly, and Rita, Catherine Byrne and Geraldine Kearins. [250]

Mrs. Kelly, who was also present, was worried that *'People will say Keogh Square is gone: what do you want with a youth centre now? We need one now more than ever before.'* Later they succeeded in building a club which became the Parish Centre after the Oblates took over pastoral care of most of Inchicore.

By December 1968 only 55 houses and cottages remained in Keogh Square. 170 families had been re-housed elsewhere even before building had gotten underway. The demolition continued inexorably during 1969. Patrick Pearse had once said, at the funeral of O' Donavan Rossa, *'The Fools, the Fools, they have left us our Fenian Dead.'* Dublin Corporation made no such error; they bulldozed the most important block of all- the Officers' block - in which the 1916 leaders were courts martialled. It was the last block to be demolished, as though they were waiting for someone to object… and **no one did.** There was, it has to be said, a small group of Sinn Fein picketers who carried placards with comments such as *'Griffith Barracks Next,'* *'228 down 20 to go,'* calling generally for more housing. The Corporation demolished the Officers' block and for some inexplicable reason retained the adjacent mortuary chapel which was of no historical importance. The local people seemed more upset by the loss of the old guardhouse facing onto Emmet Road. Finally, the vast former British Army barracks, where children lived or died in high icy rooms with stuffed sinks and filthy lavatories, perennially out of order, were gone. Eileen O' Brien borrowed a line from Countess Markievicz in her summation for the Irish Times, when she said that the bulldozers had *'done a good day's work for Ireland.'* All that remained were the school buildings, mortuary chapel, the Church and the statue of the blessed virgin which used to stand, *'a mournful accusation to the rest of the city, amid the refuse blown by the wind and the under-nourished ill-clad children.'* [251]

Sinn Fein demonstration for more housing.

St. Michael's Estate

John Sisk, Kevin Boland and Mr. P.D. Tully, director of Ardglass

Minister of State Kevin Boland cuts the tape alongside Mr. P.D. Tully.

The new complex of 8 and 4 storey flats was constructed by Ardglass Ltd. They were built on the Balancy system used in Ballymun and the parts of the houses were manufactured there and conveyed to Inchicore by lorry. Accommodation would be provided for 346 housing units including 70 old folks flats. Soon, lorries, each carrying 4 or 5 sections of the new flats from the factory in Ballymun could be seen arriving at the 14 acre site. By the end of January 1970 the first of the tenants began to move in. It was originally intended that there would be 5 X 8 storey blocks, 4 X 4 storey and 4 X 2 storey old folks maisonettes, a total of 13 blocks. However, the residents of Connolly Avenue objected to the proposed block 13 which was to be built in close proximity to their houses. They claimed that it would obstruct the sunlight and also be an invasion of privacy. Instead, the fifth 8 storey block was scrapped and two extra 4 storey blocks were constructed further to the west of the Avenue, close to the canal.

The site where the planned 5th block of 8 storeys was to be built.

The history of St. Michael's Estate is remarkably similar to that of Keogh Square and it seems that no lessons were learned by any of those concerned. In the beginning, as with Keogh Square, the new flats looked really well; indeed, the complex was described as a 'model housing development.' Each flat was self contained with bathroom and toilet facilities; it was centrally heated, with the pipes running underneath the floor and there was hot water on demand, day or night; the rooms were spacious and well laid out; the upper storeys had a panoramic view encompassing the Royal Hospital, the Wellington monument in the Phoenix Park and far beyond.

354

Squatting was a problem from the start. In one week alone, 12 new flats were occupied by squatters. When a certain Mr. Hynes went to take possession of the flat assigned to him by Dublin Corporation he found a squatter and his family in occupation. He appealed to the civic guards who were outside, but they were unable to act. Taking matters into his own hands, he gave the squatter a few punches and boldly evicted the whole family.

Flooding 1978.

The difficulties with St. Michael's Estate were not- at the beginning, at any rate- to do with bricks and mortar. No matter how many challenges the people of any area have to face, over time a community spirit will prevail. So it was with Keogh Square, and a certain code of conduct existed among the people towards one another, even if it did not extend to those outside, and especially not to strangers who ventured into the Square. However, by the time the new project was completed, many families of the old Keogh Square, including the more community-minded, had been relocated in one of the vast new housing schemes such as Ballyfermot. Tenants to St. Michael's came from various parts of the inner city. Few of these families remained long enough for any kind of settled community to develop; they moved to a better location as soon as they had accrued enough housing points. Then in the mid 1980's, a surrender grant of £5,000 was offered to enable people to buy their own houses. New housing schemes had been built in Tallaght and Clondalkin. This led to a general exodus from St. Michael's Estate and the area lost a lot of its leaders. Others, who could not afford to buy a house, availed of inter-transfers; usually an unofficial fee for 'moving expenses' would be offered as a softener in such cases. In this way there was a constant turnover of new tenants in the area. Of course, some remained until the very end and of these a few had lived in Keogh Square or had family who were 'Barrackers.'

Because the Estate was built on the former site of Keogh Square the social stigma remained and greatly affected the prospects of young people seeking employment. What makes an area a ghetto is neither the style of building nor the range of amenities, but the economic profile of the people in it. If a place has a disproportionate number of households on low incomes it will also have more than its fair share of other problems. In the latter days of St. Michael's Estate the unemployment rate was 80% with the majority of the residents living on Social Welfare. Certainly the youths felt deprived even though they were considerably better off than their predecessors in Keogh Square. Incidences of burglary and handbag-snatching were frequent. Want, coupled with boredom, a feeling of uselessness- of being left on the scrapheap- led to the obsession with joy-riding and later the use of drugs. The scourge of joyriding was first and became a nightly event ending always with the car being set on fire. These cars were usually dumped in the flats by outsiders, after they had used them for whatever purpose for which they were stolen, and were left for the local lads to drive up and down. Then, when the Gardai arrived on the scene, it was locals who would get into trouble.

There was far worse to come in the 1990's with the flood of heroin into the area. This was an epidemic. It did not matter who you were or how well brought-up your offspring were. Those who were quick to judge other families were often left to regret their words and reflect on their own situations. Drugs were being couriered in by bus and car and taxi from outside sources. The problem escalated whenever there was a shortage of supply- 'a drought.' Addicts from all over Dublin would converge on Inchicore in the hope of a drop; pitiful creatures who looked like famine victims; but there was no pity or sympathy for them at that time, only revulsion and fear. This was understandable, when people were fighting (a losing battle) to keep their own children clean. Women had to step over addicts on the balconies and hallways in order to get into their flats. Sometimes the addicts would have needles hanging out of their veins and there would be blood everywhere. It seemed that the drug barons were targeting disadvantaged areas as the teenagers there were vulnerable and of least importance in the public psyche. Who would care what happened to the children of such an area? Had an estate in Dublin 4 been targeted in the same way the entire Garda force would have been in constant vigil, but policing in St. Michael's Estate was minimal.

Fortunately some people did care. Chief among them was the local Chemist, Mr. Boles who put his reputation and his business on the line, in the face of great adversity, in order to provide treatment for the afflicted teenagers. Many middle-aged men and women living in the area today owe their lives to this man. Another was Linda Kavanagh of the Worker's Party, who also encountered opposition when she campaigned for the provision of a centre for drug misusers. Protests outside the premises on Emmet Road failed to deter Ms. Kavanagh and her dedicated workers. The Inchicore Community Drug Team continues to serve the area and in addition provides counselling services for the families of those affected. The centre was named, The Kavangah House in memory of its late founder. Other groups still in operation are The Youth Centre and The St. Michael's Family Resource Centre, an anti-poverty organization offering support and advice in a friendly atmosphere.

At this stage other problems, in the very nature of the planning and structure of St. Michael's, begin to show. The towers were built with the stairwells in the middle. This divided each floor into two, providing easy hiding places or escape for muggers, joyriders or drug pushers. Bollards had to be installed at the St. Vincent's Street entrances to curb joyriding escapades. Cutbacks in the 1980's had resulted in deterioration of the whole estate. Most of the lifts were constantly out of order; this meant tenants had to climb as many as 16 flights of stairs (2 per floor) with shopping, prams and sometimes furniture. Leaks from the roofs were another feature, with trickles of brown water streaming down decorated walls of people's homes and even into the flats below. Central heating, once considered a great boon became a nuisance when people realised that that there was no way to control the temperature. Cables for piped television housed in presses on the balconies were constantly interfered with by non-paying cable users plugging in and reducing the signal strength. The glass in the fire doors on many of the landings had not been replaced. Many of the stairwells were badly lit, rendering it a dangerous and frightening place to be at night. A serious problem in the drainage arose with sewage coming up into the lavatories at ground level. Some of these flats had to be permanently evacuated. The worst block of all was block 8, colloquially known as H Block or Hell's kitchen. This was the favourite haunt of drug users who squatted there and frequently set the flats on fire.

The playground was stripped of all apparatus leaving the surrounding railings; every few months the Corporation would send a team of painters to renew the paintwork on the railings of this redundant play area- a totally pointless exercise. The real joke was that landings were only painted once every seven years; the balconies and the exteriors of the flats covered in graffiti and flaking paint were rarely refurbished in the 40 year history of St Michaels.

Eventually in 1992, IR £1 Million for refurbishment was sanctioned under the Remedial Works Scheme. What is, I have found, more than just an urban legend surrounds the attainment of the promise of this grant:

'In 1992 (named individual, resident of St Michael's Estate[*]) had a meeting with Bertie Ahern. She trapped him in a lift in block eight and the outcome of that was a commitment for IR £1 Million for the refurbishment of St Michael's Estate…And that is what actually started the process. (Former resident & activist St. Michael's Estate).'[252]

Certainly, people in the area will remember receiving a leaflet announcing the IR £1 Million pound. Of course it was a week before a General Election. After three or four years of negotiations the money was still not forthcoming and none of the refurbishment plans materialised. While some people wished to remain on the site once it was refurbished a lot of others had had enough and wanted houses built there instead. Dublin City Council had made up their minds from as early as 1998 that demolition was inevitable. From that time onwards an unwritten, but very apparent policy of de-tenanting was in place. There was a stay on allocations while those seeking transfers out of the estate had their transfers prioritised. The eviction of up to 70 families on anti-social grounds and the transfer of other tenants to the Senior Citizens flats and the newly built Emmet Crescent dramatically reduced the population from 220 to about 55 Families. The immediate result was the spectacle of boarded up flats. What little maintenance and policing that had existed then ceased altogether. This added further pressure on the remaining tenants to leave.

With the demolition of St. Michael's Estate imminent there were also a series of plans drawn up for the redevelopment of the site. However, as with the refurbishment plans, and despite the best efforts of the newly formed St. Michael's Estate Regeneration Board, one by one these plans were scrapped. Most disappointing of all was the failure of the Public Private Partnership scheme for regeneration in May 2008; a consequence of the collapse in the property market and in particular, Brendan McNamara's construction business. Finally in November 2010, a Dutch company, Bam, took possession of a two acre site at the canal end of the former complex and began preparatory work for the construction of 75 residential units, a mix of social and affordable housing; phase one of the regeneration of the 14 acre site. Since then, a special Dublin City Council Task Force has worked with the Board to find solutions to continue with the project. On 26th February 2013 about 200 former residents gathered to witness the demolition of the final block of flats in St. Michael's Estate.

---

[*] Yes, of course it was Rita Fagan.

Liam Cosgrave, former Taoiseach and son of a 1916 leader held at Richmond Barrack at the launch of the restoration project: also Aengus O'Snodaigh TD. and Catherine Byrne TD.

Late in 2013, a grant was secured for the renovation of the Gymnasium and unit 3 of the three remaining units of Richmond / Kehoe Barracks. The CBS School had closed its doors in 2006 and all three units were allowed to deteriorate. Unit one was taken over by the HSE for use as a medical centre and beautifully restored. It is hoped that the remaining two will be restored and put to use in way that will reflect the historic and social importance of this site. In 1960, Kilmainham Jail lay in ruins and but for local voluntary workers it would have been lost to the nation forever. Today it is one the main tourist attractions in Dublin. It is also part of a rich heritage trail together with the Royal Hospital and the Irish War Memorial Gardens. The Gymnasium and units of Richmond Barracks could be integrated as part of that trail. It is hoped too, that the development of the remainder of the 14 acres, today a grass field, will continue and that when it does, lessons of the past will have been learned. Otherwise we will all be back to Square one.

The Gymnasium today with, from left: Eadaoin ni Chleirigh, Richmond Barracks Advisory Committee; Ruairi O'Cuiv, Public Arts Officer, D.C.C.; Liam O' Meara, author; Piet Chielens, 'In Flanders Fields Museum,' Belgium; Ray Yeats, City Arts Officer; Martin Mac Donagh, D.C.C.

Richmond Barracks Movement of Troops

Regt.No	Title	Date In	Out	To
1st.	Royal Cheshire Light Infantry Militia	01/1814	02/1816	Chester
3rd.	Royal Lancashire Militia	03/1814	06/1815	England
74th.	Highland Foot	03/1816	06/1817	Strabane
94th.	Scotch Brigade	03/1817	03/1818	Belfast
50th.	Queen's Foot	06/1818	01/1819	West Indies
91st.	Argyllshire	01/1819	08/1820	Jamaica
42nd.	Royal Highland	05/1819	08/1820	Kilkenny
7th.	Royal Fusiliers	12/1819	08/1820	London
29th.	Worcestershire Foot	08/1820	05/1822	Mullingar
81st.	Royal Lincoln Volunteers	08/1820	09/1820	Quebec
39th.	Dorsetshire Foot	08/1820	03/1821	Cork
77th.	East Middlesex Foot	08/1820	11/1822	West indies
31st.	Huntingdonshire Foot	08/1820	01/1823	Armagh
40th.	2nd Somerset Foot	11/1820	03/1823	N.S.Wales
33rd.	Duke of Wellington's Foot	03/1821	04/1821	Jamaica
52nd.	Oxfordshire Light Infantry	07/1821	05/1822	Tipperary
13th.	1st. Somersetshire Light Infantry	09/1821	07/1822	E. Indies
86th.	Royal County Down Foot	05/1822	05/1823	Athlone
71st.	Highland Light Infantry	05/1822	10/1822	Fermoy
3rd. Bn.	Grenadier Guards	05/1822	08/1822	London
19th.	1st.Yorkshire North Riding	07/1822	05/1823	Sligo
2nd.	Queen's Own Royal Foot	07/1822	10/1823	India
1st. Bn.	Grenadier Guards	08/1822	08/1823	England
55th.	Westmoreland Foot	11/1822	02/1823	South Africa
15th.	Yorkshire East Riding	01/1823	11/1823	Waterford
66th.	Berkshire Foot	03/1823	04/1823	Enniskillen
23rd.	Royal Welsh Fusiliers	05/1823	12/1823	Gibraltar
1st. Bn.	Coldstream Guards	07/1823	08/1824	Knightsbridge
79th.	Cameron Highlanders	10/1823	07/1824	Kilkenny

77th.	East Middlesex Foot	10/1823	02/1824	Jamaica
84th.	York and Lancaster Foot	12/1823	09/1824	Clonmel
31st.	Huntingdonshire Foot	01/1824	07/1824	E. Indies
88th.	Connaught Rangers	07/1824	08/1825	Corfu
75th	Stirlingshire Foot	07/1824	10/1825	Newry
25th.	Yorkshire King's Own	07/1825	10/1825	W.Indies
78th.	Highlanders Ross-Shire Buffs	07/1825	02/1826	Ceylon
58th.	Rutlandshire Foot	10/1825	05/1826	England
66th.	Berkshire Foot	10/1825	07/1826	Birr
34th.	Cumberland Foot	05/1826	05/1827	Templemore
73rd.	Perthshire Foot	07/1826	01/1827	Waterford
26th.	Cameronians	01/1827	07/1827	Kilkenny
72nd.	Duke of Albany Foot	05/1827	10/1827	London
61st.	Gloucestershire Foot	07/1827	10/1827	Ceylon
36th.	Herefordshire Foot	07/1827	09/1827	Royal Bks.
5th.	Northumberland Fusiliers	09/1827	10/1827	Royal Bks.
69th.	South Lincolnshire Foot	10/1827	10/1827	Mullingar
56th.	East Essex Foot	10/1827	04/1828	Londonderry
17th.	Leicestershire Foot	04/1828	05/1828	Dundalk
17th.	Leicestershire Foot	05/1829	05/1830	Newbridge
64th	2nd. Staffordshire Foot	05/1829	06/1830	Belfast
32nd.	Duke of Cornwall Light Infantry	05/1829	06/1830	Quebec
4th.	King's Own Foot	06/1830	09/1830	Liverpool
76th.	Cameron Foot	06/1830	10/1830	Beggars Bush
9th.	East Norfolk Foot	09/1830	05/1831	Clare
87th.	Royal Irish Fusiliers	10/1830	11/1830	Cork
70th.	Surrey Foot	11/1830	09/1831	Kilkenny
76th.	Cameron Foot	12/1830	04/1831	Limerick
92nd.	Gordon Highlanders	05/1831	10/1831	Clare Castle
21st	Royal Scots Fusiliers	09/1831	10/1831	Bath & Bristol
28th.	Nth. Gloucestershire Foot	10/1831	06/1832	Maryborough
50th.	Queen's Own Royal Foot	10/1831	12/1831	Newbridge
60th.	King's Royal Rifle Corps	12/1831	07/1832	Belfast
43rd.	Monmouthshire Light Infantry	05/1832	04/1833	Wexford
80th.	Staffordshire Foot	06/1832	09/1832	Belfast
50th.	Queen's Own Royal Foot	06/1832	09/1832	Birr
81st.	Royal Lincoln Volunteers	08/1832	09/1832	Templemore

68th.	Durham Light Infantry	10/1832	07/1833	Newry
52nd.	Oxfordshire Light Infantry	10/1832	06/1833	Newry
90th.	Perthshire Foot	10/1832	08/1833	Kilkenny
59th.	2nd. Nottinghamshire Foot	06/1833	04/1834	Liverpool
83rd.	County of Dublin Foot	08/1833	04/1834	Nova Scotia
52nd.	Oxfordshire Light Infantry	09/1833	10/1833	Royal Bks.
74th.	Highland Foot	11/1833	04/1834	Drogheda
1st.	Royal 2nd Bn	04/1834	10/1834	Athlone
47th.	Lancashire Foot	04/1834	09/1834	Gibraltar
81st.	Royal Lincoln Volunteers	10/1834	09/1835	Kilkenny
46th.	South Devon Foot	10/1834	01/1835	Belfast
90th.	Perthshire Volunteers Light Infantry	02/1835	07/1835	Ceylon
85th.	King's Light Infantry	05/1835	08/1835	Beggars Bush
89th.	Princess Victoria's Foot	05/1835	08/1835	West Indies
14th.	Buckinghamshire Foot	07/1835	10/1835	Pigeon House
93rd.	Sutherland Highlanders	10/1835	10/1836	Newry
91st.	Princess Louise's Argyllshires	10/1835	11/1835	Newbridge
12th.	East Suffolk Foot	03/1836	09/1836	Athlone
71st.	Highland Light Infantry	05/1836	10/1836	Beggars Bush
77th.	East Middlesex Foot	10/1836	09/1837	Malta
95th.	Derbyshire Foot	11/1836	09/1837	Newry
80th.	Staffordshire Foot	03/1837	03/1837	N. S. Wales
46th.	South Devon Foot	03/1837	09/1837	Gibraltar
94th.	Argyll and Sutherland Foot	09/1837	06/1838	Ceylon
38th	1st Staffordshire Foot	09/1837	08/1838	Mediterranean
79th.	Queen's Own Cameron Highland	06/1838	03/1839	Liverpool
96th.	Regiment of Foot	08/1838	01/1839	Liverpool
97th.	Earl of Ulster	02/1839	08/1839	Athlone
88th.	Connaught Rangers	05/1839	09/1840	Malta
19th.	1st.Yorkshire North Riding	09/1839	03/1840	Royal Bks.
64th.	2nd. Staffordshire Foot	11/1839	12/1839	Cork
56th.	West Essex Foot	12/1839	12/1839	Belfast
38th.	1st. Staffordshire Foot	12/1839	12/1839	Cashel
97th.	Earl of Ulster	12/1839	01/1840	Royal Bks.
47th.	Lancashire Foot	01/1840	02/1840	Malta
19th.	1st.Yorkshire North Riding	03/1840	06/1840	Mediterranean
20th.	East Devonshire Foot	06/1840	12/1840	Kilkenny

86th.	Royal County Down Foot	09/1840	12/1840	South Africa
98th.	Prince of Wales	12/1840	11/1841	Singapore
84th.	York & Lancaster Foot	12/1840	08/1841	Newbridge
42nd.	Royal Highland (Black Watch)	04/1841	11/1841	Glasgow
45th.	2nd. Nottinghamshire Foot	07/1841	08/1842	Gibraltar
58th.	Rutlandshire Foot	07/1841	11/1842	E. Indies
78th.	Seaforth Highlanders	11/1841	03/1842	India
7th.	North Hampshire Foot	08/1842	09/1842	Royal Bks.
69th.	South Lincolnshire Foot	11/1842	04/1845	Canterbury
54th.	West Norfolk Foot	04/1843	10/1843	Athlone
60th.	King's Royal Rifle Corps	06/1843	02/1844	Kilkenny
36th.	Herefordshire Foot	07/1843	07/1844	Newry
34th.	Cumberland Foot	10/1843	07/1844	Athlone
56th.	West Essex Foot	08/1844	12/1844	England
32nd.	Duke of Cornwall Light Infantry	06/1844	05/1845	Athlone
73rd.	Perthshire Foot	09/1844	12/1844	Royal Bks.
6th.	1st. Royal Warwickshire	12/1844	07/1845	Mullingar
67th.	Wiltshire Foot	12/1844	02/1846	Templemore
44th.	East Essex Foot	04/1845	06/1846	Newry
64th.	2nd. Staffordshire Militia	08/1845	04/1846	Kilkenny
47th.	Lancashire Foot	03/1846	10/1846	Cork
59th.	2nd. Nottinghamshire Foot	02/1846	10/1846	Limerick
83rd.	County of Dublin Foot	10/1846	05/1847	Kilkenny
3rd.	East Kent Foot	11/1846	01/1847	Royal Bks.
13th.	Somersetshire Light Infantry	01/1847	09/1847	Birr
92nd.	Gordon Highlanders	08/1847	12/1847	Limerick
85th.	King's Light Infantry	09/1847	08/1848	Templemore
49th.	1st. Royal Berkshire	10/1847	10/1848	Templemore
74th.	Highland Foot	12/1847	04/1848	Linenhall
60th.	King's Royal Rifle Corps	01/1848	07/1848	Thurles
55th.	Westmoreland Foot	04/1848	06/1850	Waterford
2nd.	Queen's Royals	07/1848	05/1850	Newry
40th.	2nd. Somersetshire Light Infantry	10/1848	10/1850	Cork
71st.	Highland Light Infantry	04/1850	05/1852	Kilkenny
31st.	Huntingdonshire Foot	04/1850	10/1850	Royal Bks.
89th.	Princess Victoria's Foot	11/1850	09/1851	Clonmel
62nd.	1st. Wiltshire Foot	04/1851	03/1852	Athlone

39th.	Dorsetshire Foot	03/1852	09/1852	Clonmel
17th.	Leicestershire Foot	05/1852	04/1853	Royal Bks.
81st.	Loyal Lincoln Volunteers	04/1852	03/1853	Kilkenny
91st.	Argyllshire Foot	03/1853	04/1854	Limerick
63rd.	West Suffolk Foot	04/1853	08/1854	Turkey
21st.	Royal Scots Fusiliers	10/1853	08/1854	Turkey
90th.	Perthshire Light Infantry	11/1853	11/1854	Crimea
3rd.	West York Militia	08/1854	04/1855	Waterford
48th.	Northamptonshire Militia	08/1854	04/1855	Mediterranean
60th.	King's Rifles 3rd Bn	09/1854	07/1855	Curragh
109th.	County of Dublin Militia	02/1855	07/1855	Curragh
96th.	Regiment of Foot	04/1855	09/1855	Curragh
93rd.	Roscommon Militia	09/1855	09/1855	Beggars Bush
40th.	2nd. Somersetshire Light Infantry	10/1855	06/1856	England
60th.	King's Royal Rifle Corps	08/1856	12/1856	Bengal
18th.	Royal Irish Regiment	08/1856	09/1857	Curragh
55th.	Westmoreland Foot	09/1856	07/1857	Ship Street
77th.	East Middlesex Foot	10/1856	07/1857	N. S. Wales
94th.	Argyll and Sutherland Foot	09/1857	10/1857	India
60th.	King's Royal Rifle Corps	07/1857	09/1857	India
16th.	Bedfordshire Foot	06/1857	09/1857	Dundalk
77th.	East Middlesex Foot	10/1856	07/1857	N. S. Wales
2nd Bn	Coldstream Guards	08/1857	10/1858	London
53rd.	Shropshire Militia	11/1857	12/1857	Royal Bks.
30th.	Cambridgeshire Foot	12/1857	10/1859	Chatham
55th.	Westmoreland Foot	05/1858	07/1859	Aldershot
14th.	Buckinghamshire Foot	12/1858	05/1859	Curragh
5th.	Middlesex Royal Elthorne L.I.	06/1859	11/1859	Aldershot
20th.	East Devonshire 2nd. Bn.	06/1859	09/1859	Curragh
76th.	Regiment of Foot	10/1859	11/1860	Waterford
2nd.	Staffordshire Militia	12/1859	08/1860	England
60th.	King's Royal Rifle Corps	10/1860	04/1861	Canada
36th.	Herefordshire Foot	10/1860	05/1861	Curragh
61st.	Rifle Brigade 1st. Bn.	04/1861	12/1861	Canada
17th.	Leicestershire Foot	05/1861	06/1861	Curragh
47th.	Lancashire Foot	06/1861	06/1861	Athlone
40th.	2nd. Somersetshire Depot	07/1861	10/1861	Birr

58th.	Rutlandshire Depot	07/1861	01/1862	Curragh
65th.	2nd.Yorkshire North Riding Depot	07/1861	11/1861	Birr
15th.	Yorkshire East Riding	09/1861	12/1861	Canada
11th.	North Devonshire 1st. Bn.	12/1861	09/1863	Royal Bks.
15th.	Yorkshire East Riding	01/1862	02/1862	Nth. America
45th.	Nottinghamshire Foot	02/1862	03/1863	Curragh
58th.	Rutlandshire Foot	09/1862	05/1863	Beggars Bush
19th.	1st. Yorkshire North Riding	04/1863	09/1863	India
84th.	York & Lancaster Foot	07/1863	09/1864	Belfast
11th.	North Devonshire Foot	07/1863	09/1863	N. S. Wales
86th.	Royal County Down Foot	09/1863	09/1863	Beggars Bush
12th.	East Suffolk.2nd. Bn	10/1863	07/1864	Bengal
32nd.	Duke of Cornwall Light Infantry	10/1863	05/1864	Waterford
49th.	1st. Royal Berkshire	07/1864	07/1865	India
49th.	Princess Charlotte of Wales	08/1864	05/1865	Mullingar
41st.	Welsh Foot	09/1864	08/1865	Bengal
29th.	Worcestershire Foot	01/1865	06/1865	Malta
60th.	King's Royal Rifle Corps	02/1865	03/1866	Nth. America
8th.	King's Foot 1st. Bn.	08/1865	12/1865	Newry
59th.	2nd. Nottinghamshire Foot	11/1865	03/1866	Birr
61st.	Gloucestershire Foot	12/1865	06/1866	Curragh
64th	2nd. Staffordshire Foot	12/1865	03/1868	Templemore
60th.	King's Royal Rifle Corps	01/1866	03/1866	Malta
92nd.	Gordon Highlanders	03/1866	09/1866	Royal Bks.
52nd.	Oxfordshire Light Infantry	04/1866	12/1867	Limerick
48th.	Northamptonshire Militia	04/1866	12/1867	Fermoy
3rd.	East Kent Foot	06/1866	09/1866	Malta
75th.	Stirlingshire Foot	09/1866	09/1866	Kilkenny
21st.	Royal Scots Fusiliers	09/1866	08/1867	Enniskillen
83rd.	County of Dublin Foot	12/1866	04/1867	Gibraltar
69th.	South Lincolnshire Foot	04/1867	09/1867	Canada
63rd.	West Suffolk Foot	08/1867	02/1868	Royal Bks.
39th.	Dorsetshire Foot	08/1867	04/1868	Kinsale
74th.	Highland Foot	09/1867	02/1868	Gibraltar
72nd.	Duke of Albany Highlanders	02/868	09/1868	Limerick
71st.	Highland Foot	04/1868	07/1868	Gibraltar
66th.	Berkshire Foot	04/1868	02/1869	Curragh

9th.	East Norfolk Foot	07/1868	06/1869	Warley
16th.	Bedfordshire Foot	02/1869	06/1869	Curragh
15th.	Yorkshire East Riding 2nd. Bn.	06/1869	07/1870	Jersey
17th.	Leicestershire Foot	06/1869	01/1870	India
47th.	Lancashire Foot	01/1870	09/1870	Nenagh
61st.	Gloucestershire Foot	03/1870	01/1870	Jersey
59th.	2nd. Nottinghamshire Foot	03/1870	08/1870	Limerick
16th.	Bedfordshire Foot	05/1870	09/1870	Canterbury
43rd.	Monmouthshire Light Infantry	06/1870	09/1870	Fermoy
9th.	East Norfolk 1st. Bn.	06/1870	09/1871	Cork
70th.	Surrey Foot	08/1870	10/1870	Royal Bks.
58th.	Rutlandshire Foot	08/1870	08/1871	Curragh
10th	North Lincolnshire 1st. Bn.	09/1870	11/1871	Cork
11th.	North Devonshire 1st. Bn.	10/1870	08/1871	Curragh
40th.	2nd. Somersetshire Foot	08/1871	09/1872	Bombay
64th	2nd. Staffordshire Foot	08/1871	03/1872	Limerick
62nd.	Wiltshire Foot	08/1871	08/1872	India
16th.	Bedfordshire 1st. Bn.	11/1871	08/1872	Jersey
80th.	Staffordshire Volunteers	12/1871	01/1872	Singapore
20th.	East Devonshire 1st. Bn.	01/1872	08/1872	Newry
106th.	Bombay light Infantry	01/1872	02/1872	Gurnsey
97th.	Earl of Ulster	08/1872	07/1873	West Indies
108th	Madras Infantry	08/1872	09/1873	Bombay
4th. Bn	Prince Consort's Own Rifle Brigade	08/1872	07/1873	Royal Bks.
3rd.	East Kent 2nd. Bn.	07/1873	05/1874	Limerick
34th.	Cumberland Foot	07/1873	03/1873	Carlisle
46th.	South Devon Foot	11/1873	06/1874	Royal Bks.
100th.	Prince of Wales Royal Canadian	05/1874	06/1876	Aldershot
29th.	Worcestershire Foot	06/1874	06/1875	Channel Isl's.
27th	Inniskilling (detachment)	03/1875	04/1875	Curragh
61st.	Gloucestershire Foot	04/1875	06/1875	Gurnsey
35th	Royal Sussex Foot	06/1875	10/1875	West Indies
60th.	Rifles 4th Bn.	07/1875	06/1876	Fermoy
90th.	Perthshire Light Infantry	07/1875	11/1876	Limerick
1st.	Royal Scots 1st. Bn.	09/1876	05/1877	Curragh
7th.	Royal Fusiliers 1st. Bn.	11/1876	04/1878	Templemore
9th.	East Norfolk 1st Bn.	05/1877	04/1878	Birr

47th.	Lancashire Foot	04/1878	08/1878	Curragh
21st	Royal Scots Fusiliers 2nd Bn.	04/1878	09/1878	Curragh
3rd. Bn.	Rifles	08/1878	01/1880	India
77th.	East Middlesex Foot	09/1878	05/1879	Beggars Bush
82nd	Prince of Wales Volunteers	05/1879	03/1880	Aldershot
104th.	Bengal Fusiliers Foot	03/1880	12/1880	Curragh
3rd. Bn.	Rifle Brigade	04/1880	06/1880	Curragh
80th.	Staffordshire Volunteers	06/1880	09/1880	Royal Bks.
57th.	West Middlesex Foot	09/1880	12/1880	Aldershot
1st. Bn.	Coldstream Guards	12/1880	03/1882	Chelsea
2nd. Bn	Coldstream Guards	02/1881	08/1882	Egypt
1st Bn.	Scots Fusiliers	02/1881	03/1882	London
3rd. Bn.	Rifle Brigade	10/1881	08/1882	England
13th.	Somersetshire Light Infantry 1st. Bn.	02/1882	08/1883	Enniskillen
2nd. Bn	Prince of Wales Leinster	07/1882	07/1882	Curragh
3rd. Bn.	Grenadier Guards	08/1882	09/1883	Woolwich
71st.	Highland light Infantry 1st. Bn.	08/1883	12/1883	Beggars Bush
3rd.	East Kent Foot 1st Bn.	08/1883	07/1884	Buttevant
2nd. Bn	Scots Fusilier Guards	09/1883	08/1884	London
1st. Bn.	Grenadier Guards	08/1884	09/1885	London
3rd.	East Kent 1st. Bn.	09/1884	12/1884	Malta
32nd.	Duke of Cornwall Light Infantry	10/1884	12/1885	Malta
1st. Bn.	Scots Guards	10/1885	09/1886	Chelsea
2nd.Bn.	Welsh Foot	12/1885	09/1887	Tipperary
2nd.Bn.	Grenadier Guards	09/1886	09/1887	Chelsea
1st. Bn.	West Yorkshire	02/1887	10/1888	Fermoy
1st. Bn.	Royal Dublin Fusiliers	07/1887	08/1887	Mullingar
1st. Bn.	South Wales Borderers	09/1887	11/1889	Balls-Bridge
2nd.Bn.	Coldstream Guards	09/1887	09/1888	Chelsea
2nd.Bn.	Scots Guards	09/1888	09/1889	Chelsea
	Queens Own Royal West Surrey	07/1889	01/1890	Aldershot
3rd.Bn.	Grenadier Guards	09/1889	11/1890	London
2nd. Bn	King's Royal Rifle Corps	01/1890	11/1891	Gibraltar
1st. Bn.	Grenadier Guards	12/1890	08/1891	Chelsea
1st. Bn.	Coldstream Guards	08/1891	09/1892	London
32nd.	Duke of Cornwall 2nd Bn.	11/1891	09/1893	Beggars Bush
1st. Bn.	Scots Guards	08/1892	08/1893	Chelsea

2nd.Bn.	Rifle Brigade	09/1893	10/1895	Aldershot
2nd.Bn.	Grenadier Guards	10/1893	07/894	England
2nd.Bn.	Coldstream Guards	09/1894	09/1895	Pirbright
2nd.Bn.	Scots Guards	09/1895	04/1897	Chelsea
1st. Bn.	Durham Light Infantry	11/1895	09/1898	Aldershot
2nd.Bn.	Hampshire Foot	01/1897	09/1897	Cork
1st. Bn.	Argyll & Sutherland	09/1898	10/1899	South Africa
1st. Bn.	King's Own Scottish Borderers	10/1898	11/1899	India
2nd.Bn.	South Wales Borderers	09/1899	12/1899	Ship Street
4th. Bn.	Argyll & Sutherland	01/1900	02/1900	South Africa
3rd. Bn.	Argyll & Sutherland	01/1900	05/1900	Ballyshannon
3rd. Bn.	Royal Irish Fusiliers	05/1900	08/1901	Royal Bks.
	East Lancashire Foot	07/1900	01/1902	Royal Bks.
	West Riding Foot	07/1900	02/1901	Beggars Bush
4th. Bn.	King's Liverpool Foot	07/1900	12/1900	Cork
4th. Bn.	Rifle Brigade	01/1901	03/1901	Portobello
	East Surrey Foot	02/1901	09/1901	Royal Bks.
5th.	Northumberland Fusiliers 4th. Bn.	04/1901	12/1902	Royal Bks.
	Irish Guards	07/1903	07/1903	London
2nd.Bn.	Royal Irish Rifles	02/1903	07/1904	Portobello
78th.	Seaforth Highlanders 2nd. Bn.	04/1903	10/04	Aldershot
4th. Bn.	Royal Irish Fusiliers	10/1904	02/1906	Portobello
1st. Bn.	Royal Berkshire	09/1904	02/1908	Curragh
56th.	Royal Essex 2nd. Bn.	04/1907	08/1914	France
	Royal Irish Constabulary	09/1907	02/1909	Phoenix Park
1st.Bn.	Rifle Brigade	01/1910	10/1911	Colchester
	R.A.M.C. No 14 Co.	01/1910	08/1914	B.E.F
	Cavalry Depot			
	11th., 4th., 8th.,13th., Hussars	03/1910	08/1914	France
5th.	Lancers	11/1910	08/1914	France
1st. Bn.	Queen's Own Royal West Kent	10/1911	04/1914	France
4th. Bn.	Royal Dublin Fusiliers (reserves)	08/1913	08/1914	Queenstown
5th. Bn.	Royal Dublin Fusiliers (reserves)	08/1913	08/1914	Queenstown
5th.	Royal Inniskilling Fusiliers	09/1914	05/1915	Basingstoke
3rd. Bn.	Royal Irish Regiment (reserves)	08/1914	09/1916	Templemore
6th. Bn.	Prince of Wales Leinster	08/1914	09/1914	Curragh
10th.Bn.	Royal Dublin Fusiliers (a few men)	04/1916	05/1916	Royal Bks.

2/6th.	Sherwood Foresters	05/1916	06/1916	Galway
3rd. Bn.	King's Own Royal Lancaster	04/1919	07/1919	
1st. Bn.	King's Own Royal Regiment	07/1919	12/1922	Shorncliffe
2nd. Bn.	Prince of Wales Volunteers	10/1919	06/1920	Palestine
2nd. Bn.	Welch Regiment	06/1920	12/1922	Colchester
	Duke of Cornwall Light Infantry	07/1921	09/1921	London
	King's Shropshire Light infantry	04/1922	12/1922	Tidworth

Present at Handing-Over December 1922

King's Own Royal Regiment	April	1919	December	1922
The Welch Regiment, 2nd. Bn.	June	1920	December	1922
King's Shropshire Light Infantry	April	1922	December	1922

Kehoe Barracks

1st. (Old) Bn. Infantry	August	1922	August	1924
55th. Battalion	August	1922	August	1924
16th. Infantry Battalion	December	1922	August	1924

August 1924, given over to Dublin Corporation.

Sources and Bibliography

Registrum de Kilmainham: preserved at the Bodleian Library Oxford

The Complete Peerage, London, St. Catherine Press, 1945.

Dictionary of Canadian Biography, Uni. Toronto Press, 1983.

Dictionary of National Biography, Oxford Uni. Press, 2004.

Calendar of Ancient Records of Dublin, Edited by Lady Gilbert, 1913- Dublin.

Sketches of History, Politics, and Manners in Dublin, and the North: John Gamble.

Citizen Lord-The Life of Edward Fitzgerald, Stella Tillyard.

That Damned Thing Called Honour- Duelling in Ireland 1570-1860: James Kelly.

Recollections of a Soldier-diplomat: Hon Frederick Wellesley.

A Brief Review of his Grace the Duke of Richmond, Lord Lieutenant of Ireland 1807-1813: Stewart and Hope.

Historical Records of the British Army-various vols*:* Richard Cannon.

Hidden Dublin, Deadbeats, Dossers and Decent Skins: Frank Hopkins.

A New Dictionary of Irish History- D. Hickey & J.E. Doherty.

A History of the City of Dublin, Warburton, Whitelaw, and Walsh, 2 volumes, Cadel and Davies, 1818.

The Traveller's New Guide Through Ireland: Gumming, 1815.

Balloon, An Authentic Narrative of the Aerial Voyage of Mr. Sadler across the Irish Channel: W. H. Tyrrell, Dublin, 1812.

Pettigrew & Oulton street directory, 1835.

Thom's Directories, from 1850, continuous.

Dublin Historical Record, 'Dublin Military Barracks', Comdt. P.D. O' Donnell, Sept. 1972.
ibid: 1956-57 Kilmainham Jail by A. J. Nowlan.

Richmond Barracks, George Campbell, former teacher CBS Inchicore, revised by Shay Hurley; unpublished: Military Archives.

Encyclopaedia of Dublin, Douglas Bennett; Gill and Macmillan, 1991.

Across a Century, Oblate Fathers Centenary Record, 1956. 'Inchicore and District', Patrick O 'Sullivan.

Dublin, The Fair City, Peter Somerville -Large; Hamish Hamilton.

An Cosantoir, 'Martello Towers' - July 1982, pg. 218.

Inchicore, Kilmainham and District, Seosamh Ó Broin; Cois Camóige.

The Goodness of Guinness, Tony Corcoran, Liberties 2005.

Old Inchicore and Kilmainham, Vol. 1. Michael Conaghan, ed. 1990.

Dublin's Suburban Towns, 1834-1930, S. O' Maitiu, 4 Courts. Press.

Janey Mack Me Shirt is Black, Eamonn Mac Tomais, O' Brien, 1982.

Report of the Trial of Hugh Fitzpatrick, 1813. National Lib. of Ireland.

Wellington, The Years of the Sword, E.Longford (E.H.Pakenham, countess of Longford) 1969.

A Story of a Soldiers Life, Garnet Joseph Wolseley.

The Life of Lord Wolseley, Maurice and Arthurs.

All Sir Garnet; a life of Field-Marshal Lord Wolseley, by Joseph H Lehmann; London, J. Cape, 1964.

Sir Garnet Wolseley: Victorian Hero, by Halik Kochanski; London, 1999.

Scraps, or, Scenes, Tales and Anecdotes from Memories of my Early Days,' Alexander Fraser Saltoun. Vol. 1. 1883.

The Life of James Thomson (B.V.), Henry Stephens Salt.

The Life and poetry of James Thomson B.V., J. Edward Meeker.

The Laureate of Pessimism, Bertram Dobell.

A Long Defeat": A Brief Life of James Thomson (BV), Dick Sullivan.

Places of the Mind, the Life and Work of James Thomson, B.V. Tom Leonard, Jonathan Cape, London, 1993.

The Victorian Army at Home: Alan Ramsay Skelley.

The Sessional Papers: the House of Lords, 1854-55.

The memoirs of Private Waterfield, soldier in Her Majesty's 32nd Regiment of Foot (Duke of Cornwall's Light Infantry), 1842-57.

The Greatest of the Fenians, 'John Devoy and Ireland;' T. Dooley.

Heroic Option, Desmond and Jean Bowen- Pen & Sword Bks. 2005.

Britain & Her Army, Correlli Barnett, Cassell and Co. 1970.

A New Ireland, vol. 5, Ed. by W. E. Vaughan.

A Treatise on Mineral Waters, by Ml. Ryan, 1824.

Kilmainham, The Bastille of Ireland: Kilmainham Jail Restoration Society 1970.

A History of Kilmainham Gaol, Pat Cooke; OPW, 1995

The Church of Ireland in Victorian Dublin; John Crawford Four Courts Press, 2004.

Surveying Ireland's Past- Multidisciplinary Essays, Ed. Howard B. Clark, Jacinta Prunty and Mark Hennessy.

373

History of Dublin Catholic Cemeteries, W. J. Fitzpatrick.

Dublin Burial Grounds, Vivien Igoe.

Kilmainham Memories, Tadhg Hopkins, Ward Lock, 1896.

Memorials of the Dead- Dublin City & County, Vol. One, 'Goldenbridge Cemetery:' Dr. Michael Egan; National Archives.

A History of Kilmainham Gaol, 'The Dismal House of Little Ease,' Freida Kelly, Mercier Press, 1988.

Reminiscences of General Sir Thomas Makdougall Brisbane; by himself.

Trifles in Poetry, including Hermit's Minstrelsy: Charles O' Flaherty- R. Carrick, Dublin 1821.

Kilmainham, 'The history of a settlement older than Dublin:' - Colm Kenny, Four Courts Press, 1995.

Dublin, The Deposed Capital- Mary E Daly, Cork University Press.

With the Connaught rangers in Quarters, Camp and on Leave: Gen. E.H. Maxwell.

Gleanings and Reminiscences, Frank Thorpe Porter, A.M., J.P.: Hodges, Foster & Co. Grafton St.1875.

Cabinet of Irish Literature- Read.

A Military History of Ireland, Thomas Bartlett, Keith Jeffery.

The Neighbourhood of Dublin, Weston St. John Joyce.

Witnesses, 'Inside the Easter Rising;' Annie Ryan, Liberties Press.

Lockout Dublin 1913: Padraig Yeats.

Disturbed Dublin: the story of the great strike of 1913–14: A. Wright.

From Behind the Closed Door, Brian Barton; Blackstaff Press.

The Easter Rising: Michael T Foy & Brian Barton.

The Heart of Dublin, Peter Pearson; O Brien Press, 2000.

Under the Starry Plough, Recollections of the Irish Citizen Army: Frank Robbins.

Life Among Convicts, Charles Bernard Gibson, 1863.

Sister Magdalen Kirwan - a link with the Invincibles, Sr. Teresa Delaney, *Journal of the Old Tuam Society*, volume one, 2004.

The Month: an illustrated magazine of literature, science and art, 1865.

Hanna Sheehy Skeffington, The Irish Feminist: Leah Levenson, 1986.

The Annals of Dublin; E.E O'Donnell, Currach Press.

Irish Regiments in the Great War; Timothy Bowman, 2003.

For Valour, the history of Southern Africa's Victoria Cross Heroes: Ian S.Uys.

A History of the Irish Working Class, by Peter Berresford Ellis.

4 Years Service in India, John Ryder 1853.

Vestiga, Charles à Court Repington.

Stirring Incidents in the Life of a British Soldier, Thomas Faughnan.

A Most Delightful Station: the British Army on the Curragh of Kildare, Ireland 1855-1922: Con Costello.1996.

Recollections of an Irish Rebel: John Devoy.

The Politics of Irish Literature: Malcolm Brown.

Fifty Years of Army Music: John MacKenzie-Rogan.

Making saints: religion and the public image of the British Army, 1809-1885: Kenneth E. Hendrickson.

History of the Scottish Highlands, Highland Clans and Scottish Regiments. John S

Keltie F.S.A. Scot.

The Prince of Wales Leinster Regiment: F.E. Whitton.

Dublin's Suburban Towns, Séamas Ó Maitiú.

The Field day anthology of Irish writing: Irish women's writing and traditions:
Seamus Deane, Andrew Carpenter, Jonathan Williams.

Great Parliamentary Scandals: five centuries of calumny, smear and innuendo:
Matthew Parris, Kevin MacGuire.

The Botanic Garden. Part II, containing the *Loves of the Plants*: Erasmus Darwin.

Sir Charles Dilke: a Victorian Tragedy, Roy Jenkins.

The Lost Prime Minister: a life of Sir Charles Dilke: David Nicholls.

Another Icarus, Percy Pilcher and the Quest for Flight: P. Jarrett.

Random Records of a Reporter: The Phoenix Park Murders, J. B. Hall.

Report on the Sanitary Conditions of the Richmond Barracks, Rogers Field.

The Boer War, Thomas Pakenham.

David and Goliath: The First War of Independence, 1880-1881,
Duxbury, Geo. R (Johannesburg: SA National Museum of Military
History, 1981).

A History of the Eleventh Hussars, (1908-1934): Capt. L.R. Lumley.

The Queen's Own Royal West Kent Regiment - 1914-1919: C. T. Atkinson.

Shot at Dawn, Executions in World War One by Authority of the British Army Act:
Julian Putkowski

Francis Ledwidge, The Poems Complete: edited by Liam O'Meara.

Francis Ledwidge, Poet, Activist and Soldier: Liam O'Meara.

The Sprig of Shillelagh, Journal of the Inniskillings, 1916-17.

Dublin Historical Record: "From Ballsbridge to the South Dublin Union":
A. Kinsella, read to The Old Dublin Society, 7th Dec. 1994.

Reminiscences of Five Years Service of an Irish Volunteer: P. Doyle.

Uncommon Valour: Paul O Brien.

Rebels, Voices from the Easter Rising: Ferghal Mc Garry.

The Rising, Ireland, Easter 1916: Ferghal Mc Garry.

Guerrilla Warfare in the Irish War of Independence: Joseph Mc Kenna.

Agony at Easter, The 1916 Irish Uprising: Thomas M. Coffey.

Michael Collins and the Making of a New Ireland: Piaras Beaslai

Richmond Barracks, Lost Chapters of our National Story: St Michael's Estate
Regeneration Board Development Plan.

The Rising: the complete story of Easter Week: Desmond Ryan.

Easter Rising 1916, Birth of the Irish Republic: Michael McNally.

A Short History of Ireland, Jonathan Bardon.

Campaigns and History of the Royal Irish Regiment: Brigadier General Stannus
Geoghegan, (Blackwood & Sons 1927).

Supreme Sacrifice, The Story of Eamonn Ceannt: William Henry.

Last Words, Piaras F. Mac Lochlainn.

The Sinn Fein Rebellion Handbook 1916.

Peter Paul Galligan- One of the Most Dangerous Men in the Rebel Movement:
Kevin Galligan.

Recollections of the Irish War: Darrell Figgis.

Emmet Hall, From Lockout to the Rising in Inchicore: Liam O'Meara.

Eamon de Valera: T. Ryle Dwyer.

Cnoc An Enaigh, Hill of the Marsh (Stories of Knockananna from Yesteryear)
Ordnance Survey Ireland (Editor), Military, *Tom Kehoe*: Shay Courtney.

With Michael Collins In The Fight For Irish Independence: Batt O'Connor.

Sleep Soldier Sleep, Diarmuid O' Connor.

Seventy- Seven of Mine Said Ireland: Marin O' Dwyer.

John Charles McQuaid: Ruler of Catholic Ireland: John Cooney.

Just Joe, My Autobiography: Joe Duffy

*Empowering Communities in Disadvantaged Urban Areas: towards greater
Community Participation in Irish Urban Planning? Part One:* Andrew MacLaran,
Vanda Clayton, and Paula Brudell.

Newspapers and Periodicals

An t-Oglach
Hibernian Magazine, 1911
The Freeman's Journal
Saunders Weekly News Letter
The Dublin Evening Post
Dublin Evening Mail
Dublin Morning Register
Carrick's Morning Post
Limerick Evening Post and Clare Sentinel
The London Derry Journal
Faulkner's Dublin Journal
The Leeds Mercury
The Southern Cross, New Zealand
Cork Mercantile Chronicle
The Dublin Builder
The Irish Builder
Dublin Penny Journal
Dublin Historical Record
The Times London

The Irish Times
The Irish Independent
The Globe
Blackwell's periodical
The Dublin University magazine
The Irish Review
The Philanthropist
History Ireland 1998
Everybody's Magazine, Vol. 39, 1918
Inniu, Nov. 22nd 1946

Archives

The National Library of Ireland.
Church of Ireland Library: Records of the Garrison Chapel of Richmond Barracks-
1857-1922.
The Walshe Papers (The National Library of Ireland- Manuscripts).
The Allen Library, Dublin.
The National Archives. Bishop Street, Dublin.
The National Archives, Public Records Office, Kew, Richmond, UK.
Military Archives, Cathal Brugha Barracks, Rathmines, Dublin.
Bodleian Library Oxford: *Registrum de Kilmainham* (1326-1339)
Argyll and Sutherland Museum, Stirling Castle Scotland.
Durham County Record Office, UK.
Essex Regiment Museum, UK.
Royal West Kent archives.
The Rifles (Berkshire and Wiltshire) Museum, UK.
Y.M.C.A, Cadbury Research Library, Birmingham. UK.

The Occasional Croak and Chirp

4.40am. and Paradise
multitudinous chirping of birds
- that I would pull back the veil
to gaze
at this Garden of Eden

but I know as I lie here -
the third floor -
behind that curtain
is a graveyard

5.45, the cry of a child
and the thump
of awakened parents
a work weary sleep robbed father pleads
In the name of Jesus !

while in the graveyard
life continues

with the occasional croak and chirp

Liam O'Meara
St. Michael's Estate, circa 1990

Notes

1 *Croke Papers*, John Wilson Croker, Vol. 1. Pg. 150.

2 *Citizen Lord, the Life of Lord Edward-* Stella Tillyard, pp 28.

3 Lennox-Charles: *Encyclopaedia Britannica,* Walter Yust- 1956.

4 *Scores and Biographies,* A. Haygarth, 1862.

5 *A Dictionary of Canadian Biography,* pg. 490.

6 *A Popular History of Ireland*, Book 12, Thomas D'Arcy Magee.

7 *Sketches of History:* John Gamble.

8 *Gleanings and Reminiscences ,* Frank Thorpe Porter.

9 *Hidden Dublin,* Frank Hopkins, 2007.

10 *Sketches of History:* John Gamble.

11 *The Walshe Papers,* National Library of Ireland.

12 *Hidden Dublin,* Frank Hopkins, 2007.

13 *A Popular History of Ireland*, Book 12, Thomas D'Arcy Magee.

14 *The Times,* the Duke of Richmond's words quoted by Wellesley Pole to the House of Commons, March 8th, 1811.

15 Both quotes: *A New Ireland, Vol 5:* essay *by* S. J. Connolly.

16 *Goodwood House*, quoted in the visitors souvenir book.

17 *Waterloo, the Hundred Days,* David Chandler 1980.

18 *Wellington, The Years of the Sword*, E. Longford.

19 Alessandro Barbero, *A History of the Battle of Waterloo*, Alessandro Barbero: Atlantic Books, London 2005.

20 *Defying Napoleon,* Dr Thomas Munch-Petersen, U.C.L, Sutton Publishing, Also: *Napoleon's Danish Plot,* Tom Kelly, *Daily Mail,* Apr. 14th 2007.

21 *Calander of Ancient Records*, vol 9 pp359.

22 *The Freemans Journal,* March -July 1800.

23 *The Freemans Journal*, Jul 28th 1800

24 National Archives, Kew: Mapping Dept., War Office MPH1/1050/2-4.

25 *Parliamentary Papers*, 1847: pp. 169, 'Return from barracks in the UK. relating to the dates of erection , materials, etc.'

26 According to the *Treble Almanac, 1813.*

27 SPO, and also quoted by P.D O'Donnell.

28 quoted by P.D. O'Donnell.

29 *History of Dublin*, Warburton ,Whitelaw and Walsh, 1818.

30 *The Royal Lancaster Militia*, J.G. Rawstorne; Longman, 1874.

[31] *The Freeman's Journal,* July, 1814.

[32] *The Freeman's Journal,* Nov. 2nd 1816.

[33] *Carrick's Morning Post,* March 1817.

[34] *The Botanic Garden. Part II, containing* the *Loves of the Plants*: Erasmus Darwin; quoted in *Balloon, An Authentic Narrative of the Aerial Voyage across the Irish Channel-* Windham Sadler- 1812, W.H. Tyrrell, Dublin.

[35] *Carrick's Morning Post,* 31st October 1816.

[36] *Dublin Evening Post,* November 7th 1816.

[37] *Trifles in poetry including Hermits Minstrelsy*: Charles O'Flaherty: R Carrick Dublin 1821.

[38] *Annals of Dublin,* 1824.

[39] *Freeman's Journal,* January 1817.

[40] *Freeman's Journal ,* July 6th 1820.

[41] *The Freeman's Journal,* 4th and 11th. Dec. 1817. Identical reports in *Dublin Evening Post* and *Faulkner's Dublin Journal.*

[42] According to the *Cork Mercantile Chronicle,* 5th Dec.1817.

[43] *A History of Kilmainham Gaol, Dismal House of Little Ease,* Freida Kelly.

[44] Dublin Historical Record, A J Nowlan, vol 15, 1956-57- reports of Inspector General of Prisons Irl. 1818, Kilmainham Jail archives.

[45] *Freeman's Journal,* 11th December 1817.

[46] A History of Kilmainham Gaol, Freida Kelly.

[47] *Wikipedia* and also :www.pdavis.nl/NamesJ.htm.

[48] *Dublin Evening Post,* June 6th 1817.

[49] *The History of Scottish Highlands,* John Keltie.

[50] *Historical Record of the 39th or Dorsetshire Regiment, of Foot,* Richard Cannon. Also, see website of Patricia Downes *'Michael Keenan, 1797-1846: Soldier Settler, 39th Regiment of Foot.'*

[51] *Military Miscellany: comprehending, a history of the recruiting of the army, military punishments...by* Henry Marshall.

[52] *Convicts & the Colonies,* A.G.L. Shaw, Melbourne University Press, 1981

[53] *ibid*

[54] *Encyclopaedia of Dublin,* Douglas Bennett; Gill & Macmillan, 1991 Also Thom's Directory 1835-1850.

[55] *The Story of a Soldier's Life,* Sir Garnet Wolseley.

[56] Public Records ML 137:published in Vol. for 1898.

[57] 4 page letter ,1885: MS106; Repository: Woodson Research Center, Fondren Library Rice University, Houston, TX .

[58] Wolseley collection; letter to his wife 28th Sept. 1882: W/P 11/23.

[59] Wolseley collection; letter to his wife, November, 1884, 24-7.

[60] Maurice MSS 2/2/18.

[61] *Who Was Who*, 1897-1916.

[62] RHK minutes, 1/1/7, p.109 (1795)- National Archives.

[63] *Freeman's Journal,* Oct 16th 1829.

[64] *Freeman's Journal,* Oct 29th 1829.

[65] 'The Tragic Tale of Stamer O'Grady and Captain Smyth of Ballintatrae, George Newcomen, The New Ireland Review, Vol 10, Sept-Feb. 1898-99.

[66] *Dublin Military Barracks,* Comdt P.D. O'Donnell.

[67] *A History of the Irish Working Class*, by Peter Berresford Ellis.

[68] *Freeman's Journal,* January 6th 1838.

[69] *Freeman's Journal,* May 10th 1839.

[70] *Scraps, or, Scenes, Tales and Anecdotes from Memories of my Early Days:* Alexander Fraser Saltoun .

[71] *Scraps, or, Scenes, Tales and Anecdotes from Memories of my Early Days:* Alexander Fraser Saltoun .

[72] *With the Connaught Rangers in Quarters, Camp and on Leave*; Gen. E.H. Maxwell.

[73] *Freeman's Journal,* September 7th 1840.

[74] *Connaught Journal,* October 8th 1840.

[75] *The Times London,* November 22nd 1841.

[76] *The Cork Examiner ,* June 8th 1842.

[77] ibid, November 17th. 1843 .

[78] *Memoirs of a Private Soldier,* Private Waterfield.

[79] *4 Years Service in India,* John Ryder 1853.

[80] Reminiscences of General Sir Thomas Makdougall Brisbane; by himself.

[81] *Freeman's Journal,* April 23rd 1845.

[82] *Saunders Newsletter,* 14th May 1845.

[83] *Richmond Barracks,* George Campbell.

[84] *Freeman's Journal,* March 25th 1847.

[85] *Morning Chronicle ,* Jan 9th 1855.

[86] *The Nation ,* Feb 17th 1855.

[87] *Gleanings and Reminiscences,* Frank Thorpe Porter.

[88] *Report of the Wantage Committee* (1892), p151.

[89] *The United service Magazine,* 1846.

[90] *Report of the Commission on the War in South Africa,* (1904), p43.

[91] *Report on the Commission on Recruiting,* (1867), p7.

[92] Sessional papers: printed by the House of Lords, 10th May 1855.

[93] *Twenty Years Recollections of an Irish Police Magistrate:* F. Thorpe Porter.

[94] A *Most Delightful Station* – C. Costello, 1996.

[95] *History Ireland.* Autumn 1998.

[96] *Everybody's Magazine ,* Vol. 39, 1918.

[97] *Irish Homes and Irish hearts,* Frances Margaret Taylor.

[98] *The Irish Times,* July 11th. 1859.

[99] *The Irish Times,* May 23rd 1862 .

[100] *The Month: an illustrated magazine of literature, science and art:* 1865.

[101] *The Irish Times,* Dec 19th 1868.

[102] *Staffordshire Sentinel,* 15th June 1875.

[103] *The English Magazine,* 1890 vol 7 pp 665-667.

[104] *Places of the Mind,* Tom Leonard.

[105] *Places of the Mind,* Tom Leonard.

[106] The Life of James Thomson, H Salt.

[107] The Laureate of Pessimism: Bertram Dobell.

[108] *A Long Defeat: A Brief Life of James Thomson (BV),* Dick Sullivan

[109] The Irish Times, January 12th. 1861.

[110] *The Irish Times,* Feb 2nd 1861.

[111] *The Irish Times,* May 11th 1864.

[112] *Parliamentary papers, Volume 43.* The Sanitary Report.

[113] *Recollections of an Irish Rebel,* John Devoy.

[114] *Recollections of an Irish Rebel,* John Devoy.

[115] *The Politics of Irish Literature,* Malcolm Brown.

[116] *Home Rule: An Irish History 1800-2000:* Alvin Jackson.

[117] *The Road of Excess,* Terence de Vere White.

[118] History of the Dublin Catholic Cemeteries William J. Fitzpatrick.

[119] History of the Dublin Catholic Cemeteries William J. Fitzpatrick.

[120] History of the Dublin Catholic Cemeteries William J. Fitzpatrick.

[121] *Recollections of a Soldier Diplomat:* Frederick Arthur Wellesley.

[122] *Recollections of a Soldier Diplomat:* Frederick Arthur Wellesley.

[123] *Recollections of a Soldier Diplomat:* Frederick Arthur Wellesley.

[124] *The Irish Times,* April 7th 1865.

[125] *St Jude's Parish Church. Kilmainham, centenary booklet, 1864-1964.*

[126] *The Irish law times and solicitors' journal:* Volume 1 - Page 735.

[127] *The Irish law times and solicitors' journal:* Volume 1 - Page 735.

[128] *Making saints:* Kenneth E. Hendrickson.

[129] *The Irish Times,* Nov. 14th 1867.

[130] *The Irish Times,* Feb. 3rd 1868.

[131] *History of the Scottish Highlands:* Vol 5, John S Keltie, F.S.A. Scot.

[132] *The Irish Builder*, Jun. 1867.

[133] *The Irish Times, Jun, 12th 1868.*

[134] *Dublin's Suburban Townhips,* Séamas Ó Maitiú.

[135] *The Irish Times, Oct.16th 1869 .*

[136] *The Times,* Apr. 16th 1870.

[137] *The Irish Times,* Dec 13th 1871.

[138] *The Irish Times,* Dec 18th 1871.

[139] *The Irish Times,* Sep. 19th 1873.

[140] *The Prince of Wales Leinster(Royal Canadian) Regiment:* F.E. Whitton.

[141] *The Irish Times,* Mar 25th 1875.

[142] *The Irish Times,* Apr 7th 1876.

[143] *For Valour, the history of S. Africa's Victoria Cross Heroes:* Ian S.Uys.

[144] *For Valour, the history of S. Africa's Victoria Cross Heroes:* Ian S.Uys.

[145] *The Irish Times,*Feb 20th 1879.

[146] *Vestigia,* Charles à Court Repington.

[147] *Vestigia,* Charles à Court Repington.

[148] *Vestigia,* Charles à Court Repington.

[149] The Leeds Mercury, May 15th 1883.

[150] *Freeman's Journal,* Oct 31st 1885.

[151] *Sir Charles Dilke: a Victorian Tragedy, Roy* Jenkins.

[152] *Great Parliamentary Scandals,* Matthew Parris.

[153] *The Times,* Jan 26th 1886,The House of Commons Report.

[154] *The Times,* Jun 21st 1889, The House of Commons Report.

[155] *Report on the Sanitary Conditions of the Richmond Bks:* Rogers Field.

[156] *Report on the Sanitary Conditions of the Richmond Bks:* Rogers Field.

[157] *The Times, Aug 27th 1889,* The House of Commons Report.

[158] *The Irish Times* Oct 4th 1889.

[159] *The Irish Times* Oct 16th 1889.

[160] *The Irish Times,* Sep 30th 1890

[161] *The Irish Times,* Dec. 7th 1883.

[162] *The Freeman's Journal,* Aug . 31st 1895.

[163] *Another Icarus, Percy Pilcher and the Quest for Flight:* Philip Jarrett.

[164] *The Boer War,* Thomas Pakenham.

[165] The Irish Times, Oct 26th 1899.

[166] *The Irish Times,* Oct.28th 1899.

[167] *The Boer War,* Thomas Pakenham.

[168] *The Phases of the Anglo-Boer War, 1899-1902,* Andre Wessels.

[169] *The Boer War,* Thomas Pakenham.

[170] *The Times,* Jul 18th 1903.

[171] *The Irish Times,* Dec 19th 1903

[172] *Naming names: who, what, where in Irish nomenclature*: Bernard Share.

[173] *The Times,* Feb 3rd, 1905.

[174] *The Irish Times,* Jan 8th 1906.

[175] *The Times,* Sep 7[th]1907.

[176] *The Irish Times,* Dec 18th 1907.

[177] *The Irish Times,* Feb 7th 1908.

[178] *Parliamentary Papers, Commons Debates*, 6th Apr 1908, vol. 187, pp 899.

[179] *A History of the Eleventh Hussars,* Capt. L.R. Lumley.

[180] *William Partridge* by Hugh Geraghty.

[181] *Lockout Dublin 1913:* **Padraig Yeats.**

[182] *Freeman's Journal* January 14th 1914.

[183] *The Irish Times, "An Irishman's Diary,"* by Jim Cantwell.

[184] *Shot at Dawn*, Julian Putkowski.

[185] *The Queen's Own Royal West Kent Regiment - 1914-1919:* C. T. Atkinson.

[186] Bureau of Military History, Witness Statement 280, Robert Holland .

[187] *Under the Starry Plough:* Frank Robbins.

[188] Bureau of Military History, Witness Statement 733, James O'Shea.

[189] *Reminiscences of Five Years Service of an Irish Volunteer:* Peadar Doyle.

[190] Bureau of Military History, Witness Statement 1511, Gerald Doyle.

[191] Vane, Sir F., Letters to his Wife, April -May 1916: Columbia Record Office,The Castle Carlisle.

[192] Vane, Sir F., Letters to his Wife, April -May 1916: Columbia Record Office, The Castle Carlisle.

[193] From an account held at Military Archives, Cathal Brugha Barracks..

[194] *Under the Starry plough:* Frank Robbins.

[195] *Guerrilla Warfare in the Irish War of Independence*: Joseph Mc Kenna.

[196] Bureau of Military History, Witness Statement 186, Thomas Doyle.

[197] Bureau of Military History, Witness Statement 280, Robert Holland.

[198] *Michael Collins and the Making of a New Ireland,* Piaras Beaslai.

[199] *Last Words* Piaras F. Mac Lochlainn.

[200] Capuchin Archives.

[201] *Inniu,* Nov. 22nd 1946, Piaras Beaslai.

[202] PRO document WO 71/345.

[203] *The Rising: the complete story of Easter Week:* Desmond Ryan.

[204] Bureau of Military History, Witness Statement 687, Monsignor M.J. Curran. Also MS .Fr. Columbus Murphy, Capuchin Archives, Dublin.

[205] *Seventy Years Young: Memories of Elizabeth, Countess of Fingal.*

[206] *Easter Rising 1916, Birth of the Irish Republic:* Michael McNally.

[207] Bureau of Military History, Witness Statement 268, Liam T. Cosgrave.

[208] *A Short History of Ireland,* Jonathan Bardon.

[209] Bureau of Military History, Witness Statement 1019, Sir Alfred Bucknill.

[210] From William Wylie's unpublished handwritten autobiography.

[211] Bureau of Military History, Witness Statement 1511, Gerald Doyle.

[212] *Supreme Sacrifice,* William Henry.

[213] Letter, Michael Mallin, can be viewed in Kilmainham Museum.

[214] *With Michael Collins In The Fight For Irish Independence:* Batt O'Connor.

[215] *With Michael Collins In The Fight, etc:* Batt. O'Connor.

[216] *Eamon De Valera,* Frank Pakenham Longford (Earl of), T. P. O'Neill.

[217] *With Michael Collins In The Fight, etc:* Batt O'Connor .

[218] Letter from Mr Justice de Valera to the author and in his possession.

[219] *Eamon De Valera,* Frank Pakenham Longford (Earl of), T. P.O'Neill.

[220] Bureau of Military History, Witness Statement 979, Robert C Barton.

[221] Bureau of Military History, Witness Statement 423, Vincent Byrne .

[222] Bureau of Military History, Witness Statement 979, Robert C Barton.

[223] Bureau of Military History, Witness Statement 687, Monsignor M.J. Curran. Also, *Peter Paul Galligan,:* Kevin Galligan .

[224] *Eamon de Valera*: T. Ryle Dwyer.

[225] *Inchicore , Kilmainham and District:* Seosamh O' Broin.

[226] *The Sinn Fein Rebellion Handbook, 1916.*

[227] *The Sinn Fein Rebellion Handbook, 1916.*

[228] *The Irish Times,* June 16th 1916.

[229] *Recollections of the Irish War:* Darrell Figgis.

[230] *The Times,* Sept 8th 1919.

[231] *The Irish Independent,* June 30th. 1922.

[232] *Cnoc An Enaigh, Hill of the Marsh, Tom Kehoe:* Shay Courtney.

[233] *Cnoc An Enaigh, Hill of the Marsh, Tom Kehoe:* Shay Courtney .

[234] *Freeman's Journal,* 19th Sept. 1922.

[235] *Seventy-Seven of Mine Said Ireland:* Martin O' Dwyer.

[236] MS, National Library of Ireland.

[237] *The Irish Times,* 19th Mar. 1923.

[238] *An t-Oglach,* April, 1923.

[239] *Freeman's Journal,* 17th Apr. 1923.

[240] *Irish Independent,* Sept. 17th 1923, "Old Comrades Tribute."

[241] *Freeman's Journal, 29th July 1924.*

[242] *The Times* and *The Irish Times,* Dec. 1st 1924.

[243] *The Irish Times,* May 1st 1926, " St. James's Parish."

[244] *A Secret Diary of Fr. Mc Carthy.*

[245] Dáil Eireann debate : 2nd Feb 1971 (online).

[246] *Just Joe, My Autobiography*: Joe Duffy

[247] *Sunday Independent, :* 15th Oct. 1967.

[248] *John Charles McQuaid: Ruler of Catholic Ireland*: John Cooney.

[249] From a letter to the author by the late Fr. Power.

[250] *The Irish Times,* Nov 11th 1968.

[251] *The Irish Times,* Feb. 13th 1970: 'Goodbye to Keogh Square.'

[252] *Empowering Communities in Disadvantaged Urban Areas (etc)*: By Andrew MacLaran and others.

The Author

Liam O'Meara was born in Dublin in rooms overlooking the Brazen Head Inn at the rear and the river Liffey at the front. He is best known as a poet and has won a number of awards including: the Hugh MacDiarmid Trophy (Scottish International); the George Henry Moore gold medallion; the Gerard Manley Hopkins, the Tipperary Theatre Arts prize, and Premio Città di Olbia (Italy).

In recent years he has worked as a researcher with the Liberties Living Heritage group and has produced a trilogy of books on old Dublin. Liam has spent many years researching the life and works of poet Francis Ledwidge. In 1995 he co-founded (with Michael O'Flanagan) the Inchicore Ledwidge Society and since then has edited a number of books of the poet's writings, both poetry and prose: *Francis Ledwidge the Poems Complete*, *The Best of Francis Ledwidge*, and *Legends of the Boyne*. He has also written his own biography of the poet and a play based on the poet's life.

He is currently a member of the Richmond Barracks Advisory Group formed for the restoration of the gymnasium and recreation room of Richmond Barracks.

Other Works by Liam O'Meara

The Bayno, 100 Years of the Iveagh Trust Playcentre.

Zozimus, The Life and Works of Michael Moran, blind poet of Dublin.

Within and Without, Dublin Churches of St. Nicholas, exploring the Manx connection.

Burned All My Witches: an autobiography in verse.

Emmet Hall, from the Lockout to the Rising in Inchicore.

Francis Ledwidge, Poet, Activist and Soldier.

To One Dead, a play based on the life of Francis Ledwidge.